THE
PENGUIN
BOOK OF
ETIQUETTE

MARION VON ADLERSTEIN

THE
PENGUIN
BOOK OF
ETIQUETTE

The complete Australian guide
to modern manners

VIKING

VIKING

Published by the Penguin Group
Penguin Books Australia Ltd
250 Camberwell Road, Camberwell, Victoria 3124, Australia
Penguin Books Ltd
80 Strand, London WC2R 0RL, England
Penguin Putnam Inc.
375 Hudson Street, New York, New York 10014, USA
Penguin Books, a division of Pearson Canada
10 Alcorn Avenue, Toronto, Ontario, Canada M4V 3B2
Penguin Books (NZ) Ltd
Cnr Rosedale and Airborne Roads, Albany, Auckland, New Zealand
Penguin Books (South Africa) (Pty) Ltd
24 Sturdee Avenue, Rosebank, Johannesburg 2196, South Africa
Penguin Books India (P) Ltd
11, Community Centre, Panchsheel Park, New Delhi 110 017, India

First published by Penguin Books Australia Ltd 2002

10 9 8 7 6 5 4

Design by Debra Billson, Penguin Design Studio
Illustrations by Tracie Grimwood
Typeset in 10.5/16.5 pt Legacy Serif Book by Post Pre-press Group, Brisbane, Queensland
Printed and bound in Australia by McPherson's Printing Group, Maryborough, Victoria

National Library of Australia
Cataloguing-in-Publication data:

von Adlerstein, Marion.
    The Penguin book of etiquette: the complete Australian
    guide to modern manners.

    Includes index.
    ISBN 0 670 87757 3.

    1. Etiquette – Australia. 2. Australia – Social life and
    customs – 1990– . I. Title.

395.0994

www.penguin.com.au

The publishers wish to thank Huon Hooke for his kind permission to reproduce
the food and wine suggestions on page 284. 'The Social Code' by Barbara
Cartland first appeared in her *Book of Etiquette*, Arrow Books, London, 1972.

CONTENTS

For my parents,
Eileen and Ernest Aylward,
who would have been amazed

INTRODUCTION

Something unusual happened to me at the supermarket the other day. The place was packed and people were anxious to grab what they wanted and get away. As I waited my turn at a plastic bag dispenser, the elderly woman ahead of me tore off a bag and, instead of keeping it to herself, offered it to me with a smile. The gesture was spontaneous and completely unexpected. I know it sounds piffling, but this minor moment put a shine on the day. As I went about my shopping I found myself being more thoughtful of others than is my usual state of mind in the free-for-all known as the supermarket. It was a simple demonstration of the therapeutic power of courtesy. I bet she felt just as pleased as I did.

More than once during the writing of this book, I have had my doubts about its relevance to the way we live now, but that incident reactivated me. We have become so used to everyday indifference, discourtesy or aggression that a simple act of kindness is the beam thrown by Shakespeare's little candle: it shines like 'a good deed in a naughty world'. I am sure that many of us don't mean to be rude. We are just unaware of the other person. Indifference becomes automatic. Before it becomes too entrenched to dig out, it's up to all of us to do something about it.

To restate the basics, the argument for behaving courteously goes like this. We live in a herd. The herd grows bigger every day. In order to organise the herd so that it rises above the law of the jungle, we must have rules of civility. If one member of the herd antagonises the others, they are likely to be antagonistic in return. Bad behaviour generates ill-will. But if that member of the herd is kind and thoughtful to the others, their attitude and responses should be similarly well mannered. Courtesy is catching.

So far so good. Having the right attitude is the starting point but it's not all. Intentions must be made clear so there is no misunderstanding. There has to be a behavioural 'language' endorsed by the herd and understood by everyone. That language is etiquette, the right way of doing things. Not everyone is taught this language, or is smart enough to pick up a working knowledge, and too few of us ever become fluent.

I find it a bit sad that etiquette as a word has become the subject of ridicule. We seem to be embarrassed by it, perhaps because we associate it with class and snobbery. The concept of etiquette, as we know it, is said to date from the court of Louis XIV (1643–1715) when a ticket or card (for which the French word is *etiquette*) was posted outlining the rules of courtly behaviour. The upper classes invented etiquette and they guarded it from common use with every weapon they could muster. The need for exclusivity made them clutch it like a sword. They built it around themselves, like moats and turrets, as a defence against the masses at the gates. Upper-class etiquette is powerful stuff, otherwise those in the know would have spread the word widely instead of keeping it to themselves. But in this age of mass communication, etiquette's out of its ivory tower and available to everyone.

Not in its old form, though. Like the written and spoken word, etiquette must evolve with the times and be useful and realistic. No language can remain static. What I've tried to do here is to redefine it for this era and for the country where we live. I started out by studying what the great pioneers on the subject have written. I measured that against what I see and hear around me, what experts in various fields have told me and the points of view of just about everybody I've spent time with over the five years it's taken me to reach this point.

Ah, yes, it has taken me half a decade to finish this book. As the years between gestation and birth began to add up, I kept on finding new areas to explore and that meant new chapters to add. My saintly executive publisher, Julie Gibbs, who commissioned the work, magnanimously extended the deadline twice. My friend and agent, Fran Moore, who is the essence of calm, kept me from panic by assuring me that more important than meeting a deadline was that it had to be right.

As the book grew organically and took on a direction of its own that was more like a guide to life than the etiquette books of the past, my clever and patient editor, Kirsten Abbott, made the observation that what most people are concerned about now is different from the priorities of half a century ago, when straight stocking seams and perfectly matched accessories were a serious matter. Ours is a more complex world. The rules are not as straightforward any more. We have a wealth of cultural diversity and that means we need to learn and respect what matters to people whose beliefs and backgrounds are different from our own. So much is available to us now – in material goods, lifestyle choices, information, entertainment – and we have to be informed enough to deal with it. Parenting is more pressured than it was when roles were defined in simpler times, when multi-generational families sat down at a table for every meal and the TV dinner was yet to be invented. What is best for children is often obscured by other issues in these times of individual aspirations and self-realisation for all. These are some of the realities I've tried to address.

Above all, the book is for Australians, in all our cultural diversity, living in Australia in the twenty-first century. Its aim is to help you steer yourself through contemporary life, avoiding as many pitfalls as possible. You don't have to follow the advice in this book slavishly but you should know what is correct, so you can make an informed decision about whether to agree with it or not. Unless you know the guidelines, how can you stick to them, or deviate from them? Ideally, courtesy is fed to you with your mother's milk. If you start learning good behaviour in the cradle it becomes second nature, as though instinctive. As with any language, you're never too old to start studying but the later you leave it the more difficult it is to master.

I was fortunate in having parents whose watchfulness and care shaped me into a well-mannered child, although I was a bit of a show-off. We were poor but we were cherished. The opening of a song that was around at the time of my birth describes our family perfectly: 'Nice people with nice manners but got no money at all.' I grew up with twin blessings from my parents. The first was the unconditional love that makes children grow into confident adults. The second was the set of good manners that I remember used to make adults smile indulgently, a terrific incentive for me to keep on behaving well.

After that little piece of self-promotion, let me assure you that I am just as capable of lapses as you are. We are all human. At times during the writing of this book, I have been thunderstruck at my hide in passing myself off as an authority on how to get through life doing absolutely everything right with a minimum of offence. Nobody gets it right all of the time. All we can do is try.

Chapter One

HELLO WORLD

It is perfectly acceptable to scream at the top of your voice the moment you enter the world. All the best people do. (They say that Italians make exceptional opera singers because they bellow at birth.) Be grateful that, in these enlightened times, those in attendance do not turn you upside down and smack your bottom as they did to generations of your forebears. That is one of those traditions that's been reviewed and found wanting. Unlike the ten commandments by which most of us live, customs and etiquette need to be assessed as each new generation lifts what they need from the past to suit the world in which they find themselves. Your turn will come.

In the cradle is where it all begins, but for now your job is to eat, drink, sleep, put on weight and be a source of wonder to your mum and dad whose hopes and dreams you embody. Little do they know how completely you are about to change their lives.

WE'RE HAVING A BABY

As a first-time mother, the moment you find out you really are pregnant, your first instinct might be to announce it to the universe. Give it some thought before you do. Under normal circumstances, the father should be first to receive the good news, then both sets of parents.

However, it's wise not to spread the word beyond your immediate families until the pregnancy is at least three months old. Mainly because during the first three months of a normal pregnancy, the risk of a miscarriage is greater than at any other time. The fewer people you tell the less explaining you'd have to do if something went wrong. Your figure will not change in a discernible way, at least to outsiders, so it's easy to keep mum. Also if you have a job, it's important to choose the right time to tell your boss and your colleagues, particularly if you are planning to go back to work after parental leave (see page 6).

THE BABY SHOWER

As your waistline begins to expand, preparation for the birth usually involves the extended family and close friends. One of them might offer to put on a social event known as a baby shower. If you experience health problems during your pregnancy, it might even be wise to delay this occasion until after the birth but, if the signs are positive, there's every reason to prepare for the baby's arrival with a low-key celebration.

The purpose of the occasion is for guests to bring presents, not necessarily expensive but invariably practical. Useful gifts include a jumpsuit, bedding, bootees, bunny rug or plastic bath. A generous impending grandparent, aunt or uncle might give a year's subscription to a nappy laundering service. Because first-time parents have to start from scratch in equipping a nursery and providing the layette, a relative or friend who doesn't intend to have another child might fix up and offer pre-loved nursery furniture, a pram or stroller.

Because many women now have Monday-to-Friday jobs, you could hold the shower at an informal lunch in a private garden on the weekend. A generation ago, the shower would have been held in the afternoon and only women invited but events such as this now involve everybody, including children.

THE BIRTH

Needless to say, you should listen to your doctor's advice on how to prepare yourself physically and mentally for the birth.

There are plenty of informative books available, and there are usually good local prenatal services, where you will find a midwife or mothercare nurse who can help and advise in the months before the baby's arrival.

After the birth, if you feel like thanking the professionals who helped you with the delivery, a letter is all that's necessary. If you'd like to do more, and you can afford it, send flowers, wine or chocolates for the staff in the ward to enjoy.

CHOOSING A NAME

The choice is entirely personal. It may be influenced by tradition, duty, sentimentality or fashion. Some people have firm ideas before the child is born. Others wait to know a little of the newborn's character before attaching a suitable name. Whatever you decide on, try not to make the name a burden for your pride and joy. Be wary of fads and steer clear of the fancies some celebrities foist on their unlucky offspring. Choose a name the child can wear easily and endow with his or her own character. It is sensible to choose two given names so that, if necessary, the child can have a preference later.

Do take note of the initials that arise out of these names and beware of unfortunate acronyms, especially if the middle name starts with a vowel. School children are merciless in their glee at finding convenient tags for their peers in the playground. For example, Natalie Ursula Thomas would quickly be labelled NUT. Patrick Oscar O'Neill, Deborah Iris Martin and Bernard Oliver Theodore would be sitting targets for ridicule.

REGISTERING THE BIRTH

Every birth must be recorded officially in state government records and this should be done within three months. The hospital supplies the form but the responsibility for filling it in and lodging it at the Registry of Births, Deaths and Marriages lies with the parents. There is no fee involved.

BIRTH ANNOUNCEMENT

Unless the paparazzi are hovering at the birth of a celebrity's offspring, a child's first appearance in print is usually a paid advertisement announcing the birth in the classified section of the morning newspaper. In general, public announcements of this kind should never be flowery or otherwise overdone, however elated the family might be. The aim is to be clear and concise. For example:

> PEERLESS   To Adam and Eva, a daughter, born 10 July.

In the case of an adoption, the advertisement might read:

> PEERLESS   To Adam and Eva, an adopted daughter, born
> 19 February in Calcutta.

If the father or his whereabouts are unknown, or the parents are separated or divorced and have agreed that the mother would take sole charge of the child, the advertisement might read:

> PEERLESS   To Eva, a daughter, born 10 July.

THE BABY VIEWING

In its first few weeks of life, your baby will be stared and cooed at by a succession of faces, some of whom will later become familiar, others who are there simply because everybody loves a new baby.

To avoid frequent and unscheduled visits by interested well-wishers, consider having an event called a 'baby viewing', a little party at home, say from four to seven one midweek afternoon, primarily for friends and acquaintances who may not be close enough to be invited to a religious service, if there is to be one (see pages 11–25).

While the baby sleeps in its crib your guests are invited to tiptoe in, only two or three at a time, to be enraptured, while the rest sip tea, soft drinks or sparkling wine and nibble finger sandwiches and cakes in the living room or the garden. The proud father should be in attendance and grandmothers, aunts and close friends should make themselves as useful as possible, attending to the baby if it wakes and ensuring that guests are well looked after.

As a guest, you are not obliged to bring a gift but if you choose to do so, you can make it something for the child, the mother or the father. There is no precedent for this sort of gift. Appropriate presents range from an armful of home-grown roses to a bottle of very special wine to be opened on the child's twenty-first birthday. The father might be given a cigar (the most prized is the Cohiba from Cuba) and the mother some luxurious fragrance, body lotion or soap. Presumably you will not utter profanities such as 'Never mind, ugly ducklings do turn into swans' or 'I hear that big ears are a sign of intelligence' but just sweet nothings, such as 'How beautiful', 'Look at the tiny hands' or 'I think she takes after both of you.' This is not the time for handing out advice either, even if you are a veteran of many successful deliveries. In fact, volunteering your opinion is never appropriate. Wait until you are asked. A new mother is anxious enough already without being given conflicting opinions on whether or not she is doing the right thing.

Once everybody has had a good look at the baby and is satisfied to leave, parents, child and any siblings can now settle down to being alone and getting to know each other.

PARENTAL LEAVE

Under the law, if you have been with a company for at least a year you are entitled to fifty-two weeks of unpaid parental leave, as long as you have given your employer at least ten weeks' prior notice. The same applies to the father of your child, if he is planning to replace you as the primary carer for part of the time. Parental leave also applies to the adoption of a child under the age of five years. You are entitled to return to your job once the break is over. If that job no longer exists, you must be given one that is as close to it as possible in status and pay.

Although this sounds straightforward, it is not necessarily so. If your job is fairly routine, then going back to it should not be complicated. But if you have a creative or executive role, the readjustment might not be so easy. Some management styles are fluid, tailored to individual talents and capacities rather than having people fit into a rigid structure. One person's absence might mean the whole pattern changes, as in the turn of a kaleidoscope. A year down the track could make the workplace quite foreign or intimidating to someone who has been at home with a baby.

Be prepared for that if you choose to take a whole year off. Otherwise you might have to consider shortening the length of time you take for parental leave and make other arrangements for baby care. Just because the law says you may have a year off work doesn't mean you must do so. It is simply one possibility.

THE NEW FATHER

There is a charming song from the 1930s called 'Remember Me?' in which a new father tries to attract the attention of his wife, who is so preoccupied with their first baby, she has forgotten all about him.

While roles in marriage and partnerships may have changed since those days, there is still a grain of truth in what that light-hearted lyric conveys. Men sometimes do feel alienated after the arrival of a child so it's important not to let the situation become one of 'two's company, three's a crowd'.

As the father, share some of the practical aspects of the baby's needs, as well as the cuddling, cooing and crooning. Be fair with the chores. Nappy-changing and endless loads of washing should be shared, along with the regular household chores of shopping, cleaning, cooking and ironing. Make yourself as self-sufficient as possible.

Depending on individuals, their characteristics, skills, responsibilities and beliefs, it might be preferable for you as the father to take parental leave from your job, at least for part of the first year after the birth, so that your partner can go back to work. In the early weeks, a mother is hard to replace but, as the months go by, a change of primary carer might be beneficial all round. At least then you'll both know what it's like to experience each other's roles – breadwinner and home-maker – and that leads to tolerance and understanding of the pressures and rewards of both.

In any case, find time to bond with your new son or daughter by strolling in the park together regularly. It may be too soon for bedtime stories, but singing or humming a lullaby or two is comforting for both of you and a fine way of getting your offspring to recognise your voice and associate it with happiness.

SIBLINGS

If there is another child in the family, the new arrival should be welcomed as long as good groundwork has been put in ahead of time. The elder one should know, well ahead of the day, that a new baby is on the way and be involved in the preparations. An only child has a big adjustment to make in sharing with another so, as parents, be sensitive to his or her need to be included, reassured and given attention. Depending on the age, an elder child often takes well to a role of responsibility so don't hesitate to confer some appropriate duty. And don't stint on praise for a job well done.

SOCIAL LIFE WITH A BABY

The power of the newborn over your entire life is awesome, particularly if this is your first child. Enormous adjustments have to be made and new friendships are likely to result. Your social life, in the first few months at least, will probably revolve around other parents of infants and toddlers. The ability to exchange experiences with mothers and fathers in a similar situation to yours can be very reassuring. You share each other's everyday concerns and triumphs. You speak each other's language.

However, don't neglect your childless friends whose private and business lives have not changed. If you don't feel up to inviting them home to dinner, or even for coffee, keep in touch by telephone, if you can find a mutually convenient time to make the call. That is a problem. Your best hour might be in the middle of somebody else's most pressing work hours, or after the two a.m. feed, a very anti-social time unless your friend lives in a distant country. Email is an excellent modern solution because you can send messages at any time without the risk of disturbing anybody.

GOING OUT

As a new parent, try not to be too housebound. Make arrangements to meet other parents with their babies at a restaurant that accommodates baby carriages and tolerates baby cries. There are such places and they deserve your patronage. Otherwise, if you have a treasure of a mother, mother-in-law, aunt, friend or a trusty nanny or babysitter, you might be able to sneak away for an hour or two on your own, or to meet someone for lunch. There is no rule dictating when you are permitted to leave your baby in someone else's care because that is dependent on your nature, the character of the baby and the calibre of the other person (see also pages 26—32). One thing is certain: you must be able to trust the carer implicitly.

On the subject of breast-feeding in public – at a restaurant, on public transport or at a picnic with friends – this is a choice best left to individuals. However, nursing mothers should be aware that it might embarrass some people, especially anyone prudish.

Crying in public

The only way an infant can express a need is by yelling. It's up to you to know whether it's a cry for food, attention or a change of nappy. As you and your child get to know each other, you start being able to tell what certain cries mean and when they are likely to occur. That means you can time your outings to coincide with the quiet periods. That's the theory anyhow.

Realistically, though, you can't always control your public appearances and inevitably there will be times when your baby screams to the rafters at the worst possible moment. Don't fuss. All babies cry. It's perfectly natural. What you should do is remove yourselves – from the restaurant, dining room or wherever – and find a quiet place nearby where you can correct the problem and calm the child. You can't expect others to put up with the never-ending wailing of your offspring, even if you have grown used to it. The cry of a child is very penetrating. Nature has made sure that it unnerves adults because that means they will attend promptly to the cause of the distress.

BABY ON BOARD

Flying overseas with an infant can be blessedly uneventful when the little one is too young to know what is going on. So don't worry unnecessarily if you have to take a long journey by air. A good airline trains its staff to handle the needs of parents and babies so think of them as your helpers, on the ground and in the air.

This is the procedure.

- When you make the airline booking, make sure they know you are travelling with an infant.
- Request a bassinet with mattress, pillow, blanket and sheets.
- Make sure they confirm that you have a bulkhead seat; that is, one with no seats in front of it, and space enough for the bassinet.
- If you are bottle-feeding, bring enough formula to last the distance. The flight attendants will help prepare, heat and wash bottles if you ask them to.
- A good airline will have a stock of strained baby food on board its aircraft. Double-check that this is so when you make the booking.

At the departure lounge, you will be invited to board the aircraft before the main bulk of passengers. A member of the cabin crew will help you with your bags, settle you into your seat and make sure you have everything you need. Certain washrooms on the plane will have fold-down changing tables, and during the flight you should be given a kit that includes items such as a changing mat, bib, nappy and disposable face wipes.

Even so, don't trust to luck. Make sure you take more than enough baby needs from home to last the entire journey. Flight delays do occur and human error might mean that nobody notices until after take-off that somebody forgot to load the baby food.

THE KNOW-ALL

They are everywhere, not just within the family or among your in-laws. Know-alls are on the street, in the supermarket, at the pharmacy, in the park and in the queue at the post office. They lie in wait to dish out advice on everything to do with mothering and the healthy growth of a child. The moment they see you with a baby, strangers who would not normally give you the time of day feel compelled to acquaint you with their thoughts on child rearing. Their first offence is usually to be wrong about the sex of your pride and joy. Do not lose your temper. These foolish things are a test of your good manners.

To your well-intentioned family and friends, say that you are following your doctor's orders and you believe it would be foolish to do otherwise. (Indeed, it would.) If it's to do with your choice of clothes for the baby, the decoration of the nursery, and the routine you have put in place, finding a polite reply is more challenging. Don't lose your nerve. Be serene but firm. For moral support, include your partner's opinion by saying confidently, 'Ben and I chose it together' or 'Ben and I find this way suits us best' or simply 'We like it this way.'

Here's what you could say to strangers as you smile sweetly: 'Thank you for your opinion' and leave it at that. White lies are permissible in these circumstances, so 'I appreciate your interest but, actually, I'm a paediatrician' or 'My first baby? Goodness, no, he's my fifth!' should be enough to ward off most know-alls.

THE BABY BORE

There is no limit to the love you should give your child – anyone who is cherished from the cradle is deeply privileged – but there is a limit to how many stories your long-suffering friends and relations can bear. Do be aware of the difference between telling the odd little anecdote and being a baby bore. Grandparents can be just as guilty of this sort of tiresome talk. Make an effort to keep up with what's going on in the outside world so that you can participate in general conversation beyond the limits of the nursery.

CEREMONIES AND CELEBRATIONS

A child's first formal public function is the one that honours him or her by acceptance into whatever religion or community the family belongs to. There is no particular age at which a child should be christened, but if there is an heirloom christening robe, the younger the better before the baby outgrows it. Three or four months is a popular age for christenings, although the date chosen might depend on more practical matters, such as when all the members of both families can get together. (Remember that the naming ceremony of religions other than Christianity should not be called christenings.)

Families who do not follow any formal religion are free to invent their own naming ceremonies, with or without professional celebrants. Such an event could occur anywhere and at any time but, given the broad age span of people likely to be there, it's sensible to hold it during the day in a place where children can run around freely, and the elderly can sit in comfort. A barbecue in a private garden and a picnic in a public park are two possibilities. The thought that every member of the immediate family, as well as each very close friend, has a part in the child's life might mean there is no need to nominate one or two in particular to be spiritual guardians, the equivalent of godparents in a religious service.

At one such service I know about, everybody paid some kind of tribute to the child, by reading a piece of poetry, singing, dancing, playing a musical instrument or delivering a tender little monologue. Literature is rich in inspiration. Look up William Blake's 'The Divine Image' and his 'Songs of Innocence' ('Little Lamb, who made thee?'). There are poems of whimsy such as Edward Lear's 'The Owl and the Pussycat', and sentimental ones, like Robert Louis Stevenson's 'Romance' ('I will make you brooches and toys for your delight') and Robert Burns' 'A Red, Red Rose'.

A stanza or two from *The Rubáiyát of Omar Khayyám* ('underneath the Bough, A Jug of Wine, a Loaf of Bread – and Thou Beside me singing in the Wilderness') is an appropriate offering from someone worldly wise. Judith Wright's 'Woman To Child' is a touching, reflective piece for a new mother to read. Banjo Paterson is at his witty and irreverent best with 'A Bush Christening', a pacy ballad about a ten-year-old who thinks his belated christening means he'll be branded, like a colt.

The point of an occasion such as this is to acknowledge and honour this new human being, bestow a name and to celebrate life.

A TRADITIONAL CHRISTENING

If you are irregular or lapsed churchgoers but still wish your child to be received into the church or place of worship, choose a suitable one and introduce yourselves to the priest or minister. If he or she agrees to perform the ceremony, you will be expected to attend a few services immediately before the date of the ceremony to show good faith. It would be discourteous not to do so. It would also be polite to continue to attend services, at least for a short while afterwards.

Christianity is by far the most dominant faith in Australia and the majority of Christians are Roman Catholic, with Anglican (previously Church of England) a close second. The Uniting and Presbyterian Churches also form part of the broader Christian make-up of our eclectic society. So here is a broad outline of what happens at a christening. The priest or minister at your local church will be able to explain any specific details particular to that church.

Godparents

For members of most Christian churches, a very early consideration, perhaps even before a child is born, should be the choice of godparents. This decision is a tricky one. The role of a godparent is to look after a human being's spiritual wellbeing all through the growing years to maturity and even beyond. Although not necessarily a blood relation, a godparent becomes part of the godchild's extended family. It makes sense to choose someone of the same faith as the family. There is no official role for godparents in either the Presbyterian Church or the Uniting Church in Australia because both these Protestant churches place responsibility for the child's spiritual upbringing with the parents. You may appoint godparents if you wish but, technically, they are not necessary.

Godparents are expected to bestow gifts at the christening and on important milestones, such as birthdays, graduation and marriage. While only part-time, it is virtually a lifetime job. Tasks godparents are not expected to undertake are the payment of any bills involved in the ceremonies throughout a godchild's life, nor are they required to be adoptive parents if the child is orphaned.

Only someone very close should be asked to take on the responsibility of being a godparent. Instead of asking anyone directly, be tactful to avoid the embarrassment of a refusal. Say something like 'If we asked you to be Angela's godparent, would you think it wonderful or terrible?' There is no limit to the number of godparents a child may have but the usual number is two – one woman, one man. If one of them is a wild card, say someone loved but free-spirited, or footloose, therefore unreliable, you may wish to choose another, more dependable, person as well.

If you are asked to be a godparent and you are reluctant, now is the time to be honest. Don't be tempted to take on something you know you can't carry through and say so, in the gentlest way you can. Tell them how honoured and flattered you are that they think you suitable, but you do not feel equal to such a responsible role.

Should gays and lesbians be godparents? Certainly, if they are your relations or close friends. Because most homosexuals remain childless, they often make the most doting and caring of godparents. Because they often have full social lives, they can be interesting and amusing company. Because they represent a way of life that may be very different from the parental one, they broaden a child's experience of the world and teach valuable lessons in understanding and tolerance. Because they do not have the demands usually made on the financial resources of parents, they can be generous givers and, while this should never be the primary reason for choosing a godparent, it is reassuring to know that a godparent will not be unduly burdened by the expectations of the godchild as time goes by.

Invitations to the christening

In planning the christening, the first person to speak to is the priest or minister at the church where you worship to settle on a suitable time and date because a christening or baptism usually takes place in a church, often within a normal Sunday service or during mass. You should also discuss fees and the use or otherwise of still and video cameras, flashlights and tape recorders.

A christening is an intimate rather than lavish affair, and invitations may be made by telephone, fax, email, posted handwritten letter or printed card, or a combination of these. The priest who conducts the ceremony, and spouse, if there is one, must be invited to join the party afterwards, although they may not come. If it is a small gathering, involving only godparents, family and close friends, one of the most efficient and personal ways of inviting anyone anywhere is to make a telephone call first, followed up with a handwritten invitation that reads something like this:

> *1 Swans Way*
> *Swankton*
> *24th October*

Dear Kay and family,

Adam and I are delighted that you can join us at St Mark's on Sunday, 3rd November, at 3 o'clock for Angela's christening, and at home afterwards for ablutions of another kind. See you then.

Love, Eva

What to wear

If there is a family christening robe, this is the day when the child, whether boy or girl, should wear it. If there is no such heirloom, the new dress should be white, the symbol of purity, although it need not be elaborate. Parents, godparents and guests wear whatever they would to a normal church service. Put on something bright and cheerful to mark the occasion.

Ceremonial procedure

The ceremony takes place beside a font in the baptistry of the church. Traditionally parents played a secondary role to the godparents but that has changed. Now the mother may hold the baby as the priest performs the naming ceremony and the father may wipe away drops of holy water after it has been sprinkled on to the child's forehead. They also recite the baptismal vows, along with the godparents, undertaking to guide the child on the Christian way. The indignity of being showered with water is often the signal for an outburst of fury on the part of the blessed one and this tantrum will form part of family folklore, one of those moments recalled with affection and told and retold as the child grows up. For a Roman Catholic, a certificate of baptism is essential throughout life because without it he or she is not regarded as a member of the church, therefore cannot take communion, go to confession, be married or take any other sacrament in the church.

Afterwards, everyone goes to the parents' house, where the newest member of the church is fed and put to bed, to sleep while the others toast its health and good fortune, as they enjoy a lunch or afternoon tea of light finger food from a buffet. Champagne or other sparkling wine is appropriate at a christening party and perhaps a tier saved from the parents' wedding cake (see page 244). Since most parents at this time should not be expected to make a night of it, thoughtful guests will linger no more than an hour or two.

Christening presents

It is customary to give something that lasts. Godparents of the Roman Catholic faith often give a medallion of the Virgin Mary. Other time-honoured gifts, brought to the house after the ceremony, are: a spoon, a pusher, a cup or a bowl, all in sterling silver and perhaps hand-engraved with the celebrated one's initials; a small portfolio of blue-chip shares; a tiny gold bracelet; a silver frame; a handsome photograph album; a proper teddy bear; the video just taken in church. Windowshop at Tiffany & Co for inspired ideas realised in sterling silver. My favourites are a rattle shaped like dumbbells and an elephant moneybox.

Saying thank you

A child's parents do the thanking, in ways appropriate to the gift and the occasion. Written acknowledgements of these gifts is obligatory. The letters need not be long but they must be promptly written and sent. It is perfectly acceptable to buy decorative cards as long as they are blank. A printed 'Thank you' is no substitute for something personal, warmly penned and sincerely meant.

CEREMONIES OF ALL KINDS

As for practices that welcome the newborn into particular religions, they are as varied as the countries in which they are practised, and subdivided endlessly between sects, social and ethnic groups and, with immigration, adapted to conditions in the adopted country. There are also strong cultural differences. For instance, the Chinese believe that a child born in the Year of the Dragon is particularly fortunate, therefore the birthrate increases noticeably in those years. What follows here is a brief look at some of the traditional rites and ceremonies of various religions. Obviously some of the ceremonies are no longer practised in full, but the information here will give you a general idea of what to expect at such an event.

No matter what sort of religious ceremony you attend as a guest, don't attempt to use a camera, flash or tape recorder unless permission has been given by the authorities and the parents. If you are not of the same religion as those conducting the service, follow the lead of others in sitting and standing but bear in mind that you are not required to participate in prayers, songs or communion.

THE BUDDHIST BABY

There is no birth ceremony for Buddhists although initiation and naming ceremonies may occur in certain Buddhist sects. Buddha taught that earthly existence is transient and that suffering is caused by desire. People are required to repeat the cycle of life and death until they can be released from it. Through self-discipline and meditation in life, one can ultimately reach nirvana, a sublime state of enlightenment after death, and an end to the suffering inflicted by life.

In China, a person's age dates from conception, not birth, but it is not considered a good idea to choose a name until the child is born. The Chinese have many superstitions surrounding pregnancy and birth. One of them is that certain foods eaten for a week before conception determine the sex of the child: carrots, lettuce, mushrooms and bean curd produce a boy; fish, meat and pickles result in a girl. Another is that the unborn child is a girl if her mother's stomach is rounded, a boy if the stomach is a bit pointy. A reception for family and close friends takes place a month after the birth. Traditional gifts are nutritious foods for the mother and toys, clothes, gold jewellery and perhaps a Buddha image for the child. In gratitude for presents showered on the newborn, the parents bestow hard-boiled eggs in red-dyed shells, along with rice cakes, as symbols of new life, good fortune and family completeness. Take care not to lavish compliments on the babe because it might draw unwanted attention from evil spirits.

THE GREEK ORTHODOX BABY

The priest at the church where the family worships should be invited to visit mother and child as soon as possible after the birth to offer prayers. On the fortieth day after the birth, when the mother has adjusted physically and mentally, she and her husband take the child to the church for thanksgiving.

Baptism is a great social event for the Greeks. Confirmation is given at the same time and godparents play as important a part as parents in promising to guide the child's religious development. Although it doesn't matter at what age baptism takes place, the child should be robust enough to undergo full immersion three times and anointment with the chrismation, a preparation of olive oil and perfumes from the Patriarch of Constantinople, head of the Orthodox Church.

Traditionally, the best man at the parents' wedding becomes godfather to the first boy and first girl born to them, although there is no hard and fast rule; these days a woman may be the most important godparent. The role in the Greek Orthodox Church is taken very seriously and the child becomes part of the godparent's family.

The godparent buys a totally new outfit for the child, including shoes, socks, hat and underwear. He also provides a gold cross (or gold sovereigns) and the bottle of olive oil, the large towel, large sheet, hand towel and fresh soap that will be used in the ceremony. The godparent also provides for each guest a little sack of five sugared almonds on which is tied a medallion of the madonna or the baby Jesus for a girl or a cross for a boy.

As the ceremony begins the mother holds the baby while the priest offers blessings. The child is taken from the mother by two women members of the immediate family, undressed at a special table, wrapped in the towel and handed to the godparent. After more blessings, the priest dips the child to the neck three times in holy water and drizzles water over the head. He then anoints the body all over with oil before handing the poor mite, usually screaming, back to the arms of the godparent, who holds the sheet and towel ready to receive their precious charge. The priest makes a sign of the cross over the child's mouth, forehead, the soles of the feet and the palms of the hands. Then he snips off a lock of baby hair, puts on the new singlet and places the medallion or cross around the infant's neck. The child is then dressed in the rest of the new clothes by the two women.

When all the members of the congregation file up to the altar to shake hands and congratulate the christening party, they are each given the sugared almonds and a chocolate from a silver tray, provided by the parents.

After the ceremony, there is usually a party where life is celebrated exuberantly with food and wine and, sometimes, music and dancing. Rather than the traditional big feast, there is now often a cocktail party instead. Children are always included.

THE INDIAN (HINDU) BABY

In the fifth month of her pregnancy, the mother-to-be is given a sari shower, the equivalent of the baby shower except that the presents are for the mother, not the child. She is presented with saris and sweets (for the craving pregnant women are supposed to feel) and her friends put flowers in her hair. Traditionally in India, an itinerant trader who dealt in bangles would be summoned. As many as twenty bangles might be bought and given to the honoured one. The practice is carried on in a minor way in Australia but the bangles have to be bought from more conventional sources. The whole purpose is to make the woman, who is beginning to change in shape and weight, feel good about herself.

In former times, for health reasons, mother and child were kept away from contact with outsiders during the first eleven days after the birth and only the mother was permitted to touch or handle her baby. That is why the priest does not come to the house to bless them until the twelfth day. Within three months, he visits the house again for the naming ceremony. He says prayers and writes the baby's name with a gold ring on a big platter of uncooked rice. The father dips the ring in milk and places it in the baby's mouth three times. The first boy is named after his paternal grandfather, the second boy after his maternal grandfather. The first girl is named after her father's mother, the second after her mother's mother. Food is served but no alcohol.

To celebrate each stage of the child's early development – its first word, its first steps – special food is prepared.

THE ISLAMIC BABY

Because its doctrines and practices are not widely understood, some explanation of what Islam stands for is appropriate here. Mohammed, the last of the prophets, who was born at Mecca in 570 AD, received his first revelation at the age of forty from God (Allah) through Archangel Gabriel. This revelation, which lasted for twenty-three years, is known as the Qur'an (Koran). Islam is not a stand-alone religion but a continuation of the message that originated in Judaic-Christian belief.

The Qur'an (Koran) forms the basis of every Muslim's faith and practice. The Sunnah is a second source of authority for Muslims. It is a record of the practice and example of how the revelations contained in the Qur'an were put into practice by Mohammed during his lifetime. These two texts set the standards by which most Muslims live today. Their focus is on piety, modesty, charity and moderation, on living in harmony with family, neighbours and the environment, and on the concept of justice. Muslims believe in the same holy books as Jews and Christians and revere all the prophets, from Adam and Joseph (Yusef), to Solomon (Sulaiman) and Jesus (Isa).

Like other religions, Islam spread to many communities throughout the Middle East, Asia and Africa. Some of these communities incorporated their own cultural practices into their interpretation of Islam, which accounts for widely different procedures from one group to another. Some perform rites that are abhorrent to other communities and have no basis in Islamic law.

Islam is not just a religion but a way of life. How a Muslim thinks and behaves in life, in relation to implementing Allah's word, is crucial in determining whether the final judgement will send him or her to a state of grace in heaven or to damnation in hell.

Islam attaches great importance to the family unit. According to

Islamic practices and teachings, a child should be conceived in goodness and joy, so the act between a man and a woman must be more than just a sexual encounter. Prayers are said beforehand and the interaction between them should be loving and considerate.

The first words a child hears after birth is the kalimah, 'Allah akbar', a declaration of faith that 'God is the greatest', there is only one God and Mohammed is His messenger. These words are said into the baby's ear by a member of the family – it doesn't matter which one. The hair of the child is shaved and the weight of it in silver is given away in charity. If the child is a boy, he will be circumcised, preferably at the time of birth, with a very sharp, sanitised instrument by a skilled person. Girls are not meant to be circumcised. Female genital mutilation has no basis in Islamic law or practice.

Contrary to common belief, carrying an evil eye to ward off danger or prevent a jinx is not endorsed by Islam, which forbids superstition. It is a pre-Islamic cultural practice in some countries.

Within seven days, the child is named. The best names are thought to be those whose roots lie in positive words, including the ninety-nine descriptions of Allah, or the names of prophets, angels or Islamic heroes. They include Abdullah (Servant of Allah), Abdurrahman (Servant of the Most Merciful), Abraham (Ibrahim), Moses (Mousa), Dawud (David) and Salahuddin, after Salahuddin Alayoubi, a warrior who played a key role in regaining Jerusalem during the Crusades. Because the Virgin Mary is highly respected by Muslims as the mother of the prophet Jesus, girls are sometimes named Mariam, which is Arabic for Mary.

To celebrate the birth, one or two sheep are killed and shared with family, friends and neighbours at a ceremony called an *aqiqah*. Some of the meat is given to the poor or needy. Although there is no Islamic requirement to do so, and depending on what is appropriate to their means, guests usually bring gifts of clothing or other goods for the baby. Some give money. The provision of gifts is an act encouraged by

Mohammed as a way of fostering bonding and compassion between people.

THE JEWISH BABY

For a newborn child to be considered Jewish, the mother must be Jewish. Although mixed marriages are frowned upon they do happen and even if the father is not Jewish, the child still is. Not so if the father is Jewish and the mother is of another faith.

When a boy is eight days old, circumcision (the surgical removal of the foreskin of the penis) is performed at home, at a hospital or in the synagogue and he is given a Hebrew name in a ceremony called *brith milah*, meaning 'the covenant of circumcision'. This ceremony formally welcomes the child into the covenant between God and the Jewish people. Orthodoxy requires all male guests to cover their heads with a hat or a yarmulke (skull cap) and women to wear modest clothing. The ceremony is usually followed by a celebration for family and close friends, who bring small gifts for the child.

Jewish girls have it a lot easier. A girl's naming ceremony takes place during a regular Sabbath (Friday evening or Saturday morning) service in the synagogue when she is a month old. She is given her Hebrew name and received into the community when her father is called to read from the Torah during the service. There is usually a reception at home afterwards.

There are many Progressive Jewish ceremonies to welcome a baby girl into the religious community, which are done at home and involve lighting candles, or pouring water over the baby girl's feet, as Abraham did for his guests to welcome them just after he was circumcised. There are also some Orthodox Sephardic communities that pass the baby girl among the guests, and each offers the baby a blessing.

A charming Jewish tradition is to plant a cedar tree to celebrate the birth of a boy and a cypress for a girl. The tree grows with the child and is made into the *chuppah* (marriage canopy – pronounced 'hoopah') under which he or she will be married.

THE JAPANESE BABY

Soon after being born, a child is taken by the mother with the extended family to a Shinto shrine to be received into the community and blessed by the priest in a ceremony known as *Hatsumiya-Mode*. A faith rather than a religion, Shinto, which means 'the way of the gods', originated in Japan even before writing was introduced in the fifth century. It is based on the worship of elements of nature, both tangible (trees, rocks) and intangible (fertility, ancestors). According to Shinto, the world is wonderful and people are intrinsically good. Badness is caused by malevolent spirits.

The worship of Shinto does not conflict with other beliefs, therefore many of its followers practise more than one faith. They say that the Japanese are born according to Shinto, live by the teachings of Confucius and die as Buddhists.

When children are aged three, five and seven, they visit the shrine again to receive blessings aimed at keeping them out of harm's way. This ancient ceremony, known as *Shichi-Go-San*, was instituted when life spans were so short that few children reached maturity.

SOME CUSTOMS WORTH COPYING
Sugared almonds

The Italians call them *confetti*; the French, *dragée*. Since as far back as the second century BC, sugared almonds have been a symbol of joy at the birth of a child. According to *Larousse Gastronomique* this practice originated among influential families in Ancient Rome. Now it is widespread among Catholic families in France, Italy and Spain, and Orthodox families in Greece, where sugared almonds in white, pink or blue are given to each guest at the christening. They are exquisitely packaged in decorative little tulle bags or special boxes, sometimes with the child's name on the front.

Croquembouche

Since for the French, like the Italians, no occasion is complete without an elaborate lunch, the christening is celebrated with champagne, expensive foods such as lobster, and some kind of magnificent cake. It might be the typical croquembouche – a pyramid of cream- or custard-filled profiteroles made of choux pastry with a crackling glaze – or something even more fanciful, such as a cradle made of almond paste. Although the croquembouche, which means 'crisp in the mouth', was a treat enjoyed by the privileged in mediaeval times, it was introduced to the wider community by the famous eighteenth-century chef, Antonin Carême. His amazing set pieces, such as minarets and pagodas, have inspired pastrycooks ever since but the festive concoctions of today are usually less ornate.

Sweet things

Traditionally in Germany, baby clothes are pegged to a washing line strung by neighbours across a village street, or from house to house, to announce the birth of a child. Nowadays, a giant toy stork in somebody's front garden also signifies a new baby in the house. Italians proclaim a birth with pink or blue ribbon draped around the front door. At a baby viewing in the Netherlands, pink-and-white or blue-and-white aniseed-flavoured biscuits called *muisjes* are always served. After a christening in Sweden, the Lutheran pastor gives the family a candle that is intended to be lit at the anniversary of the christening.

Chapter Two

GROWING UP

The family structure of father as provider and mother as home-maker is declining with each census. Judging by the enthusiasm a lot of women have for paid work, it's safe to assume that the old model is not even the most attractive one except, perhaps, for women in unskilled jobs. Financial independence has made many women wonder what benefits marriage can bring over more informal partnerships, especially since, on average, women who work the same hours as their husbands still do much more than a fair share of domestic chores. Marriage is no longer the necessary social prerequisite for parenthood either, so it's not surprising that one-parent and de facto families are on the increase.

WHO LOOKS AFTER BABY?

When children are very young, the question of whether or not both parents should have full-time jobs is not easily answered. There are convincing arguments for and against. If, as a parent, you own your own business or work from home, you might be able to have a young baby with you all or most of the time. But sweet babies quickly grow into demanding toddlers who need constant supervision and stimulation, essentials an adult workplace cannot offer, unless it has a pre-school department.

Economically, two incomes are sometimes a necessity, which at least eliminates the need to make a choice. But if money is not your primary reason for wanting to go out to work, there will be times when it's only human to feel a bit guilty. If that is the case, beware of any tendency to over-indulge your children. Instead, try to make the most of the time you do spend together and be vigilant about the care they are being given when you are not there.

A possible choice is a loving, healthy and competent mother or mother-in-law. But extended family members – aunts and grandparents – may be unable, unwilling or too far away. Besides, family relationships are intricate, delicately balanced and easily upset. You might find that doting grandparents, although well intentioned, start to take over, leaving you without the ultimate say in how your children are being raised. On the other hand, they might be enjoying lives of their own so much after raising a family, they may not relish going through it all again.

NANNY AND BABYSITTER

Nannies and babysitters might not be perfect but, because your relationship with them is a commercial one, at least you are the person who chooses them, makes the rules and sets the standards. You are in control. Or so you hope. Another possibility is an au pair, a young woman, usually foreign, who lives with a family for one or two years while she learns the language. The term is French and it means 'on a par' or 'on equal terms'. Although she is not a servant, an au pair repays her keep and pocket money by helping with light chores and some babysitting. It's a good set-up if you can find the right person. Look under 'Nannies' in the Yellow Pages or try the Internet.

Whether your search is for a nanny or a babysitter, the require-ments and responsibilities are the same. The only variable is the length of time that person spends with the child. You must be absolutely sure that your child is in safe hands before you engage anyone. Rely on word of mouth and specialist agencies rather than classified advertising pages. Go to reliable sources for recommendations: friends and family members, neighbours, your colleagues at the office. The corner shop, if you have a trusty one, can be a very effective personnel department for household help.

If you do run an advertisement or respond to one, make sure you ask for references and then follow them up diligently by calling the people who wrote them for verification and enlargement. Some refer-ences (see pages 166–167) can mislead unless you read between the lines and you should not take chances with what, perhaps, is the most important staff appointment you are ever likely to make.

Once all these steps have been taken, the final selection should be based on your own instincts and the child's reactions. Even after you have employed someone, be watchful until you are absolutely sure your babe is receiving the best possible care in your absence.

I have friends who found the perfect solution. When a child was born to the young woman, who runs her own very demanding business, her mother gave up her full-time job to become the paid nanny to her grandchild, giving peace of mind and great joy all round. But not every-one is in a position as happy as that one.

Live-in or day help?

How closely you welcome the nanny, or any permanent or semi-permanent staff, into your family is a matter of personal choice. But be cautious of too much intimacy. This should be a businesslike exchange. It's wise to keep a distance between employer and employee without affecting superior airs or being thoughtless or unkind. Courtesy belongs to every relationship in life, starting with those under your own roof.

Any live-in nanny must have comfortable quarters near her charge. She must have her own bathroom, television set, clear hours of work and of leisure. It is normal also to supply her meals. You should formalise the agreement with anyone you employ in your house. Think of it in the same way as you would when you appoint someone at the office. A contract of employment is a good idea if only to clarify the duties on both sides.

If you have live-in staff, your house should be reasonably large so that their quarters are distant from your own. If your living arrangements don't have that capability or you do not feel comfortable about having staff around twenty-four hours a day, then part-time helpers are the answer – either a local person, a couple or a team of professionals who come regularly.

Clarify the rules

The nanny must be briefed thoroughly about every aspect of the routine you wish your child to have, including the content and timing of meals, where and when outings should occur, when the child should be bathed and put to bed.

You must agree between you precisely what she is to do, if anything, apart from attend to the child or children. Light cleaning or cooking are not part of a traditional nanny's responsibility but that is subject to negotiation. Define the requirements right at the start, and make sure her payment is acceptable to both of you.

Important telephone numbers must be on hand at all times in case of emergency: your mobile, your office, the family doctor, close relative, fire brigade, local police station, taxi company, trustworthy neighbour. When you go out in the evening, be sure to leave the telephone number of the place where you will be.

From the start, a routine should be established to give the child a sense of security. Make sure the nanny knows what level of discipline you expect for the child. Consistency is important. There's no point asking the nanny to monitor and correct her charge's behaviour if you then indulge any lapses.

In exercising discipline, be firm, fair and benign, in the hope that it does not occur to the child to defy you. Good parents and carers practise what they preach, knowing that the lessons that have a lasting effect are taught by example. Any inconsistency will be noted and remembered. Parents who are consistently well behaved, in public and at home, have every chance of raising well-behaved children. A good nanny will be aware of these standards and will know how to supervise your child in your absence.

FATHER AS PRIMARY CARER

For some reason, it's tempting to feel sorry for single men who have custody of their children. We think of them as curiosities but they're not as rare as we may think. According to a 1999 report published by the Australian Bureau of Statistics, there are more than 60 000 lone-father households in Australia with children under the age of twenty-four. While the figures don't show how many have help from nannies, grandparents and other family members, these men are still the primary carers, playing the part of both mother and father. We're not surprised when women take on this dual role, so we shouldn't find it strange that a man should do it. If you are one of them, full credit to you when you cut school lunches, join the mothers waiting at the school gate in the afternoon and set a good example for your children at home.

CHILDCARE CENTRES

There are plenty of good centres that look after babies and very young toddlers, but you may feel the optimum place for children under the age of three is at home, for health reasons as much as any other. Little ones need to build up resistance to germs before they mix with too many outsiders, otherwise they are vulnerable to colds and whatever other minor maladies are lurking around. If you are friends with the mother of a child the same age as yours, you could share the costs of employing someone to be with them both at home until they are old enough to go to a childcare centre.

Creches, nursery schools, day care centres, pre-schools and kindergartens come under the blanket term of childcare centres. They are places that offer day care to children who are too young to go to proper school. Their standards and facilities are as varied as the individuals who run them, so be prepared to shop around before you trust your child to one of them. The best recommendation is word of mouth from other parents whose priorities you share.

If you are planning to send your child to a specific independent school later – that is, a private rather than government-run school – find out if it has a kindergarten that takes children from the age of three. If you have other children, it also has the great advantage of being a one-stop drop on the Monday-to-Friday parental chauffeur service.

Failing that, as a starting point get in touch with the National Childcare Accreditation Council in your state (www.ncac.gov.au) for basic information, including government-accredited childcare centres in your area.

Visit the properties in person. At a good facility, you should be made to feel welcome at any time into an atmosphere of openness and human warmth. The children should be clean, absorbed in whatever they are doing and comfortable with the staff. Apart from that, take note of the following.

- Make sure the hours are compatible with your own and determine what would happen if ever you were late in arriving to pick up your child.
- Check that the centre is clean, suitably equipped and the building and its facilities are well maintained.

- Ask for a copy of the centre's aims and procedures regarding each individual child and make sure that what you want is provided.
- Ask if you can inspect the kitchen and see examples of the menus served each day to make sure meals are nutritious and well balanced.
- Make sure you find it easy to communicate with these people, that they'll take your point of view seriously and keep you in touch with the day-to-day goings-on of your child, including any problems.

When you've made a choice but before you make a commitment, take your child along to see how well he or she takes to the centre, the staff and the other children.

SIBLINGS

If your first child is still a toddler, many experts counsel against announcing that a little brother or sister is on the way until you have been pregnant for at least six months, otherwise the waiting time will seem endless, therefore frustrating, to the child. Make sure any changes you make to the nursery are done well ahead of the birth and before the secret's out. That way, your toddler will not know there is an ulterior motive behind his or her promotion from a cot to a bed. Once you've shared the news, involve your child in all the preparations, including your visits to the doctor, and shopping for the new baby.

The choice of who looks after your firstborn while you are in hospital is a very important one. Ideally, it means the child should stay at home rather than having to be farmed out to aunts or grandparents. If that's not possible, make sure your little one is familiar and happy with the carers, and their home, well ahead of time.

BEING FAIR TO EACH CHILD

With more than one child, there will always be a degree of rivalry between them. Do your best to be a step ahead of it and to keep it at a healthy level. The fear in each child's heart is that, if you lavish too much attention and care on a new baby, or another brother or sister, your love will run out.

Love has no finite measure, like a ball of string or a loaf of bread. It has no 'use by' date, like a carton of milk or a jar of peanut butter. In fact, it is self-generating. The more you give, the more you receive and the more you have to give. If you can impart this abstract idea to your children it might help them avoid the deadly sins of envy and jealousy.

Find ways of spending time alone with each of your children in the normal course of things so that you have a chance to talk, one to one. Without your having to say it, your actions will tell them how important they are to you. Go out and hire a video together; ask for help in choosing a gift for someone; stop off at a café on the way home from school.

Quarrels between siblings are inevitable. Unless they come to blows, leave them to sort things out for themselves. It's part of learning. Besides, it's not a good idea to apportion blame unless you have witnessed what caused the altercation. Some human beings are manipulative enough to appear innocent when they are guilty, and these techniques are learned very early.

It's more complicated if your brood includes stepchildren or an adopted son or daughter, but the principles are the same. Try not only to be fair but to be seen to be fair to each child, and try not to show favouritism, even if one behaves like an angel and the other is the devil incarnate. At the same time, if one child shows signs of talent in a particular field, encourage the expression and direction of that aptitude.

Being fair does not necessarily mean giving each child precisely the same thing. One child's treat might be another's penance. Your son's aptitude for music should not mean that your daughter has to have piano lessons when she'd rather be fiddling with a microscope. Knowing the scope and the limitations of each of your children is the first step in encouraging their natural abilities and applying them to something worthwhile and rewarding long-term.

STEPCHILDREN

Because stepfamilies are made, not born, their success is the result of goodwill, hard work and patience (see also pages 398–401). You can't create an instant happy family from the remnants of a marriage broken by divorce or death, so the important thing is not to rush it. Let relationships evolve. Never force a stepchild to call you mum or dad. Let that happen automatically, if at all. Your given name, or its diminutive, will do very well unless the child invents a suitable one.

If you can start out afresh in a home of your own that neither family has lived in before, that is ideal. You're working from scratch to build a place that has no history for any of you, only a future. Make sure each child has a personal space in this house, preferably a private bedroom, but that depends on circumstances and each individual's age.

A united front by the parents is essential to the stability of a stepfamily. Children will be divisive, if you let them, but if they know that whatever one parent, step or otherwise, says and does will be endorsed by the other, it might make them feel frustrated at first, but they'll know where they stand and that leads to a sense of security.

As a stepmother, never criticise your stepchildren's mother or her family and keep in direct touch with them in situations of shared access. The same goes for a stepfather. When your stepchildren have to be disciplined, it is not your place to take on that role initially. Leave the discipline to the genetic parents, at least until you know you have gained the children's trust and respect. Avoid confrontation. Sit down and talk things out if there's disagreement over rights or habits. Try to find out what's motivating their behaviour rather than be provoked by it.

Make sure that your stepchildren have time alone with your spouse, just as you should plan to do things alone with your own children on a regular basis. But for most of the time, gather them all together as a total family. Do things together that you can all enjoy, whether it's seeing a movie, going bush for a weekend, or barracking for the budding soccer star of the family on a Saturday afternoon. Pitch in together on Clean Up Australia day. Celebrate milestones that you alone share: the date you moved into this house, or the day you brought home a puppy from the lost dogs' home. As time goes on, try to bond with your stepchildren, too, and find small things you can share alone together.

ADOPTED CHILDREN

In the past, a stigma was attached to the birth of a child whose mother was unmarried, whether or not the father was unknown. Many of these children were candidates for adoption for economic or social reasons and their origins kept quiet. One joyous outcome of the relaxed liaisons we now enter into is that a child born out of wedlock is so commonplace it goes unremarked. Skeletons in the closet are fewer now in most families than they have ever been. Let's hope they soon disappear altogether.

Hiding the truth from an adopted child is not a good idea. Every child has the right to know whose genes he or she carries, as much for practical reasons, such as potential health risks, as emotional ones. Besides, it will all come out one day, as the truth tends to do, and that can be a terrible shock to a young adult who had no idea that his or her origins were other than what you said. You will never be trusted again.

The broad facts of adoption can be given in a very positive way to a young child: 'We wanted you so much, we went all the way across the world' or 'We waited five years for you' or 'Your mother loved you so much, she wanted the best for you and she couldn't afford to give it, so she asked us to do that for her.' Show how carefully you have kept all the precious documents relating to the adoption. Make sure you have photographs and, possibly, a video of the child as a babe in your arms and any other moments that indicate how important the child is to you and your family. I know a couple who have framed the little satin baby shoes their newly adopted daughter wore when they brought her home to Australia from India.

As the child grows, expect more questions about the circumstances of the birth and the whereabouts of the natural parents. Answer these questions honestly and don't stand in the way if the child wants to get in touch with the mother and father, if they are still alive and agreeable to the contact.

Whatever the origins of your children, foster a sense of protectiveness in each one for the others by giving the firstborn a feeling of being a kind of second-in-charge to you when the next one is still a baby. This should in no sense be a heavy obligation on the elder child, but more a privilege in being trusted as your ally and confidant. That's an attractive role model for the rest. Create an environment in which a newcomer will be welcomed and treasured, no matter where she or he comes from.

A PLEASING CHILD

From pre-school to puberty, children should be schooled not only in the three Rs and other academic, artistic and scientific essentials, but in decorum. They must develop the conscience that tells them right from wrong. All this does not happen automatically but only after persistent persuasion by parents, carers and teachers with no lapses allowed. A well-behaved child knows what it's like to please other people. People smile on children with approval when they sit up straight at the table and say please and thank you and that makes children happy and secure. They should be taught to stand up immediately an adult guest enters the room, to offer their hands when they are introduced and not to address a grown-up by his or her first name unless invited to do so. In this way the groundwork is laid for the development of a young human being into an attractive, charming and well-mannered person. When we grow up and realise what these efforts entail, our gratitude should be boundless for the good work put in on our behalf by our own parents.

Patiently but relentlessly, children have to be encouraged – again and again and again – to put their toys away, to wash their hands before meals, to sit still at the dinner table and, if they need to leave it, ask to be excused before they do. Limits should be put on time spent viewing television, videos and computer games, and a child should go to bed at a fixed time every night.

As a parent it's important to remember the power of actions over words. If your own behaviour is at odds with what you expect of your children, don't be surprised if they become disobedient and disrespect-ful. If you want your lessons to hit home, practise what you preach.

CHILDREN AT THE TABLE

A friend of mine is a teacher at a private boys' school in Sydney and he is sometimes in charge of groups of boys aged between ten and twelve on weekends away. The boys are expected to do various chores, includ-ing helping to set the table for dinner. My friend says that some of them have no idea where to set implements as simple as a knife, fork and glass at each table setting.

If children rarely sit at a table to eat their meals with the family, how on earth can they be expected to grow up with even a rudimentary grasp of the table manners and settings outlined in Chapter 12? Incon-venient though it may be, you must make time to sit down together at the dinner table as regularly as possible, once you feel they are old enough. Young children usually need to eat dinner earlier than their parents, so your communal table might have to wait until weekends.

Sharing food at a well-laid table is a great communing and civilising ritual in many societies. Although most of us do it from time to time, noshing in front of television has nothing to do with communing. This is the prerogative of people when they are alone, although I know plenty of loners who dine at the table just as they would if someone else were there.

Teach your children to pass food to others before they help themselves and to wait until their elders start eating before they tuck in. They should be taught not to interrupt adults but to wait for a pause before they open their mouths, and then only when there is no food in them. The ability to sit still and listen is a very important survival skill at every stage in life, so the sooner it is acquired the better. Make sure they ask your permission to leave the table when they have finished eating. I was at a get-together not long ago where a ten-year-old waited for a pause in the conversation before asking his father, 'May I change the subject?' From that moment, he had us all in thrall.

BEHAVIOUR IN A RESTAURANT

As their behaviour at the table becomes more controllable, children should be taken out quite regularly to a restaurant that caters for them. Hopefully, they might be shocked by the antics of some of their contemporaries, who roll on the floor, play chasey and yell at the top of their voices without restraint, until one of their parents blows his or her top and the whole outing turns into a fiasco. This is not a happy scenario and, unfortunately, it is not rare. An undisciplined child is an unbearable barbarian.

The more experienced children become at going out to restaurants, the more at ease they feel and the better behaved they should become. Because children are insatiably curious and very observant, they take notice of the way other people handle their forks, spoons and cups, the way they speak to waiters and each other, the way they pay their bills. This is an excellent opportunity for parents to point out praiseworthy table manners. It doesn't take long for children to differentiate between good and bad conduct. Reward your child for behaving well, not necessarily by gifts or sweets, but by expressions of approval and perhaps little privileges.

TOILET TRAINING

Don't expect it to happen before a child is two or three years old and on no account force it. Never decide on a date by which the mission must be accomplished, such as the birth of your next child, and ignore busybodies who express surprise that your scion is still in nappies. Wait until there are indications of receptiveness to learning, such as a curiosity about people using the toilet, or an expressed desire not to wear nappies any more.

Give praise when your child tells you the nappy is wet or dirty, more praise when he or she says it while it's happening. Cross your fingers that this will very soon lead to an alert before the deed is done. In that case, head straight for the potty. Take the training slowly and never seem daunted by setbacks. Keep in touch with your doctor if you worry that things are not proceeding normally. Up to about the age of five, it's not unusual for children to wet the bed occasionally. The Internet has some excellent sources of advice for parents on matters such as this, so log on for guidance and reassurance.

MUCKING UP

A model child is a figment of the imagination, the outcome of a sincere wish by parents that their diligence will result in exemplary behaviour on the part of their children at all times. If a child is not disobedient sometimes, that's cause for worry.

Children like to test the boundaries that you have so carefully constructed by pushing them, sometimes just a little bit, sometimes in a way designed to shock. You are unshockable, though, aren't you? At least, that's the way it should appear to them. When your son comes home from school having increased his vocabulary by one or two choice four-letter words, and practises them out loud with an enthusiasm he would never apply to his homework, what do you do?

In a child up to the age of five, ignore swear words and they should go away. But with, say, a ten-year-old, the incident can be the catalyst in opening up a whole area involving appropriate language and morality. Sit down and ask questions in a reasonable way, such as 'Where did you hear that word? Do you know what it means? It's not a word we say in front of other people. It degrades private parts of the body, the parts that are sacred and we keep to ourselves. There are certain rules about language, as there are about behaviour. You don't pick your nose, belch or break wind in public because it's gross and offensive. If you use ugly or obscene words and actions, people will think less of you.' Be open, take the mystery out of it, involve your children in rational discussions and leave them with plenty to think about.

If the naughtiness is simply to do with your daughter not washing her hands before she comes to the table, or your son leaving his room in a mess, move quickly to reinstate obedience. Relaxing the rules, even once, creates a precedent that makes them harder to enforce next time.

UNDERMINING INFLUENCES

In many ways, outside forces are against you in your attempts to teach your children good manners. Take prime-time television and the way teenagers, and sometimes whole families, are depicted in many sitcoms and some commercials. How often do we see teenage children feeding their faces as they loll on sofas with their feet on the coffee table. Or cutesy pre-pubescents giving their parents and teachers a bit of lip in fractured language.

As adults, we may appreciate the humour of precocious boys and sassy girls engaging in smart dialogue, but when you think of the message being delivered to an impressionable young audience, it's not so funny. If children grow up believing this kind of television, it will seem to them that sloppiness and bad manners are standard behaviour. As a parent, no matter how vigilant you are about monitoring what your children watch, you can't supervise them all the time – for instance, when they're at a friend's house. But try to balance their viewing so that they see plenty of programs that show people being civilised to each other.

POCKET MONEY FOR CHORES

As soon as they are old enough to have a sense of responsibility, children should be required to take on chores to earn their pocket money. Lapses must not be tolerated unless the circumstances are exceptional: emotional stress, physical illness, pressure of impending exams, or as a reward for especially good behaviour. Decide who does what by discussing it as a family. Being dictatorial will be counter-productive and could cause resentment or sibling rivalry.

A child's first obligation is to keep his or her space neat and tidy. After that, apportion tasks such as setting the table, washing up, making beds, dusting, sweeping the yard and cleaning the car fairly and to those best suited to them. If your daughter likes the garden, let her do some digging, watering and weeding. If your son likes to cook, ask him to help you in the kitchen and teach him how to set the table properly. Change the responsibilities around from time to time so that repetition doesn't lead to boredom. Don't inflict the burden of work on a child who is too young for it but watch the child's capabilities develop and introduce small jobs gradually. It's amazing how quickly they understand what pay is all about.

When you entertain adult friends at home, involve your children as co-hosts. Give them tasks they find easy and pleasurable to do. Little ones can be made to feel very grown-up if they are given the responsibility of passing around a plate of food.

Older children can be recruited as waiters and kitchen hands, valuable training for part-time work when they're university students and for later in life. As for what you pay them, that depends on their ages and levels of skill, but don't be stingy if they've done the job willingly and well. Be generous with praise as well; it's a great motivator.

PARTY TIME

By the age of two, most babies are on their feet, almost out of nappies and ready to party. Keep birthday parties for toddlers small and manageable. Five little friends, at most, if the occasion is intended for the child rather than the parents. At this age, a larger number might get out of hand or detract from the birthday child. A party of six two-year-olds is manageable, as long as there are several adults to lend a hand, solve problems or, better still, head them off before they start.

Because most children at this age still have a nap between two and four in the afternoon, a good time for a party is from eleven in the morning to one. The invitations go out two weeks ahead of the date by telephone or in writing. Anticipation will be kindled in the tinies if each receives a pretty or amusing card in the mail, so try to make an effort to start the excitement well ahead. It is customary for each child to bring a birthday gift and to go home with treats.

If the day is lovely, the party can be held outside. Tie balloons to the front gate of the house and to the front door to make the place special for everyone. Set a table under the trees with ribbons and bows, balloons and a cloth that will survive spills and smudges. Since some of the little ones will still be in nappies, turn a guest room into a changing room, with a sheet of plastic, a big bath towel placed on the bed and a box of tissues nearby.

APPROPRIATE FOOD

Simple is best. Although packaged potato chips and other savoury snacks are not the things parents wish their children to eat, they are popular with the toddler set. Peanut butter spread on bread cut into triangles, circles or stars also goes down well and, for some children, strips of fresh carrot and celery, along with fresh fruit, such as strawberries, bananas, orange segments and wedges of apple. Fairy bread and butterfly cakes provide a bit of magic. Make sure there is plenty of pink lemonade, orange juice and milk.

Adults may be given a choice of wine, beer, coffee, tea, mineral water, nuts and finger sandwiches. The centre of attention should be the cake, highly decorated, very fanciful and bearing the appropriate number of candles, which are lit by a doting adult and blown out by the birthday child (with help, if necessary) as the grand finale to the event.

AMUSEMENTS

Be wary of hiring an entertainer, such as a clown or a fairy godmother for children as young as these. I know of a party where the pirate was so convincing, two children went home in hysterics. Decide instead to revive simple games you remember from your own childhood. There's plenty of time later for more sophisticated distractions. In Pass the Parcel, the children stand in a circle and pass a wrapped gift from hand to hand while music is played, and when it stops the person holding the parcel is allowed to unwrap one layer. Whoever is in charge of the music must time it so that each child receives a present. Another game for toddlers is Statues. When the music stops each child must stand as still as possible. If the weather turns bad and the party has to move indoors, you might have to resort to other games. Musical Chairs, Blind Man's Bluff and Pin the Tail on the Donkey are good stand-bys.

TUSSLES

Few parties for two-year-olds are the model of decorum that may (or may not) come later in life because civilising the human being takes a lot longer than two years and much of the charm of babies is that they are guileless. The party can start to get boisterous when the party child declares 'I want that one' and snatches the colouring book from a parcel won by another child, who bursts into tears and wants her mother, who has gone shopping for half an hour. Somebody pushes someone, who starts to scream and sets off everybody else.

Mothers, fathers and grandparents should move in without chastisement or fuss to distract each child in some way. Tears are dried. It is gently explained that good children should not take toys that belong to other children and, besides, look at the treasures each of them has.

THE PARTY'S OVER

Two hours is more than enough time to exhaust everybody at a toddler's party so you should wind up the proceedings at one o'clock. Send each child home with the present from Pass the Parcel plus little treats, such as a chocolate Freddo, a fairy ring (for girls), a Batman and Robin souvenir (for boys), a slice of birthday cake and a balloon. A note of thanks for the gifts should be sent to each child who attended. The parents of the guests should also write their thanks for a lovely party and for the take-home trophies. Have your child beside you when you pen these notes and encourage his or her contribution. It is also a good idea to read the thank-you letters you receive. In this tactful way and before it even begins to make much sense, a child is introduced to the obligations and rewards of being a well-mannered person.

NO VULGAR DISPLAYS, PLEASE

As children grow, the birthday parties that mark their progress can be themed to fit their interests and level of education at a particular time. However, beware of undue ostentation and extravagance, designed more to outdo others than to honour your child. No matter how well-off you are, buying in the catering and entertainment for a hundred children can never be as joyful for your own as involving them creatively in every aspect of planning a party for a handful of true friends. Besides, how do you top an extravaganza next year, and the year after? Children grow into sophisticates soon enough. Keep the wonder and innocence children have in small things for as long as possible.

Fancy dress

Party themes that have been a great success in my family include medi-aeval knights and ladies with a homemade cardboard castle as the centrepiece. Dressing up as a member of the cast in a blockbuster movie is another winning formula, along with a video of the movie and festive lunchboxes for the viewers.

Perhaps our most successful party – certainly it was the most graphic – was the one for a twelve-year-old where we all dressed as punks, when the cult was still shockingly streetwise. The table was set with butcher's paper on which were scrawled ghoulish names of guests: Billy Rotten and Maggotty Meg. Food was dyed purple and green, with eggs painted like eyeballs. There was plenty of leather, chains, safety pins and coloured hair. A conservative grandfather wore a ripped T-shirt, fake tattoos and had his hair spiked with pink gel. It succeeded in linking the generations as though we were all of one age. It certainly made the children realise that the oldies were not so old after all.

SHARING

As these early years go by, a child begins to be aware of several important things. The first great lesson to be learned from birthday parties is that each person has a day of being feted and it's your turn on your birthday. The other children will bring you presents and they receive small gifts in return. When you become a guest at somebody else's birthday party, you are the one who hands over a gift that you yourself would probably adore to keep. This is when you learn the second great lesson: how to share with others and the pleasure of giving. Children should be encouraged to do this willingly, even if it's painful. Nobody should ever know they feel anything but generosity and great pleasure in giving and, if they practise long and hard enough, that's exactly what they should come to feel.

SCHOOLING

Big decisions must be made about which schools will provide suitable education for your children at every stage of their growing years, from the time they are barely out of nappies until their late teens. What works for the younger ones – a school's physical proximity to where they live, for instance – might not be so important later, when academic standards and individual needs are paramount.

In some families, tradition is important, too, particularly if it relates to private schools where the same lessons have been drummed into the heads of generations of the same blood line. Along with recording the arrival of a new member of such a family at the Registry of Births, Deaths and Marriages, the parents also put the baby's name down at the chosen school for inclusion with the intake of pupils in five or so years' time.

Whether or not that custom exists in your family, there's plenty to think about before you send a child to a particular school. The question of public or private schooling must be answered first. Public schools offer education free of charge whereas independent schools charge fees that vary a great deal from one to another. It's not always lack of money that prompts parents to send their children to a public school. Some believe that learning to mix well with people of different backgrounds and beliefs will give the child a wider perspective than can be gained from moving among children of a similar social and economic level.

So much depends on the individual school, its aims and standards. There is little doubt that independent schools can give children invaluable extras in and outside the curriculum such as languages, drama, music and a variety of sports. But there are also many public schools that stand out from the crowd academically and socially, and are known for the achievements of the pupils they send on to seats of higher learning. And remember that there are many people who make a success of their lives no matter where and for how long they received a formal education. Over and above instruction at school, the values and attitudes of parents at home are a deciding factor in whether or not their children reach the goals they set for themselves.

FIRST DAY AT SCHOOL

No matter how busy parents might be in their business or social lives, there are times when nobody can fill their shoes. One is on a child's first day at school. At least one parent should take the new pupil to school and be there again when school's out to listen to the day's doings and be free with praise and the child's favourite food. Parents must be willing members of the audience at school concerts and enthusiastic barrackers on sports days.

CHILD SAFETY

Many Australian children now are driven to and from school by car, not necessarily because parents want to pamper them but because children seem to be more vulnerable on their own than they were a generation ago. In those days, children and their friends went to school by public transport, although they were cautioned never to speak to strangers. That is more than ever a golden rule for all children.

Shepherding young children whenever they go out and protecting them from harm is a fundamental parental role. It's equally important not to be over-protective and to know when to encourage independent thought and action. Being close to them and sharing their everyday experiences helps you arrive at informed decisions about when they can be trusted to go by themselves to the corner shop, or to visit a friend who lives two streets away. Shielding children from reality for too long leaves them unprepared when you are not around.

GIVE UP THAT SEAT

When children do travel by train or bus, whether they are alone or with you, they should be prepared to give up their seats readily for their elders (see also page 64). They should not put their feet on the seats. They should not eat or drink as they ride or as they walk along the street. If they want to eat something in a public place, make sure they know that they should find a park bench or a wall and sit down before they start to consume.

Well-brought-up children do not sit on the footpath or on the steps of a city building. Exceptions may be the vast banks of steps in front of some civic buildings, such as an art gallery, museum or library, but the primary purpose of these steps must be borne in mind: they are there to give access to that building. So children sitting there should keep to the sides, out of the flow of pedestrians.

APPEARANCE

Some schools require their students to wear a uniform and that does away with having to make daily choices and accommodate childish preferences. After hours and at weekends it's a different matter. Unsuitable though you think a certain kind of dress might be, try to see it from your seven-year-old's point of view. Be firm but fair. Yes, you may wear your fairy wings to the supermarket. No, you cannot go bare-armed in this weather. Yes, you must wear that sweater your grandmother knitted when we go to see her today. Yes, you may wear jeans to Simon's party as long as they are clean.

When you shop for their clothes, respect the preferences of your children. Don't make them wear things they hate. Clothes are more than a means of keeping warm and staying modest. They are a key to identity. Being at one with the peer group is imperative in the minds of most children, so make sure you approve of the peer group to which yours belong. And remember, *you* dress for your peer group, too.

DIFFERENT SETS OF VALUES

When your children begin to visit the homes of friends they make at school and at play, they'll probably notice ways in which these households differ from their own. It's important to point out to them that not everybody has the same values and standards, that differences between families are perfectly normal, that we all have a right to live as we please as long as we don't harm others, and that these differences should be respected. Tell them about the rich variety of human life, the evolution of traditions and the value of heritage.

Children love stories of the past, so tell them what you know of your own family heritage, what you remember of your forebears and trace the connection from then until now. You could make this clear by drawing a family tree with a bud on the end of a different twig for each of your children. It's a way of helping them understand that within your own family you live by certain principles, you believe in them, they have always worked for you and these are the values you expect of them.

HEADING OFF TROUBLE

It is important to watch for any changes in the behaviour of children of school age because they could indicate that all is not well. For instance, if your son suddenly doesn't want to go to school it could be because he's having difficulty with lessons or relationships. Perhaps he's being bullied by another child, or victimised in some other way. If that is the case, don't ring the bully's parents. Discuss it with the form teacher and try to resolve it before it becomes too important.

Some bullies are born and some are made. If you notice that your child likes to intimidate others, start at the earliest possible age to say that this kind of behaviour is not acceptable in your family and make sure that your own behaviour as parents is not giving the wrong message. Try your best to make sure he or she does not become a victim either. The best way to do that is to keep telling your children how worthwhile they are; a child with high self-esteem does not readily become a victim.

In a class of perhaps thirty children not everybody will have your own standards of behaviour and your children must accept that difference and learn to deal with it. If you are summoned by the principal, which indicates that the matter is serious, don't approach the meeting with a belligerent or defensive attitude because all the school is trying to do is enlist your help in solving a problem.

A DIFFICULT TEACHER

Some people are compatible, some are not. If your child has trouble getting along with a particular teacher, try to find out exactly where the trouble lies. Is it the subject matter of the lessons? Do other children in the class have these problems? Does your child feel picked on, discriminated against or unnecessarily pressured? Are there any specific incidents the child can describe that indicate something wrong with the teacher's attitude or behaviour? Be as well informed as you can before you take the matter any further.

Parent–teacher interviews are held regularly in most schools. If you can wait, that is the ideal time to air any anxieties you have and listen to the teacher's point of view. If the matter is too urgent to be delayed, make an appointment to see the teacher as soon as possible and raise the subject, face to face, in a calm and reasonable way. It could be that the child is not equal to the level of the lessons and needs tutoring to catch up. Or perhaps he or she has no interest in the subject, or is inattentive, or disobedient. If what you hear still leaves you with question marks about the integrity or competence of the teacher, you should take your concerns to the school principal.

LEARNING ABOUT DRUGS

Opportunities to raise the subject of drug abuse arise fairly regularly in everyday life, if you are alert to them. The ravaging effects of drug abuse on a person in a movie, on television or in real life are an ugly sight for children, but exposing them to this reality is a necessary counter-balance to any impression they might be given that drugs are cool, associated as they are sometimes with glamour and celebrity (see also pages 93–98).

A derelict person on a park bench is not an attractive role model for a child, but rather than condemning them, encourage your children to feel compassion and perhaps start developing a social conscience. Syringes in the street are a grim leftover from the sordid practice of shooting up in a dirty alley; use the sight of them as an example to explain the dangers.

Without being heavy-handed about it, you can make sure your children have no delusions about the negative effects of drugs. Encourage their questions and never dodge the difficult ones. Most of all, set an example. If you use illicit drugs, or abuse legal ones, your words of caution will fall on deaf ears. Also remember that children's first experiments with drugs often result from raids on the medicine cupboard in the family bathroom.

LEARNING ABOUT SEX

The instruction of minors in the very grown-up subject of procreation is a challenge that requires courage and delicacy. Customs and views vary widely between ethnic and religious groups and from one family to another. What must be said, though, is that teaching a child about sex is primarily the responsibility of that child's parents or guardian. School teachers play a part, but it should be second lead. Whatever the circumstances, no child should reach puberty in a state of ignorance about what is happening to her or his body.

As a parent, you should answer questions about the birds, bees, babies and the human body directly. Be honest but tactful. In the early years, answer only enough to satisfy the child. However, it is important to be prepared; you will know when your child is ready to hear the full story. When friends and school mates tell your children amazing stories about sex, they should feel comfortable in talking to you about it without fear of your disapproval, evasion or ridicule. That kind of trust comes about if you always take pains to encourage them to tell you anything at all without ever appearing to be shocked. From the time your children begin to reason, they should be made aware of the parts of their bodies that should never be violated and made to feel confident about telling you of any threatening incidents, no matter who they may involve.

As children develop, parental teachings should go beyond the biological and cover the emotional aspects of adulthood, the powerful forces that can get people into so much hot water. The mechanics of the sexual act are one thing but the fact that they may be overwhelmed by the desire to do it can seem ludicrous to pre-pubescents. The connections between desire, intercourse and pregnancy are not always obvious, but it's worth pointing out that when the time comes falling in love clouds the issue, heightens the experience and masks the machinations of nature (see also Chapter 9).

Your daughter should look forward to menstruation if you have told her it will mean that she is no longer a child but a woman. While she should not be misled about the discomfort that is often experienced before and during menstruation, it should not be exaggerated or referred to as 'the curse', or any other such pejorative term.

Similarly, your son should be made aware of the changes in his own body by his father. By this stage boys and girls should know that sex can result in more than a pregnancy. It can transmit diseases, at least one of which is life-threatening. Once enlightened, they should conclude that only a fool would have sexual intercourse without using a condom. At sex education classes in many schools, students experience the condom first hand by putting it on a banana. It may be crude but it clarifies any misunderstanding.

EXPLAINING DEATH

Children brought up in the country learn about the great physical realities of life at an early age. Birth, reproduction and death hold few mysteries for kids reared on a farm. Not so their city counterparts, who are often so cut off from the earth they think that eggs come from cartons and chickens from the local takeaway. However, opportunities to prepare a child for the notion of death exist in the effect of the seasons on plants and insects in your own garden, and in the death of a family pet who must be given a respectful send-off. Take time to explain the life cycle of leaves and flowers. Point out the physical differences between something that's alive and something dead.

LOSS OF SOMEONE DEAR

Of the many sometimes conflicting emotions that overwhelm us when someone we love dies, the primary one is a dreadful sense of loss. Children feel that, too, even the little ones, but because their comprehension of death is confused, it is all the more frightening. First of all, they need reassurance that they are loved and will be taken care of; that they are not about to die; that you as a parent are not about to die; that they are in no way to blame for the death of the loved one.

Try to keep the household routine running as normally as possible. Don't shield your children from your own grief but allow them to be part of it and to know that their own feelings of bewilderment and sadness are shared. Include them in discussions about the funeral arrangements and use your own discretion about whether or not to let them witness a burial. Perhaps that depends on the age of the child.

Answer their questions as clearly and honestly as you can using language appropriate to their age. How you explain death will depend on your own beliefs, but do choose your words carefully. 'God has taken him from us' might make God seem like an enemy. 'She has gone to live in heaven' might make the child feel guilty at having driven her away. 'He's gone to sleep' could make the child afraid of going to bed. 'She's gone on a trip a long way away' could cause the child to worry because she didn't say goodbye; it also leaves a sense of incompletion when the traveller never returns.

Above all, don't misunderstand the reactions of your children to an important personal loss. The fact that they do not seem to be affected may not be a true measure of how they feel. Sometimes it's impossible to express deep sorrow in words. Just be there and be supportive. That can be beneficial all round. Staying close to your children can help you cope with your own bereavement.

Chapter Three

EVERYDAY ENCOUNTERS

Trivial though they may seem, the little things we do every day to maintain an orderly existence are the substance of life. We must breathe clean air, eat fresh and nutritious food and keep ourselves fit and healthy, just to be able to stay in this world. We must take on the pressures of earning money so that we can keep ourselves and our families fed, housed and clothed. As well as that, we must try to live in peace within our families and among neighbours, friends, acquaintances and perfect strangers. Courtesy is not just for special people and special occasions, it's for everyone, every day. Being punctual when you meet a friend for lunch, wiping your feet on the front doormat, turning off your mobile telephone before you enter someone's home, taking off your sunglasses when you meet a friend in the street and offering food to others before you help yourself are the automatic actions of a well-brought-up person.

HOME AND HEARTH

Within our own four walls, we are free to set and maintain our own standards but only up to a point. Because we are part of a community, we have obligations to be considerate of others, particularly the people next door.

THE PEOPLE NEXT DOOR

In dealing with the neighbours, be warm and helpful but not meddlesome or too chummy. 'Neighbourly' is the term for it. No better opportunity for small talk exists than the dialogue between neighbours, with the weather, the gardens, the maintenance of gutters, the pests invading the citrus trees, and the increasing rates as first-rate topics that lay fruitful common ground.

Where there are children of similar age in the street, they should be invited to each other's houses to play and encouraged to become good friends. Apart from there being safety in numbers, membership of a little group helps encourage a spirit of camaraderie, loyalty and an awareness of the needs of others. It means that other parents know who your children are and perform a kind of neighbourhood watch over their welfare. That makes daily living more pleasant all round.

When new people move into the house next door, it is a friendly gesture to knock on the door at a time when you know they are up and about, introduce yourself and say you hope they'll enjoy living in their new street. Whether you are as hospitable as Americans, with their gifts of home-baked cookies, is another thing. It is never wise to be too intimate with neighbours. You may be forever pestered by someone fond of dropping in unexpectedly – the most tiresome of all social horrors – or there could be a falling out for some reason and you're stuck with an enemy on your doorstep.

When you plan a big party of some kind, let the immediate neighbours know in advance there'll be some noise but try to make sure it is subdued by a reasonable hour. In some cases, the neighbours might be invited to the party if you like them, which solves all problems.

Border skirmishes

Potential problems between neighbours – intrusive branches or roots of a tree, inconsiderate builders, loud music, who pays when the fence has to be renewed – must be handled with grace and courtesy if possible. Try to avoid a confrontation. Taking a stand forces the other party to do the same, which means somebody has to lose face if a solution is to be found.

If the roots of a tree next door are clogging up your drains, the best procedure is to get the problem verified and fixed temporarily by a plumber, then talk politely to your neighbour explaining the difficulty. You should hope to reach agreement about the solution before you apply to the council for permission to have the tree removed. Rather than cut down a beautiful and mature tree, your neighbour might prefer to share the costs of regular visits by the plumber to trim the offending roots. Whatever happens, try to reach a compromise rather than take an inflexible position.

How to make a complaint

On the other hand, if you have a legitimate complaint, such as a building under construction intruding on your land or causing damage to your property, you can ask the council to intervene. But the council cannot help if you object to other people's builders walking across your roof, or if your neighbours spend their weekends blasting the district with noise all day long. One way of dealing with that is to talk to the others who live nearby and approach the offending household as a group. Be polite, reasonable and firm. Rather than launch a direct verbal attack on the person, direct your quarrel at the action. For example, instead of saying, 'Get those yobboes off my roof' or 'Turn that effing music down', rephrase it as 'My roof is fragile and the insurance company has warned me not to let anybody walk on it' or 'Your music is so loud we can't hear ours, and that's a bit unfair, isn't it?' In an apartment building, the best procedure is to complain to the body corporate or to the agency that manages the building.

When not to mind your own business

It's difficult to know when, if ever, to interfere with what is going on next door, but if a dog whines all day when its owners are at work, for example, it is advisable to let them know. They might not realise how miserable the animal is without them. If it becomes clear that an animal is neglected – sometimes people go away for a few days without having made proper arrangements for household pets – you should call the RSPCA. If domestic violence involves children, then it is your responsibility to report it to the appropriate authorities.

BORROWING

Try not to prevail on other people for the use of something that belongs to them. Certainly do not make a habit of it. If you must borrow something, whether it's a handkerchief, a book or an umbrella, you must return it in good condition as soon as possible. Since it was a favour, it is courteous to add a thoughtful gesture of your own. For example, if you do borrow from a neighbour the proverbial cup of sugar to make a cake, give a piece of your cake to your benefactor when you pay back the cup of sugar. The handkerchief must of course be laundered beautifully before being returned. The book must not have the corners of pages turned down or stains from food or drink; it must be in much the same state as it was when it was delivered into your care.

If the favour was a big one – borrowing a car or boat from a relative or close friend – make sure it is immaculate, inside and out, and the tank is full of petrol when you give it back. That's the least you should do. The thoughtful borrower will find something else that will express gratitude and be received with pleasure: flowers, a potplant, a bottle of wine, music recorded on cassette tape.

Some people are reluctant lenders. If you are one of them, be assured that you are not obliged to part with anything. But instead of an outright refusal, do try to be ready with a plausible excuse for saying no: your computer is being serviced or you'll be working flat out on it for the next week or so. Your bicycle has been a bit wobbly lately and on no account would you jeopardise the safety of the other person by lending it. Be pleasant but stick to your guns and hope that eventually these requests will cease. 'Oh, I'm just about to use it myself' is a handy, if desperate, response in most cases.

Borrowing and lending money is not advisable between relatives and friends. If you need a loan, go to a bank or other institution set up for the purpose. If you know someone who is desperately short of a sum of money that you would not miss, instead of lending it, give it and forget all about it.

GARBAGE

On average every year, each one of us in Australia produces one tonne of waste material that includes six billion plastic bags. We are second only to the United States in our ability to make rubbish. That is a shameful record, particularly since there are positive things we can all do immediately without any real difference to the way we live.

1   Cut down our use of plastic bags.
2   Recycle plastic containers, paper, glass bottles and cans.
3   Dispose of all rubbish responsibly, whether it's the remnants of a picnic or the wrapper of a chocolate bar. Throw them in a bin – preferably a covered one – but never in bushland, on the beach or in the street.

Make sure your rubbish bin at home has a secure lid so that when you put it out for collection it cannot be raided by birds or animals. If you have an open bin for recyclable materials, make sure papers and plastics are secured so they don't blow about the streets. That kind of civic responsibility is not only a courtesy to the environment and your neighbours but to the garbage collectors, who do unpleasant but essential work, the value of which goes largely unacknowledged.

DOMESTIC PETS

For many people, a home is not a home without at least one dog or cat, sometimes both, and maybe a tortoise, a few guinea pigs, two budgies and several goldfish. Looking after other creatures can give children a sense of responsibility, even though the proper and consistent care of an animal is usually left to the parents.

Before you have an animal as a family member make sure you know what you are in for, and be prepared to accept the responsibility. Animals are not inanimate objects to be collected like cars or paintings or prized trophies for display. Never give an animal as a present to someone unless you have asked that person and you are absolutely sure it will be received with enthusiasm and given a loving, permanent home. Each year, the RSPCA across Australia receives about 153 000 unwanted, neglected or abused animals, of which 72 000 are dogs and 59 000 are cats. Don't add to the statistics.

What ownership entails

Apart from being officially registered, just like human beings, fed special foods and taken periodically to the vet for check-ups, dogs must be walked on a leash at least once every day (you must carry with you the means of picking up their excrement), bathed once a week and given proper training in heeling, sitting and other commands. Cats also must be registered and fed special foods. They must be combed, provided with immaculate litter trays and given places other than the carpet to sharpen their claws. Water bowls must be refilled daily. Like humans, all animals must know the boundaries of their territory and have clean, comfortable bedding. Unless you are prepared to love it, whether it's a dog, cat, rat or pony, don't be tempted to buy it.

You must also decide before you undertake this obligation what you're going to do with the animals when the family goes on holiday. Unless you plan to take them with you or you have a reliable relative or close friend to look after them, it's best to get them used to being sent to reputable kennels or catteries by starting when they are young and adaptable. For older animals, incarceration in a cage can be a traumatic experience, however irreproachable the care. Some breeders will accept their pedigreed four-legged products back as temporary boarders and that is ideal.

If you are not planning to breed from your animals, they should be de-sexed. Ask your vet for advice on when that should be done. It might be sooner than you think.

Dogs

The first decision is what kind of dog. Characteristics vary enormously between one breed and another. The difference between a lapdog and a working dog is so great, they might as well be different species. Whether the dog is to be kennelled outside or allowed to sleep on the rug beside your child's bed should also be a factor in determining the breed.

Mind you, you might not have a choice. If a litter of puppies is born to the terrier-collie cross next door, fate will have decided for you because there's probably no way you'll dissuade your children from pestering you for one. Otherwise, check the Yellow Pages for dog breeders, or go to the RSPCA, where many an animal-lover has found a grateful, loyal and lifelong friend.

Whatever the dog's origins, it should be given a collar with a tag identifying its name and your telephone number.

Cats

A cat is not really a suitable pet for children, who are often too boisterous for feline comfort. It will bond more easily with an adult. Yet happy cohabitation with children is possible because cats are very clever at distancing themselves from potential trouble. Claws are the problem in cat encounters with children too young to comprehend the danger. (Never even contemplate the cruelty of having a cat's claws removed; they are essential to its independence and survival.)

If a cat and dog grow up together they often become great friends, not realising that they're meant to be natural enemies. In such a family, the right kind of dog can be the willing butt of infantile pranks, patiently putting up with any amount of hugging and tail-pulling, letting children ride on his back and dress him up as a baby. His compliance takes the children's attention away from his feline friend, who may be left in peace. Like the dog, a cat must have a collar with an identification tag.

Although cats are by nature nocturnal, they are also predators, which is why they should be kept inside at night. A cat trained from the age of three months will eventually become resigned to staying indoors, even when the moon is full and caterwauling fills the night air. That's better than nests being raided or half-dead birds fluttering helplessly in the jaws of your triumphant tabby.

Animal etiquette

When you have guests in your house, make sure they are not greeted by a moist nose prodding their crotch the moment they walk through the front door, or pleading eyes beside their chair at the dining table. Unless your guests declare themselves to be besotted with animals, keep your four-legged friends away from them for the duration of the visit. Some people are allergic to dogs and cats; some have phobias about them. Be sensitive to their susceptibilities.

Cats often but not always take themselves off the moment the doorbell rings. If yours does not, just make sure the guest on whose lap it threatens to sit will welcome it. Some cats have an infallible instinct for targetting the one person in the room who wants nothing to do with them. Head that off if you can and if the animal insists, remove it from the room.

As a guest, never bring your own pets with you to somebody else's house unless you are specifically invited to do so. However beautifully trained they are, there will be disruption of some kind. In a smart flat in London years ago, several of us waited for a minor diva to arrive for supper after a performance. With a flurry she finally made an entrance with her little Maltese terrier who, in over-excitement, straightaway peed on the white carpet.

TARDY TRADESPEOPLE

Why is it that, even with the immediate access mobile telephones can give, the company that sold you an item of merchandise usually cannot give you a more precise delivery time than 'sometime' on a certain day? So you cancel all obligations and wait in all day. Even then, your wait might be in vain. Next time, as a precaution, don't pay up front. Make it cash on delivery in the hope that it will speed things up. Good luck.

Many tradespeople also don't turn up when they say they will. These are bad business practices that should not be tolerated. When you approach a plumber (or electrician, builder, painter, carpenter) for the first time, and he doesn't return your call, make a second call, just in case the first message got lost somehow. If it is not returned, find another plumber because this one is never going to get any better.

There are responsible tradespeople, if you make the effort it takes to find them. When you do, you'll wonder why you put up with unreliability all this time. Don't support bad habits. Give your business to people who deserve it. That way, standards must improve for everyone. I have often thought that a little list of the best and most reliable tradespeople would be a great gift to newlyweds. It's taken me years to assemble mine.

When a team does come to work on your premises, it is not obligatory to offer them tea or coffee and biscuits but it is hospitable. If you are having a sandwich in the kitchen at lunchtime, you might like to ask if they'd like one, too, if you feel comfortable about it, particularly if there are only one or two of them and they happen to be working in that area. Although many tradespeople bring their own food and drinks, your offer will be seen as a gesture of goodwill. It will set the mood for the duration. Your consideration is likely to be repaid by the respect they show in tidying up after them and being as unintrusive as they can be. Apart from that, keep out of their way and let them get on with what they are doing without interruption until the end of the day, when they'll feel rewarded if you express approval for the job they have done.

OUT AND ABOUT

As our cities become more and more populous, some people feel that their anonymity in the crowd is a licence to behave selfishly and rudely. Don't be tempted to copy them, however stressed or frustrated you might feel. Think how unhappy their lives must be. Make yourself feel better by doing somebody else a kindness.

PUBLIC TRANSPORT

Taking a bus, tram or train presents a wonderful opportunity for spectators of the human comedy. Do it regularly and you receive excellent instruction in tolerance.

If you are an able-bodied person you should feel morally obliged to give your seat to someone who is not as young or nimble as you are. Pregnant women, elderly people and the disabled should never have to be straphangers. A young child should sit on the lap of an adult rather than occupy a seat when other people are standing. Students should nurse their backpacks. These are fundamental niceties of behaviour on public transport.

Always have your fare, or your ticket, ready when you board and try to have the correct amount of money when you pay. Wait until departing passengers have left the vehicle before you board. Don't push. Abide by the rules, such as those that prohibit eating or drinking as you ride. Respect other people's space in crowded vehicles, whether you are seated or standing. Be careful how you handle a broadsheet newspaper in the confined space. Take a lesson from travellers on crowded buses in New York city and the tube in London at peak hour: strap-hangers fold the whole broadsheet vertically, with the front page facing outward, so that it's half the width. Then they just open the pages, one at a time and fold them back on each other, keeping the long thin shape.

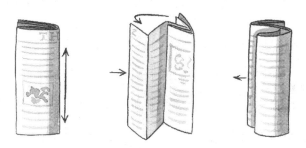

Say 'Excuse me, please' and smile if you need to manoeuvre past the person seated beside you and when you squeeze through a crowd to get to the exit. Dispose of spent tickets in a litter bin, not in the street. As you leave a bus, it's an old-fashioned courtesy to thank the driver.

ON THE ROAD

The rules of the road are very clear. Anybody who merits a licence is supposed to be familiar with what is permissible and what is not for the person in the driver's seat. How pleasing it would be if reality measured up to the theory.

Never exceed the speed limit, even when you think there are no police around, and never drive when you have been using an illegal substance or drinking more than a glass or two of alcohol. Don't honk the horn unless it is absolutely necessary – say, to warn a pedestrian who appears not to have seen you coming. Don't try to beat the lights as they turn from amber to red. Don't rev up a reluctant engine to an ear-splitting pitch at six o'clock in the morning. Turn down that ghetto-blaster. Unless you qualify, on no account park in a space designated for disabled drivers. When you know another car is waiting for a space that's about to become free, don't attempt to steal it.

Make sure your mobile telephone is one that fits into a speaker system in the car, so it does not have to be hand-held; it should be used only when absolutely necessary if there are passengers. Nothing should ever be thrown out of the car window. Small rubbish bags kept in the glove box are practical for refuse destined for the garbage bin when you get home or for a bin provided in a public place.

Road rage

The fact that anger is one of the seven deadly sins does not seem to worry many people who drive cars and exhibit lack of control at what they perceive to be an outrageous personal attack or stupidity on the part of another driver. Road rage has become a nasty side effect of traffic congestion and the general pressures and frustrations of urban living.

It's unpleasant enough for anyone to witness, but its effect on children is more complicated. If people in other cars do it, it may be seen for what it is: bad behaviour. But if their parents do it, they might think it's perfectly okay. Children observe and imitate the behaviour of their parents when they are behind the wheel of the family car and that is a very good reason to contain your wrath, even when other drivers behave abominably.

Do not shout, mutter oaths or attempt to compete with dangerous drivers. Don't lose your cool, even in traffic jams or when you can't find a place to park. Listen to something serene on the radio or cassette tape that helps you rise above the racket outside.

TAXIS

Anyone who takes taxis regularly knows that there are as many good, pleasant drivers as grudging, bad ones. But when they're bad, they can be truly horrid! If you are one of them, this message is for you.

- Don't pretend to know where you're going if you're not sure. Look in the street directory before you turn on the meter.
- Tell the passenger in broad terms which route you plan to take and make sure there is agreement on it.
- In high summer, close the windows and turn on the air-conditioning.
- Silence those back speakers.
- When you know there is a queue at the rank ahead, don't pick up an opportunist who has ducked around the corner to head you off.
- Don't attempt to multiple hire unless there is a genuine shortage of cabs.
- Don't grumble when a passenger wants only a short ride.

Not all passengers are models of good behaviour, either. If you are one of them, this message is for you.

- When a cab stops for you, smile and say 'thank you' as you get in. It sets a pleasant tone for the ride.
- You are not obliged to abide by the old Australian egalitarian custom of sitting in the front seat beside the driver. It might be more comfortable for you both if you sit on the back seat, particularly if you have bulky bags or packages.
- Don't leap into a cab when you know someone has been waiting for it longer than you.
- If you book a taxi by telephone, be ready when it arrives. If you change your mind, telephone to cancel.
- If you travel on an unfamiliar course, don't assume the driver is deliberately lengthening the journey. An experienced cabbie can predict traffic patterns fairly accurately and it's often quicker and cheaper to take a less obvious route.
- A taxi is not a bar or café, so don't eat or drink there.

ON THE STREET

Traffic lights and zebra crossings are there to preserve the safety of pedestrians and to prevent traffic accidents. As a pedestrian, don't cross the road unless the green light says 'walk', and make sure drivers have seen you and been given plenty of time to slow down before you set foot on a zebra crossing. Taking risks of this kind are more than silly; they are unfair on perfectly law-abiding drivers who might find themselves in a pile-up or on a charge of knocking somebody down.

Crowded city pavements are very chaotic now because people amble all over them instead of keeping to one side. I remember when a white line used to be drawn down the middle of city footpaths in Sydney and people walked to the left of it, just as they drive on the left-hand side of the road. Such sensible procedures have long vanished. The footpaths may be wider but the crowds are more muddled. Look at the way people line up on the kerb, facing each other like opposing armies ready to ape the Charge of the Light Brigade when the lights change to green.

On escalators, we used to stand on the left so that somebody in a hurry could pass on our right. But that simplicity has been complicated in some places by signs advising us to stand on the right. That is practical in countries where you drive on the right-hand side of the road, but not in one where we drive on the left. This kind of confusion adds unnecessarily to the frustration of trying to get around in a civilised way in our cities.

Anyone on a bicycle, rollerblades or a skateboard should have the necessary protective gear and should be aware of their designated zones. Crowded footpaths are not the place for them.

CHECKOUT CAPERS

Apart from on the road, one of the best places to learn about the laws of the jungle is the supermarket. Because people feel they are anonymous there, they are often inconsiderate or downright rude. It is amazing how oblivious of others many people are, when they stand gawping at the shelves or gossiping with their trolleys sticking out across the aisles so that nobody can pass. Think of shopping at the supermarket as a lesson in life.

At the checkout, there is sometimes a game of bluff, often instigated by a wily person who pretends ignorance. While it is churlish of someone with a mountainous load not to let someone with a carton of milk and a loaf of bread go ahead, this expectation should not be automatic. Either a polite request should be made or an invitation extended. Most supermarkets have checkouts dedicated to people with a limit of eight or twelve items and shoppers with large loads should not be expected to stand aside for a series of opportunistic queue-jumpers. It is perfectly okay to put a stop to this passing parade by politely but firmly pointing out the checkouts for people with few items.

SMOKING

Legal restrictions and social pressure have combined to limit the places where smoking is permitted and it's reasonable to assume that the habit will ultimately go the way of snuff-taking. Until that happens, smokers should take great care in where and when they choose to light up and non-smokers must avoid taking the high moral ground too readily. Telling others what to do can be an addiction just as heady as puffing tobacco.

Do not smoke indoors in a public or private place unless you know that it is legal and, if so, that it will not offend anybody else. When you need to smoke, go outdoors. Never blow smoke in the direction of anybody else and don't toss your butts out indiscriminately; first make sure they are not still smouldering before you put them in an ashtray or the rubbish bin.

Whether or not you are a smoker, don't talk about it all the time. Non-smokers, especially ex-smokers, often become bores about how awful smokers are. Smokers often become bores about their guilt. This kind of talk gets nobody anywhere. As with politics and religion, talking about it endlessly is not likely to change anybody's mind so leave it alone.

EMBARRASSING MOMENTS

If I had spinach between my teeth, crumbs around my mouth, smudged mascara, something suspicious up my nostril (probably a bit of tissue) or my fly undone among a group of people, I would like a kind friend to draw my attention to it, rather than titter about it and leave me in blissful ignorance.

How should my friend do it? Well, rather than shout about it for everyone to hear, a whispered aside should do the trick. If that's not possible, the next best way to indicate there's a minor mishap is by sign language. First you catch the person's eye when nobody else is looking and then perform a subtle little bit of mime. If you know how to play charades it should be easy.

EXPERTS IN YOUR LIFE

Every adult needs the support system of a handful of professionals who can be relied upon for expert advice at certain times. The basics are: a doctor who is a general practitioner, a dentist and a solicitor (along with barristers, they are now called lawyers). This key group used to include the bank manager but the role of such people has been taken over by computers now, so they don't count on a one-to-one basis any more. Add to these the chemist, hairdresser and dry-cleaner. Depending on your circumstances, you might also need an accountant, stockbroker, veterinary surgeon, florist, personal trainer, beautician, manicurist, alternative medicine practitioner such as an acupuncturist, and so on.

How do you find these people? In the same way as you find a reliable plumber or painter: word of mouth. Don't trust to luck with professionals. The matters they handle are too important, sometimes a matter of life and death.

THE DOCTOR

Forty years ago, ethical behaviour was an important aspect of what students of medicine were taught at university. Today it is just as important, except that its emphasis has shifted. Whereas in the past the focus was on ethical behaviour within the medical profession, it now also deals with the relationship between doctor and patient and the rights of the individual.

Ethical doctors abide by a handful of principles in their dealings with patients. They are to do with respect for your right to informed consent (nothing can be done without your full knowledge and approval), confidentiality (what the doctor knows about you will never be divulged to anyone else), beneficence (the doctor will act only for your good) and justice. Choose your doctor very carefully. He or she must be someone in whom you have faith and trust. Try not to chop and change around too much because the more your doctor knows about you, the more informed and efficient the care is likely to be.

Imbalance of power

Most of us feel a bit uncomfortable when we enter a doctor's surgery because, whether we realise it or not, we feel powerless. The doctor is powerful. We are not. It's an imbalance the profession would like to correct because no human being, no matter how well qualified, is omniscient. There are many things the medical profession does not know. The more equal you feel, the more comfortable you will be in the presence of the doctor, and the more open and honest the communication. That helps with the diagnosis and the doctor's ability to decide on the right treatment. The old-fashioned local GP (a species fast becoming obsolete) knew the family's entire history, medically and otherwise, and that was a huge advantage.

One of the reasons why many of us don't have the family doctor any more is because we tend to move around at different stages in our lives and new connections have to be made. The best way to choose a doctor – and any other professional, for that matter – is on the recommendation of someone you trust.

How informal the relationship turns out to be depends on the two individuals involved. My own doctor tells me that when a new patient comes into her surgery, she says, 'Hello, I am Dr X.' If the newcomer says, 'I'm Mrs Y', their exchange will continue to be formal, at least until they get to know each other better. But if the reply is 'I'm Sally Y', my doctor then says, 'I'm Margaret X' and they proceed on first-name terms. On the doctor's part, it's an offer to equalise the power. Some people accept that offer, some don't.

When you have an appointment with your doctor bear in mind the following.

- Make a list of all the things you want to say and take it with you. It's easy to forget when you are in the presence of someone powerful.
- Don't lie about anything. What is the point? Presumably you are there to be treated for some medical problem, so how can the correct treatment be prescribed if you haven't been honest in talking about your symptoms, your diet, your habits, or whatever.
- Certain words may have one meaning for the doctor and a different meaning for the patient, so try not to misinterpret what the doctor says. For instance, take the word 'shock'. To the patient, it might mean a jolt or a fright, but the doctor might be using it in the context of blood circulation. Don't be embarrassed to ask questions to make sure you understand exactly what the doctor means.
- Don't be antagonistic. You're not confronting an enemy but someone who is trying to help you. If you don't like this doctor, find one with whom you feel compatible.
- Keep an open mind about your problem. Sometimes people can get

a fixed idea in their heads, which leads to their following a certain line to the exclusion of all others. It might lead to a dead-end.

· Don't expect the doctor to know everything or be disappointed when he or she can't give you a black-and-white answer.

For example, if your condition is difficult to diagnose, ask the doctor to tell you what you *don't* have. Sometimes the answer can be a big relief.

HOSPITAL

Never let someone close to you go into hospital alone. It is an alienating experience, no matter how comfortable the hospital and charming the staff. The procedures are often dehumanising, turning a person into a patient, just a body in bed number three, room six, ward ten. Not knowing what is to come physically can be terrifying. See your charge to his or her quarters and make sure that nothing is wanting before you leave.

If you are the patient, take plenty of distractions with you, whether books, magazines, crossword puzzles, embroidery or some hobby. It might sound strange, but hand-rolling the edges of linen squares to turn them into table napkins is a task that gives me a great sense of calm. I took the paraphernalia for this activity with me once when I went to hospital and the head sister attributed my speedy recovery to what she termed my 'meditation'. I had never thought of needlework as a mantra but because it is repetitive I suppose it has a similar effect.

Some people are good patients and some are bad. I see no point in being cantankerous. Submit with grace. The people around you are trying to help you and the more you cooperate – the more often you smile and say 'please' and 'thank you' – the happier everyone will be, most of all you. Don't try to rule the roost, run the show or tell the experts how to do their jobs. That's not your role. Lie down. Be quiet. Instead of complaining about being bored, think how lucky you are to be able to watch daytime television without feeling guilty.

Visiting the patient

I'll never forget the comment of an eight-year-old I know when her friend asked if she could go with her to see her aunt in hospital: 'It's not a cocktail party, you know' was the wisdom that came out of the mouth of this babe. How true. It is no cocktail party unless the patient is in hospital for something minor (or joyous, like the birth of a child), is in good spirits and has a private room. Most confinements in hospital are not so jolly.

Visiting a friend who is ill is commendable, provided the attention is welcome. First establish whether the patient wants visitors and respect that decision. It is very bad form to try to intrude on someone who does not want visitors. Once you know your visit will be welcome, ring the ward sister at the hospital to ask if there are fixed visiting hours. Find out the most appropriate time to drop in, ideally when others are unlikely to be at the bedside. It's very irritating for someone who is bedridden to be a spectator at an animated social exchange between visitors who seem to have forgotten why they came.

Ask what the patient would like you to bring. Cut flowers are not always the answer. An elderly friend of mine who adored flowers became terribly worried when the masses of blooms that surrounded her bed were not attended to properly and she herself was too ill to do anything about it. Some flowers are more suitable than others. I remember asking a dear one which flowers he would like me to bring and suggesting marvellous red and orange lilies that were in season at the time. 'No', he managed to say, 'too aggressive.' So I brought baby roses.

A tasty morsel of food might be relished, as long as there are no dietary restrictions. Smoked salmon sandwiches and a good cappuccino can be a great treat after the blandness of hospital food. If the patient is well enough and the hospital permits alcohol, tiny bottles of French champagne are a delicious treat. If you take fruit, try to find something manageable, such as bananas, mandarins, cherries, grapes or dates rather than big pieces that need a knife. Magazines and books of short stories are often more suitable than something that needs sustained attention, although that depends on the person, the malady and the treatment.

Be cheerful but not hearty. Don't overwhelm with your vitality. That can be exhausting. Never sit on the bed unless you are invited to do so, and then with care and a minimum of movement. Don't cry, sigh or look miserable. Don't tell woeful tales or talk about disasters. In your attempt to entertain or keep the conversation going, don't yakkety-yak at length about people the patient does not know and probably has no desire to.

Don't stay too long. A number of fleeting calls is far better than one very long one. Try to be useful. When a person is confined to hospital there are sometimes little things that could make life more pleasant: a scarf or a wrap fetched from home, hand lotion, something more luxurious than the standard-issue soap. Perhaps you could offer to do their laundry, bring the mail from home, pay bills that might be outstanding or make telephone calls. Lying in a hospital bed gives a person a lot of time to dwell on perceived problems and magnify the minutiae of life. Taking burdens off a patient's mind is a wonderful aid to recovery.

Chapter Four

THE DANGEROUS YEARS

You've watched it elsewhere in nature and now you see it in your own offspring in puberty. Suddenly a carefree youngster turns into a restless adolescent experiencing physical changes and new emotions. Preoccupation with body image, the need for privacy, mood swings and endless time on the telephone are perfectly normal. You are witnessing a human being in transition. An adult is frantically signalling to get out of a body not yet mature enough to cope with the full responsibilities of being grown-up in our complex society.

EXPECT REBELLION

In order to grow to full independence, a human being must question the family that nurtured him or her. Spirited exchange can be beneficial to you as well as a safety valve for your teenager, whose point of view is worth your consideration, even if you disagree with it. The important thing is not to drive it underground or it will fester and emerge later as a mid-life crisis or an unseemly belated outbreak of some other kind. As a parent, you have to be content with the knowledge that the greatest success you can have in child-rearing is to produce a fully fledged adult who will one day be able to fly the coop and spread his or her wings in the world.

KEEP THE BONDS INTACT

Youth is a time of idealism and it can be uncomfortable for you as a parent when your children notice the discrepancy between what you are, what you do, what you say and what you expect of your young. Think of it from their point of view. You are boring because you are predictable; you have to have been to bring them up with some stability and consistency. Now they blame you for it. Try not to be hurt by what seems to be their ingratitude. Move on with them, keep an open mind, stay a step ahead of them, if you can. Don't compare them with the shining light you remember yourself to have been at their age. You were not perfect either. Ask your mother.

As a teenager, try to understand your parents' concern for your wellbeing and safety. When they insist on knowing where you're going and with whom and what time you'll be home, they're not trying to spoil your fun but to protect you from danger. As a parent, it's perfectly realistic to set a curfew for nights out. It's also a good idea to know who their friends are. The best way to do that is by encouraging them to entertain at home. Make yours the house where they are comfortable to congregate. Don't hover or be too vigilant, though, because you must trust your children for them to be able to gain a sense of responsibility. Once you are satisfied that the company they are keeping is good, you can leave them to their own devices, up to a point, depending of course on your own beliefs and cultural heritage. It's all a matter of balance and it's up to you to strike the right one.

THE NEED FOR PRIVACY

As a parent, it's important to keep in touch with what your children are doing all the time, which does not mean being stealthy or prying. Ideally they should have rooms of their own and their privacy must be respected. Never enter a teenager's room without knocking and waiting for a reply. Never open their mail, eavesdrop on their conversations, joke about their personal dramas or read their diaries without permission. Those are the actions of enemies, not allies.

Head off the pranks that younger children may play on the teenager by talking to them about the necessity of respecting each other's private space and personal possessions. Make sure they show similar respect for the teenager's friends when they ring or call at the house. The little ones are of course intrigued by the change in this person they emulate. They feel the loss of attention that goes with a teenager's growing preoccupation with the outside world. Watch that the needling doesn't become tiresome. But maintain house rules to do with expected chores, access to the telephone, the computer and the car.

DATING

As a parent of a teenage girl, make sure you meet the boy she plans to go out with, and know where they are going. If possible, give your daughter a mobile telephone and check that she has enough cash for a taxi home, if necessary. If he arrives to pick her up in a car, he must not honk the horn and sit out there, waiting for her to come running, but park the car and ring the doorbell. Your daughter should open the door and ask him inside to meet you for a few minutes. You should make an effort to be welcoming, informal and not obvious in your appraisal of him; no looking him up and down or asking searching questions about his background. Remember, it's only a date, not a lifelong commitment.

It is appropriate, though, to ask him to bring your daughter home by a certain time. What time that is will depend on her age and where they are going. If it's to a rock concert, be realistic about the time it might take to leave the venue and negotiate the traffic. Ask your daughter to ring if they look like being late.

If the boy does not have access to a car and your daughter does, it is still imperative for you to meet him before they go out together. Since presumably he is used to taking public transport, insist that he come to the house before they go off in the car. To state the obvious, make sure they understand that driving and drugs (including alcohol) do not go together. If they are going to be drinking, it's best to take taxis or public transport and leave the car at home. If one or both youngsters are on their P plates, it is illegal for them to consume any alcohol at all if driving.

Traditionally the expenses to do with going out should be met by the person who asked, although now it's sometimes more realistic to share the costs. For instance, tickets for a special event, such as a concert by a famous entertainer, can be expensive. To avoid any awkwardness there must be a clear understanding at the outset about who is going to pay. If funds are limited, it's best to be frank about it rather than risk running up unaffordable bills or have the embarrassment of running out of cash. If the two are keen on each other, going to a movie by public transport can be as rapturous as a costlier night out.

At the end of the evening, the boy should take the girl home to her front door and wait until she is safely inside before he leaves. Whether or not she invites him in for a cup of coffee is a matter of individual choice and circumstances, and subject to the approval of her parents.

DATING MANNERS

Opening the car door, walking on the kerb side, pulling out the chair for a girl to sit on, and standing up the moment she gets up to leave the table and again when she returns to it were automatic actions of well-mannered boys and men until at least the middle of the 1960s. Since then, for a number of reasons, these courtesies have all but disappeared. Certainly many of them do not make sense in the modern world: walking beside a woman to protect her from mud that the wheels of horse-drawn carriages kicked up at her ankle-length skirt is hardly necessary now.

But what has replaced them? In many cases, the sight is not pretty. One of the worst, and this happens with shocking regularity, is for a chap to stride ahead, leaving a sheila to trail along like some grateful canine. Whichever side of her he chooses to walk on, it should not be in front (unless they are going downstairs, in case she might fall) or behind (unless they are going upstairs), but at one side of her or the other. By all means walk arm in arm, or hold hands, unless the path is narrow, or you are obstructing the passage of others, in which case you must go single file.

Since a man is usually physically stronger than a woman, he must look after her, especially in crowded streets and empty alleys and car parks at night. When he sees her home, he should wait until she is safely inside her own front door before he leaves. Protectiveness is one of the most attractive male characteristics. A man who is truly confident in himself will have no qualms about being gentle with a woman and a woman must not misunderstand and read this as patronising or demeaning. She must have the grace and self-possession to accept being treated in a thoughtful and civilised way. Whoever is the stronger of the two, whether male or female, should do the protecting. If you are both of equal strength, then protect each other. For homosexuals and lesbians, just choose the role that best suits each partner.

TURNING DOWN A DATE

One of the sadnesses of life is that infatuation is often one-sided and romantic advances by one person are not always welcomed by the other. If a boy asks you for a date and you don't want to go out with him, don't be brutal; let him down gently: 'Thank you, but I'm not allowed out midweek and we're going camping at the weekend' or 'I'm on standby for babysitting' or 'I've got to study or I'll never get through my exams.' If he doesn't take the hint and keeps on asking, you'll probably have to finish it by saying you've started to go out with someone else, whether you have or not.

The same situation can happen in reverse, when a girl's overtures are not welcomed by a boy. As a boy, you should find excuses similar to the ones mentioned above rather than deliver an outright no. And don't boast about it to your mates.

SAYING NO GRACEFULLY

Sexual intercourse with an under-age person is a criminal offence. The legal age of consent in Australia varies, depending on the sex of the two people and the state or territory where they happen to be (see below). It's important to be aware of those limits if you are partnering somebody young whose precise age you do not know, or if you know your partner is below the legal age, or if both of you are, and you find yourselves so carried away by passion you forget all caution and have sex in a parked car or some other public place after dark and risk being caught.

Even so, no matter what the age group, when a boy pays for an evening out it does not automatically include sexual favours. He should not expect it and neither should the girl, unless they are equally smitten. Turning someone down can be hurtful, especially to an inexperienced and unsure person, so do it with tact and kindness. If the idea of going to bed with them on the first date is distasteful to you, be honest enough to say so. But if this is not your first date and you find the boy unattractive, a white lie is better. You could say, 'I'm not ready to go that far yet' or there's always the old standby, 'It's the wrong time of the month.' If you don't want to see him again, say, 'I like you very much but not in that way' and if he still pursues you later, it might be best to pretend to have met someone else rather than encourage him to hope that some day it might be the right time of the month.

Age of sexual consent

The minimum legal age for sexual intercourse in Australia depends on your sex, the sex of your partner and where you happen to be.

In all states and territories, it is an offence for a carer in charge of a mentally ill or handicapped person to have sex with that person. It is also illegal for anyone with authority over someone under the age of eighteen to have sex with that person. Needless to say, it is against the law to have any kind of sexual contact with anyone of any age who is a lineal descendant. The sexual activities of Australian citizens abroad are also governed by Commonwealth legislation that fixes the age of consent for both heterosexuals and homosexuals to sixteen years.

Apart from that, people having sexual intercourse in the following places must be at least as old as the ages shown (these were correct at time of going to press), with some exceptions, such as in Queensland, where anal sex is prohibited with anybody under the age of eighteen.

	Male with female	Male with male	Female with female
ACT	16 years	16 years	16 years
NSW	16	18	no law
NT	16	18	no law
QLD	16	16	16
SA	17	17	17
TAS	17	17	no law
VIC	16	16	16
WA	16	21	16

CAN HE/SHE STAY OVERNIGHT?

Infatuations, crushes and other romantic attachments are inevitable during the teenage years and it's anybody's guess how long they will last. Usually, though, many ships pass in the night before they tie up together so, as a parent, whether you love or hate your teenage offspring's current object of desire is probably not going to matter much in the long run. Be accommodating, even if the idea that this person might become a relative one day appalls you. On the other hand, don't place too much hope in the long-term viability of a teenage twosome you feel is made in heaven. It's early days yet.

Whether you permit the lovebirds to spend the night together under your own roof is up to you to decide. One thing that can be said in its favour is at least you know where they are. Younger children should be made aware of the overnight guest as a matter of course and without undue emphasis. They should understand that they must respect the privacy of the pair and not burst in without knocking. If you know the parents of the beloved, it might be wise to ring them discreetly. Mention that you're thinking of letting the teenage couple spend the night together at your place and hope they have no objection.

Who's responsible for the condoms is a thoroughly modern and sensible concern. While those who wear them should be the ones to acquire them, a sensible girl will have a supply as well. It's not a question of trust, it's to do with taking proper precautions against pregnancy and disease that can be fatal. The wise parent makes sure there are reliable condoms in the bathroom cupboard, just in case.

HOMOSEXUALITY

All children are curious about sexual differences, often at a very young age. Their perfectly normal games of doctors and patients should not be regarded as sinister unless you have good reason to suspect that they are. After puberty, same-sex experiments do not necessarily indicate homosexuality in a girl or boy but merely exploration and confusion due to rampant hormonal change. At this age there is fertile ground for sexual inquiry but any amorous attachments are often broken once these young people move into the wider world.

However, sometimes such predilections do not disappear and the person must come to terms with his or her own homosexuality. There are sad tales of boys and girls who grow well into adulthood in fear of admitting their sexuality, even to their parents or sometimes themselves. There can be terrible ramifications from this denial, including marriages of deceit, lifelong depression and guilt, which can impact severely not just on the person but on all those close to them.

The attitude of parents of gays and lesbians is vital to their children's ability to become well-adjusted adults. Parents should make every effort to engage their children's trust, regardless of sexuality, and to give love unconditionally. It is unfair for parents to pretend not to know, to place obstacles in the path of openness, to cause children to feel ashamed of their sexual preferences, or to pressure a homosexual to marry and devastate his or her own life as well as that of someone else. Repression can lead to unhealthy practices and self-destructive behaviour.

If you suspect that your son or daughter is gay, ask about it openly and be prepared to accept the answer, whatever it may be, without any sign of shock or disapproval. It is more difficult for your child than it is for you to open up the subject because he or she probably fears rejection. The more reassurance you can give of love, admiration and respect, the better. Don't be afraid to ask questions and express any worries you may have about what you perceive a homosexual way of life to be. Be a good listener. It's also important not to feel that you are somehow to blame, that you've done something wrong. Plenty of research on homosexuality indicates that sexual preferences are not the result of upbringing. Also, there are many ways of living happily, and marriage with children is only one of them.

To heterosexual couples with children, homosexual liaisons sometimes seem fragile and insecure. In fact, there are many homosexual unions that are as long-lasting and firmly based on fidelity as an ideal marriage is expected to be.

As a young person who is gay or lesbian, you probably have a pretty good idea of how your parents would react to the knowledge. If you want to keep in close touch with them, you'll probably have to raise the subject sooner or later. Parental love is sturdy and resilient. Even if your parents are hardliners in their beliefs, they should come around with time because the last thing they truly want is to lose touch with you. Meanwhile, the support and loyalty of friends, regardless of age and sexual preference, can be just as enduring as kinship and often even more rewarding. Try not to let your sexual orientation dominate your life. Above anything else, we are all human beings. Whether we're female, male or somewhere in between is secondary.

TEENAGE PARTIES

Teenagers are restless, sometimes awkward socially and not necessarily great conversationalists. At a party it's best to give them room to move. These are the years of wild infatuations, romantic notions and unpredictable liaisons. Give them the chance to gravitate to people they find attractive or with whom they feel at ease.

If the gathering is at your house, you'll need to establish the balance between being a vigilant parent and giving the youngsters their space. Although you don't want to cramp their style, make sure you know whether there's alcohol or not and how much is being drunk, and what time people are expected home. And of course, guests should be on their best behaviour, no matter how relaxed the occasion.

If the party is for a grander occasion such as a swish sixteenth birthday, some forethought will be required to make it memorable – for all the right reasons.

A few precautions are necessary in taking control of the party and not letting go of it. The best way to handle an incident is not to let it happen, which is why having some dependable adults circulate among the crowd is a good idea.

There are two main problems. The first is security. Gatecrashing is a sport among teenagers and the party could be mobbed. News of an impending party spreads like a bushfire by word of mouth, telephone, email or just by osmosis. If the party is big, hiring professional security guards ought to be considered. Invitations should always be in writing so starting and finishing times can be specified. Here is an example of an invitation.

(Given name of guest, handwritten)

Please join us to celebrate
Angela's Sixteenth Birthday
from 6 p.m. to 11 p.m. on Saturday 10 March 2001
1 Swans Way, Swankton

All drinks will be provided so please do not bring a bottle

RSVP Angela Peerless Telephone 0931 6409

Please bring this invitation with you or we won't let you in!

Guests must be required to present their invitations to gain entry. Unless everyone is familiar with the address, it's a good idea to include a map and precise directions with the invitation.

Alcohol abuse is the other big problem, along with illegal drugs. The invitation should also make it clear that guests are not required to bring alcoholic drinks because they will be provided. If people do bring alcohol, it should be taken away from them at the door and given back to them when they leave. A bar should be set up with either professional waiters or parental volunteers, preferably male, to dispense drinks instead of leaving it to the crowd to help themselves. Anyone caught attempting to use drugs should be asked to leave immediately. The teen host or hostess must take some responsibility for establishing the boundaries of behaviour for his or her friends at the party.

PARTY PREPARATION

- Let the neighbours know in advance. Invite them, if you are on social terms.
- Check that the first-aid kit is in order.
- On the evening, be sure to have on hand a list of everyone who is coming, along with their addresses and telephone numbers. These details might be needed in a hurry.

If the party-goers are under eighteen, it's a good idea to invite their parents for a pre-party drink. That gives the hosts a chance to find out which children are permitted to drink alcohol, which are not and how each of them plans to get home. It has advantages for the parents of the young guests as well, by giving them an opportunity to get to know the hosts and be reassured that their children are in responsible hands.

In planning a menu, bear in mind that many young people now are vegetarian. Finger food passed around first, followed by a simple buffet supper, is a good solution, although there should be enough chairs for everyone to sit down if they wish. Make sure you have plenty of soft drinks, including a fun non-alcoholic fruit punch. (For a guide to drinks and how to estimate quantities, see pages 291–292.)

Among venues outside the home, a ferry hired to cruise a river or harbour can be a good idea. Departure and arrival times are predetermined, waterborne craft are virtually impossible to gatecrash and alcohol consumption is limited to what is on board.

YOUNG DRIVERS

At the age of eighteen, a person is legally an adult, with an adult's rights to vote and to get a driver's licence (see below). Even so, parental hosts should have a sense of responsibility towards guests of this age and remember that provisional licence holders are not allowed to drink and drive (they must have zero blood alcohol levels) during the probationary period. They should also make sure they know the transport arrangements of everybody else when the party breaks up. Non-drivers should not be turfed out into the night without a taxi or a lift in somebody else's car.

AGE AT WHICH YOU CAN OBTAIN A LICENCE

ACT	17	SA	$16\frac{1}{2}$
NSW	17	TAS	17
NT	$16\frac{1}{2}$	VIC	18
QLD	17	WA	17

GIFTS

Birthday gifts are usually brought to the party and either opened when they are given, put in a special place for opening later in the evening, or kept for opening when the guests have gone. In any case, a handwritten letter of thanks must be sent to each giver as soon as possible after the party.

Appropriate presents a sixteen- or seventeen-year-old should be pleased with include: clothing, music, books, toiletries, fragrance, video games, gift vouchers from favourite stores, movie money, annual cinema membership (very reasonable), magazine subscriptions, driving lessons.

At eighteen, the gifts could be something more lasting: jewellery, luggage, art, books, sports gear, important wine, special courses or classes. And perhaps symbolic, such as an expensive watch for a young man and heirloom silver for a young woman, although only family and very close friends can be expected to give as lavishly as this.

WHEN A PARTY GETS OUT OF HAND

If an invited guest is causing serious trouble, the first move is to look at the guest list, call the offender's parents and ask them what they would like you to do; they might choose to collect him or her themselves. If they are unavailable, somebody at the party should volunteer for escort duty. Should the culprit refuse to go quietly, a level-headed mediator rather than a hot-head should be asked to try to calm the situation. In any case, ease the person away from the main party so as not to spoil other people's fun.

Gatecrashers must be dealt with swiftly. There is usually someone at the party who knows them and that person must be involved in facilitating their exit. If necessary, threaten to call the police. The last resort is to make that call and hope it's a quiet night on the local beat.

THE FORMAL

At the end of Years 10 and 12, a great social event known as The Formal takes place, usually on a Friday or Saturday night before the serious examination period starts. The teenagers dress up like ladies and gentlemen and are expected to behave that way, more or less. It's an exciting time. For most girls, this will be their chance to choose their first formal dress. In fact, the planning may start months ahead if the girl is to find the right dress, or have it made, and to accessorise it properly. A word of caution about footwear: if you're not used to ankle-wrecking high heels, don't use this gala event to try them out. Start practising well ahead of time, or settle for something pretty and closer to the ground. For the boys, since many are still growing, it's sensible for them to hire a tuxedo for the night rather than make the big investment a permanent one would require. (Keep that gift for the twenty-first birthday.) An alternative is to wear something groovy but not showy.

Depending on the individuals, their circle of friends and the school, plans might be made to go in groups, or in couples within groups. It's as acceptable for a girl to ask a boy to partner her as it is for him to ask her but, whatever happens, it should be done well ahead of time and whoever does the asking must be prepared to pay whatever expenses – transport, for instance – the event will involve.

On the evening, whoever calls for the other should do so at the front door and be asked in to meet the parents. The boy gives a corsage to the girl. She gives him a flower to wear in the buttonhole of his jacket (*boutonnière* is the debonair French word for it). No other gifts are expected.

Groups often congregate at somebody's house beforehand for drinks or they meet somewhere picturesque to be photographed. Sometimes friends share a room or suite at a hotel to prepare for the evening and to crash in afterwards. Sharing the hire of a limousine gives the evening a great sense of occasion and keeps reckless revellers away from a driver's seat.

The main event often takes place in the ballroom of a big hotel or in a reception centre where a photographer will be in attendance to make sure the evening is immortalised for countless photo albums. The standard format of a formal dinner is followed. If there are to be speakers, they may include the head boy or girl, selected teachers and perhaps a graduate from the previous year.

Nobody imagines that when the dinner is over it's time to go home, so parents should address this reality ahead of time and decide whether or not to impose a curfew or place any other restrictions on their young. Post-formal parties can kick on until dawn in private houses, nightclubs or on the beach. Only you can decide whether or not your child is mature enough to handle it.

HOLIDAYING WITH FRIENDS

At the end of Year 12, when serious exams are over and before the start of summer jobs, tertiary education or a career, older teenagers may need a release from the pressures of study, discipline and parental control. A good way is a holiday shared with friends in the peer group. This is often known as 'schoolies week'. It need not be far away: maybe camping in the bush, sharing a flat at the beach, or taking over the weekender of someone's parents. It's a time when parents must trust, however uneasy they may feel, and children should honour that trust.

To persuade your parents to let you go, make sure they know all the people you'll be holidaying with, precisely where you are going and when to expect you home. Given their approval, make sure you take a mobile telephone and enough money for an emergency (to get home, for instance). Ring as soon as you get there to assure them you have arrived safely and call them again if there are any changes to your plans.

PEER-GROUP PRESSURE

Without parental supervision, you are on your own in making choices about what you do and how you behave. Sometimes a peer group exerts a powerful force over its members, who might be pressured into doing things that go against their own beliefs. By all means, cooperate with the group in a spirit of camaraderie, accepting the common view on minor things, such as which beach to swim at, what food to buy and who has the bathroom next, but take care not to step outside your own moral boundaries. Stick to your guns on things that matter to you and if that is not respected by the others, you're in the wrong group.

THE ROCK CONCERT

Central to the lives of most teenagers – and subteens – is music that is almost invariably at odds with anything their parents and other adults enjoy. Video clips, magazine coverage of rock groups, and live appearances have a powerful effect on young people, influencing the way they look, feel and behave. Bands with the most appeal are usually those that aim to shock and incite rebellion. Lead singers in these bands become godlike objects of passion, to be worshipped, emulated and mobbed.

A rock concert where there is no reserved seating can be a dangerous place for young women, and men, too, if they are not built like rugby players. The prospect of seeing in person an adored singer or band provokes a level of excitement that overwhelms some individuals. When emotion overrides rational thought, the pressure of a crowd of five thousand pushing towards the stage is a terrifying possibility.

Most people caught up in this hysteria are without malice and entirely unaware of the danger of what they are doing. Under normal circumstances they would respect other people's space; on a crowded train, for example. But fuelled by ear-splitting music, dazzled by the spectacle and taken out of reality by the exhilaration of the moment, an individual is lost in the will of the herd. With most challenges in life, forewarned is usually forearmed, but here it probably won't help much when someone enters the trance-like state induced by this kind of group dynamic. The sheer numbers can also make things more difficult.

A well-managed rock concert will have at least one security guard for every hundred people and sometimes half as many again, depending on the kind of event. They do their best to head off trouble before it starts. For instance, they will try to stop 'surfing' (when a person is picked up and passed from hand to hand over the heads of the crowd) around the mosh pit, because people can get hurt by flailing limbs, particularly if the surfer is a hefty guy in boots with steel caps. The surfer, too, risks taking a dive head-first to the floor if hands are suddenly not there to keep him buoyant.

Even with vigilant security, surfing does happen, especially if the crowd is so dense it becomes too chaotic to be policed properly. Etiquette for guys in the mosh pit dictates that you must lend your support to the person, most often a male, who is being passed around and protect any girl who is near you. Should the person fall, you are expected to help get him or her to their feet. But in the frenzy, etiquette is easily forgotten. The mosh pit is a dangerous place for men as well as women.

SURVIVAL TACTICS

1   Don't go to a rock concert unless you have a pre-purchased ticket for a reserved seat. That means you have your own space and nobody else is allowed to encroach on it.

2   You'll be searched for knives and alcohol by security guards before they let you in. Don't wear or carry anything that could be considered a weapon; for instance, a heavily studded belt or dog collar, thick chains or spiked boots.

3   If you are a guy, dress for combat. Worn jeans and an army windbreaker will do. Before you leave home remove eyebrow, nose and ear studs and any other body jewellery. Wear old

runners that you can afford to lose. Anchor your hair under a back-to-front baseball cap.

4 If you are a girl, don't wear expensive clothes and avoid anything too revealing. Being in close proximity to other people, you're likely to be touched when you don't want to be. Avoid anything that could catch you around the throat, or be torn off, or knocked off. A T-shirt is better than a backless halter; jeans are better than a mini-skirt. Wear sneakers or gym shoes rather than Doc Martens, boots, or anything spindly or uncomfortable.

5 Have a handful of tissues in your pocket when you go to the toilet, in case the paper has run out.

6 Say no to anyone offering you drugs.

HOW TO GET AN AUTOGRAPH

Famous stars have bodyguards to protect them from any kind of danger. If a bodyguard is unsure of your intentions as you approach, he must automatically assume the worst, if he's doing his job properly. So, rushing at your idol means you'll be blocked by the guard and you'll never get an autograph.

The correct procedure is to queue politely at the public point nearest to the backstage exit and hold your pen and autograph book, or program, where they can be seen. The star will more than likely come over and sign because you are non-threatening and what you're after has been made quite clear. (For more details on meeting famous people, see page 438.)

DRUGS

A paradox in the nature of human beings as we grow older is our ability to remember the good things and forget the bad, particularly when they relate to our own behaviour. Remember your own experiments a generation or so ago? That doesn't mean you should be indifferent to what your children are playing around with. Set the boundaries and make sure they know what they are and why they must be respected. By now you've hopefully given them the self-esteem and confidence to be able to resist peer pressure and say no.

SMOKING

Tobacco was yesterday's temptation and its use lingers on, despite the body of medical evidence that points to its disastrous effects on health. Some young people take up the habit because their parents do it. Conversely, others smoke because it is frowned upon by their parents and other worthies. Make sure your children know about the damage tobacco does to the body. All you can hope is that its attractions will fade as good sense takes over.

DRINKING

In moderation, alcohol has a great deal going for it. It is synonymous with goodwill, pleasing to the palate and conducive to socialising. It helps people relax. Good wine is a happy partner to good food. It is integral to ceremonies and rituals as diverse as taking holy communion in the Catholic Church and the launching of great ocean liners. When children grow up with wine on the dinner table they seem to have less interest in abusing it later than people to whom it has always been forbidden. But its dangers are very real, especially when it is coupled with driving, a situation that happens all too often and with disastrous results.

Getting drunk at one time or another is almost a rite of passage for teenage boys and girls. If it's a rarity, there's no reason to be concerned, as long as your hapless young pisspot is in responsible company that will get them home in one piece. The experience and its aftermath might be the only lessons necessary to ensure it doesn't happen again. But if it becomes regular, make a time to talk it through in a calm way, not when he or she is still under the influence or suffering and remorseful next day. Do it in cold sobriety. Try to find out what drives the behaviour, whether it's the company, a certain set of circumstances, or something more deep-seated. If you feel it is more serious than you can handle, ask your doctor to recommend a trustworthy source of professional help.

ILLEGAL SUBSTANCES

Tobacco and alcohol are subject to misuse but they are still legal, at least for people over the age of eighteen. As we know, today's drugs such as ecstasy, heroin and cocaine, are not just addictive; they are also illegal. Acquiring them means being underhand and mixing with people on the wrong side of the law. There is also no way of knowing whether the drug is pure or whether it has been mixed with something else, and if so what and in what proportion. The risks cannot be over-stated. Nobody will ever know for sure how many deaths from drug overdose are deliberate and how many are accidental.

Not everyone who uses these drugs, even relatively regularly, becomes a helpless addict but there is always that danger. Who can tell who will be the one? The slogan 'just say no', however worthy and idealistic, is somewhat simplistic. If everybody else is doing it, it's hard to say no when you are seventeen. People who are high on life naturally have no need for a synthetic boost. Keep them busy. Praise their accomplishments. Build their self-confidence. Idleness is a risky state for a teenager.

As a parent, all you can do is try to steer your children towards benevolent company and activities that will help them fulfil their aptitudes and ambitions. Try to keep them involved in family activities as well as giving them freedom to gravitate to the people and pastimes they enjoy. Encourage them to move in a number of different circles, not just one group, so that they don't become totally identified with one set of values and practices to the exclusion of all others. If that group exerts a bad influence that must be stopped, or if it disintegrates for some reason, your teenager will be left without friends and that is a vulnerable state for anyone to be in.

FAMILY DISCUSSIONS

Raising the subject of drugs with your children shouldn't be hard if you have created an environment in which views of all kinds can be aired within the family without fear or inhibition. By the time your children are teenagers it would be surprising if the subject hadn't been raised and talked about, many times, in an everyday sort of way. No big deal. As they grow older, they understand more about the implications of drugs and their effect on the body and mind so it's crucial to keep the subject out in the open.

To initiate a discussion about drugs, choose an unhurried time when you are alone together and raise the subject in an indirect way. If you suspect your child might be experimenting with or exposed to drugs, don't confront. Coax. Say something like, 'You seem a bit distant lately. Is there anything you want to tell me?' or 'Jean thinks there might be drugs at the party on Saturday night. Do you think there will be?' The aim here is to foster an exchange. Listen carefully and sympathetically but never hesitate to make your own position clear on what is and is not acceptable. Rather than lay down the law, though, give options. Involve your child in the decision-making that will have such a profound effect on his or her life.

Try to avoid confrontation because that means both sides taking a stand and being inflexible. Talk it through. Try to come to a compromise that appeases everyone, set limits that are fair yet firm. Children need a framework that tells them where they belong. To them it means you care, and if you care about them they must be of value. Self-esteem is a powerful defence against drugs.

As a teenager, or anyone else for that matter, if you genuinely believe that such drugs should be decriminalised or legalised, then work legitimately towards changing the law. Involve yourself in peaceful demonstrations, recruit people to your cause, instigate some kind of reform movement, write pamphlets, give speeches, or take whatever action is necessary to bring your point of view to a wider audience. But work within the law, not outside it.

SIGNS OF DRUG USE AND ABUSE

To be able to read the signs, you need to know the effects different groups of drugs have on the human body. Here are the main ones.

Narcotics

These painkilling substances extracted from the poppy include heroin and opium, which are highly addictive. The more they are used, the greater the dosage required to achieve the euphoric state called a 'high'. By slowing down all the body's functions, including heart rate and bowel movement, opiate narcotics induce lethargy and loss of interest in food, sex and just about everything else except how and where to get the next hit.

Stimulants

Whereas narcotics slow the body down, amphetamines, including cocaine and ecstasy, rev it up, which is why they're given names such as 'speed' and 'uppers'. The over-excitement they cause comes from high blood pressure and their effect on the central nervous system. This heightening of activity wards off the need for sleep and food. Users sometimes need to chew gum to cushion their teeth from the rigours of excessive grinding. Exhaustion, anxiety, insomnia and acute depression are often the after effects, along with an intense desire for more stimulation. In the case of cocaine, nasal and general breathing problems can result.

Hallucinogens

Marijuana and LSD belong in the category of mind-altering drugs that slow reflex action and affect the way the world is perceived. Hallucinations, blurred vision, paranoia and hunger are among the common symptoms. Afterwards, through delusions and flashbacks, the mind seems to be more affected than the body, although increased weight is sometimes a result.

Sedatives

Sedatives can be found in most homes in Australia, either in the drinks cupboard or bar or the bathroom cupboard. Alcohol is one of them. Others are sleeping pills and tranquillisers, which are often prescribed to calm the central nervous system in order to relieve anxiety and stress. Symptoms of abuse include slurred speech, vertigo and lack of concentration.

Inhalants

The kitchen, bathroom and garage are amply stocked with chemicals which, if inhaled, manifest themselves in various ways, from delirium to apathy. The products include glue, petrol, paint thinners and some substances that come in aerosol containers. Sniffing can lead to eye, throat, lung and brain damage, unruly actions and irrational behaviour.

DON'T ASSUME THE WORST

As you can see from these descriptions, many drugs have similar outward symptoms. In a mild form, some of them are just like normal teenage behaviour. Sulking, self-centredness and adopting the unkempt appearance of street rabble are the baggage of many teenagers who have never touched drugs.

Be that as it may, you would not be a caring parent if you weren't watchful and fearful of any indication that something as insidious as a drug is taking hold. If you see a glaring change in your teenage child, such as uncharacteristic furtiveness or the sudden arrival on the scene of a different set of friends, do your best to find out what is going on, not by prying but by talking. Whatever you do, don't do anything to lose your child's trust. Don't raid a teenage bedroom for evidence. And don't assume anything until you know the facts.

Chapter Five

LEAVING THE NEST

O nce children who live at home begin to earn their own money, they should be required to pay for their board and keep, whether or not their parents are well-off. This is not unreasonable or unkind. It's sensible and realistic. Their launch into the outside world and their adjustment to it will be much easier if they understand what is expected of them. University students living at home should be expected to do jobs around the house in lieu of rent. The most important survival skill parents can give their children is self-reliance and there's no better starting point than expecting them to help pay their own way.

INDEPENDENCE DAY

There is no specific age at which a young adult should leave the family home to live somewhere else. Too many factors are involved. Some children mature faster than others. Some crave independence, others prefer to linger within the security of the family. Money determines whether or not many young adults can afford digs of their own. Cultural and religious beliefs sometimes prevent young people, particularly women, leaving home until they are married.

MOVING OUT

When the time comes for a young adult to leave home, all that parents can do is be as supportive as they can, if not with money, then with goodwill and the assurance that there will always be a bed at home, no matter what. If they are moving into a flat to share with friends, a few household items, such as plates and pots, sheets and blankets, are usually welcome, along with simple recipes for nutritious dishes and practical help with the physical move.

A sensible first step for a university student is to move into a college on campus where you can be semi-independent, yet safely tucked up in a contained and familiar community. Some colleges have allegiances with certain schools or religions. In most of them, you have your own room. Whether all or only some meals are provided depends on the college and how many of its students go home at weekends. You are expected to do your own washing and to keep your room clean and tidy. So much of life at this time centres around your studies, your friends and your social life at college that it's a natural place to perch for at least a year.

EMPTY NEST

As the parent, be willing to help but try to resist meddling in your child's new arrangements, volunteering advice without being asked or criticising what you see. If it's your last child who has just moved out, think of your empty nest as a place to redecorate, or to trade in on something smaller and more manageable. Do the things that weren't possible when you were bringing up your children. You are now free to travel, learn new skills, dine out, go to the theatre and work seriously on your golf handicap or your prowess at bridge. Volunteering your services to help people less privileged than you are might be a very satisfactory way to redirect your instincts for nurturing and protecting. For some parents, these years present a new lease of life with a sense of freedom every bit as heady as that being experienced by their young. But not all parents feel that way.

As the child, try to understand the enormity of the change in your parents' household once you have left and be tolerant of their need to know where you are and what you are doing. A regular telephone call is immensely reassuring. And don't do it only when you need something. Ring for the sake of having a chat and try to sound as though you're interested in their everyday doings, even if you are not. You must realise that, to your parents, you will always be their child, no matter what your age.

Giving something back

Make sure your visits home are not always accompanied by a swag of washing, a request to borrow the car or a plea for funds. It's inconsiderate to appear to value your parents only as material benefactors. Try bestowing something on them for a change, for no reason other than as a token of your love and respect: something as simple as a bunch of the flowers your mother particularly loves, or a clipping from the paper that will interest your father. Ask them if there's anything they need that you can fetch: the dry-cleaning, a stack of Medicare forms or items that might not be easy to find in local shops. If you can afford it, take them out to dinner. Keep your own record of important dates, such as their wedding anniversary and birthdays, rather than having to be reminded.

THE RELUCTANT FLYER

It's reasonable to assume that in most cases the desire for freedom comes from the child. However, the reverse can happen if the contented chip-off-the-old-block shows no sign of wishing to move out as the years start adding up. Sometimes mum and dad are longing for some independence of their own and, after all those years they've spent catering to your needs and wants, they deserve it. As parents, however much you love being with your adult progeny, it doesn't necessarily follow that you want it all the time and under the same roof. This can present a dilemma and you might hesitate in making the first move because you fear you'll be thought uncaring. The way to convince yourself that a parting of the ways is natural is to note how decisive other species are in turfing out their young.

Apparently Australian boys are particularly attached to the comforts of home – regular food, an efficient laundry service and an understanding attitude towards a friend staying overnight. If this is the case with your son, examine your own motives for making your home too attractive to leave. Beware selfishness masked as benevolence. Unless there are physical or mental disabilities, it is neither fair nor healthy for an adult to be kept in a state of childish dependence. Long-term, it's a disaster.

Talk openly about these things, if you can. It could be that your scion thinks you would be offended if he or she chooses to move out. Perhaps finding a civilised alternative is not easy, given the high costs of accommodation and the limits of most young people's budgets.

LIVING WITH OTHERS

Sharing a flat is a popular solution, not just for financial reasons but for the experience of learning about human beings in their great diversity. There's adventure, excitement and a sense of liberation in taking responsibility for yourself after all these years of living within the protection of your family. You quickly realise that most others do not live, think or act like you and your family do, and that is a good thing. Living with others broadens your perspective on the world.

Choosing a compatible flatmate is not as easy as it may seem.

When you live under the same roof, friends you dearly love do not always turn out to be what they seemed when you knew them less well. It's a pity to jeopardise a firm friendship by expecting too much of it, so beware of rushing headlong into what you imagine will be absolute harmony with someone you've known virtually all your life but never lived with before.

BEING THE LODGER

If you have never lived away from home before and you are not able to board with relatives or friends of your family, it might be wisest to look for a room in a flat or house already owned or leased by somebody else. That way you can gain experience without taking on a big obligation. It also means that the house rules have been laid down. Ask precisely what these rules are before you agree to take the room.

For instance: what does your rent cover, apart from the room? What happens about common expenses, such as telephone calls? Are electricity and gas included? Is there an extra charge for heating or air-conditioning? Do you pool your housekeeping money or take care of your own expenses? Do you share the cooking and, if not, which is your shelf in the refrigerator, pantry, cleaning cupboard? Is there a roster for the washing machine? Who does which household chores and how often? What is the procedure for inviting friends in for drinks or dinner? Is there a curfew?

CONSIDERATE FLATMATES

Once you are installed, remember the following courtesies. Keep all your belongings in your own room, not strewn all over the flat. Don't help yourself to other people's newspapers, CDs, books, magazines or anything without first asking. Never enter anybody else's room unless invited. If you borrow somebody else's food, replace it the same day. Leave the kitchen spotless. If somebody else has left a mess there, work around it and raise the subject openly with your flatmates; on no account clean it up – unless it happened because of an emergency – or you'll be doing it for the duration of your stay. Be careful to write down legible telephone messages for your flatmates and make sure they get them. If you enjoy music, make sure your flatmates do too before turning up the sound.

OVERNIGHT BEDMATES

I'm told that taking a lover to bed in a flat shared with others is now acceptable behaviour, as long as the guest does not intrude on other people's space. But do make sure your flatmates agree to it. If so, the guest must not commandeer the entire sofa or monopolise the television or video. Inhabitants take precedence for the bathroom and there should be no sounds of merrymaking from the bedroom. The current fashion for promiscuity notwithstanding, inviting a one-night stand home to a flat shared with others is out of line.

BOSS OF THE HOUSE

If you like taking responsibility and you feel you can handle it, you might prefer to lease a flat yourself and choose your own tenants to share it. Before you decide to do that, remember that you're going to have to pay the rent whether other rooms are let or not, so make sure you have enough to cover all contingencies, including the bills for running costs that are inevitable every month or quarter. A great virtue of this sort of set-up is that you're the one to decide what the house rules will be. Make sure they are fair, workable and clear to everyone (see page 103). The big disadvantage is that at any time anybody can move out at short notice – to travel, shack up with someone, get married, go home to the family – leaving you to look for another suitable flatmate.

Set the standards

Always be open about any annoyances or concerns you have with what someone else has done or not done. Although it's tempting not to raise a touchy subject, it's better done sooner than later, when it could turn into an unpleasant confrontation. Be rational and matter of fact. Don't let emotion cause you to say things you do not mean or will regret later. Don't inflict unnecessary hurt. The person who remains cool will always be in control. If the other person has done something truly dreadful, continues to default on the rent, or is just not compatible with everybody else, you are the one who will have to send the culprit packing. Being a landlady or a landlord is a role for grown-ups.

First trip abroad

A smooth way of easing yourself, or your child, out of the parental home is to work towards the big trip abroad. Living and working in another country is invaluable to a receptive young mind and there is no better time than now, before life gets too serious and commitments stand in the way.

Where to for the first-time traveller? The world's your oyster. Step one, think carefully about what you'd like to do and then research the subject. The Internet is a great starting point, along with the tourist offices and consulates of the countries that interest you.

EXPERIENTIAL TRAVEL

Travel with a greater purpose than just sightseeing is a wonderful way of experiencing life in a foreign country, for a few months, weeks or years. Camp America, a spin-off from the American Institute for Foreign Study, recruits foreign staff over the age of eighteen for summer camps all over the United States. Volunteers on the program are well looked after and it's a great way to meet new people.

Idealism prompts those fit enough to work for their keep in kibbutzim in Israel and you don't have to be Jewish to be accepted. As well as teaching you the local parlance, many language schools, from Japan to Italy to Guatemala, offer to find suitable accommodation either with a family (the best way to further your fluency) or in a flat or hotel. Although you must be an American citizen to join the Peace Corps, there are other altruistic organisations, such as Australian Volunteers Abroad, that place Australians where they can do some good in the world.

Traditionally, many young Aussies head off to do a two-year working holiday in the United Kingdom. Many other countries now have similar permits, and are worth investigating for a different kind of experience.

GENEROUS GIFTS FOR THE TRAVELLER

Apart from material presents on a special occasion, such as a twenty-first birthday, there are others that parents and close relations can give to provide intangible benefits in the form of experiences that will never be forgotten by a young person who longs to see the world. Any of the following are ideal: a round-the-world airline ticket; a return airline ticket to an exciting destination; a Eurail Pass; a good backpack; a phonecard that enables the traveller to make international telephone calls to the value of a predetermined amount; a fistful of US dollars, a currency recognised virtually everywhere in the world.

CHOOSING AN AIRLINE

Shop around to find the best deal in airline tickets. It might not be direct from an airline, but through a carefully chosen travel agent. Airlines sell their tickets to licensed travel agents at wholesale rates, leaving it to individual agents to decide what mark-up they will put on the retail price. This can vary from one agent to another. You can also do your research and make bookings on line.

Be cautious of settling on the cheapest airfare because not all airlines are of similar standard and safety should be your first consideration. Choose the airline and its connecting partners on the basis of 1) their safety record, 2) the condition of their fleets and

3) their reliability in honouring bookings, so that you're not at risk of being off-loaded unexpectedly.

CONTACTS OVERSEAS

If your family has connections overseas, you or one of your parents should write letters telling them of your impending arrival. Do not dream of turning up unannounced on anyone's doorstep. Neither would it be correct to wait until you arrive in the foreign city to introduce yourself on the telephone, a sloppy habit that unfortunately is all too prevalent.

After some pleasantries and family chitchat, a letter written by one of your parents would include a paragraph that goes something like this:

> *We are finally launching Angela into the outside world on the 27th of next month. She is over the moon at the idea of seeing Los Angeles and New York on her way to London. May I ask her to get in touch with you when she gets to Los Angeles? It would give me great peace of mind to think that she knows someone there.*

The letter should go off well ahead of your departure, so that there is time for replies and, perhaps, gracious invitations for you to stay or come to dinner. If both parties have fax facilities or email addresses, they are perfectly acceptable modern means of communication. There is also something exciting and satisfying about the swift despatch and instant arrival of a message and the speedy reply to it. Your parents should be prompt with their letter of thanks:

> *You are a true and treasured friend to offer Angela a room at your house. I cannot imagine a warmer welcome for her.*

Regardless of whether or not you accept these invitations, it is important that you also write a letter of thanks to each person before you set off.

> *Dear Mrs Sparkles,*
>
> *Thank you so much for inviting me to stay with you when I get to Los Angeles next month and for offering to meet my flight. You are very kind and I am delighted to accept. I arrive on PossumAir flight PA100, at 3 p.m. on 27th April. Mum has told me so much about you, and the time you worked together in New York. I long to meet you and to hear more.*
>
> *I look forward to seeing you soon. With appreciation and best wishes,*
>
> *Angela Peerless*

As for how long you stay, do remember this bit of Venetian wisdom. Q: What do fish and good house guests have in common? A: After three days they go off.

It is also courteous to take a gift to your hosts. It need not be expensive but it should be thoughtful and appropriate to your age and financial circumstances. An impecunious student can get away with a pot of pawpaw ointment, teatree soap or perhaps a box of macadamia nuts from a duty-free shop at the airport on departure from Australia. However, if your parents choose to send something, make sure it's light to carry; a scarf is ideal.

After you have been a guest in someone's house, whether for a few nights or just for dinner, always send written thanks from your next stop. Just a postcard will do.

STEP-BY-STEP PLANNER

As the day draws near, you start having anxiety dreams of being lost in space. Calm your nerves by making endless lists, ticking off items as the deeds are done.

You will need a passport that's valid for at least three months after your planned return to Australia. To apply for one, telephone the Passport Office in your capital city or collect the forms from a post office. It can take up to eight weeks to receive your passport.

Through YHA Australia you can join Hostelling International, a wonderful network that gives you access to a cheap bed almost anywhere in the world. More than that, these hostels are a mecca for interesting young (and not-so-young) people of many nationalities, fabulous places for forming new friendships and hearing about the best hostels, restaurants, sights, bargains, night life and all the little tips and tricks to help make your journey more rewarding. These are places where you also hear the latest news about temporary jobs, such as bartenders in Spain, grape-pickers in France and waiters in popular summer and winter resorts.

YHA offices are in all state capital cities. You fill in a form, your application is processed and you receive your membership card on the spot for a very affordable fee.

Once you can answer yes to the following, you're well on the way to having a wonderful trip.

1   Do you require visas for the countries you plan to visit? If so, have you applied for them? A visa is obtained through the relevant consulate. Rules, timing and fees vary from one country to another but, in general, you will need to lodge your passport, at least one passport photograph and a completed application form at the consulate.

2   Do you have at least six spare passport photographs of yourself? Take them with you. You never know when you might need them.

3   Have you been immunised against diseases that are present in the countries you visit? Remember that a course against malaria usually has to be started some time ahead of your arrival in the danger zone. Immunisation can be done by your

family doctor, or you can visit a clinic that specialises in this field of medicine, such as Travellers' Medical & Vaccination Centres, where reliable advice is given on precisely the kind of protection you need for any destination in the world.

4 Have you had a medical check-up recently?

5 If you are on regular medication of any kind, do you have enough of it to last the trip? If not, do you have a prescription that can be interpreted by a pharmacist overseas?

6 Have you had a dental check-up recently?

7 Have you taken out health insurance cover for the journey and do you know who to contact if you need to use it abroad?

8 Have you taken out luggage insurance cover?

9 Have you decided which method you will use to obtain money abroad: a) traveller's cheques; b) charge card/s; c) a card keyed to your bank account so that you can draw on it from a network of ATMs around the world?

10 Are your charge cards valid?

11 Have you bought from your bank some cash in the currency of your destination/s? Make sure you're familiar with the value of the notes before you leave.

12 Have you made arrangements for bills to be paid in your absence?

13 If you plan to communicate with family and friends through email, does your service provider permit you to log on at the cost of a local telephone call instead of an international one?

14 Do you have an Internet service provider (ISP) that allows you to send and receive email messages no matter where in the world you happen to be?

Plans confirmed

Now, have your whole itinerary typed clearly and comprehensively, leaving plenty of space for notes and changes in the margins. Include addresses, telephone numbers, arrival times, as well as departure times.

Once it's in black and white, you'll be able to identify any gaps or inconsistencies. Double-check everything. Do not leave a thing to chance.

Your travel agent should give you a computer printout of your itinerary to confirm flight details but it will show only the bare bones of the trip you plan. It's advisable to do one yourself that includes addresses and telephone numbers.

Here's an example of an itinerary.

ITINERARY

Angela Jane Peerless Melbourne/Los Angeles/New York/London/Paris
27 April to 15 July 2003

Sun 27 April 8 p.m.	*Depart Melbourne PossumAir Flight PA100*
3 p.m.	*Arrive Los Angeles Airport*
	to be met in Arrivals hall by Mr and Mrs Sparkles
	transfer by their car to 2500 Santa Ana Breezeway,
	Beverly Hills tel (310) 060 7752
Thu 1 May 11 a.m.	*Depart Los Angeles Flight zyx*
2 p.m.	*Arrive JFK Airport, New York*
	transfer by bus to City terminal, then by taxi to
	Jake Blum's loft at 1275 Pink Street, SoHo,
	New York, NY 10012 tel (212) 006 5306
Fri 2 May	*Find a youth hostel or cheap hotel in SoHo or TriBeCa*
Sun 4 May	*Move to youth hostel*
Sun 11 May 10 p.m.	*Depart JFK Airport Flight xyz*
Mon 12 May 11 a.m.	*Arrive London Heathrow Airport*
	to be met by Mrs James Witherspoon and taken
	by tube to 42 Posche Mews, Chelsea SW3
	tel (020) 005 0586

Wed 14 May	*Depart Witherspoons' house to share flat with Julie Jiggles at Flat 4, 130 Gorblimey Way, Pimlico SW1 tel (020) 006 3987*
Sat 31 May	*Depart London with Julie, Damien and Frannie on the Eurostar to France for six weeks' backpacking on the continent*
Sat 12 July	*Return to London (Pimlico address) and look for work*

TO THE PHOTOCOPIER!

Take two photocopies of each of the following and leave one set with a reliable and accessible person at home and plan to pack the other set in a safe place, separate from the originals: every page of your passport that has anything on it; every page of your airline ticket; serial numbers of your traveller's cheques; health insurance documents; luggage insurance documents; immunisation certificates; and itinerary.

BASIC TRAVEL EQUIPMENT

What you take with you depends on where you're going and what the weather's likely to be when you get there. Will you need to dress for chilly northern Europe in March as well as steamy cities where it's hot all the time, such as Bangkok, Singapore and Kuala Lumpur? If you're planning a long trip, to keep your load reasonably light and manageable, it's a good idea to pack what you need for the first few months and buy extras as you need them. Remember, when you're moving around you don't need a lot of clothes. You need adaptable ones, good survivors that are easy to care for (see page 113). And you certainly do not need a lot of baggage.

Experienced travellers agree that ideal equipment includes the following.

1   A good, sturdy backpack that suits your build and is as lightweight as possible. The ideal kind has a detachable day

pack that's small enough for day trips and sightseeing, and to conform to airline regulations for carry-on baggage. Make sure both these packs are identified, inside and out, with your name and contact details. If the backpack does not have an inbuilt locking device, buy a padlock and keep the key on your keyring.

2 A money belt for your travel essentials: passport; airline ticket; money (traveller's cheques and cash); charge cards; international phonecard; keyring.

Travel wardrobe

Comfort is paramount, particularly if you have long train or bus journeys planned, so choose your pieces carefully. Don't take clothes that are pale or crushable; they do not survive well on a long journey. You'll need items that are easy to wash and dry and don't show the dirt.

The best colour scheme for a cold climate is student black or navy or grey that you can dress up or down at will. In hot countries, khaki, camel and beige are more suitable. Take one pair of proven comfortable shoes that will last the distance and one pair of smarter shoes for cities or for going out at night.

In Muslim countries and in any country where people are devoutly religious, a woman is not respected if she shows a lot of bare skin. Pack a lightweight scarf that you can use to cover your head or shoulders if necessary.

On flights as lengthy as those we need to get us to other continents jeans are uncomfortable. Knitted fabrics of good quality and substantial weight are the best travellers. They're more flexible and less likely to crush than other fabrics. Footwear must be comfortable too, as feet tend to swell on planes. Wear your money belt and do not take it off until you get to your final destination. Do remember that it's always cool as high in the sky as you'll be, even over the Equator, so don't dress for climates at stops on the way, unless you're leaving the aircraft there. Most terminals are air-conditioned. When you arrive at your destination, looking like a student puts you into an international league of like-minded travellers who are appropriately dressed anywhere.

In-flight bag

Put the following into your day pack for taking on board the flight: toiletries bag with miniatures of skin-care products, make-up, comb, toothbrush, toothpaste, tissues, face cloth; panty liners or a clean pair of underpants; any necessary medication; inflatable pillow; reading material; Walkman; currency converter; address book; ballpoint pen.

Check-in bag

Pack the following in your backpack to be checked in before you board your flight and not seen again until it's on the carousel at your final destination: two sets of underwear, if they are lightweight enough to dry overnight, but otherwise take three sets; one pair of cheap thongs to wear in the hostel shower; pocket knife with scissors; sleeping bag and sheet (optional – most youth hostels provide blankets but you often have to hire sheets); lightweight raincoat; small torch; chamois or hand towel; mini sachets of detergent; clothes line (excellent ones are available from travel equipment shops). Pack the clothes and shoes that you won't be wearing on the plane. (For further advice on successful travel attire, see pages 358–359.)

If you're planning to look for work, take a basic business outfit, including a suitable pair of shoes. And don't forget your references.

Before you leave check with friends, your travel agent or a guide book to see if there is anything peculiar to the destination. For example, travellers to Russia used to be advised to take bath plugs, which were apparently absent from hotel bathrooms there.

DO'S AND DON'TS OF AIRLINE TRAVEL

Don't try to carry too much on board. It's burdensome for you and unfair on your fellow passengers. Do smile and be pleasant to the flight attendants. That way, they'll be nice to you, too. Don't put your day pack in the overhead locker unless it's absolutely necessary. Put it under the seat in front of you because it's accessible at all times and it's a great footrest in economy class. Don't curl up in the foetal position for the flight. Instead, stretch in your seat, reaching your arms high above your head, flexing your back and straightening your legs. Do drink lots of water. Don't drink too much dehydrating alcohol, coffee or tea. Don't eat too much. Pounce on the salads and fruit. Do walk briskly around the airport terminal at stopovers. Don't dawdle and don't sit down; there'll be plenty of that when you re-board. Do treasure the transit card given to you at stopovers. Otherwise there'll be a terrible fuss when you try to re-board. In these times of stringent security, you might hold up the plane and your fellow passengers will hate you for it. Never part with your valuables, even to go to the toilet on the plane. Always take your money belt with you. Flight attendants can't be vigilant at every seat.

STREETWISE

Do be cautious, especially if you are a young woman travelling alone. Plan ahead so that you have a place to stay each night and you know how to get there. Australia is a safe country and children who grow up here can be vulnerable when they travel to less fortunate places in the world. Don't be too trusting. Never leave your bag unattended. Never agree to carry anything for someone who approaches you at an airport terminal. On your arrival somewhere, ignore any touts who are after your business and take a public bus or a registered taxi. If you need advice about the legitimacy of the transport on offer, ask a uniformed employee of the airline on which you travelled.

Don't ask for trouble by standing on a street corner gawping at a map, an attitude that tells passersby you are a stranger and a naive one at that. Japan is one of the very few places in the world where you feel safe enough to walk around the streets at any time without fear of being mugged. Try to blend in with the locals and always walk purposefully, even if you haven't a clue where you're going. Try to study a map in private. If you get lost, go into a café or some other place where you can sit down in a corner and work out where you are. (For more tips on travelling safely, see page 361.)

Respect local customs and sensitivities. For instance, you are still expected to cover your arms when you enter a church in Italy and to dress modestly in a Muslim country (see page 113).

As for advice on what to do if you are feeling scared, that depends on where you are and what the threat is. If you're being followed or harassed in some other way and you are in a country where the police force is trustworthy, find a policeman or a police station. If you do not trust the authorities, go to a big international hotel, one with a known and reputable brand-name, such as Hilton, Inter-Continental, Hyatt, Sheraton or similar, explain your worry to the concierge and ask if the security guard would shoo away whoever is pestering you. Take a taxi from there to wherever you are staying. If you are ever in a hotel where you receive unwanted telephone calls, report them to the resident manager or concierge straight away.

If you are in serious trouble, go to the Australian consulate or embassy. If there isn't one in that country, prevail on the embassy of a friendly, English-speaking nation, such as New Zealand, Canada, the UK or the USA.

Sometimes when travelling, you just feel lonely or homesick and need cheering up. That's the time for a treat. Instead of yet another hostel, check into a good hotel and indulge in a foam bath, a towelling robe and a good sleep in.

Now for the final check.

- Money belt: Passport? Airline ticket? Charge/ATM cards? Traveller's cheques? Cash?
- Pocket of your day pack: Itinerary? Luggage keys? House keys? Address book? Pen? Something to read?

- Backpack: Have you identified it, inside and out? Have you locked it? Where's the key?
- Now, quickly – What's your passport number? What's your PIN number? What's your flight number?

Bon voyage!

Chapter Six

MODERN
COMMUNICATION

At its most basic, communication between human beings is in person, a direct exchange between two or more people. That's how it started out and, despite technology, face-to-face encounters are still the most satisfactory means by which we get along with each other. In private, people confide things they would never put in writing or voice on the telephone. When you look someone in the eye, it's difficult to be anything but honest although, as anybody who reads the daily newspaper knows, there are people who rise to that challenge without any problems at all.

Human beings are social creatures. As well as needing to belong to a group, we are also inquisitive and adventurous. We love novelty. Most of us like the stimulation of meeting new people and the possibility of making new friends. That would be impossible to do without a common language and a set of rules for putting it into practice. That set of rules is called etiquette.

INTRODUCTIONS

Fear not. Everybody makes mistakes in introducing people. The more relaxed you are about it the better. If you make a mistake don't worry about it and certainly don't fuss. Apologise, if you feel that is appropriate, and get it right next time.

Speak clearly so that both parties can hear what you are saying. An important point to remember is that, as with written communication, you must be consistent about the use or non-use of titles. In other words, say you are introducing two of your friends, an older one titled 'Lady Smith' and a younger one titled 'Mrs Jones'. If you refer to your friend Smith as 'Lady', you must refer to your friend Jones as 'Mrs' when you introduce them. Otherwise, it's Wendy Smith and Harriet Jones.

In Australia we tend to be far more informal than people in most other societies, but it is wise to stick to formality with your superiors in business and with anybody you are meeting socially for the first time, particularly foreigners. Unless you have been introduced on first-name terms, wait until you are asked to use the newcomer's given name.

Be cautious of using the term 'Christian name'. Not everyone is a Christian, so a better term is 'given name'. Even 'first name' can be misleading, since some Asian countries place the surname first and the given name second. For correct forms of address for practically everyone you can think of in the world, see Chapter 20.

So here's what you're supposed to do and say.

1   Although there are exceptions (see point 2), men are introduced to women. Formally, you would say, 'Mrs Watson, may I introduce Mr Chapman.' Less formally, you might say, 'Elizabeth Watson, this is David Chapman.' Informally, it might be as simple as, 'Liz, this is David.'

2   If the man is very well known, the other person is introduced to him. For example, 'Professor Turner, may I introduce

Mrs Foster.' Less formally, you might say, 'Joshua Turner, this is Kay Foster.' Informally, 'Josh, this is Kay.'

3   Younger women are introduced to older women. Formally: 'Mrs Martin, may I introduce Miss Balafas.' Less formally: 'Jo Martin, this is Dimitria Balafas.' Informally: 'Jo, this is Dimitria.'

4   Younger men are introduced to older men. Formally: 'Mr Groves, may I introduce Mr Jang.' Less formally: 'Kenneth Groves, this is Yun-Sik Jang.' Informally: 'Ken, this is Yun.'

5   Children are always introduced to adults. The adult's title should be used unless you know that he or she prefers not to have it mentioned. 'Mr Waks, I don't think you have met my niece, Penny.'

6   When you introduce people of the same sex and similar age, the one who is less important should be introduced to the other. Formally: 'Dr Noble, may I introduce Mr Ord.' Less formally: 'John Noble, this is Ian Ord.' Informally: 'John, this is Ian.' It's a tricky one, this, if you are introducing two people with big egos so be careful who you choose. If you want to be the soul of tact and wriggle out of it, you might say, 'I'm sure you two notables must know each other already' and leave it to them to introduce themselves.

7   Couples should be introduced separately, not as a unit, even if they are married and the wife has taken her husband's name. Formally, she is Mrs Jeremy Burton. Informally, Sarah Burton. If the wife uses her maiden name in business, she may or may not want to use it in private life. Find out before you make the introductions. If she prefers her maiden name, then formally she is Ms Sarah Lo.

8   If a woman is a widow, she is still addressed by her late husband's name – that is, Mrs Jeremy Mason. If she is divorced, it is not correct for her to use her former husband's given name, so she becomes Mrs Susan Mason.

9 Before you leave two people you've just introduced to rummage for some topic they might have in common, give them a lead: 'Dr Noble has just done some interesting research on the common cold.' 'Mr Ord has signed up for the Peace Corps in Africa.' 'The Burtons have just moved here from Adelaide and they're looking for a house.'

WHAT TO REPLY WHEN YOU ARE INTRODUCED

'How do you do' is the formal response from both sides when two people are introduced. On no account take it as an enquiry about your health and reply 'I'm well' or, worse, 'I'm good.' (When a young friend of mine was in her teens and her father asked her how she was, she said, 'I'm good.' His reply was 'I'm glad you're good, but are you well?') A popular response is 'Hello' which should do in occasions other than strictly formal ones; some people say 'Hi' but that is too casual for anything other than the most informal occasion. It is permissible to say, 'I'm delighted to meet you at last' but 'Pleased to meet you' is an absolute no-no.

OFFERING YOUR HAND

According to tradition, a man should wait until a woman extends her hand before he does. That is obsolete now. It is courteous for either, or both, to hold out a hand unless a woman is introduced to a man whose religious faith prohibits him from touching women. This applies to some, but not all, Muslim men, and to priests of certain religious orders so, if you are unsure, it's wise to wait and see before you attempt to shake hands.

SOMEONE WITH A DISABILITY

If a person you are meeting for the first time is disabled, a handshake might not be appropriate. Wait until a hand is extended to you. In any case, disregard the disability as much as you can and behave as you normally do with anyone you meet. Converse directly with the person, don't patronise, ask searching questions about the disability or use flattering expressions, such as 'you are very brave'. By all means offer help, if it seems to be needed, but on no account push it. Wait until you are asked and then abide by any specific instructions.

REMEMBERING NAMES

It is both an art and a science. If you weren't born with a talent for remembering, master it by scientific means. It takes discipline and practice but it can be done, even if you're Miss Forgetful or Mr Absentminded. Here are techniques that work for some people. Try them on for size.

- Repeat the name of the person you have just met the moment you shake hands. 'How do you do, George.' Use the name again in the next-but-one sentence. 'George, I couldn't agree more.' Don't overdo it, though. It irritates some people.

- Silently repeat the name of the person you have just met fifteen times but try not to look as though you're adrift in another world and keep your lips still.

- If possible, write the name down as soon as you can. Some people have to see a name before they can remember it.

- Associate the name with a rhyme: Mary contrary; Tom the pom; Ray the gay; Derek the cleric; Chi likes tea; Rod the god; Rob the nob; Sam the lamb; racy Tracy. Make sure any irreverence remains unspoken.

- Identify the name with the person by thinking of something striking in that person's appearance: Ruth has red hair; Alan is taller than everybody else; Katrina with a fabulous sapphire ring; Jodie in tortoiseshell specs; Joe who combs his hair over that bald patch.

Guests whose powers of recall are wanting are very grateful for a second chance, so the thoughtful host should look for opportunities to repeat people's names in general conversation: 'Sandra, I've seated you beside

Pria at the table, so come and meet someone else before we sit down.' 'I thought so, too, Marco.' 'Helga, you are a mine of information.' 'Maggie, may I tempt you?' 'As Dr Wang was saying . . . '

Whatshisname

When you are with a friend – say, in the street – and you are greeted by a person whose face you know but whose name escapes you, on no account disregard your friend when you stop to chatter. You must make some form of introduction.

Your best bets are these. Perform a one-way introduction, with 'This is my colleague, Teresa Saunders', and hope the stranger will say her name and that Teresa has the sense not to whine 'But you haven't told me her name.'

Or you can make the preamble to an introduction so lengthy, by saying flattering and explanatory things about Teresa, that before you're finished they'll be shaking hands rather than have you rattle on.

If you have to admit that you've forgotten the name, get out of it by telling a whopper, such as: 'I thought it was you but somebody told me you'd gone to live in New York.' 'You've lost so much weight, I didn't recognise you at first' (but not if the person is too thin). 'Forgive me, I was miles away.' 'You look impossibly young, what have you done?' (but never to someone who clearly has had something done).

On the other hand, this sort of subterfuge can be avoided if you are the one whose name has been forgotten. If it becomes apparent to you that the person you're about to greet hasn't a clue who you are, never be crass enough to put that person on the spot by asking, 'Do you remember me?' Simply extend your hand and say, 'I'm Kylie Betts and we met at Philip Engelberts' product launch.'

INTRODUCING YOURSELF

Awkward though you may feel at a big reception where you cannot find a single familiar face, except perhaps the host, take courage and

introduce yourself to someone who looks sympathetic. Look around
for a person who needs rescuing as much as you do and introduce
yourself. This enterprise is usually more successful if you select another
loner, or a couple who seem isolated, rather than try to crack a jolly
group who have a lot to say to each other. It's also wise to be careful not
to intrude on well-known people who are comfortable and secure in
their celebrity and might question what motivates an approach by a
complete stranger. (For more details about conversation starters, see
pages 334–336.)

Dining with strangers

When you are a guest seated at a table in a private house and you
haven't met the people on either side of you, introduce yourself,
whether or not there are place cards. Similarly, at a large gathering,
such as a fund-raising dinner or any commercial event where strangers
are seated at tables of ten or eight, be the first to stand, extend your
hand and introduce yourself to everyone else at your table. It breaks the
ice and opens the way for a pleasant exchange with everyone there so
that nobody is left out.

Needless to say, in introducing yourself, never preface your name
with Mr, Mrs, Ms, Dr, Lord, Lady, or any other title or honorific. Just
say your given name and your surname. Better to be open and modest
than stuffy or boastful.

Table-hopping in restaurants

If you pass someone you know on the way to your table in a restaurant,
pause for a moment if you know them well, but don't introduce the
person with you and don't linger, as though waiting for an introduction to everybody else at the table. Best of all, just smile, say hello and
keep moving.

There are times when people go to a restaurant hoping to discuss
intimate personal matters or confidential business affairs in private.

You can usually tell from their placement (in the corner) and from their body language if this is the case. Don't intrude or even attempt to catch their attention. If eye contact is inevitable, smile, wave and forget about them.

At the sighting of a famous person in a restaurant, do not stare and do not approach their table to gush, or to ask for an autograph. Behave as you would with someone unknown.

ELECTRONIC COMMUNICATION

There are many tools of communication now at our fingertips but the missing link is widespread understanding of how to use them properly. I don't mean in terms of technical skill – even five-year-olds have mastered that – but in terms of courtesy. The etiquette of using a mobile telephone, for example, is yet to be heeded by many people to whose ears these devices are so often glued. That shouldn't surprise us, really. Most people have not yet learned to use the normal telephone in ways that do not offend or inconvenience others.

THE TELEPHONE IN BUSINESS

In his vast experience of corporate telecommunications, the Sydney broadcaster Brendan Walsh has found that all a customer wants from a business call is 1) a prompt response from 2) a real person who 3) can make a decision. How simple that sounds. How rarely it is achieved.

If you are in the front line of all incoming calls to your company, you will have been told what your response is to be. You probably say something like 'Good morning, Bigtime Partners' or 'Bigtime Partners; how may I help you?' If the company is a large one, such as a department store, the briefer your message the better; each extra word takes up precious time and could result in calls banking up unnecessarily.

Your role overall is to be welcoming and efficient, to stay calm and not to leave callers in limbo. If they decide to wait on the line for someone, keep going back to reassure them every twenty seconds that they haven't been forgotten.

When the telephone rings at the desk and you are not the receptionist, your first words when you pick up the receiver should be a greeting, such as 'Good morning' followed by 'this is' and your first name and your surname. It's not enough to say Sophie or Flora or Nicky.

If the call is for someone else, do not leave the caller wondering what's going on while you search the office for your colleague.

Do not ask a caller to 'Hang on a sec' while you answer the other line unless you have an old-fashioned telephone system and you are the only person there. In that case, be quick and apologise to both parties. Otherwise, let the second caller leave a message on voice mail.

Return calls promptly, on the same day if possible. If you cannot make the call yourself, ask an assistant or a colleague to call to explain your silence and take a message if necessary.

When you leave a message for someone to call you back, leave your number and your name, including your surname. It always amazes me how few people, particularly women, use their surnames in business. In leaving these details on voice mail, speak clearly and slowly and repeat the number and the name, if it's an unusual one.

In taking a message for someone from a person you do not know, don't presume to be on first-name terms, particularly if you are a receptionist, secretary or personal assistant.

Try not to say the dreaded words 'no problem'. (In the seventies, the phrase 'no worries' always made me terribly worried.) A friend of mine is invariably tempted to reply: 'I wouldn't have asked you if I'd thought it would be a problem' but he is too polite to do so.

The flexibility of voice mail

The great virtue of voice mail is that it is easy to change the message as often as required yet so few people in business bother to make the effort. Instead, they leave the same message, which goes something like

'I'm either on the phone or away from my desk. Please leave your name and number and I'll get back to you as soon as possible.' But that tells the caller nothing. 'As soon as possible' should be dropped entirely. How much better would it be to say, 'I'll be in a meeting until midday. If you leave your name and number I'll call you before one o'clock' or 'Please leave your name and number because I check my voice mail every hour' or 'I am on leave until Monday, 7th of September. Please press 0 to speak to reception.' Don't use gobbledygook, such as 'I'll be at A.T.E' or 'I.T.B.' or some other esoteric place.

Hello! Anyone at home?

The worst abuse of telecommunications is the company that forces you, while you wait on the line for someone to answer your call, to listen to a series of platitudes, usually advertising the so-called advantages of the products or services in which the company specialises. Almost as bad is the inane repetition by a recorded voice assuring you that someone will be with you 'shortly'. A voice that says, 'All of our operators are busy' convinces me that there is but one lone person fielding a score of irate callers – that is, if there is anyone there at all. Being ear-bashed while you are a captive audience is an appalling imposition; silence or serene music would at least permit us to busy ourselves with something else while we wait. And wait and wait.

This is not an advance in communication. Nor is the call-waiting system that permits the interruption of your conversation with an announcement that another caller is queuing for you. These foolish things try our patience and our manners.

I am not an enemy of the technology known as IVR (interactive voice response) by which your call is answered by a recorded voice chanting words like 'For bookings, press one. For administration, press two. For marketing, press three . . .' and so on. At least it aims to get you to the right person speedily. I also see no reason why anyone should not screen calls, whether in business or at home. It is not always convenient to talk on the telephone. You might be trying to meet a deadline, head off a problem or organise your time efficiently. You might be waiting on one particularly urgent call. Just make sure you return the screened call as soon as you are able.

THE PRIVATE TELEPHONE

It is not necessary to state your name when you answer the telephone at home. A simple hello is all you need say. Otherwise, most rules you practise at the office also apply to your off-duty use of the telephone, with some additional considerations.

Before you make a call to a private number, give some thought to the time of day when it might be most convenient. If there are young children in the house, six o'clock in the evening is usually not a good time, however well it might suit singles. If you know that someone entertains often, do not place a call at lunch or dinner time. Calls before nine in the morning are inconvenient for most people, although if you are sure that summoning a close friend at eight a.m. will be welcome, go ahead. In any case, no matter what time you telephone, always ask if it is convenient before launching into whatever you have to say. If you sense that the person on the other end of the line is distracted or anxious to get away, bring your call to a fast finish. When calling overseas, check the time difference so you don't wake someone at four a.m.

A flick of the finger can mean you disturb a stranger by dialling the wrong number. Apologise before replacing the receiver and dialling again.

Before you use the telephone in somebody else's house, always ask permission. Never make an interstate or overseas call unless you use a phonecard, reverse the charge, or have some other way of making sure the call will not be debited to your host's account.

Nuisance callers should be cut off immediately. Don't listen any longer than it takes to establish the nature of the call, then hang up. If it is repeated, call your phone company to report it. The appropriate number is listed in your telephone directory.

Rules for the answerphone

Keep the outgoing message as brief as possible. My own preference is a pithy 'To leave a message, please speak after the beep.'

Unless you want to invite burglars, don't tell the world 'We're not here right now.' On the subject of security, I quite like the idea of a dog barking in the background of the recorded message. Not a little yelp, but a gutsy bass baritone from, say, a German Shepherd.

To leave a message, wait until after the signal. Be brief. Speak clearly. If you need to leave a number, say it slowly.

Do not tell your life story to the answerphone. Apart from the tedium of the playback, it will cut you off after a short time, perhaps without giving you time to leave a contact number.

If you ask for your call to be returned, remember to say thank you.

MANNERS AND THE MOBILE

We know the advantages of the mobile phone, which are many, particularly for people whose jobs take them away from base for much of the time, or for emergencies when you are away from home. But I can't think of anybody who needs to be a slave to the telephone every waking moment of the day or night, especially since calls need never go unanswered when technology gives us the facility to store messages for later.

People who are courteous are aware of how intrusive a mobile telephone can be to those around them. They understand the protocol. However, we have all been subjected to users who are so insensitive, they seem to feel that making themselves and their cellular phones a public nuisance somehow gives them status. I can remember sitting in comfort in a hushed and thinly populated lounge at Heathrow Airport reading a book when a man sat in a chair at right angles to mine, took out his telephone and rang everyone he could think of to tell them where he was. He was so loud and intrusive I had to move. Why do so many people shout into their mobile telephones? They remind me of old American movies that show country bumpkins doing the same when the telephone was first introduced.

Anyone investing in a mobile phone must be aware of the great etiquette of turning it off. You should do this automatically before entering a private house for a formal social engagement, any party venue, a lecture hall, business presentation, restaurant, theatre, concert hall, cinema, aircraft, church, hospital and any sports area where the players might be put off their game, such as a tennis court or golf course. It should go without saying that a mobile telephone does not belong at a wedding, birth ceremony, funeral or other tribal ritual, whether or not it occurs in a hallowed place.

For reasons of safety, it is against the law for the driver of a car or truck to use a mobile telephone while the vehicle is moving unless it is hands-free. The penalty for breaking this law is upwards of one hundred dollars.

NETIQUETTE: NICETIES ON THE INTERNET

The opening up of this fabulous communications universe does come with its own rules of etiquette, known as netiquette, the means by which netizens (citizens of the net) explore cyberspace without offence to each other. These rules are outlined in various publications on sale at bookshops and on web sites accessible to all netizens.

Anyone familiar with the golden rules of conduct in general should not need any further instruction. The intention is the same. Be aware of the needs of others even though you cannot see them and probably do not know them. Respect everyone equally. Just because you can be anonymous on the net should not prompt bad behaviour; that is the province of cowards and sneaks. Snooping on somebody else's email is as unethical as opening mail of any other kind when it does not belong to you. There is also no excuse for rudeness and it pays to be aware that, when you send a message to someone on the net, you can never be sure where it will end up. It is so easy for the recipient to store it and to post it into other email boxes at whim.

Of course, fear of being found out should not be the motivation for behaving well, whether on the net or on the ground. Set your own standards and keep to them.

Email

Composing a message to be sent by email is not as similar to writing a letter as it might seem at first. Think of it as a cross between a letter and an old-fashioned telex or telegram, particularly in business. Some people are inundated with legitimate emails, plus junk emails, every day so don't make yours laborious or it might be read only sketchily and perhaps even misinterpreted. A kind of shorthand is sometimes used for phrases that often recur, from FYI (for your information) to TTFN (ta-ta for now), so it's a good idea to become familiar with them.

Another thing about email is that it has spawned a sign language of its own, using what are called emoticons to try to put some warmth into what is visually a static and colourless piece of communication. Emoticons are rudimentary smiley faces, made on the keyboard. You have to look at them sideways to recognise each face and what it indicates.

Some of the most basic are these, but there are plenty of others and no end to the inventions of a creative mind.

SYMBOL MEANING

:-)	*happiness*
:-D	*laughter*
:-(	*sadness*
:-0	*shouting*
;-)	*winking*
B-)	*cool (sunglasses)*
:-l	*indifference*

Using these symbols is not obligatory. I personally find them a bit naive but if you are at a loss for words and you want to be friendly or amusing, they might work for you. Children can have a great time inventing more, including some kind of logo to accompany their signature. As an adult, though, be cautious of their over-use in business because they could become tiresome.

Be careful not to use all CAPITAL LETTERS in an email because it indicates anger and is called 'shouting'. Some people use all lower case but I suspect that's because they haven't been trained to touch-type. If you are skilled at the keyboard, use upper and lower case characters, as you would in a normal letter. If you are besieged by emails, all you can try to do is reply immediately, keeping what is called the 'thread'. That means you should attach your reply to the communication you received so that its recipient, who might be just as swamped with emails as you are, does not lose the plot.

THE NEW RADICALISM: PUTTING PEN TO PAPER

Is handwriting dead? Not quite. Although, except for the signature, it is not often seen in letters any more. Other means of writing words and speaking to each other across continents and oceans have taken over the world and most of us are out of practice when it comes to picking up a pen and putting down our thoughts on anything lengthier than a shopping list.

Although the venerable practice of writing and receiving letters and invitations has been well documented, it's probably due for an update. Let's review the traditional laws that govern it, starting with the personal wardrobe of stationery, to see how relevant they are to us in Australia now.

Before we start, though, it must be stressed that it is not obligatory to have printed stationery. Plain paper will do, as long as it is a pale colour and of good quality. Relegate paper with lines on it and the sentimentality of fancy florals and other fussy motifs to the world of childhood.

STATIONERY WARDROBE

By January 2002, fifty-five per cent of Australian households had at least one personal computer (PC). One of the side benefits of the computer desktop with printer is its ability to produce rudimentary letterheads in your chosen font, type size, layout and colour. Moreover, you may print only a few at a time and change the content at will instead of having to order hundreds from a professional printer. All it costs is the paper and ink.

Although these sheets made by loving hands at home are not quite a substitute for writing paper printed from a copperplate engraving, they are splendid for everyday household correspondence and any missives you send by fax.

Apart from that, if you can afford it, beautiful writing paper – which snobbery decrees must never be called letter paper or notepaper – is one of the most rewarding indulgences on which to spend money. At its most traditional, it is plain white or cream (pale blue or grey are acceptable but less formal) with a perceptible watermark when you hold it up to the light. It is a little smaller than A4 in size and thick enough for your writing not to show through on the other side. Your address, telephone number and whatever else you wish to include are set in a Roman type (that means the letters have serifs) and printed in black or the almost-as-okay dark blue. They may be centred at the top or split, with the address positioned at the right and the telephone number at the left.

Traditionally, all your stationery would have been stamped from a die that was in fact an engraved copper plate. The craft of hand engraving does still exist here but stationers who can do it are rare. Less expensive and readily available is flat or raised printing (thermography).

Here are some of the main models of printed personal stationery.

AN INFORMAL   This is of the same weight, colour, typeface and content as your letterhead but folded to half size for shorter notes or invitations. Your name and address are engraved on the outside. You write your message on the inside and, if necessary, continue it on the back.

AN AT HOME CARD   Traditionally, this card carried the name of a woman only, whether or not she was married. That could be misleading for a married woman today. I see no reason why the names of wife and husband should not be printed on the card. The RSVP and the address are positioned at the bottom left-hand side of the card. I would also include the telephone number as a courtesy to someone who needs to leave it with the babysitter or in case of an emergency. In colour, the card should match your letterhead but the traditional type is copperplate (script) lettering. With its sparse words, this card is adaptable to all sorts of social events. You fill in the rest according to the type of event.

> *Mr and Mrs Adam Peerless*
> *at Home*
>
>
> *R.S.V.P.*
> *1 Swans Way*
> *Swankton Vic. 3142*
> *9585 4444*

A CORRESPONDENCE CARD   This very useful piece has your name and address in one line across the top. If you want a streamlined collection of stationery and you don't entertain all that often, you might prefer this to an At Home card.

> *Mr and Mrs Adam Peerless, 1 Swans Way, Swankton, Vic. 3142*

The possibilities are almost endless, as any good stationer will be happy to show you. Your choice depends very much on your way of life. Whether or not you follow these guidelines to the letter is up to you. For many of us, too much formality may seem alien in a country as relaxed as ours. Something more imaginative or more fun might be preferable: a monogram, family coat-of-arms or a cleverly designed personal logo, for example. Unless your address is likely to be permanent, though, consider the wisdom of investing in stationery that might be obsolete well before your stocks of it have run out.

If you can afford envelopes lined in tissue paper, do so. They stand out happily among the commercial wrappings of junk mail and those with windowpanes that signal bills. Needless to say, do not waste these special sleeves on everyday business mail, such as posting cheques, returning forms or entering competitions.

An essential accompaniment, according to tradition, is the fountain or cartridge pen filled with black or navy blue ink. However, I think this is optional rather than essential. So much fiddling around. Although I believe the ballpoint pen should be wielded only to fill in forms in duplicate or triplicate, I find that disposable felt-tipped pens retain the character of the handwriting without the high maintenance of a fountain pen. And when they run dry, you throw them away.

A word here about addressing envelopes. Time was, addresses were penned in script, with commas and fullstops perfectly placed and each successive line indented a little further than the one above. That has now changed with the use of high-speed electronic processing equipment to sort out all the mail. This technology is intolerant of punctuation, underlining, illegible handwriting or any format that does not match its program.

Ideally, the equipment prefers an address of three lines only.

- Write the name of the person intended to receive the letter on the top line.
- Start the second line immediately beneath the beginning of the line

above. Do not indent it. Write the number and name of the street. If you want to include a house name, start the second line with it. A flat or apartment number should also be placed on the second line.

- The last line should always be the suburb or town printed in capital letters plus the abbreviated state name and postcode.

Ms Angela Peerless
3/165 Burke Avenue
COSMIC BAY NSW 0202

If the letter is to be sent overseas, the name of the country should be written in capital letters on the last line. Do not confuse the processing equipment by trying to shoehorn an overseas area code into the four boxes on the envelope. In fact, for overseas mail, it's best to buy airmail envelopes.

If the address on the envelope is typewritten instead of hand-written, it is not necessary to type the postcode in the four boxes. Just leave a few spaces on the bottom line after the abbreviated state name before you type the code.

For a guide to the correct form of address for various people, from the nobles and notables of Europe and Asia to career couples and the people next door, see Chapter 20.

BREAD-AND-BUTTER LETTERS

Not everybody is a born wordsmith but that should not inhibit anyone from writing letters. The best are those that come from the heart, how-ever simple the wording. A friend of mine cherishes this one, from an eleven-year-old:

To Dear Jane
Thank you for letting me use your seat. The ballet was wonderful.
I'm very sorry you were sick. I hope you get better soon!
Love from Lucy

If you start the habit early, writing should not be a terrible chore. Bread-and-butter letters do not have to be lengthy. If you are better at graphics than you are with words, apply that talent to your letters. I still have the dove a talented friend of mine painted with a few brush strokes in gold and black on white to thank me for giving him dinner one evening.

LETTERS THAT SHOULD NEVER BE SENT

THE CIRCULAR   A lengthy and often boring report on a year in the lives of a person or family. This is inflicted on every major or minor acquaintance. Do not be tempted to think that this is an acceptable substitute for a personal letter. It is not.

THE DOOMSAYER   Although sometimes a letter must convey bad news, a pessimistic diatribe is the last thing anyone deserves to receive. Letters aimed at depressing or unduly worrying somebody should be posted in the dustbin.

THE ANONYMOUS MISSIVE   If it's worth writing, it's worth owning up to. It's cowardly not to.

AN EMOTIONAL COMPLAINT   Sleep on it before you send it. Things sometimes seem different next day.

THANKS

Whenever you accept a written invitation, after the event you should write a letter of thanks promptly. Say how much you enjoyed the food, the company and the whole occasion, make a personal observation, such as the beauty of the table or something interesting that was said or done and thank them for including you before you sign off.

A formal thank-you for dinner could go something like this:

Dear Mr and Mrs George,

It was a great privilege for me to have been your guest on Monday. The whole evening was special, not just because of the beautiful setting and the superb food, but because you made me feel so at home.

What an amusing storyteller Mr Franc is and how charmed I was
to find him so approachable.

Thank you for an event that I shall remember always.

Yours sincerely,

Angela Peerless

A handwritten letter of thanks is always appreciated, no matter how informal the occasion. Among friends, keep it light and straightforward.

Dear Antonia and Scott,

Peter and I enjoyed every minute of our evening with you,
consuming indecent quantities of delicious food and just being on your
home ground. I always love being in your house because it is such an
unmistakable reflection of its owners.

Kay and I are thinking of meeting for lunch in town on Thursday.
Any chance you might join us?

Love, Sabrina

Thanks for a wedding present

Within a month of their return from the honeymoon newlyweds should put their thanks for wedding gifts in writing. Traditionally it was the bride's responsibility but now that so many couples have jobs outside the home, they should share this chore. When a gift is very special, you might want to enthuse a bit.

Dearest Lucinda,

You are such an angel! Paul and I were speechless with joy when we
opened your beautiful and generous gift. Thank you from the bottom of
our hearts for all your good wishes and for being there to share our
wedding day. You must come to dinner very soon and we'll bore you with
our honeymoon snaps.

Love, Rachel

CONDOLENCE

The difficulty of finding the right words to express your sympathy should not prevent you from writing a letter to someone who's having an unhappy time. (For examples of appropriate bereavement letters, see page 483.)

To a colleague who has lost a job

Dear Harriet,

To reiterate what I said when you left yesterday, I want you to know how much I have enjoyed working with you these past two years. Your humour has sustained us all and, sadly, nobody will ever be able to fill that gap. Just remember, you are fabulous! Onward and upward!

If you can, make the most of this time of freedom because, knowing your capability and energy, all too soon you'll be committed to stern disciplines again. Thank you for your friendship. I know we'll stay in touch.

Ciao for now,
Tracey

APOLOGY

What to do to say you are sorry and how you do it depends on the deed. If it was bad behaviour, sending flowers with a card that reads 'I am deeply sorry and hope you will forgive me' is about as much as you can do. In other situations, something along these lines would be appropriate:

Dear Janet,

I promise not to go on about it but just let me apologise once again for my clumsiness last night, the one flaw in an otherwise perfect evening. Trust me to pick your best crystal instead of a kitchen glass to

knock over. A replacement should be delivered by the end of this week.
I'll call you at the weekend to make sure.

With thanks for your tolerance,
Adam

CONGRATULATIONS

When fortune smiles on someone close to you, show your generosity of spirit in writing. If it has to do with the announcement of an engagement or impending marriage, remember the fine old tradition of offering congratulations to the man but never to the woman; to her you say, 'I hope you'll be very happy.' I quite like the old-fashioned nicety of this distinction. For some sort of public achievement, something along the following lines would be appropriate:

Dear Zoe,

News of your promotion made me feel so proud, you'd think I had something to do with it! All I can claim is to have recognised exceptional ability in you from the cradle. Freddy and I send you our congratulations and our love.

Moira

INTRODUCTION

When someone you know well moves to another city or another country where they have few or no contacts, it is a great kindness to introduce them to people you happen to know there. Do this only if you know both parties well because a letter of introduction carries your personal endorsement of the characters and personalities of both parties.

Never force newcomers on to anyone unless you know they will be welcome. Any Australian who has lived abroad for a length of time in one of the great cities knows how tiresome it is to have a steady stream of unknowns from home who have somehow got your address, all hopeful of a bed, a dinner or at least a drink at your expense. Dear friends are a different matter, although they should be careful not to expect to be feted and fed without reciprocating.

How you word a letter of introduction depends very much on the people and the circumstances but, whether you convey it by post, fax or email, do send it well ahead of the date of the person's arrival to give the recipients time to reply. Write another letter for the person who you are introducing to deliver by hand, perhaps with a small but thoughtful gift from you (see page 108).

KEEPING IN TOUCH

As the use of email becomes more widespread it is very easy to keep in touch with colleagues, friends and even children anywhere in the world. But there are people, particularly the elderly, who do not have access to modern technology and may become isolated because of it. A note penned and posted in the lunch hour is all it takes to make somebody feel they are part of your life.

> *Dear Nan,*
>
> *When I looked at the courtyard this morning and saw the first snowdrop, I thought of you. Remember when you let me dig some up from your garden?*
>
> *They seem to flourish here. Wish I felt the same. I am burdened with boring work this week but my great consolation was finding the pricey Italian sunglasses I thought were lost forever. Guess where? In the glove box. Talk about your forgetfulness! You're nothing on me. Hope you are well and that we see you soon.*
>
> *Love, Helen*

Whichever words you choose and no matter how brief they are, do put them down in writing and post that letter. There is no excuse for lapsing, even if you are very busy. But be careful of over-zealousness. A friend of mine in the travel industry has a cautionary tale. Once, before

taking off for abroad, he knew he'd be too busy to write thank-you letters after several dinner engagements that week, so he penned them all
beforehand. He gave them to a friend with instructions to post them
after he'd left the country. They were posted immediately and arrived
before the events had taken place. His hosts dined out on that for
weeks.

Chapter Seven

MANNERS IN BUSINESS

The overall aim of any commercial enterprise is to make money for the people who own it. In the case of not-for-profit organisations, the aim is to make money for a particular cause. There are many complex ways of achieving these simple aims but, in the end, whether you're in electronics, education, marketing, medicine, finance, food, big-time mining or small-time retailing, the success or failure of your business depends on people. Even someone who owns and runs a company must rely not only on employees but on the customers who buy the goods or use the services the company provides. None of us works in isolation. We are all interdependent. Courtesy and kindness help smooth the way in business, just as they do in private life. Equipping yourself with some basic professional niceties will stand you in good stead, whatever your line of work. And in this fast-paced era, your good manners may well set you ahead of the pack.

APPLYING FOR A JOB

Anyone who works, or plans to work, should keep a binder with plastic sleeves in which relevant papers can be filed. It is so much easier to put a presentation together quickly if all the elements are in one place. If you have a computer at home, store the information there but be sure to keep a back-up, too, on a floppy disk or on paper. This information is too precious to be put at risk. Early in your career, or even before you have one, start filing all references, reports and awards related to your academic or professional life plus examples of your work if appropriate. From time to time, update the record of your education and job experience, otherwise known as a résumé, or curriculum vitae (CV) in Latin.

BLUEPRINT FOR A RÉSUMÉ

There is a standard way of putting this information down clearly and concisely for a prospective employer. Your computer program might even have an example form for you to copy. It should not be hand-written but typed on a word processor in a clear and business-like way. Keep it as brief as possible – one or two pages at most. Use a font, size, style and layout that make the words as clear and legible as possible.

At the top of the first page, put your full name, address and contact telephone number and, if appropriate, fax number and email address. Include date of birth, marital status and nationality if you wish, although they are not necessary.

Under the heading 'Professional Experience' itemise the positions you have held, starting with the most recent and working back. Include precise dates and a brief summary of what each job entailed.

Following that should be another heading, 'Education', under which you give a brief rundown of your schooling, working back from your most recent studies. Include any degrees, special awards, honours or roles you held within the school or university. Also mention any part-time courses you have taken, such as evening classes.

The next heading will depend on what else you feel it would be advantageous to include. Perhaps the heading could be 'Interests and Activities'. List the ones that show your capabilities in a positive light; for example, secretary of a club, captain of a sports team, volunteer at a crisis centre or member of a fund-raising committee dedicated to a good cause.

Finally, under 'Referees', give the names and contact details of two or three senior people with whom you have worked who will be able to vouch for your ability and character. If you are just starting out in the business world and have no such contacts, give the names of reputable people who know you well: the head of your school, a professor at university, anyone of accomplishment who is a long-standing friend of your family, your parish priest or other spiritual leader. Always seek permission of these people before you include them and remember to thank them verbally or in writing and to keep them in touch with your progress.

Make sure your résumé is beautifully presented, with no literals, no smudges and no dog-eared edges. Attach to it photocopies of any references you think might help; do not risk losing the originals by entrusting them to anyone. Keep all this paperwork immaculate in a plastic sleeve, preferably in a loose-leaf file where it can lie flat and be ready to send out as soon as you need.

WHERE TO LOOK FOR JOBS

Word of mouth is by far the best way of learning about a job vacancy but not everyone has access to insider knowledge. If you are employed and you want to move, take trusted friends and colleagues into your confidence by telling them you are looking for a job but don't shout it from the rooftops or you may not be in employment for long. Whether or not you are employed, if you have contacts at a high level in business, now is the time to use them but only to seek advice; do not jeopardise a friendship or other close relationship by applying undue pressure. The more people who are aware of your search, the more likely you are to hear about something suitable.

You might prefer to use the services of an employment agency (colloquially known as a head-hunter), particularly if you are a senior executive. There are plenty of them listed under 'Employment Services' in the Yellow Pages of the telephone directory. Centrelink (formerly the Commonwealth Employment Service, or CES) is a good source of more general work.

In the meantime, don't hang around waiting for the telephone to ring. If you have access to the Internet, click on 'Employment' and see what turns up. Study the classifieds in the daily newspapers and in specialised publications applicable to your field of endeavour. The fact that an advertisement is likely to generate a lot of replies could be an advantage if you handle yourself competently and intelligently verbally and in writing. You should aim to get your foot in the door for a face-to-face interview with the person or group who will make the final decision, although you might have to go through a series of checks before you get there.

GETTING AN INTERVIEW

First impressions matter in all aspects of life, particularly in a job application and interview. When you know there is a vacancy for a job you would dearly love, find out all you can about the company and its business. Showing interest in a particular company – not just a job anywhere – is impressive to a potential employer. You'll be one step ahead if you are informed.

If you are required to send in your application, write a letter to accompany your résumé and the other paperwork outlining your credentials. Bear in mind when you write this letter that its primary objective is to get you an interview. Be clear, concise and positive. Your letter might go something like this:

3/106 Bayside Drive
Wicksworth Vic. 3614
Telephone 0980 3721

6 May 2003

The Director of Human Resources
Axel, Potty & Purdy Pty Ltd
GPO Box 983456
Melbourne Vic. 3001

Dear Sir or Madam,
I should like to apply for the position of Marketing Services Officer advertised in today's edition of The Age.
After three years of experience as Personal Assistant to the Director of Marketing of Tinker & Tinker Inc., I feel I am qualified to move on to a more responsible role. Your company's reputation for innovation is widespread and it would be an honour for me to become part of its dynamism.
My résumé is attached, together with copies of three references. Since I am currently in employment I would appreciate your keeping this application confidential.
I welcome the opportunity to present myself to you in person and look forward to your reply.

Yours faithfully,
(signature)
Angela Peerless

Once you have sent in your application, make sure you are easily accessible by telephone. Giving your business telephone number may not be a good idea if you work in an open-plan office where there's little privacy but, if you give your home number, make sure it has the ability to take messages efficiently and that there are no embarrassing greetings on the answering machine.

WHAT TO WEAR

When you secure an interview, start making decisions about your appearance and be comfortable in presenting the best of what you are. Consider the company's corporate culture and dress accordingly.

Have a dress rehearsal in front of a mirror. Try sitting down to see how far your skirt or trousers ride up. If you decide to wear a skirt, you must wear pantihose or stockings. Socks worn with trousers in business should be mid-calf- or knee-length and match the pants rather than the shoes. Don't forget to check how you look from behind as well as in front. People who would be far too discreet to look you up and down when you are face to face usually have no compunction in giving you the once-over from the rear.

As a business outfit, a good suit cannot be bettered. Nothing flash but not too dull, either, depending of course on the kind of work you do. We're thinking corporate here. If you're in the arts and entertainment, looking colourful or outrageous might be your admission ticket to work. In fashion and design there is a look that you will know how to put together if you're equal to the job. Dressing appropriately tells so much about you. Overalls on the candidate for a sales job in computer software are as misguided as a conservative suit and tie for an art director in an advertising agency.

In any case, pay meticulous attention to grooming. Clean hair and fingernails, polished shoes in good repair and immaculate clothes are fundamental. Take a neat bag with a notebook, pen, diary (in case you're required to make another appointment) and any papers that might be necessary. Make sure you do not have to fumble or rummage through your bag to find something.

GETTING THE JOB

Be there on the dot of the appointed time. If in doubt, arrive early and walk around the block or sit in a coffee shop until it's the right moment to present yourself. Although arriving too early can make you feel a bit awkward, it's a lot better than being late.

Mind your manners with the receptionist and anyone else you meet on the way to being ushered into your potential employer's office. Leave your right hand free of chattels to offer it to the person interviewing you. (For more on greetings and introductions, see pages 119–125). Wait until a seat is offered before you plonk yourself down and then sit up straight. Smile and look your interviewer/s in the eye. Do not lead the interview. Be courteous, open and friendly in a businesslike way. Never gush and don't smoke.

Although in general it is better to say too little than too much – a chatterbox can be irritating and off-putting – do answer questions with a bit more than yes or no. Enlarge on it with relevant facts or observations but keep to the point. Don't be evasive or flippant.

Do not boast. It is better to underplay your achievements than crow about them. Don't sell yourself short either, or hide your light under a bushel. Be calm and confident about the things you know you do well and be kind to yourself about your failings. In fact, put them right out of your mind unless asked specifically. Then think of them not as failings but just as things in which you are less qualified or less interested than you are in everything else.

When it becomes clear that the job is yours for the taking, don't hesitate to ask pertinent questions relating to procedure, what will be required of you, to whom you report directly in the hierarchy, the structure of your salary package and the details of your superannuation, which all employers are by law required to pay. Showing a keen interest in the company and its wellbeing will be to your credit. Keep your questions focused on the job, not on how many sickies, holidays or smokos are due to you.

If you do not get the job, you would not be human if you did not feel disappointed but don't be disheartened. Something even better might be just around the corner and the more interviews you have the more practised you become at anticipating questions and being prepared to answer them confidently.

NO-NO QUESTIONS

There are certain questions that should never be asked at a job interview. Human rights, anti-discrimination and equal opportunity legislation in Australia forbids prospective employers from basing their decisions on anything other than merit. While there are minor variations from one state to another, according to Commonwealth law your race, colour, sex, religion, political opinion, national extraction, social origin, age, medical record, criminal record, marital status, impairment, disability, nationality, sexual preference or trade union activity do not count unless they have an immediate bearing on your ability to do the job, therefore questions about them are irrelevant. People who test positive to HIV or AIDS must be given an equal chance with other applicants as long as their state of health does not affect their ability to handle the work required.

If your prospective employer does put any of these questions to you, field them tactfully rather than indignantly, with something like, 'I don't think that has any bearing on my ability to do the job' or 'I have been told that questions of that kind are discouraged by law.' If your interviewer insists on answers, I don't think you want that job but, if I were you, I would bring the incident to the attention of the Anti-Discrimination Board in your state.

SUCCESS AT THE OFFICE

From the start, the more pleasant you are to everyone the easier it will be to settle into your new workplace. Don't be afraid to ask questions to do with your work but stay away from anything too personal in office hours, unless there is a crisis and you can be genuinely useful.

Be the soul of discretion. If you have a problem with your boss, tell your boss, not the whole office. In fact, come out in the open with any of your colleagues if you feel there are difficulties between you. Don't be tricky. Don't tell tales behind someone's back. Steer clear of gossip and be wary of anyone who tries to winkle confidential information out of you. Change the subject by asking a question that switches the focus back to everyday business: 'I've been meaning to ask you for the web address of so and so' or 'You're a fund of knowledge about these things: where are the ink cartridges kept?' or 'What is company policy on borrowing reference books from the library?'

Always regard anything told to you behind closed doors as confidential. If you're bursting to tell someone, wait until you get home and share it with your nearest and dearest who, being your loyal and trusty ally, should make sure it goes no further. Someone you can rely on to keep mum at home is a healthy safety-valve for the pressures of business.

Keep your workspace clean and tidy and your valuables under lock and key when you're away from your desk. Be helpful to colleagues and friends and generous in your willingness to come to the aid of someone who is overloaded, although be wary of being exploited by a lazybones. Willingness to help develops a spirit of camaraderie. Some of the strongest friendships in life start at work.

WHAT NOT TO CALL PEOPLE

Although we Australians are just as informal in business as we are in private life, unless you are at a very senior level wait until you are absolutely sure that your boss wishes to be on first-name terms with you before you decide to use Tom, Dick or Harriet. Women joining companies at board level are sometimes faced with a very different challenge. Whereas a toey young male executive would not hesitate to address a venerable chairman by his given name, a woman who is schooled in paying respect to elders might be reluctant. Be brave. Thrust out your hand and say, 'How do you do, John.' If you create a precedent by calling him Mr, don't hold your breath waiting for him to ask you to use his given name. In any case, when you mention your boss to others in business, always refer to him or her as Mr, Mrs or Ms. In alluding to colleagues, use the surname as well as the given name: 'Jacinta Wells is in charge of marketing that product' gives her far more importance than 'Jacinta looks after that.' The same principle applies when you introduce yourself to others. Offer your hand and say, 'Hello, I'm Angela Peerless', not just 'Hi, I'm Angela.'

If your position calls for a personal assistant, never refer to her as 'my girl' or yell for him, as though he's some personal slave. Get to your feet, put your head around the door and say, 'When you've got a minute, Georgina, let's go through the agenda for tomorrow.' Don't demean him or her with words like dear, lad, pet, luv, sonny or any other term of endearment applicable to children. Show respect, courtesy and kindness to everyone, from the cleaners to the members of the board, and that's the way you'll be treated in return.

CHIEF COFFEE CARRIER

Unless making tea or going out for a tray of cappuccinos is one of the specifications of the job, it should not be expected from the boss's personal assistant or the most junior member of the staff. If coffee-carrying is necessary from one employee, it must be part of that person's job description. Otherwise, everyone should look after themselves or take turns in getting sustenance for the immediate group. It's up to the group to determine the fairest way of managing this trivial but massively important part of daily office life and everyone should be sensitive to the rules and take part dutifully.

When a colleague's workload is particularly heavy and deadlines loom, the least you can do is fetch a sandwich and a cup of coffee, no matter what your place in the hierarchy. More than once I have seen the co-founder of a very successful homewares company buying sushi from a Japanese restaurant to take back to everyone at the studio for lunch. No wonder morale is so buoyant in the people who work there.

TURN UP ON TIME

Present yourself on time for meetings. Tardiness is a discourtesy to others, whose work must then lie unattended while they cool their heels waiting for the arrival of someone who makes a habit of being late. If you are the most senior person at that meeting, or you are the one who has called it, start proceedings on time unless the absent party is crucial to the purpose of the discussion. The risk of missing out on vital information should spur the latecomer to be punctual next time.

THE CONFIDENCE TO SHARE

Never use the word 'I' if you can use 'we' instead. 'We' is a team word, 'I' is a selfish one. Don't be the one who earns the nickname Mimi ('Me! Me!'). Share your achievements because rarely are they the outcome of the efforts of just one person. Kindness does not demean, it ennobles. Generosity of spirit is catching, too. It creates a positive environment, fostering high morale and the pursuit of excellence in everyone, a state of grace that should be an important goal for any company.

If you are in a position of responsibility for other people, never be afraid to employ somebody who is smarter or more talented than you are. Their accomplishments will reflect well on you in the eyes of your superiors, who will see you as a good manager and a confident human being. Encouraging the development of someone means that one day you will probably lose that person to another department or another company, but growth is the nature of living things, which is why trying to hold people back simply does not work. Let them fly, then encourage the next set of fledglings.

Not all hatchlings turn into birds of paradise, though. Some are bone idle or bored or unmotivated or unqualified or just undisciplined. Bad behaviour must be corrected, in the interest of other employees, and that means cautioning the offender in private as soon as possible.

A DIFFICULT COLLEAGUE

There's one in every office, so be prepared for the person who borrows your stapler, wastebasket, notepad or pen and never returns it; who spies on your emails, distracts you when you are busy or starts nasty little rumours. Try not to be drawn into conspiracies or distracted from your own work. Try not to lose your temper. Be professional, pleasant but removed, although don't suffer in silence: 'My pen has walked again . . . in your direction, Kevin?' or 'If you're going to stationery, Sybil, I'd be grateful for replacements for that stack of envelopes you borrowed yesterday.' Analyse the troublemaker's behaviour and try to find the cause. It could be envy, or just a clumsy plea to be noticed and included.

If the someone offends by constantly biting nails, picking teeth, sniffling, shouting into the telephone or giving off unpleasant body smells from the mouth or underarms, somebody will have to say something. It's difficult for a colleague to do it without causing resentment and an uncomfortable environment from then on. The one best placed to broach the subject is the person's immediate superior, who should take the employee aside and say something like 'Derek, you are probably unaware of it, but you do have a habit of . . . ' or 'I realise you have a wonderful voice, Lotte, but it does carry in an open-plan office, so can you tone it down a bit?' or 'Bill, I know you shower every day but an anti-perspirant is pretty important when we work as closely as we do in this office' or 'Annie, your breath doesn't seem healthy lately. Do you need time off for the dentist?'

THE OPPOSITE SEX

This is a minefield so tread carefully. The most important thing about dealing with someone of the opposite sex at the office is to be sensitive to individual beliefs and feelings. Keep sex out of it as much as you can, which is not to say that women should dress like men or that a man should muscle his way through a door in front of a female colleague. Courtesy all round, please, regardless of sex. Outside office hours, you might be good friends who greet each other with hugs or kisses – perhaps even closer encounters – but leave those outside when you enter the office building. If business associates know each other well, an air kiss on each cheek is appropriate in some industries. Apart from that, a handshake should be the most intimate exchange between people of the opposite sex in a work environment.

Hands off

Sexual harassment is a nasty practice that still hangs around and must not be tolerated from anyone. If you feel comfortable, politely address the offender and let them know that this behaviour is unacceptable. Otherwise report it to your immediate boss. If your boss is the guilty one, go to a higher level. If the company is unsympathetic or uncooperative, go to the Anti-Discrimination Board in your state. The involvement of a government agency will almost certainly put fear into the offender and the company principals and get results.

Working relationships

Sexual attraction between two people at the office is an entirely different matter. Nobody wants to stand in the way of romance but do keep it outside work hours. If you enter into a liaison with someone who is already committed, particularly in marriage, you do so at considerable risk. Some of these unions end happily, some do not and when love turns bad, seeing the other party on a daily basis can be unbearable. That usually means at least one of you has to quit. Think about the consequences before you let yourself in for complications of that kind.

ETIQUETTE AT WORK

If you've been in business for any length of time, you might think that thoughtfulness, kindness and even common courtesy have become as obsolete as the electric typewriter in the modern corporate world. Sadly, it is true that many people who are civilised outside office hours revert to barbarism when they enter the portals of commerce. Sitting behind the wheel of a car in city traffic is another catalyst in a change for the worse in normally well-behaved people.

Getting into the crowded lift of a high-rise building is evidence, if you need it, of the mentality of some contemporary executives. It can be a free-for-all with brute force the winner. To the casual observer the most chilling thing is that these modern dinosaurs seem not necessarily to be deliberately rude but to be oblivious of anybody else. Except for those fawning upon the boss, anybody who stands aside for another is indeed a rarity, almost an anachronism, especially if it is done with a smile. How long since someone other than a paid doorman held a door open for you?

Mind you, more than one man has told me that the courtesy of opening a door or standing back for a woman to go first has been received with hostility. I cannot fathom why anybody – woman or man – should feel demeaned by a gesture such as this. Perhaps it depends on how it is done. If it is accompanied by a patronising appraisal of her body or some facetious remark, then the gesture is not courteous but impertinent. Sometimes, isn't it true that it's not so much what is done but how it's done that matters?

KILLER INSTINCT OR KINDNESS?

Is success in business dependent on ruthlessness? I don't think so. Although the 'killer instinct' is a much admired quality in boardrooms around the world, it is heartening to notice that the success – if any – of brutal people in business is often short-lived. It's usually people of subtlety and courtesy who succeed in the long-term. Because they are aware of others and make them feel they are valued, these long-term achievers also receive respect, admiration and affection.

Ambition is an admirable thing but it should never be naked or it becomes ugly. Everybody in business is dependent on the cooperation of others and the success of the whole should be credited to everyone who contributes to it, even in a minor way. The team is all. How much more pleasant and productive it is if every member of the team feels the sense of achievement that is such a powerful motivator.

That is not to say that individual excellence should go unrewarded, financially and in status. Far from it. Many years ago, when I worked for a large advertising agency in New York, my creative director was responsible for an idea that won the company an important piece of new business. The very next day he was given a handsome salary increase and moved into a flash corner office with a stunning view. The message from management couldn't have been clearer. In giving him recognition, they gave everybody else an incentive to do better.

LOYALTY CUTS TWO WAYS

It might sound old-fashioned but the firm that pays you has every right to expect your loyalty. Similarly, loyalty is owed by the company to its employees. Telling tales within the office is bad enough; bad-mouthing management or your colleagues to people outside is unforgivable. Having said that, I know that many companies now do not deserve loyalty because the people who run them are themselves greedy, disloyal or uncaring towards the people who work for them. Nevertheless, just because other people behave badly does not mean that you should. That would give them power over you. Show them how it should be done by setting an example. Claiming the upper ground gives you the upper hand.

Don't demand too much of the people who work for you. Being a high-profile boss who earns a big salary is in itself motivating but it's unreasonable to expect the same drive from employees in routine jobs with little prospect of improvement in circumstances or pay. Certainly, expect them to be supportive and loyal but don't lean on them for effort over and above what they are paid for.

I truly believe that when people feel secure and happy in their work they are more creative and more productive. This atmosphere comes from the top. If confusion or incompetence or negativism exists there, it will poison every level as it filters down. You know the old saying: when a fish goes off it starts at the head.

THE ABUSE OF POWER

Some people can handle power without becoming self-important. Many cannot. Anyone who is rude to those in subordinate roles at the office, or who asks indignantly 'Do you know who I am?' of the receptionist at a hotel, a flight attendant or anyone else in the front line of a service industry has a problem. It is not easy to deal with such people; most of us prefer to steer clear and do for them only what is absolutely necessary. It's our only means of revenge. What a shame they'll never know what they are missing.

BUSINESS CORRESPONDENCE

Despite email, which is very straightforward in format and has its own protocol, people still send and receive business letters, although many nowadays are part of promotional material masquerading as personal correspondence.

A good business letter gets to the point quickly, makes its meaning clear, is concise and does not attempt to be personal unless it is between people who know each other very well. Ideally, it fits on one page.

- Make sure you spell the recipient's name correctly and that the job description is correct. The best way to make sure you get it right is to telephone that person's office for verification.
- Address a man as Mr. If the letter is to a woman, find out how she prefers to be addressed. All it takes is a telephone call to her or her assistant. If, for some reason, you cannot find out, use the title Ms.
- Different companies prefer different formats but, in general, the date is placed at the top right-hand side of the page,

under the address, although it can be ranged left, if that is the
company's standard.

- The person's name and address are typed against the left-hand
  margin.
- It is a nicety in business for the person whose signature appears
  on the letter to handwrite the 'Dear John' rather than type it.
- Type the subject of the letter in a heading, centred on the page,
  a little lower than the space for 'Dear John'.
- The opening paragraph should set the context; for example,
  'Further to our recent telephone conversation . . . ' or 'Our client
  has advised us that . . . ' or 'When we spoke last month, I said I'd
  try to contact . . . '
- The second paragraph should contain the substance of
  the letter.
- If the substance takes some explaining, you might want to split
  it into two or more paragraphs so that it is easy to read. Avoid a
  great grey mass of type.
- If the letter runs over to a second page, '/2' typed at the bottom
  right-hand corner of page 1 indicates that another follows.
  Type 'Page 2' at the top right-hand or left-hand corner of the
  second page.
- The final paragraph should constitute a call to action or simply
  sign off in a businesslike way. Do not reiterate the person's name
  here ('John, I do hope we can . . . ') because it sounds contrived,
  the kind of thing taught at some how-to-succeed school to get
  you close to the other person. It reeks of insincerity.
- 'Yours faithfully' is still the appropriate business-letter sign-off
  but few people use it now. 'Yours sincerely' or 'Kind regards' or
  'Best wishes' have become popular. Whichever you prefer, you
  might like to add a handwritten message, if you want the letter
  to be more personal.
- Your name and job description should be typed at the end of the

letter with a space left above for your signature. If you want to indicate your title, such as Ms or Dr, put it (in brackets) after your name, never before it.

WHEN THE COMPANY ENTERTAINS

To what extent hospitality is a part of your business life depends on the kind of business you are in. But whether your company plays host once a year at Christmas time or relentlessly, as it does in public relations, and whether it's a party for a hundred or lunch for four after a client meeting, you are a host, not a guest. No matter what your level in the company, it is your responsibility to make sure guests are as well looked after as they would be in your own home.

In fact, the higher you are in company status, the more willing you should be to do routine matters yourself. If you are a chief executive having drinks in the boardroom after a client meeting, it will do you nothing but good to pour drinks for your guests and for your own people, no matter where they are on the corporate ladder.

TIPS FOR THE CLIENT LUNCH

If you ask the great veteran hotelier Peter Stafford which is the best restaurant or hotel, he will reply, 'The one that knows you best' because you will be treated as the VIP you are to that establishment and given the best it can offer. In the case of a restaurant, you will also be able to speak with some authority on the menu and wine list and make recommendations. Never take a client to a restaurant where you have never been before, no matter how great its reputation.

- Establish that the kind of food served in the restaurant is acceptable to your guest.
- Always make a booking and request a specific table, if you wish.
- Call or email your client on the morning of the lunch to reconfirm time and place.

- Arrive at the restaurant a few minutes ahead of the scheduled time. Make sure you are happy with the table.
- Turn off your mobile telephone. If you're expecting an urgent call, give the telephone to the head waiter with the instruction to let you know immediately the awaited call arrives. This goes for your guest as well.

If you want to settle the bill without fuss or fanfare, give your charge card to the head waiter when you arrive with the instruction not to bring the bill to the table but to prepare it and keep it at the cashier's desk until you go there at the end of the lunch (on the pretext of going to the washroom) to approve and sign it. You may wish to add ten per cent or more to the bill when you sign or, better still, to give it in cash, a gesture that will greatly endear you to the staff.

As a guest, remember that, in contrast to social occasions when you should arrive ten to fifteen minutes after the appointed time, you should always be on time for a business meeting, even if it does take place over lunch. If you arrive before your host, wait at the bar, if the restaurant has one, or at the table. If you are offered a drink, choose water rather than alcohol.

When your guest arrives

Get to your feet and offer him or her the best seat, which is often the one against the wall with the best view of the restaurant. Seat yourself on the outside in what some people call 'the paying seat'.

If you decide to drink wine, determine your guest's preference for red or white. If you are not confident in your choice of wines, do not be embarrassed to ask the advice of your guest or the sommelier (wine waiter). Either one should be delighted to help. Inexperienced hosts are sometimes reluctant to ask the advice of the sommelier because they suspect he or she will recommend something very expensive. That is rarely the case. A good professional usually chooses something in the middle range or gives more than one recommendation, to include something at the lower end of the price range.

Strictly speaking, when you have made a decision about what to eat and the waiter comes to take your order, it is up to you to ask your guests what they have chosen and then convey their orders to the waiter before you place your own. But you may find this unsuitable and, if the group is fairly large, it's usually more efficient to let them give their orders direct to the waiter. Always wait until everyone else has ordered before placing yours.

All business meetings have a purpose and lunch is no exception. The arrival of the first course should be your signal to raise the subject you want to discuss, if it hasn't arisen before.

LUNCH AT THE OFFICE

Its degree of lavishness depends on its purpose. If it is intended to be a work session, keep the menu to sandwiches, fruit and mineral water. If it is to signal the end of a project or to celebrate a good result, it can be more sociable and relaxed. In that case, have the lunch catered and invite all those involved to the boardroom or other suitable office. The setting should be streamlined and stylish, with flowers, linen napkins and placemats, china and wine glasses.

No tricky foods

Choose a menu that does not present a potential challenge for anybody at the table and always make sure it includes dishes suitable for a vegetarian. Take into account any special dietary requirements your guests may have and cater accordingly. With its almost universal acceptability, the avocado is an excellent ally at a business lunch. Salmon is pretty safe, too. Make sure the dishes are easy to eat. No fish on the bone, globe artichokes or anything else likely to test dexterity or result in messy fingers (see pages 298-307). If pasta is served, make sure it is more manageable than spaghetti or fettuccine, which are notorious for flinging spots on ties.

Don't overdo the volume of food. Two courses are plenty. In high summer, a cold main course such as vitello tonnata or chicken salad is appropriate but in winter something warm is preferable. For carnivores, a piece of well-hung roast beef with horseradish, mustards or sauce bearnaise, boiled potatoes and salad is hard to beat. However, there are some marvellous modern alternatives to traditional food but make sure they are not too tricky and hold the chilli.

How to ask for a pay rise

In companies where management takes an ethical and humane approach to its staff, asking for a raise should not be necessary in the normal course of events because performance will be assessed regularly and rewarded accordingly. Not all businesses are based on the principle of fairness, though. On the other hand, some employees have an over-inflated idea of their own worth, or are gullible enough to believe every fairytale about what other people are paid. In many businesses, 'the squeaky wheel gets the most oil' seems to be the corporate motto and unless you speak up for yourself, more money is not likely to be forthcoming.

Most companies conduct performance appraisals regularly, once every six months, or once a year. Some require input from the colleagues of the person being assessed, some rely solely on what the immediate boss has to say. If appraisals are linked to pay in the company you work for, that is the time to raise the subject of more money. But if appraisals are not linked to pay, wait for another time to bring the subject up.

ASSESS YOUR OWN PERFORMANCE

Before you make an approach, spend some time at the weekend going through all the things you have done to benefit the company, particularly those tasks that were over and above the call of duty. Also consider the skills you have that are not being utilised and where you think they could be applied to your employer's advantage. When you are armed with these hard facts, it's difficult for a fair-minded boss to say no.

The exercise is an interesting one to go through because you may find that your contribution has not been as great as you'd like to think. In that case, be wary of asking for more pay until you have something to substantiate the request.

GETTING WHAT YOU WANT

Once you are forearmed, choose the moment carefully. Make it a time when your immediate boss is least likely to be distracted by other matters. Always make an appointment. In a very small company, or if you work for an individual, such as a doctor or lawyer, raise the matter when there's a pause in the day's work, or perhaps just before it's time to go home.

Here are some guidelines on what *not* to say when you ask for a pay rise.

1 'I need it because I want to put an extension on my house' or 'My wife is pregnant' or 'My kids' school fees are getting out of hand' or anything else that has nothing to do with company business. The first aim of a business is to make a profit for the people who own it, not to fund welfare.

2 'I deserve a raise because I've been working hard.' Perhaps, but how productive have you been? Activity is one thing, achievement is another.

3 'George is getting more than I am and he joined more recently.' That may be so, but George might have been more expensive to hire because he has qualifications that you do not have. His department might be more profitable than yours.

4 'If I don't get more money, I'll resign.' Don't deliver an ultimatum or you might find yourself on the street. Leave your boss room to manoeuvre. Be reasonable. The board of directors sets budgetary limits within which each department must operate. Be patient; any increases might have to wait for the next financial year.

5 'I'm being paid less than my market value.' The boss might call your bluff and invite you to go and take advantage of the money available in the outside world. If you then decide not to leave, you'll have the disadvantage of being thought lazy or cowardly.

6 Don't fly off the handle. Being emotional will get you nowhere.

HOW TO RESIGN FROM YOUR JOB

You might be dissatisfied with your current post, but remember that it is easier to get a new job when you have an existing one, so try not to resign before you have secured another position.

Once your new job has been confirmed, resign quickly before word gets out. This is usually done in writing, although you may want to explain your reasons in person before you hand your written resignation to your immediate boss or the person who employed you. Do not criticise your employer or the company. You never know where, when or how your paths may cross again. Leave with goodwill and courtesy, no matter what prompted your resignation.

Here is an example of a letter of resignation. It may be typed or handwritten on the company's letterhead.

26 May 2003

Mr Michael Maudlan
Marketing Director
Tinker & Tinker Inc.
3 Dampier Place
Melbourne Vic. 3000

Dear Michael, (handwritten)
  After three productive years as your assistant, I have accepted an offer to join Axel, Potty & Purdy Pty Ltd as Marketing Services Officer. The timing of my resignation is subject to our mutual agreement,

but I would like it to take effect as soon as possible.

The decision was not easy. You have been an inspiring boss and everything I know about marketing, sales and office management I owe to you. However, it is time for me to broaden my experience and move on to new challenges and greater responsibility.

I appreciate all that you and the company have done for me and hope that we keep in touch.

> *Yours sincerely,*
> *(signature)*
> *Angela Peerless*
> *Personal Assistant to the*
> *Marketing Director*

Before you leave any job, always ask for a reference. You never know when you might need it. File it away carefully with your résumé and other papers related to your professional life.

HOW TO WRITE A REFERENCE

Writing a reference for somebody very good is easy and sometimes even pleasurable if you truly believe in that person's value as an employee and you want the best for them. Writing a reference for somebody whose work you find less than adequate is very difficult. On the one hand, unless that person's performance is deliberately unproductive, it is churlish and mean-spirited to refuse to write one. On the other hand, you do not want to misrepresent that person's abilities and foist a dud on to an unsuspecting employer. The best way to read a reference is to take note of what is not there because it is a clue to the failings of its subject.

Here is an example of each of them. All business references should be typewritten on company letterhead. Because a reference is not really a letter but the writer's opinion of the ability of the subject, it is not necessary to address it with terms such as 'To whom it may concern' or

'This is to certify . . .'. Simply date it, make the statement and sign it above your typed name and title.

31 May 2003

For the past three years, it has been my good fortune to have Angela Peerless as my Personal Assistant. She has chosen to leave the company to further her career.

When Angela joined us, she was a raw recruit from university. Thanks to her bright mind, willingness to learn and winning personality, she has become invaluable to me, not only in the routine matters she was first employed to perform but in taking initiative. She is capable of handling whatever challenges come her way with efficiency and good humour.

She is quick, self-generating, creative and highly motivated. I have no hesitation in recommending her to a prospective employer who values these qualities, and envy the good fortune of the person who becomes her next boss.

Yours sincerely,
(signature)
Michael Maudlan
Marketing Director

31 May 2003

Angela Peerless has been my Personal Assistant for the past three years.
Her duties have involved answering the telephone, attending to correspondence, arranging meetings and helping to organise media presentations and product launches.

She leaves the company of her own accord.

Yours sincerely,
(signature)
Michael Maudlan
Marketing Director

AN UNSATISFACTORY EMPLOYEE

Stern measures have to be taken if someone is not doing the job efficiently. Being hauled in front of the boss or the head of human
resources is now called counselling and these are the steps a manager
should take.

1 Talk to the employee in private about your concerns that
    work standards are not being met and listen to any
    explanations. If there is a valid reason – say, inadequate
    equipment or work overload – provide what is necessary
    to promote efficiency.

2 Wait a reasonable length of time before an assessment. How
    long depends on individual circumstances, so you must be the
    judge. Then, if there has been no improvement, instigate
    proceedings for a counselling session and give the employee
    time to prepare for it. Apart from yourselves, there might be a
    witness present at the meeting. It is important for agreement to
    be reached early if there is a problem. In any case, the aim is to
    discuss the problem openly and dispassionately and try to find
    a solution. Concentrate on solutions rather than doing a post
    mortem. Set a date for a review of performance – say, a month
    ahead.

3 Keep a written record of this session, signed by you and the
    employee. It should detail date, names of participants, location,
    purpose of the session, points discussed, aims agreed upon and
    date of review. A copy should be given to the employee and
    another placed in a confidential file.

4 If there has been no improvement in a month's time, hold a
    further counselling session and set another date by which you
    hope to see results. Again, put it all in writing.

5 At the third meeting, if the situation is the same, it must be
    recognised that something will have to change. The job may be

modified, or another post more suited to the employee's ability may be offered. Otherwise, you will probably have to let the employee go but before you do that, make sure you know the company's responsibility financially and legally. Do consider giving the person the option of resigning rather than being given the sack.

THE DISMISSAL

Firing someone is unpleasant for everybody – the one doing it, the one receiving it and everybody else in the workplace. There is no painless way. But remember to be well-mannered and considerate, never brutal or unkind. If you are the one who has to despatch someone, put it as clearly yet tactfully as you can and do it swiftly. It must be done face to face. Don't take the spineless way out by putting it into a memo or doing it over the telephone. 'I'm sorry but we are going to have to let you go' is about the most sensitive way to say it.

DIGNIFIED DEPARTURE

Sometimes a company requires the sacked person to quit the job on the same day. If so, as the person in charge you must give that person the dignity of time to clear his or her desk or office. Unless an employee has done something invidious, never be a party to ordering him or her out of the building straight away, leaving others to go through private papers and possessions and bundle them into boxes for collection. That is barbaric and cowardly.

If you are the one given the sack, console yourself with the knowledge that these events can occur because of differences of personality or lack of what used to be called 'chemistry' between people. Some people are compatible, some are not. One development that often prompts a round of removals is a change of management. The incoming boss may feel threatened by employees who, through experience and track record, have access to the management level above, or to valuable clients and industry heavies. The 'new broom' may be anxious to have a fresh team of people who are easier to control and likely to feel beholden.

Remember, sooner or later being fired from a job happens to most people. Think of it as a valuable experience rather than reason for self-doubt. Although it is important to accept responsibility if your performance was not up to scratch, do not let it undermine the value you place on yourself but rather think of ways in which you can do better next time.

COMPANY GIFTS

Whether or not an enterprise has a policy of bestowing or receiving gifts largely depends on that company's business and how it relates to other outfits. It is, for instance, a mainstay of the public relations business. Gifts from clients to the people within other firms who are responsible for giving them business must be very carefully chosen so as not to be seen as payola. Sending something lavish just before a client's annual review of suppliers would be very unfortunate timing.

KEEP THEM BUSINESSLIKE

The traditional time for business gifts is at Christmas or New Year. At that time, anything that is business-related and carries a promotional message is the safest kind of present. Diaries, calendars, notebooks, pencils, calculators, mouse pads, address books, letter openers and books about company history are all safe bets. Flowers and food that can be enjoyed by the whole office are also acceptable, as are samples of the company's products, particularly if they are luxury goods. At the very least, sending greeting cards – designed specifically for the company, or whose proceeds go to charity – is a safe procedure.

WITHIN THE OFFICE

A culture of giving, or otherwise, within a company is also an individual matter. A new member of staff should be careful to ask what the procedure is when there's a milestone birthday or somebody is leaving. It is important to limit the number of occasions on which a worthy appears with a collection bag for yet another whip-around; not everyone can afford to contribute to gifts for everybody's impending birthdays, engagements, marriages, babies, resignations and retirements.

Boss to PA

It is virtually obligatory for a boss to give his or her personal assistant a thoughtful gift at the end of the year, or after a particularly punishing few weeks of concentrated work that has intruded on leisure time. Try to make that reward personal. That does not mean intimate, like sexy lingerie or underwear, but tailored to that person's preferences. If your PA likes the theatre or ballet, give a double pass to the best seats in a forthcoming production. Beware of making a stab in the dark. Unless you are sure that a particular style of tableware, decorative object, piece of clothing or accessory is the perfect choice, avoid it. Any boss who is vigilant will know the PA's favourite department store and boutique; what better than a gift voucher from one of those?

PA to boss

If you are the PA, it is not necessary for you to give anything to your boss, but there is nothing wrong with reciprocating, with the proviso that your gift is small and in no way comparable with what you are being given. Only a PA knows the predilections and peccadilloes of the boss – she loves white flowers, he's forever losing the case for his reading specs, she adores Anita Brookner's novels, he never remembers a sunscreen when he's out on his boat – and that's a huge advantage in choosing just the right gift that will give pleasure and, sometimes, amusement.

Between workmates

When a strong friendship has sprung up between colleagues, exchanging tokens of appreciation becomes automatic, but be careful not to do it in front of associates who are not as close to you. Do it outside office hours, over lunch at a café or a drink after work.

Chapter Eight

KEEPING UP APPEARANCES

Paying attention to the way you present yourself is a mark of self-confidence, optimism and respect for other people. There is no doubt that your appearance determines the way you are regarded by others, particularly at first meeting, and first impressions tend to be lasting ones. Picture your appearance as part of the general landscape and you quickly realise why looking your best is a courtesy to others. Always make an effort to be a pleasure to look at for the people you encounter, even just passersby.

NO BODY'S PERFECT

Women and men come in different shapes, sizes, proportions and colouring. What looks sensational on one person will not necessarily have the same effect on another. As soon as you begin to venture into adulthood, the first gift some kind adult should present you with is a full-length mirror that allows you to view yourself from all angles. Never leave home without seeing how you look from behind. The line of panties under slinky trousers is not a pretty sight. Bulges across the back from a bra that is too tight can spoil your entire look. Your hair may be immaculate from the front but have a mind of its own from behind. If the seat of your trousers or skirt is crumpled before you leave home, how will it look by lunchtime?

A common mistake for many young women is to try to ape the kind of physical beauty that nature has bestowed on famous fashion models and certain movie stars. You must realise that stunners like these are very rare. That's why they are supermodels and superstars. Many of them are not as good-looking in the flesh as they are in pictures. Their beauty is enhanced by clothes, make-up, lighting and photographic techniques.

There are many forms of beauty and the kind that appears on catwalks and magazine covers and in feature films is only one of them. It's impossible for us to see in ourselves the individuality that others find attractive but it's important to know that it exists. Personality, vitality and mystery are alluring qualities that bring the physical being to life. Be confident enough to accept your own uniqueness. Rather than try to change it, make the most of it. Be the best of what you are. If you are comfortable with yourself, other people will be, too.

SELF-APPRAISAL

Avoid tight clothes if you are overweight, underweight or your skin tone is not firm; fabric stretched to its capacity will accentuate the negative, not the positive. Contrary to what many people believe, oversized clothes do not make you look bigger if their fabrics are lightweight, not thick and heavy, and their colour is subdued; they soften the line and give you room to move, masking imperfections in body shape. Skinny women also look best in voluminous clothes and they can be of any weight and colour.

A neck that is too short, shoulders that are too wide or too narrow, short arms, big bottom, sway back, disproportionately large bust and many other real or perceived foibles in the body can be offset by clever tailoring or the right choice in off-the-peg garments. For example, a halter neck makes a woman's narrow shoulders look wider. If you are broad-shouldered, try a boat-shaped neckline. Similarly, don't be shy about your assets. If you have great legs, hike up your skirts. A tiny waist deserves to be accentuated. So does a long neck and a smooth decolletage.

One effective way of finding out what flatters your face and suits your shape is to take note of what you're wearing when people pay you genuine compliments. Sometimes they are not aware that the colour or cut of what you have on is what makes you look particularly attractive.

Changes in the body

With the relentless march of time body dimensions change, so gradually that you only sense them at first. Have you noticed that, every seven or so years, certain things that used to work for you are somehow not suitable any more? You look in the mirror and something is not quite right. For a woman, your eyeliner may be too dark, your hair colour too bright, your skirt too short, your upper arms not their best in short sleeves. For a man, a shirt that's too tight around the neck gives you a strangled look; if the buttons strain across your stomach, you look bloated. If you put on weight, the choice is clear: lose it or get a new wardrobe.

The ability to see yourself with some degree of impartiality takes courage, but your bravery will be rewarded by an appearance that adapts gracefully to the reality of now instead of reflecting what used to be. There is nothing so ageing as still wearing the look that suited you when you were young and nubile.

That doesn't mean embracing every new fad indiscriminately, as fashion victims do. Being in fashion no longer means adopting one particular look. There are many choices every new season. All you need do is take from them what you know feels and looks best on you. If you can't find anything, wait until next season for major purchases. Remember not to take seriously the exaggerations that pass for high fashion in reports on the collections from the fashion capitals of the world. Those shockers are designed not to be worn but to attract the publicity that is essential to the successful marketing of a fashion label and to the reputation of its designer.

DEPORTMENT AND GROOMING

Start with the raw material of what you've got: your body. Look after it with a balanced diet and exercise, but there is no need to be fanatical. Unless you are a serious athlete, excessive training is as misguided as extreme indolence because it tends to overwork the bones and over-develop the muscles. Don't invite problems for later years. Keep yourself fit and agile by integrating exercise into your ordinary routine. You don't have to make a production out of it. Take the stairs instead of the lift and leave the car in the garage if your destination is within walking distance. Eat healthy foods that you like and, if you feel that you're beginning to put on weight, foil it by eating a little less of those foods at every meal. Try to stay trim because it's much easier to maintain weight than to lose it permanently.

Body awareness is an obsession of our time. Personal trainers, regular workouts at the gym and running in the park seem to be necessary counterbalances to sedentary lives dominated by the computer. As well as pulmonary strength and muscular development that are part of modern fitness, it's important to practise the kind of fluidity we admire in cats, gazelles and ballet dancers. Flexibility, a straight back and a graceful gait are attractive physical attributes and they are necessary to the ability to wear clothes well.

Doing good old-fashioned housework – reaching up to dust bookshelves, bending down to wipe out the refrigerator, whirling about with the vacuum cleaner – is an excellent way to exercise your body as you polish up your nest. A vigorous workout on the dance floor of a nightclub counts as exercise, too, although it might be the last thing you had in mind while you were doing it.

The other imperative is good grooming, head to toe, for men as well as women. Not everyone can afford the time or the money for a weekly visit to the hairdresser, manicurist, pedicurist, masseur, and others of that ilk, but we can all make an effort to be clean and fresh. Good posture, agility, a well-scrubbed look, clean well-cut hair, bright eyes and glowing skin add up to the kind of beauty that outshines most others. Facial hair either shaved completely or trimmed into a neat shape are fundamental to a well-turned-out man. Designer stubble has had its day.

PERSONAL HYGIENE

Anyone who has ever been in close proximity to other people on public transport will know just how offensive body odour can be. A good underarm deodorant or anti-perspirant helps lengthen the effectiveness of the ablutions of men and women, but it is not a substitute. At the risk of stating the obvious, everybody should take a bath or a shower at least once a day, and those who do strenuous physical work, exercise vigorously or play sport should shower as soon as possible afterwards.

Bad breath is another anti-social emanation which, if it persists, might be a symptom of medical or dental problems that should be seen to. If it is just the aftermath of a rich dinner, a breath freshener might help. Some people find the smell of garlic offensive, although with our changed eating habits, many more of us are immune to the side effects of consuming this pungent bulb because we eat it ourselves. Fresh parsley can be an antidote to the smell of garlic, which is one of the reasons why the two ingredients often appear together in recipes.

Wash your hands before you begin to prepare food, before you sit down to eat and after you have finished eating. Always have clean fingers and clean nails before you use cosmetics or touch anything that should be completely sterile, such as a baby's bottle.

Always wash your hands after you have been to the lavatory, no matter how minor the activity, and that applies to men as well as women. Whenever you go out, make sure you have a handful of tissues in your pocket or your bag for those times when you are faced with an empty toilet roll in a public lavatory.

In private houses or anywhere men and women use the same facilities, men must take care not to leave drips on the edge of the toilet bowl or on the floor. If random droplets do occur, they should be wiped away with toilet paper. Always put both lid and seat down after you have made sure everything has been flushed away successfully. An old-fashioned method of dispelling the whiffy after-effects of an evacuation of the bowels is to strike a match and let the sulphur act as a fumigant. So it's a good idea to make sure there is always a box of matches in the bathroom.

If the flushing device in a cistern refuses to work when you have done the deed, cover the evidence with a few leaves of fresh paper. If you are in a private house, tell your host or hostess discreetly. If you're in a public place, all you can do is pre-warn the next person and report the malfunction to an attendant if you can find one.

If you are in an area where the plumbing is not connected to the public sewer, don't put sanitary pads or tampons into the lavatory or you might wreck whatever system is in place there. Seek advice from your hosts. If you are the host, make sure your guests are acquainted with any idiosyncracies in the plumbing.

BEAUTY-BOX MAINTENANCE

Bags gather dust. Pots of eyeshadow get smudgy. Brushes and combs gather hairs. Sponges and applicators show their recent history.

Wear and tear on the contents of our bathroom cupboards and make-up bags is considerable and it's easy not to notice. Others do, though, and to an outsider it's not attractive. Housekeeping on your personal products is as important as it is on your house. Try to have a clean-up every so often.

APPROPRIATE DRESS

Since about 1920, clothes for women and men have become more and more relaxed and that is a good thing, up to a point. While it is important to feel at ease in what you wear, comfort should not predominate at the expense of appropriateness or propriety. The jeans you wear to take the dog for an early-morning run in the park may also take you shopping at the supermarket but they will not impress the human resources manager of a big corporation or get you through the front door of a long-established club. Clothes you wear for slopping around at home on a Sunday morning should be left at home when you go out.

When you present yourself at sombre occasions, make sure what you wear is suitably deferential and sober. Black is no longer obligatory at a funeral, although it is still appropriate, along with any dark colour and, in some religions, white; never appear in flamboyant jewellery or ties or bright colours, unless it was the will of the deceased (see also page 482). If you have to appear in court for any reason, show respect for authority and earn credibility for yourself by dressing neatly and conservatively.

Always make an effort to wear something special to a friend's birthday party, the opening night of an opera or play, a smart restaurant or even to dinner at somebody's house. You're part of the entertainment so dress for it. In most places, the more attractive you look, the more you'll be held in esteem. It might not be fair, but it's true. Despite the adage 'don't judge a book by its cover', that's exactly what most people do.

DEFINITIONS OF DRESS

Letting people know what they are expected to wear is essential when you host any occasion. Be as clear as possible in what you mean. If the party has a theme, the invitation might read 'The theme of the evening is Carnival in Rio, so please dress accordingly.' 'No denim' is a bit brutal but at least it's precise. 'Formal' is a tricky one because how you interpret it seems to depend on what age you are. To many teenagers, it means a tie of any sort. To their parents, if it applies to an event after six p.m. it specifies black tie; for one during the day, it means morning dress. Many and varied are the guidelines on contemporary invitations. Let's try to clarify what they mean.

White Tie or Evening Dress

This sort of formality for very grand occasions is all but obsolete in Australia but it still exists in high society in Europe. The man wears black evening trousers, a matching tail coat, white waistcoat, shirt with winged collar, white bow tie and black patent leather shoes. (Top hat and cane, à la Fred Astaire, are no longer in fashion.) A woman must wear a long evening dress – short skirts and trousers are not acceptable – and long evening gloves.

Black Tie or Dinner Jacket

Formal evening wear is seen only after six o'clock. To be traditionally correct, men wear a white dress shirt, with a piqué or pintucked front (never frilled or otherwise ostentatious) with a black tie, that must never be pre-tied and stuck on an elastic band or clipped on to the collar. It must be hand-tied, according to the illustrations on the following page.

If the tie is a little rakish, never mind. That adds character and leaves nobody in doubt that it is hand-tied. The shirt has French cuffs (cuffs that fold back on themselves) and they require cufflinks, which are plain and of good quality. With this you must wear long, fine, black socks, black shoes, black trousers, braces, waistcoat or cummerbund and a black dinner jacket. Like socks, the cummerbund should be an extension of the trousers, therefore the same colour, although some men seem to like it in a lively hue with matching bow tie. An alternative to the cummerbund is an evening waistcoat. Do refrain from wearing a white carnation in your buttonhole lest somebody mistake you for a functionary. Wallet and pen are tucked into the inside breast pocket of your jacket and your handkerchief of hand-rolled white linen is tucked into a side pocket of your trousers, not frothing out of your breast pocket.

Tying a bow tie

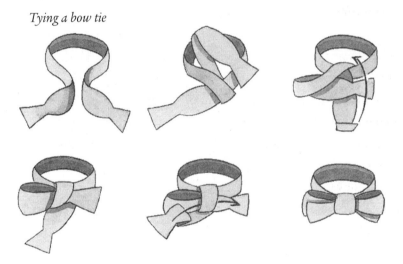

There are acceptable alternatives, particularly for the free-spirited, who may choose to wear a more modern version of the garb: a white or black silk skivvy is a good substitute for a dress shirt and tie, as a velvet smoking jacket is for a traditional jacket, particularly in cooler climes. Again, the utmost restraint is called for in this kind of dress. A white dinner jacket, also known as a tuxedo, with black trousers is acceptable evening wear in most places in warm weather. But if in doubt, you cannot go wrong with a black dinner jacket.

A woman's choice is wider and in many ways more difficult. Your evening dress may be long or short, strapless or with long or short sleeves, and in any colour, but it should be elegant rather than flamboyant and suitable for sitting in, without it spilling out all over the neighbours or crushing disastrously. Evening pants instead of a skirt are quite acceptable in most places in Australia. The outfit must also be comfortable and should not expose a lot of flesh. Your bag should be as small as possible. For an occasion like this, pile on the family jewels.

Decorations

If this word appears on any invitation it means that if you have been given a 'gong' – that is, honoured officially by the head of state of any country – you are expected to wear the orders, decorations or medals that represent that award. Unless 'decorations' appears on the invitation, it is not appropriate to wear them.

Formal Day Dress or Morning Coat

Although now rare in Australia, it's the daytime equivalent of black tie, sometimes seen at special race meetings and at the weddings of prominent people. A man wears striped trousers with braces, a cutaway grey or black jacket, white shirt, grey silk tie, waistcoat in grey, beige or black, and black lace-up shoes. To be ultra-traditional, you would also wear a grey or black top hat and grey gloves (or yellow, if your jacket is black). A woman wears a dress or suit, with skirt or trousers, of any colour, with a hat, sheer stockings, elegant but sensible shoes (particularly at the races) and a handsome bag. Gloves are optional.

Lounge Suit or Business Suit

For a man, this means matching dark jacket and trousers with a business shirt and tie. For a woman, whatever is your best garb at the office, or cocktail clothes, if it's an evening event. Cocktail dress is the kind of thing you'd wear to dinner in a smart restaurant. It could be the tailored suit you've had on at the office with a change of jewellery and accessories, or it could be a slinky little silken something, worn with high heels and a wrap.

Informal

It does not mean what it says. It just means not black tie and not necessarily a business suit. A man may wear a blazer and slacks with a shirt and tie. A woman could wear a similar outfit or the kind of dress or suit she'd wear to lunch or dinner. Neither of you should turn up in workout clothes, runners, football jerseys, shorts, thongs or anything else of that sort.

Smart Casual or Elegant Casual

To me, the looks that typify this description are the ones you see on the most fashionable streets of Milan and Rome. Fabric, fit and finish of each garment should be of the finest quality. For day, the easy style of well-cut trousers, an open-necked shirt and either a blazer or a sweater, slung around the shoulders. For evening, something similar but in silkier fabrics. Tracksuits and gym shoes may be casual but they are definitely not smart or elegant.

Come As You Are

Don't take it literally, especially if you've been replanting the garden or painting the terrace. What it means is don't put on your finery, but do come scrubbed up and neatly turned out. Chinos, well-maintained jeans, sports shirt or a superior sort of T-shirt will do, as will tailored shorts (as long as you've got decent legs).

BUILDING A WARDROBE

The principle of putting together a workable wardrobe is the same whether you are a man or a woman. You build it, piece by piece, in a calculated and disciplined way, based on what you need to wear at work, at home and at play. That means choosing a colour scheme that suits you and sticking with it, no matter what you buy. Once you have this basic wardrobe, you can add bits at whim each season to give it a kick along and bring it up to date.

BEWARE OF BARGAINS

Who among us has not made a terrible mistake at a sale? Some of us have made many. Before you leave home to go to a sale, write down exactly what you are after because, once you lose your head in the frenzy of the hunt, it is all too easy to forget what you came for. A bargain is not a bargain, however cheap, if you hate the thing when you get it home. Best to go to a sale in total sobriety on a day when you're feeling tight-fisted. On the other hand, don't pass up the perfectly wonderful thing you had not anticipated. You'll regret it for life.

WARDROBE FOR THE PROFESSIONAL WOMAN

The fact that the law on dress for women in business has not been laid down as rigidly as it has been for men is a mixed blessing. On the one hand, freedom to express your personality in the way you dress is an attractive idea. On the other, decision-making is trickier when there are fewer guidelines. It's easy to go wrong, especially when fads come and go so quickly and clever marketing and fashion hype can seduce you into buying something completely inappropriate for a day in the life of the successful business woman you are, or hope to be.

Many companies, particularly big corporations, have a written dress code for management and staff. Abide by it if you value your job. People who are seen to respect company values are taken seriously as candidates for promotion. Some rules are unwritten and it's a good idea to acquaint yourself with those, too. The women in senior roles set the standard, so it's a good idea to follow their lead. When in doubt, err on the conservative side, and imagine the day when you run the corporation and you're free to make your own rules.

Long live the suit

It's difficult to better the suit as the basis of your Monday-to-Friday wear. In fact, you could do worse than take a man's wardrobe as your blueprint. You might decide to add a dress or two, and to extend the possibilities of your suit by buying both a skirt and trousers to match the jacket. Fortunately, the decision on cut, colour and number of buttons is entirely up to you and how much you are prepared to go along with the current fashion. However, avoid skirts that are too short, tops that are too skimpy and colours and patterns more suited to poolside in the tropics or an underground bar at midnight than to an office.

There might still be some companies with regulations preventing women employees from wearing trousers but I cannot believe that such outmoded thinking can go on much longer. Well-tailored trousers are not only good-looking, they are more comfortable and more practical than skirts for many women.

Since you are going to have to look your best, week after week, your choice of colours is best limited to those that team happily together. Think of suits broken down into pieces that can be mixed with others to make fresh outfits from fewer components. Narrow your colour scheme to a few basics, then add bolts of colour to create different looks. Remember, you do not need a lot of clothes. You need to be able to put together an interesting selection of outfits from a limited number of pieces.

Colour and quality

First, decide on the two basic colours that will be your mainstays for summer and winter. One of them could be black; it's safest for style, has staying power and it works for day, night, winter, summer. It teams with just about every other colour, including navy. Those old rules about black and navy not being compatible, and shades of navy all having to be the same, don't apply any more.

If you hate black or it doesn't suit you, choose navy and camel, dark grey and khaki, taupe and beige, brown and dove grey, or whatever you feel comfortable in. In general, darkish tones are best for basics simply because they don't need to be washed or dry-cleaned as often as pale colours. Ideally, whatever else you buy should be capable of co-ordinating with these basic colours. Just as a man uses ties, pocket handkerchiefs and socks to change the character of basic outfits, you can use scarves, jewellery, socks and tights.

Second, always go for quality. It cannot be mistaken. If you choose a garment well, it will last for years and represent far better value than something cheap. Buy fewer and better clothes rather than many garments of indifferent quality. Knitted fabrics of wool, silk and micro-fibre make great travellers; bear that in mind if you spend a part of your life in airline seats and hotel rooms.

Say your basic colours are black and grey. You might choose to buy one black suit, one grey suit and one black-and-white houndstooth check suit. Buy one black tube dress and one grey dress. Be sure the cut and style makes them compatible with the suit jackets. If you can afford it, add the luxury of an extra jacket and pants in white or cream for summer.

Shirts and tops

Have at least one camisole top and one shirt in each of your chosen basic colours – that is, black and grey. Then add pale colours and strong patterns for variety. Buy a red top, if red suits you, or one in yellow, or mauve or green or cobalt blue. Buy a shirt in a jazzy pattern. If you choose white shirts, make sure you know how to keep them looking immaculate. For dynamism and a look of freshness, nothing beats a crisp white shirt, but only if it is impeccably washed and ironed. If you can't do that, then buy low-maintenance garments that need little or no pressing and travel well.

Footwear

Have at least two pairs of good-quality shoes (Italian, if you can afford it), in your basic colour, that are comfortable to wear and in a style that will not date before you've had your money's worth of wear out of them.

If you can walk in high heels without crippling yourself, go for them, but make sure they'll be practical for a long day at the office and for all the running around you might have to do. Don't wear anything frivolous at work or you might be considered too flighty to be serious about your job; save your fancy footwear for after hours. However many pairs of shoes you have, keep them in good shape by cleaning them after each outing, alternating them with other shoes so they can rest and having them repaired before heels and toes show any signs of deterioration.

Legs

Even in summer, business women are expected to wear stockings but that should not be a hardship if you work in air-conditioning. Keep a back-up supply because sheer hose is easily snagged or laddered and that lets your appearance down, particularly if you're wearing a skirt. You never know when you might be summoned to an important meeting. Some stockings and pantihose are so sheer they make you look bare-legged so make sure your legs are properly groomed. Hairy legs, like hairy armpits, are not attractive, so shave regularly or use a depilatory if you can't afford the time or money to have a leg wax.

Bags

A set of bags, rather than one, is obligatory for a day in the life of a business woman. You'll need a bag for personal items, such as keys, specs, cosmetics, wallet, and so on. Your second bag, or portfolio, is for papers and other items related to your work. If your business takes you away overnight for a seminar or a client meeting, you'll need another bag big enough to hold a change of clothes and small enough to fit under an airline seat.

They need not all match but they should be good-looking and well made. Unless money is not an issue, steer clear of an expensive bag when the cost has more to do with marketing the label than with quality. Not all highly promoted fashion names measure up to their reputation. A bag of that kind dates quickly because its design can be pinned down to a specific period and it will be superseded next year by a new model. Buy things that are of good quality, whatever the origin. They will last until they fall apart, even if the only signature they carry to their grave is your own.

In my experience, the best place to find such accessories is in the northern Italian city of Florence, where the streets are lined with boutiques specialising in leathergoods. Most often, each one is a factory outlet for the work of a family of artisans, who take pride in their designs and craftsmanship and would not dream of copying what's in the shop next door. The quality, style and value are there, though you've never heard of the brand.

Accessories

Scarves, belts, wraps and jewellery are all useful additions, particularly if your job means socialising after hours. Often, there's no time to go home and change, yet you need to look a little more dressed up than you do during the day. A change of details can make the difference: off with the tailored jacket and sensible shoes, and on with the chiffon scarf or cashmere wrap, high heels and pearls.

What 'business casual' means for women

On the days when the management of your firm allows 'casual' dress – it could be every Friday, or any day when a client meeting is not scheduled – it is important to understand the definition of the term. You are still likely to be expected to wear sheer stockings, shoes that are not too open and a top that has sleeves of some kind, unless it is covered by an overshirt or jacket. Jeans, bare midriffs, calf-length pants and garments with apertures in unconventional places might be familiar sights in the street but they are not acceptable in conservative companies. Save them for the weekend.

AT LEISURE

As for what you wear in your time off, that is up to you. It depends on your obligations, interests, activities and the way you choose to present yourself. The one essential I would advise is the little black dress. It might be a cliché but it's not easily bettered after five when you're off to cocktails, or an art opening, then on to dinner or a concert.

Another evening essential is a wrap, the perfect garment for the theatre because you needn't check it into the cloakroom – and queue for it afterwards when you want to be ahead at the taxi rank – because unless it's as weighty as a blanket, it's easily folded and kept on your lap.

WARDROBE FOR THE PROFESSIONAL MAN

What follows is an ideal, not often reached but worth aiming for, if you want to get on in a conservative profession and you are not short of money. First of all, find your tailor. In a city, there is always one (or two or three) whose craftsmanship all others are measured by. Snobbery also sometimes motivates the choice of a tailor – in certain circles the right tailor is as important as the right club – and whether or not that kind of thing influences you, it's useful to know that it might matter to people who are in a position to judge you, or to give you a job.

The eternal suit

Four or five bespoke (made-to-measure) lounge suits are the basis of a conservative man's attire. Although a suit of this sort is a big invest-ment, it makes good economic sense in the long run. Depending on the cloth, the wearer and the degree of care it is given, it should last for seven to ten years.

The perfect suit is one that fits you properly, complements your colouring and is appropriate to the occasion. Good bearing is also essen-tial to show off a well-made suit. The jacket will be hand-finished and have four buttons on the sleeve, which must be capable of being unbut-toned. A more casual jacket would have three buttons on the sleeve.

Like shoes, a suit should not be worn day in day out but rested after each outing. Unless some disaster occurs, it need not be dry-cleaned more often than three times a year and then only by someone who does it by hand, although sponging, pressing and airing outdoors in the shade on a dry, clear day should occur regularly.

An ideal suit wardrobe could comprise, in order of importance: one charcoal grey; one dark navy blue; one navy blue or grey pinstripe or chalk stripe; one grey flannel; and a Prince of Wales check in lighter grey, perhaps with a touch of blue or red in the weave.

Shirts

You'll need about a dozen shirts, in plain white, plain blue, checks and stripes, to be worn with the suits. Business shirts should always be impeccable and perfectly pressed (see pages 197–198), so make sure you have the means – or the energy yourself – to launder them properly.

Ties

How you wear your tie says as much about you as the colour and pattern you have chosen. A tie that's awry, or too long or too short for your height and girth, is not a good look, no matter how handsome it is. If you tie it properly to begin with, you shouldn't have to fiddle around with it for the rest of the day. (For how to tie a bow tie, see page 181.) Here's how to tie the most popular knots.

Single Windsor knot

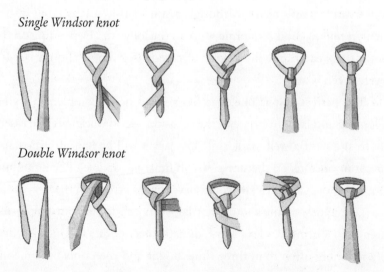

Double Windsor knot

When you wear an expensive pure silk tie, take care not to stain it with food or anything else because ties are usually wrecked by dry-cleaning. Men known for their sartorial splendour are not afraid to sling the tie they are wearing over one shoulder, or tuck a napkin under their chin, when they eat messy foods such as noodles.

Shoes and socks

Some people assess a man by the state of his shoes, so make sure they are always polished and well heeled. Eventually your wardrobe should include: two pairs of black lace-ups; one pair of black slip-ons, such as the Gucci loafer; and one pair of brown brogues in punched leather or suede. Socks should always match the suit trousers rather than the shoes, and be long enough to cover any bit of leg that is visible at any time – for instance, when you cross your legs.

Handkerchiefs

Whether or not you put a handkerchief in the breast pocket of your jacket, and to what extent it protrudes, is a matter of personal taste and temperament. Take care, though, that it does not make the pocket bulge and spoil the line of the jacket. Traditionally, the best quality handkerchiefs were of silk or Irish linen with hand-rolled edges (see page 267).

The delightfully dandified practice of tucking a handkerchief into the sleeve of a jacket at the wrist is about as rare as the sighting of a northern brush-tailed possum, although bespoke tailors in Australia are sometimes still asked to adjust the lining of a sleeve to hold a handkerchief.

Jewellery

Don't overdo it. If you wear neck chains, make sure they are nicely out of sight under your shirt. A heavy watch you might wear in the daytime is not appropriate evening wear. For night, choose something thin and elegant. In general, it is better to go for quality rather than quantity in rings, cufflinks and dress studs.

What 'business casual' means for men

'Mufti days' is the term one company uses for Fridays, the one day of the week when 'casual' business wear, rather than 'formal' business wear is acceptable in that organisation, echoing what is happening in many big corporations. ('Mufti' is the term used for what a soldier wears when he is out of uniform.)

This policy is changing, yet again, as management ponders these questions: to what extent should we modify the uniform that has served office-bearers in business so well for so long? Should mufti be permitted every day, except for those days when client meetings are scheduled?

If you work for a conservative company that has relaxed the rules of dress, do not misread the new definitions. 'Business casual' means well-tailored pants with a narrow belt, a tailored jacket that may or may not be of the same colour and fabric, shoes, socks and an open-necked shirt that has a collar and must be tucked into the trousers. It does not mean jeans, T-shirts, parkas, tracksuits, shorts, sneakers, sandals or any garment sporting a logo.

AT LEISURE

As well as tailored shorts and casual shirts, you'll also need one double-breasted navy or black blazer; one blouson jacket in leather, wool or cashmere; three pairs of trousers in grey, taupe and fawn or camel; and one pair of jeans or cotton twill pants.

Extras such as topcoats, raincoats, gloves and hats are determined by climate and way of life. The most common kind of hat now seems to be a baseball cap, but recent sightings have been reported of such threatened species as the panama, trilby, stetson, bowler, topper and boater. Smart straw sunhats are now almost de rigueur for our Australian climate.

If you are wearing a hat when you meet somebody in the street, touch the brim as a greeting; remove it if you stop for a lengthy chat with a woman. Remember to take your hat off when you enter someone's house, an office, a Christian church, the lift in a public building or when a funeral procession passes by.

PRIVATE CLUBS

Australia's leading private clubs seem to be in agreement about standards of dress for anyone who enters their portals. Whether you are a member or a guest, bear in mind that your briefcase should always be left in the cloakroom, not carried through to public rooms, and mobile telephones are very unwelcome. If you are to be a guest at a club, it's always wise to check the dress code beforehand with the member who invited you. (For required dress for sporting clubs, see Chapter 18.)

Ladies

For ladies, during the day a dress or suit, with a skirt or tailored trousers, is acceptable in most clubs. Jeans are not permitted. For receptions in the evening, a cocktail dress, dressy pants and top, tailored evening trousers with jacket, or an evening gown is appropriate. If you're unsure, it's best to stick with something conservative, in keeping with the general standards of these sorts of clubs.

Gentlemen

A dark lounge suit with a tie is expected for gentlemen and boys, unless you have just arrived from the country or a sporting fixture, in which case a blazer and tie is acceptable. If black tie is required for a club event it will be clearly indicated on the invitation. Schoolboys may wear their current school uniform. If a boy aged between twelve and fifteen is not in uniform, he may wear a long-sleeved shirt and tie. All boys over the age of fifteen must wear a long-sleeved coat and tie.

THE RACES

Dressing up dies hard at important race meetings, such as those surrounding and including the Melbourne Cup and spring and autumn carnivals in cities and towns in every state. In what is known as 'the outer' (a self-explanatory term in more ways than one), you may dress as you please, and that means anything from a footie jersey to flamboyant and outrageous dress topped by a shocking chapeau; this is where newspaper photographers prowl to get their best pictures on Cup Day. But if you are invited into the Members' Reserve, you'd better study the rules or you might find yourself denied entry, as the dress guidelines are quite strict. Although variations occur from one club to another, they are likely to be minor. Here is the dress code for the VRC (Victoria Racing Club).

Ladies, teenage girls and children

Women are 'expected to maintain a suitable standard in keeping with the dignity of the Members' Reserve. Younger children accompanied by an adult must be suitably attired.'

The most elegantly turned out women at the races wear sheer hose, practical shoes and hats that may be arresting and glamorous but never vulgar. They are clever enough to choose outfits that survive well, no matter what the day turns out to be. November weather is notoriously skittish in Melbourne and optimists in their summer get-ups have often ended the day shivering and bedraggled. Never fear that you'll be conspicuous if you take the special train that runs between Flinders Street Station and Flemington Racecourse all week. It's a fashion show on wheels.

On Derby Day, the stylish Saturday occasion that opens Melbourne Cup week, it's customary for a woman to wear black-and-white and for a man to put a cornflower in his buttonhole. A man wears a yellow rose on Melbourne Cup Day, the first Tuesday in November, when women are strikingly turned out in keeping with the carnival colours of the jockeys. On the Thursday after the Cup, women put on their pastel finery for Oaks Day, also known as Ladies' Day, and a man who rises to the occasion wears a pink rosebud. The final Saturday is family day, a relaxed outing with children, when clothes are the kind of things you'd wear to the polo (see page 430).

Gentlemen and boys over fourteen

Here the guidelines are much more specific.

OBLIGATORY   A suit, sports coat or blazer plus tie, except from 1 December to 31 March, when coats may be removed. Outside these dates, the Chief Executive may permit jackets to be removed if the temperature is too hot but you must wait for this to be announced formally.

NOT ACCEPTABLE   Any form of sports shoe, including track shoes and runners; sandals, thongs, dilapidated footwear, scuffs, slippers and any shoes without socks. Jeans, jodhpurs, shorts or non-tailored slacks. Open-neck shirts or shirts without a collar. Parkas, windbreakers, tracksuit tops, golf and yachting weatherproofs, waist-length jackets including bomber jackets, denim jackets, anoraks and bush capes. Safari suits, tracksuits. Peaked caps and beanies. Pullovers or cardigans without a jacket, rugby tops and football guernseys, even if you wear a tie.

CARING FOR YOUR WARDROBE

Like people, clothes respond to tender loving care. Never leave them in a crumpled heap or let them get too grubby before you have them laundered or dry-cleaned. Removing ingrained dirt or stains and pressing out deep wrinkles inflicts unnecessary punishment on fabrics, particularly fine ones, such as cashmere, alpaca, lamb's wool, silk and linen. If you like expensive and beautiful things you must be prepared to look after them properly.

READ THE INSTRUCTIONS

A garment bought off the peg should have a label, sewn inside the neckband or in a side seam, telling you: 1) whether or not it must be dry-cleaned or laundered; 2) if laundered, then whether by hand or washing machine at a specific water temperature; 3) whether it should be ironed and, if so, how hot the iron should be. Always read these instructions carefully.

Sometimes, certain lightweight silks and synthetics that are marked 'dry-clean only' are in fact washable, but the manufacturer has been overly cautious so as not to invite litigation over a garment that has been ruined in the wash. Sometimes a cotton fabric has a polished finish that will disappear in the wash. Disobey the instructions only if you're experienced in laundering fabrics and you're confident of a good result.

HAND-WASHING WOOLLENS

Use gentle suds in lukewarm water for hand-washing lamb's wool and cashmere sweaters. Squeeze them gently. Never wring them or you might damage them or pull them out of shape. After thorough rinsing in tepid water, roll each sweater up in a towel and press the bundle gently to extract excess moisture before you lay the sweater flat, or semi-flat on a clothes horse, preferably in the sun on a dry, windy day. Make sure it is completely dry before you put it away.

Boring though it is, acquaint yourself with the instruction manual for your washing machine before you use it and make sure the dials are switched to the right program before you do a load of washing. Make a pile of the white things and another of the coloured things and wash these two piles separately. That way, white garments should remain pristine.

HOW TO IRON CLOTHES

First, assemble the essential equipment.

- An iron from a reputable maker. Make sure it has a dial to regulate the temperature. It is not absolutely necessary to have an iron with the facility to make steam. Unless they are well-maintained, such irons sometimes spit rusty water, usually when you're ironing something white and precious. A plastic bottle for spraying water when you need it may be old-fashioned, but it's foolproof and just as effective.

- An ironing board with a tight, thickly padded cover.
- A miniature ironing board for sleeves.
- A commercial spray formulated to give body to the fabric as you iron.
- A pressing cloth for wool and cashmere garments. It should be in pure cotton or linen, big enough to cover the ironing board. It can be as humble as the remnant of an old bed sheet.

A business shirt

When some people take a shirt from the washing machine they put it on a coathanger to dry instead of whirling it in the dryer as it lessens creasing. If you do put it in the dryer, take it out while it is still damp and, if possible, iron it immediately and let it air on a coathanger.

A silk shirt should be washed by hand in gentle suds and luke-warm water. Rinse, then pat it dry in a towel; do not put it in the dryer. Roll it up and place it in a plastic bag in the refrigerator. Iron it damp, with the arrow on the temperature regulator pointing to the word 'silk', and take care not to iron in creases. If you do make the mistake of ironing in a crease, spray it with a little water before pressing again.

Shirts made of synthetic or part-synthetic fabrics are easy to maintain but are generally not as good-looking as those in natural fibres. Despite wash-and-wear tags, they usually do need a light press with a warm-to-cool iron before they look smooth enough to wear.

Pure cotton and linen shirts may be ironed at relatively high temperatures, but be careful not to scorch the collar. Best to err on the safe side and lower the temperature. If the shirt is embroidered, iron the embroidery on the wrong side so that the pattern stands out in relief on the right side.

TEN STEPS TO A PERFECTLY PRESSED SHIRT

1 Holding it by the collar, shake the shirt out and rest the collar, wrong side up, on the ironing board. Iron the wrong side of the collar. If the collar does not have an inside layer of stiffening,

you might need to give it body by spraying it with the commercial spray – not too much or it might stick to the iron and leave a brown deposit.

2 Turn the shirt over and iron the right side of the collar, taking care to work inward from each end. This is because sometimes the outside of the collar is a bit bigger than the inside and a crease can result. It's best if the crease is in the middle of the collar at the back of your neck when you put it on, not in front where everyone can see what a slapdash presser you are. If you do make a crease on the point of a collar, just spray water on it and start again.

3 Pick up the shirt with each hand pinching the back, halfway down the seam that joins it to the sleeve. Fold it across that line, so that the shoulder area lies flat and the collar stands up. Press the shoulder area.

4 Press the inside of the cuff on one sleeve. Turn the cuff over and press the outside. This is another area that is highly visible when you wear the shirt, so take care not to make creases in the wrong places.

5 Stretch out the sleeve along the ironing board and press it on one side. Turn it over and press the other side.

6 Repeat steps 4 and 5 for the other sleeve.

7 Press the back of the shirt; that's the easiest bit.

8 Press the front side of the shirt with the buttons on it. You might want to give the edge of it a stiffening from the spray to make a nice smooth front.

9 Press the other side of the shirt, being careful to keep the front edge as smooth as possible, probably with another spray or two.

10 Hang the shirt on a coathanger, even if ultimately you plan to fold it and put it in a drawer or on a shelf. The shirt should air and become completely dry before you put it on or it will start to go limp before you've left the house.

Sleeves without creases

Lots of styles in shirts and blouses do not conform to the strict rules governing the business shirt. This kind of top often looks wrong with a sharp crease down the outside of a sleeve. That's when a meticulous ironer brings out the miniature ironing board, which is narrow enough for most sleeves to slide over to be ironed.

Cashmere sweaters

1 Place the sweater flat on the ironing board with the back of it facing upward.
2 Cover it completely with the dry cotton or linen cloth.
3 Turn the temperature of the iron up to the 'hot' or 'cotton' setting.
4 Press it all over, except the basques.
5 Turn it over, cover it again with the cloth, and press the other side.

Suit trousers

For jeans and many other casual pants, the knife-edge crease down the front of the leg is not appropriate. But for a business suit, or the tailored trousers you wear with a blazer or any other traditionally cut jacket, the crease is essential.

Here's how to iron a decent pair of trousers.

1 Open the zipper and slide the thin end of the ironing-board into the top of the trousers with the backside facing up. Dampen the pressing cloth lightly, place it over the trousers and press, making sure the arrow on the temperature regulator of the iron points to the word 'wool'. The cloth is necessary in order to avoid the shiny look that results if the iron is placed directly on a wool fabric; gabardine and serge are particularly vulnerable.
2 Move the trousers around the board until you have pressed the

top of them completely, as far down as the crotch, taking care to close the zipper and flatten the fly as neatly as possible.

3 Open the zipper again and fold the trousers along the edges where you want the knife-edge creases to be.

4 Lay the trousers along the ironing board. Make sure that the creases you are about to iron in are in precisely the same place as they were when the garment was new.

5 Lift the top leg from the ankle end and fold it back, so that the inside of the other leg can be pressed first. Cover it with the damp pressing cloth before you iron.

6 Turn the trousers over and repeat step 5 on the other leg.

7 Reposition the leg so that the outside of it now faces upward. Cover it with the damp pressing cloth and iron, pressing hard on the crease that runs down the front of the leg.

8 Turn the trousers over and repeat step 7 on the other leg.

9 Depending on the type of coathangers you have, either fold the trousers over the bar of a wooden one, suspend them from the waist on metal clips, or hang them upside down from the ones that hold them between two clamped wooden slats.

10 Make sure they are completely dry before you put them on or they'll crumple the minute you sit down and your good work will have been in vain.

Chapter Nine

LOOKING FOR LOVE

Courtship might not be as formal as it used to be, but the tingling self-consciousness remains, at no matter what age boy meets girl (or boy meets boy, or girl meets girl). That's the wonder and the fright of animal magnetism. You know you're attracted to somebody by the flutter-bys in your stomach and a heady sense of being hopelessly in the grip of your emotions. All you can think of is seeing that person again.

MAKING THE FIRST MOVE

As a woman, if the whole idea puts you in a tizz imagine how much worse it is for a man who, according to all the old rules, is the one required to make the first move. Not so now, and that is a good thing because it leads you to understand how vulnerable it can make a person feel to ask somebody out. While there is nothing wrong with a woman asking a man for a date, proceed with caution. The practice is not universally accepted by males in general and the older they are the more awkward they are likely to feel about it. You might scare a conservative chap, or lead a macho liberal to get the wrong idea. As modern as they may be, a lot of Australian men are still reluctant to accept the emergence of the independent woman.

If you do not know the man you find attractive well enough to be able to assess his reaction, make it so informal it doesn't sound like a date or wait for him to make the first move. Encourage it, not by batting your eyelids or being too obvious in hanging around, but by being approachable. Be friendly. Don't try to get his attention by childish needling or coy asides. Make him feel good. Pay him a compliment.

HOW TO BE NOTICED

Say he's a colleague at the office. When you meet him in the lift, you might say, 'Great suit' or 'Like your new haircut.' Or pause at his desk to remark, 'I thought your presentation yesterday was very impressive. Congratulations.' If he's someone you see regularly near where you live – swimming in the pool of your apartment building, on your morning run, leaving for work, at a local café, shopping for supplies – smile and say hello in a neighbourly way; as time goes by, think of something relevant to chat about, even if it's just the weather, or the council's plans for some civic development. If you have a mutual friend, tell that friend how much you admire your chosen chap and hope it gets back to him. Lack of response does not necessarily mean he finds you unattractive, although be brave enough to accept that it might. It could be that he's involved with someone else, or getting over a painful love affair, or prefers the other sex.

It would be so easy, wouldn't it, if you could read the signals. But infatuation affects different people in different ways. Sometimes they blush or turn white. They might be warm or cool. They might smile, or try to avoid the adored one's eyes. Teasing or baiting is often a clue to infatuation in an immature person. So is speechlessness. Use your instincts. There's usually some electrical charge between you if the attraction is mutual. In any case, if your feelings are strong, don't miss the opportunity. It may never happen again. What have you got to lose?

HOW TO ASK

You could make it sound as though it's not anything as serious as a date with romance by linking it with a group activity. For instance, 'We're all going to watch the start of the regatta on Saturday. Would you like to join us?' or 'Ben is house-sitting this weekend and he's asked me to bring some friends on Saturday night' or 'We've booked a table at the Golden Dragon to watch Chinese New Year. Want to come?'

Traditionally, though, the form for a man asking a woman to go out with him goes something like this.

1   First decide where and when you'd like to take her out. Be decisive. On traditional first dates, reliable favourites are: going to a movie, going out to dinner or, if money is not an issue, both. But there are many other possibilities depending on your age group, the interests of the woman and your own finances. They may be physical (cycling or rollerblading in the park), cultural (concert or play), educational (a cooking class at the market or a lecture by a visiting boffin), sporting (football game, tennis match), or whatever.

2   Telephone at a civilised time. During the week, that means calling her at work, or soon after she gets home from work, but not when she's eating dinner and never after nine o'clock at night. And don't call when you've had too much to drink. On weekends, good times to ring are usually between ten a.m. and midday or at around five or six o'clock in the afternoon.

3   Make sure she knows who you are by saying your name clearly and describing when you met and perhaps what she was wearing.

4 If you know her well enough, you'll have used your imagination and chosen something that she likes to do. Point that out when you ask her. For instance, 'I know you're a fan of Rachel Griffiths, so I thought you might like to see her new movie' or 'I know you're a vegetarian and I've discovered this great new restaurant' or 'I'm going on a protest march about your favourite subject, the environment, on Tuesday week. Come and help the cause.'

5 If she says yes, do your utmost to meet her at a place most convenient to her, not necessarily to you. Make the effort to call for her at home or at her place of work. If that's not possible, make the meeting point somewhere comfortable – say, in the lobby of a big hotel or in a café, never on some windy street corner or any other exposed public area – and get there early.

    If she says no, listen carefully to the reason why. Could be that she is genuinely busy on the day or evening you've nominated and, if so, what she says should sound encouraging, not dismissive. Don't pressure her to change her mind or her plans.

6 Try twice more over the next two weeks and if she still says no, then forget it. Look around for someone else.

HOW TO RESPOND

Here are two possible scenarios.

1 The person at the other end of the line is that awful guy who's been giving you the eye when he parks beside you at your office building. You can't think of anything worse than going out to dinner with him. Be kind but firm. If you truly do not want him hanging around, say something like 'That's very sweet of you, but I'm not a free agent any more. In fact, I'm practically engaged.'

2 The person at the other end of the line is that divine guy you've been eyeing when you park beside his car at your office

building. You can't think of anything more blissful than going out to dinner with him. But you can't go, because it's your grandmother's eightieth birthday and there's no way you can miss the festivities. Tell him the truth. Say how disappointed you are and that you'd love to make it another time. Don't frighten him off by inviting him to the birthday party.

HELLO STRANGER

Picking up a stranger (aka 'pirating' in the old days) used to be an absolute no-no for nice girls but there are pick-ups and there are pick-ups. They do not have to be dangerous but never be tempted by one that is even a little suspect. Many years ago in London, I worked with a young copywriter who was also a poet. He swore that the best place to meet the right kind of girl was at an art gallery. Because art appreciation is such a high-minded pursuit, two people getting together in front of a masterpiece bears no resemblance to 'hello sailor' advances, encounters with anonymous nerds on the Internet or ads in the lonely hearts columns.

WHERE TO MEET GIRLS

If you have a sister, her friends are your first possibility. If you don't have a sister, try your cousins or the girl next door. Unless you work in an all-male environment, the place where you spend so much of your life earning a living can yield a partner who has the advantage of sharing an understanding of the demands of your job; it's also quite natural to ease into dating slowly, starting with a sandwich for lunch at the local café or a glass of wine at the pub, without commitment until you size each other up. Be careful, though, to keep any liaison outside office hours. Another possibility is to join a social, business or sporting club that accepts both sexes and widens the scope of your regular circle.

WHERE TO MEET GUYS

A very pragmatic girl I used to know reckoned that the best place to look for a mate was where there was no competition: on oil rigs, in far-flung mining centres and other outposts where women are as scarce as men are plentiful. But before you take the desperate measure of changing your entire way of life, put your brother on the case. If you don't have a brother, try your cousins or the boy next door. Then there's the office. 'Feel like a drink after work?' is an non-committal way of getting to know a colleague better. Sometimes the fellowship between two people who have worked closely for a long time can turn into something more serious, but that can cause complications unless you are very careful. Much depends on the levels at which you work. If there's a big discrepancy – say one party is a member of the board of directors and the other works in the despatch department – then beware. If you're the type to join a club or go to evening classes, that could be a good solution. Steer clear of bars and nightclubs as places to chat up strangers and never leave with them, even if you are with a girlfriend; the combination of alcohol, the lateness of the hour and what may be perceived as an easy lay is too dangerous a cocktail to be worth the risk.

ON THE FIRST DATE

Spend a lot of time and thought beforehand on choosing what to wear and making sure it's immaculate, and doing whatever else it takes to present yourself at your best. Women, as well as some men, may feel more confident if they get their hair and nails done. Preen all you like in front of the mirror. Then forget it. Few things are more offputting than someone, female or male, constantly fussing over their appearance. Approach your tête-à-tête with a positive attitude but curb your expectations and try not to be too critical. Nobody's perfect.

Don't bend the truth about yourself. Little white lies may seem innocent enough but if this turns out to be a lasting union, there'll always be a question mark about your honesty if you've been telling whoppers about your background, your accomplishments and your influential friends. Besides, snobbery, boastfulness and name dropping are very boring and downright unappealing. Keep the talk to interesting topics, but nothing too gloomy or self-absorbed.

If you're stuck for things to say, draw the other person out and be an exemplary listener. But don't be blatant. 'Now tell me all about you' can be intimidating, whereas something like 'I'm interested to know what your work entails' or 'What did you think of Bali?' makes it easy for him or her to answer because it's specific. Other subjects you can share are the places you'd like to visit, favourite books, music, films and television programs, food, pets, people you admire, things you like to do.

Just in case things turn out to be unpleasant, make sure the battery is charged on your mobile telephone and always have enough cash for a taxi home.

WHO PICKS UP THE BILL?

As for who pays for the costs of the evening, the accepted rule is that the person who asks is the one to foot the bill, unless some other arrangement has been entered into beforehand. If you object to someone else paying for you, mention it when the invitation is extended and make sharing the costs a condition of your acceptance. Stick to your agreement, whatever it is. Fighting over a bill is unnecessary and undignified. If you are troubled by generous hospitality, be the one to pick up the bill next time.

SAYING GOODNIGHT

No matter who did the asking or who paid for the evening, the man should see to it that the women gets home safely either by taking her there or, if that's not possible or reasonable (she lives on the other side of town), by seeing her into a taxi. Don't expect to be invited into her house and don't pressure her to let you in, but be content to make sure she's inside her front door before you leave. If you are invited inside for a nightcap, that is not necessarily an invitation to intimacy. It may be just a gesture of thanks for your courtesy. Or it may not. What is crucial here is that, whatever happens, it should be with the consent of both of you.

SAYING THANK YOU

Don't forget your manners the next day. If you were the invited one, ring to say how much you enjoyed the evening and, if it's true, how much you look forward to next time. If you like, you might say, 'Next time the treat's on me.' If the response is positive, ring again in a week's time with your invitation. On the other hand, if the thought of another date is unbearable, call to say thank you and leave the impression that you'll be very busy for the next little while.

LATER DATES

The second date is often much more fun than the first because you're more relaxed. The fact that each of you wants to be with the other again is flattering for both of you. You feel confident of your attractiveness. Barriers come down and there's less stress and self-consciousness. That is, if you like what you see on second viewing.

It is a well-known fact that no single gentleman should ever be without a bottle of proper champagne in the refrigerator, even if that is the only thing in there. Nor is there any reason why a single lady shouldn't adopt this habit. In this modern day, both should at least have the fixings of a good breakfast there as well.

SEX AND THE SINGLE PARENT

When you have children at home, separate your dating partners and family into two different categories. Children, particularly little ones, must be shielded from bonding closely with someone short-term.

Otherwise, when that person is no longer around, they'll have a sense of abandonment that may make them wary of attaching themselves to anyone. If and when your children meet your paramour, introduce him or her as a 'friend', nothing more, unless the relationship has become permanent and the newcomer is moving in for good.

Until then, go to bed with your lover at his or her place, or when it's your ex's turn to have the children for the weekend, or when they are staying overnight with their grandparents. Don't complicate life for them. On the other hand, don't sacrifice yourself and your own sexual needs. It just takes sensitivity and good organisation.

BREAKING UP

Some dates turn into lifelong partnerships but many don't. Sometimes it becomes apparent to one or both of you that it's just not working. Having a rational discussion about breaking up can be very hard if the desire to split is one-sided and the other person simply cannot see the problem. But try to talk it through. If you've been going out together for any length of time, you owe it to yourselves to try to end it amicably. Be careful not to destroy the past along with the future by losing your temper and saying things you will regret. Don't involve others in what is a very private matter. You do not owe anybody else any explanations and you certainly don't need anybody else's advice.

If you're the one who wants out, don't just disappear. That is the coward's way. The worst thing you can do is to leave the other person hanging there, thinking you'll call and wondering why you don't. If you can't be entirely truthful, tell a white lie that causes the least hurt. Say you need more space, time to think.

Even if you've been together overnight just once and you say you'll call next day, or later in the week, make that call, whether you want to continue the relationship or not. If you don't want to see that person

again, you could pretend to have met a former love and become infat-
uated again. You could say that you're not ready for another
attachment just yet because you're not over the last one. Or something
like that, anything to let the other person down gently. But don't say, 'I
don't want to see you again because you're a lousy lay' or something
equally offensive.

The ideal is to remain friends, if you can. That's not easy to achieve
because a relationship is often unbalanced in what it means to each
partner. On a scale of passionate to indifferent, their ratings should not
be assumed to be identical. If continuing to see each other in a platonic
way does not suit both people, it's best to drop it altogether and move
on. Comfort yourself with some old adages: 'plenty more fish in the
sea' or 'if you miss one bus, another one comes along'. It often turns
out to be true.

Chapter Ten

HERE COMES THE BRIDE

No tribal ritual brings out the best and the worst in people as much as the tying of the nuptial knot. It is fraught with complications, passions and problems in the power play between the generations, the sexes and the rellies. If it weren't for the relatives, a wedding would be bliss. But, then, it wouldn't be a wedding, would it, if it were straightforward? And for all the potential frustrations, this is still your once-in-a-lifetime chance to be the debonair groom and the blushing bride, centre of all attention and admiration. It is your day.

THE ENGAGEMENT

Before women had the independence they now enjoy, it was customary for the man to ask the woman's father for his consent. While the thought of a father handing over his daughter to another man is a hangover from the days when women were considered the property of men, it is still courteous for the young couple to seek their parents' approval, or at least let them know, before the engagement is announced to anybody else.

There is no set period for an engagement. It can last for a few months or a few years, depending on the couple and their circumstances, but at least it should be long enough for both extended families to meet and get to know each other. How close the attachment of families becomes is anybody's guess. Unless in-laws are compatible in a genuine way it's not a good idea to force togetherness. Better to keep a polite distance than to put everybody through close encounters that are not amicable or are strained.

Before you actually marry in Australia, by law you must both be at least eighteen years of age, unless there are exceptional circumstances, in which case parental and judicial consent are necessary before the marriage can take place. It is worth pointing out that, if you are the bride, once you are married you are not required by law to change your surname to your husband's. That practice is based on convention and whether or not you follow it is up to you. Whichever name you choose will not alter the fact that you are married, even if your legal name is still the one your parents gave you.

THE RING

As evidence of commitment it is traditional, although by no means obligatory, for the man to give the woman an engagement ring set with some sort of precious stone or stones. The ring is worn on the third finger of her left hand, to be joined later by the wedding ring. A diamond is traditional because of its symbolic purity, durability and the fact that it coordinates with anything you might choose to wear, but you might prefer your birthstone. It's a good idea to choose the ring together because there often has to be a compromise between what you deeply desire and what the budget can stand.

BIRTHSTONES

January	*Garnet*
February	*Amethyst*
March	*Aquamarine, bloodstone, jasper*
April	*Diamond*
May	*Emerald*
June	*Pearl, moonstone, alexandrite*
July	*Ruby*
August	*Peridot, sardonyx, carnelian*
September	*Sapphire*
October	*Opal, tourmaline*
November	*Topaz, citrine*
December	*Turquoise, lapis lazuli, zircon*

LOW-KEY CELEBRATIONS

Elaborate engagement parties are not common now. Couples are more likely to put on drinks at a parental home on Sunday afternoon, or take a hired room at a pub one evening. With a get-together as unceremonious as this, it would be misleading to issue a very formal-looking invitation, so whether you have something printed or handwrite it or invite people by telephone or email probably depends on the numbers. Don't expect gifts. If someone feels moved to bring a present, it should not be lavish. People you ask to a party of this kind are not necessarily those you'd invite to your wedding; it's not important enough to bring relatives from interstate. Best to stick to a more informal group, such as close family friends, neighbours and colleagues from the office.

Besides, an engagement does not carry the significance that a marriage does so it's a good idea to keep it low-key. If you choose to advertise it in the classified columns of a newspaper, it is traditional for the bride-to-be's parents to pay for it. Keep the wording simple. Flowery or overly emotional prose is not appropriate.

> PEERLESS – STANDAWFISH   The engagement is announced
> between Angela Jane, eldest daughter of Mr and Mrs Adam
> Peerless of Swankton, and William, only son of Dr and
> Mrs Peter Standawfish of Auckland, New Zealand.

If parents are separated, divorced or widowed, the wording may be adjusted accordingly. For instance, if the bride's parents are separated but not divorced, the wording would be:

> PEERLESS – STANDAWFISH   The engagement is announced between
> Angela Jane, eldest daughter of Mrs Eva Peerless of Swankton
> and Mr Adam Peerless of Toffs Harbour, and William, only son
> of Dr and Mrs Peter Standawfish of Auckland, New Zealand.

If the groom's parents are divorced and his mother has remarried, the announcement should read:

> PEERLESS – STANDAWFISH   The engagement is announced
> between Angela Jane, eldest daughter of Mr and Mrs Adam
> Peerless of Swankton, and William, only son of Dr Peter
> Standawfish of Auckland, New Zealand, and Mrs Roberto
> Boccherini of Bologna, Italy.

If the bride's mother is widowed and has not remarried:

> PEERLESS – STANDAWFISH   The engagement is announced
> between Angela Jane, eldest daughter of Mrs and the late
> Mr Adam Peerless of Swankton, and William, only son of
> Dr and Mrs Peter Standawfish of Auckland, New Zealand.

PRE-NUPTIAL AGREEMENTS

In situations where there is a large estate, it may be practical to draw-up a pre-nuptial agreement. Though potentially hurtful, the subject of money must be raised well before the marriage becomes a reality. If each party has substantial material assets, one or the other (preferably both) might want to draw up a pre-nuptial agreement that clearly specifies the financial arrangements that apply to the marriage.

Under federal legislation that came into force at the end of 2000, such agreements are now legally binding; before that ruling, a pre-nuptial agreement could be overruled in court. There is little romance in signing such a document, but where sizeable money is involved, you have to be pragmatic. Make sure a lawyer checks the contract before you sign it.

BRIDAL SHOWER

If this girlie get-together is to happen at all it should take place a few weeks before the wedding, probably on a weekend afternoon, with cakes and tea and perhaps champagne. Arranged by a close friend, such as your chief bridesmaid or matron of honour, it has the sole purpose of giving friends and immediate relatives the chance to bestow on you a whole lot of utilitarian objects, often for the kitchen. In fact, the old-fashioned term was 'kitchen tea'.

Suitable gifts are measuring spoons, tea towels, basins, oven mitts, aprons, cake tins, storage jars, egg whisk, rolling pin and any other item or utensil that belongs with the everyday paraphernalia of most households. If you have a hope chest, whatever you have squirrelled away there should be put on show, along with your bridal trousseau of pretty nighties, robes and dainty slippers. Like the trousseau, a hope chest, also known as a 'glory box' or 'bottom drawer', is by tradition a repository of items collected by a young woman in anticipation of marriage.

THE ENGAGEMENT'S OFF

Marriage is a hugely important obligation that will change your life. Unless you are absolutely sure you want to go through with it, don't do it, even if it is perilously late in the piece. Better a broken engagement than a broken marriage. The engagement period is intended to be a testing time to determine just how compatible two people are and sometimes engaged couples do change their minds.

A good test of whether or not you have found the right partner is to imagine what life would be like without him or her. Only if you feel you cannot live without this person should you proceed with the wedding. If either of you decides to break off the engagement, the ring and any heirlooms or expensive jewellery given by either person to the other must be returned and all presents sent back to the people who gave them to you.

If your parents announced your engagement in the newspaper, the correct thing for them to do is publish another notice.

> The marriage between Angela Peerless and William
> Standawfish will not take place.

WHO PAYS THE BILLS?

As parents of the bride, you should let the happy pair make the important decisions, such as the time and date of the occasion, the kind of wedding they want and its degree of formality, the number of guests, the venue, the menu, the decoration, the dresses and flowers. You are there to respect and implement their wishes and to make the preparation – despite the normal hitches and panics – as exciting as the day itself. It is your lot, too, to foot most of the bills.

Remember that the planning of a formal wedding can take months, or even a year or more, if it's to take place in a romantic season, a popular venue and a busy church. If you are affluent enough to be able to send your daughter off in grand style you are fortunate. If you are not, the day can be just as wonderful because a wedding, no matter what the scale, is a rite of passage that stirs the emotions in everyone. Sometimes the most enjoyable weddings are the simple ones where people express their happiness without too much formality or inhibition.

Other options are for expenses to be shared by both sets of parents, by the bride and groom or by all parties. It depends on circumstances. Traditionally, though, the expenses are divided up in this way.

THE BRIDE AND HER FAMILY PAY FOR:

- Invitations and postage
- Wedding dress and going-away clothes for the bride
- Dresses for the bride's attendants if the bride has firm ideas about what she wants and they are likely to be costly; otherwise it's reasonable to expect the bridesmaids to pay for their own dresses and accessories
- Flowers and music for the church
- Photographic and movie records of the event
- Reception costs
- Wedding ring, if there is one, for the groom

THE GROOM PAYS FOR:

- The marriage licence
- The wedding ring
- Fees and donations to the church
- Flowers carried by the bridal party
- Buttonholes for himself, best man and ushers
- Wedding cars
- Gifts for bride's and groom's attendants
- The honeymoon

An appropriate gift for a bridesmaid, if your budget permits, is a piece of jewellery that she can wear on the day. In any case, give something lasting, such as a piece of fine china, the special edition of a book or a silver frame for her chosen picture of the wedding. For the groomsmen, a pair of cufflinks, a wallet or a fountain pen is traditional.

Whether or not you exchange presents as the bride and groom probably depends as much on your financial situation as on your feelings for each other. Since it is a time when so many presents are bestowed, it might be wise to postpone giving anything more until the honeymoon or the first anniversary.

DECIDING ON THE CEREMONY

The first thing to do is to make an appointment with the celebrant or priest to determine the date and discuss the kind of ceremony you have in mind. If you choose to be wed in a spiritual place – church, temple, synagogue, mosque – bear in mind that you are on hallowed ground and behave accordingly. Relaxation of the rules over past decades means that people may marry where and how they wish – barefoot on the beach at dawn with a pet pug as bridesmaid, or dressed as pagan nymph and shepherd – but it is not appropriate to be exhibitionists in a holy place. The choice of music should be similarly appropriate. If you must have the latest rock number, play it at the reception, not in church.

That said, and depending on the particular church, the clergy often go out of their way to accommodate special needs and wishes but don't stretch their goodwill beyond acceptable limits. Presumably, the reason why you choose to marry in church is your desire to be part of a cherished tradition. If you want to deviate widely from that tradition, choose a non-sectarian celebrant and another location.

A CIVIL CEREMONY

In 1999, more people were married by civil celebrants in Australia than by ministers of religion. That is a first in our history. Given that these figures have shown a steady increase throughout the twentieth century, from 2.4 per cent in 1909 to 51.3 per cent in 1999, it is reasonable to assume that this trend will continue.

One virtue of having a celebrant officiate is that your choice of what is said and where the ceremony will be performed is wider. It could be anywhere: your own house, a public garden, an art gallery, the private room in a restaurant or hotel, on a yacht, on top of a mountain or at a famous landmark in your town or city. The tricky thing is to choose the right celebrant. Unless you already know someone you feel comfortable with – say, a woman or man who presided at a friend's wedding – look in the Yellow Pages.

Some celebrants operate within an association, such as the Australian Federation of Civil Celebrants, which can advise you on fees. It's perfectly acceptable to shop around and talk to several celebrants if necessary until you are happy to make a choice. It is the celebrant's responsibility to lodge the necessary forms with the government, just as a minister of religion would do.

The celebrant will have suggestions about what is said and the vows you make. If some are a bit syrupy for your taste, you might prefer to write your own promises. A good starting point is to study the traditional vows to determine what they mean and whether they hold special significance for you. The Uniting Church has an interesting, up-to-date version you may find useful as a guide. Or you may prefer to be innovative and choose your own words.

The Uniting Church of Australia is a progressive Christian church known for its ordination of women and for its willingness to offer its services to the community, whether people are members of the church or not. This church has a choice in the wording of marriage vows taken by bride and groom, including one that has appeal to many couples today because it's phrased in a modern way and is applicable to both of them. It goes like this.

I, William, in the presence of God,
take you, Angela, to be my wife.
All that I am I give to you.

All that I have I share with you.
Whatever the future holds,
I will love you and stand by you
as long as we both shall live.
This is my solemn vow.

A straightforward way of getting married without much ado is at the Registry Office. You must complete a form called Notice of Intended Marriage and lodge it at least one calendar month, and no more than six months, ahead of the wedding date. Each of you needs to show your birth certificate or, if that is not possible, a statutory declaration and relevant documents of identification. If either of you has been widowed or divorced, the certificate of death or decree absolute must be produced. If you decide to elope, the same procedure applies.

On the day, with two adult witnesses, the whole ceremony is usually done within twenty minutes and you walk away with your marriage certificate. The fee of about two hundred and fifty dollars covers all costs. How and where you celebrate is up to you.

A RELIGIOUS CEREMONY

For a more traditional wedding, let us assume that neither of you has been married before, that you will be married in a church or other holy place and given a reception afterwards – it is sometimes called a 'wedding breakfast' – attended by your relatives and friends. What follows is a blueprint, based on time-honoured practices, but it is not intended to be a set of commandments that must be followed. With individual rights and the choices we have now, we are free to take what we want from the past and to modify it at will. When you plan your wedding, follow your dream. Make the day exactly what you have always wanted it to be. At least one calendar month before your wedding date, the person who is to perform the ceremony will require you to fill in a Notice of Intended Marriage. He or she is also responsible for lodging the official marriage certificate with the relevant authorities within a fort-night after the wedding.

THE BRIDAL PARTY

The best man

He is the groom's minder – his brother or old friend – there to get him to the church on time and in good shape, to be keeper of the wedding ring, to charm the bridesmaids and the guests. He is efficient, close to the families involved and privy to all the arrangements so that he recognises key guests and is comfortable with them.

Ahead of time, he is the one to organise the buck's night, that tribal get-together of young stags to send off one of their kind. The best man will ensure that this event takes place a week before the wedding to give the groom plenty of time to recover.

At the reception he must make a speech that praises the bridesmaids and tell hitherto unknown and amusing stories about the groom. Telegrams are virtually obsolete now, but he reads any faxes, email messages or cards that have come from well-wishers not in attendance. It is pertinent here to note that messages of this kind should not be smutty, hackneyed or heavy-handed. If they can't be original and witty, they should be sincere.

The chief bridesmaid

She is the bride's closest friend or relative of similar age, someone genuinely loyal and loving in whom she can confide, particularly during the often frustrating times that precede a wedding when nerves are frazzled and things are said that may be regretted.

The chief bridesmaid arranges a hens' party before the wedding to give the bride-to-be her last chance to kick up her heels as a single woman. Traditionally, this was a decorous affair but modern women view themselves and the world differently and their festivities can be every bit as wild as a buck's night.

On the big day, she is watchful and efficient because her tasks are often practical ones, such as ensuring that the bride looks her best at all times, dress and veil perfectly arranged, hair and make-up in place. This is particularly important when it comes to the bride getting in and out of cars comfortably, gracefully and uncrushed. Not only does she stand by to hold the bridal bouquet when necessary, she also manages to conceal upon her person a comb, lipstick and powder compact to repair the bride's make-up. (Remember: the wedding pictures are forever.) If the chief bridesmaid is married, her title is matron of honour.

Other attendants

Groomsmen, bridesmaids, flower girls and pages are optional. The choice is often determined by courtesy. For instance, there might be a cousin who would be thrilled to be a flower girl. Or the bride and groom might each have a sister and it could be hurtful not to invite both to be bridesmaids. The number of attendants is a matter of individual choice but, unless the wedding is very lavish, too many might just be too much.

The ushers

For a grand church wedding there may be at least two ushers. Traditionally young men but now often women as well, they are members or friends of both families. They stand at the door of the church to greet the guests, hand them running sheets of the service, direct the bride's relatives and friends to the pews to the left, and the groom's relatives and friends to the pews to the right. They escort the mother of the bride, other women who arrive alone, very elderly people and any VIPs to their seats. Only those closest to the bride and groom sit in the first few rows of pews. Others sit in the rows behind. If in doubt, it's better to take a pew towards the back; you can always move forward if there is room when the ceremony is about to start.

CHOICE OF MUSIC

A bride who chooses to follow tradition to the letter, walks down the aisle on the arm of her father to the strains of the Bridal Chorus from *Lohengrin* by Richard Wagner. When the nuptial knot has been tied, she leaves on the arm of her husband to the triumphal Wedding March from incidental music composed by Felix Mendelssohn for William Shakespeare's *Midsummer Night's Dream*; it's been in fashion since the wedding of the Princess Royal in 1858.

Beautiful though they are, repetition has made these pieces rather hackneyed. There are many others that are equally appropriate and may be more inspiring because they have not been heard so often. Here are some possibilities. If you're not familiar with them, go to a record store and listen to them. There are also CDs specifically devoted to wedding music. Ask the priest or the organist at your church for suggestions, too, then choose something that suits everyone. Your ultimate choice might depend on whether you decide to have an organist, a choir, a chamber music group, recorded music, or a combination of them.

Before the bride arrives

As the wedding guests begin to gather, it's customary to create a contemplative mood with background music. Johann Sebastian Bach has some masterly pieces to do just that. They include his Toccata and Fugue in D Minor and 'Sleepers Awake'.

As the bride walks down the aisle

The important thing about the music here is that it should be serious enough to respect the solemnity of vows you are about to make and have a strong opening, so that people know to rise, turn and look at you, as you are cued to put your best foot forward. Two pieces that do this in a subtle way are 'Ave Verum Corpus' by Wolfgang Amadeus Mozart, and 'Jesu, Joy of Man's Desiring' by Bach. If you'd like a more forceful introduction, you might choose 'The Arrival of the Queen of Sheba' or a suite from the *Water Music*, both by George Frideric Handel.

While you sign the register

When the bride and groom disappear with their witnesses to sign the register, the congregation is left to contemplate the altar, the stained-glass windows and the ceiling, as they listen to music to soothe the spirit. For a single voice and/or a choir, you might consider 'Let the Bright Seraphim' by Handel; 'Ave Maria' by Franz Schubert; 'Sanctus' by Gabriel Fauré; or Mendelssohn's 'O for the Wings of a Dove', which is particularly beautiful when it's sung by a boy soprano.

Suitable instrumental works include Mozart's 'Alleluia' from *Exsultate, Jubilate*; 'Adagio' from Marcello's Oboe Concerto in C Minor; Johann Pachelbel's *Canon*; and *Liebestraum* by Franz Liszt.

Salute to the newlyweds

When the bride and groom emerge as a married couple, it's time to pull out all the stops with a truly exhilarating and triumphal work: *Gloria* by Antonio Vivaldi; 'Toccata' from Symphony No. 5 by Charles-Marie Widor; *Te Deum* by Marc-Antoine Charpentier; or *Music for the Royal Fireworks* by Handel.

Uninvited performers

In extended families, there are sometimes amateur singers or instrumentalists. They might offer to sing or play for you during the ceremony or at the reception. If you are keen for them to do so, there's happiness all round. But if you are not, then be gentle in turning them down. You could say that you had no idea they would make such a lovely offer and you have gone ahead and finalised the arrangements and booked the musicians. Say that you'd love them to bless you with their musical gifts at a small family gathering on another occasion. If you are the gifted amateur, don't offer to sing or play at a friend or relative's wedding. Wait to be asked.

PHOTOGRAPHERS AND VIDEOTAPERS

Nowadays, as a guest at a wedding, you will probably get the impression that the wedding service has been set up for the camera rather than the congregation. The reality of the day often seems incidental to the production that goes into recording it for future viewing. While it is understandable to want to have a flattering record for posterity, care should be taken that the intrusion of cameras does not detract from the spiritual meaning of the vows being taken. The bridal couple who is more aware of the camera than of the seriousness of the occasion risks appearing artificial and insincere.

It is important that the photographers be chosen carefully and briefed properly about where and when they are permitted to operate.

DECIDING ON THE RECEPTION

After you've decided on the ceremony, the next step is to select the venue for the reception. If few guests are invited, they may be received at home if the house or garden is big enough; if you plan to stage it outdoors, no matter what the season, have a marquee or some other means of shelter in case of bad weather. Unless there are many willing hands to help decorate the house, cook, lay out the food, serve it, attend the bar and clear away glasses and dishes, it's advisable to employ outside help.

For larger weddings, few family houses are able to cope with a sizeable wedding feast, so look at all the places you think will have the right atmosphere, facilities and service. Go into every last detail with each manager and ask for written quotes before you make the final decision.

Shop around. At some reception venues, once you have chosen the room you want and discussed the type of reception, whether sit-down dinner, buffet, cocktail party or whatever, the menu, decoration and every little detail, including table sizes and place cards if appropriate, you pay a small deposit when you finalise the booking and the rest two days before the wedding. The price quoted will include an estimate of the amount of drinks likely to be consumed. If people drink less than that amount, you receive a refund; if they consume more, there will be an additional bill. This practice is fairly standard at reputable venues.

BEWARE OF PITFALLS

Your budget will dictate much of what is possible but beware of places that require you to pay too much up front. There are horror stories of innocents being required to pre-pay everything – reception, wedding dress, video operator, official photographer – months ahead of time. The professionals who provide goods and services for weddings know that more money is lavished on a wedding than on any other occasion in many people's lives. The ruthless among them exploit this vulnerability by charging exhorbitant prices, so be careful. When you enquire about fees, don't let on at first that the event is a wedding; imply it's just a run-of-the-mill party and see if there's a difference in the quotes.

Understandably, as a bride you want to make all the decisions yourself but if you are sensible you will also listen to words of wisdom from your elders, most of all your mother and aunts, who have probably had a lot more experience than you have in organising events and know some of the pitfalls.

MUSIC AT THE RECEPTION

Your own tastes and the time of day should dictate the kind of music you choose to hear at the reception. Some people employ live bands, some hire DJs, others rely on recorded music. An important consideration is the level of sound. Don't have it so loud that nobody can hear anything else, just at a time when people have a lot to talk about. If you do plan to have loud music to dance to, think about holding your reception in twin rooms, one for chat, the other for dancing. That way, everybody can be happy and comfortable.

For me, there is no more beautiful greeting to people arriving at a reception than the liquid sounds of plucked harpstrings, the sweetness of violins and the pastoral purity of the flute. If you need to be convinced, listen to Mozart's Concerto in C for Flute and Harp.

THE SEATING PLAN

No matter how small the reception, if people are to be seated at tables, there must be a seating plan with a place card to indicate where each person is to sit. The seating plan should be made by a trustworthy elder who is diplomatic and aware of any affiliations or antipathies that exist within and between both families.

At occasions such as this, married couples may be seated at the same table but not immediately beside each other. Care should be taken to seat the elderly or disabled with people they know and trust. In fact, a wedding being such a tribal matter, people will probably be happiest among their kith and kin who they may not see as often as they would like. But avoid a sharp division between 'his' side and 'her' side, like troops mustered for battle. Intermingling of the bride's and groom's relatives and friends should be encouraged. The best place for children is with their parents or at a table of their own near someone with the authority to keep them in order.

The bridal table is placed where it is visible to everyone else. Traditionally, seating is along one side only, so that the wedding party face outward to their guests. If a parent of the bride or groom is widowed, the best man or chief bridesmaid should sit where that parent's partner would have been placed. If the bride's father is dead, whoever gives her away should take his seat at the table.

- If both sets of parents are alive and living together, seating at the bridal table goes like this (from left to right, seen from the guests' perspective): Chief bridesmaid. Groom's father. Bride's mother. Groom. Bride. Bride's father. Groom's mother. Best man.

- If the bride's parents are divorced and both have remarried, this is the traditional seating plan (if they can stand each other): Bride's stepfather. Chief bridesmaid. Groom's father. Bride's mother. Groom. Bride. Bride's father. Groom's mother. Best man. Bride's stepmother.
- If the groom's parents are divorced and both remarried, the seating goes like this: Best man. Groom's stepmother. Groom's father. Bride's mother. Groom. Bride. Bride's father. Groom's mother. Groom's stepfather. Chief bridesmaid.
- If both the bride and groom have divorced parents who have remarried, you need a longer table: Groom's stepmother. Bride's stepfather. Chief bridesmaid. Groom's father. Bride's mother. Groom. Bride. Bride's father. Groom's mother. Best man. Bride's stepmother. Groom's stepfather.

As with invitations, the variations here are as endless as human entanglements and commonsense should prevail. If there is acrimony between parents who are divorced, or iciness between her parents and his parents, everyone will be more comfortable if only the newlyweds and their attendants are seated at the bridal table.

WEDDING DRESS

It is true that the bride may wear whatever she chooses but the dress should be in keeping with the mood and scale of the occasion. A crinoline would be incongruous at a small reception at home, just as a dress that parades intimate bits of the bride's body is not the right thing to wear in church. When in doubt, err on the side of discretion and simplicity.

Your dress should be in keeping with your character, something that makes you look lovely and feel comfortable. A veil is customary, although not obligatory. Consider a train only if you feel easy about trailing one around. If in doubt, wear something more manageable. How you look from the back is important at any time, never more so than at your marriage, when the congregation will have plenty of time to study you from behind as you take your vows and receive blessings. In deciding on the fabric and design, consider the time of year and remember to check on what kinds of flowers are in season then (see pages 231–232).

It is traditional although by no means obligatory for the bride to wear white, the symbol of purity. Although it is reasonable to assume that few brides walking down the aisle in these permissive times are virgins, white is still appropriate, if you think of it as symbolising spiritual purity, as many faiths still do. Never choose yellow (jealousy) or green (envy) as the colour of the wedding dress.

OLD, NEW, BORROWED, BLUE

The superstitious are careful to wear something old, something new, something borrowed and something blue. The something old could be your grandmother's antique lace veil, or an heirloom handkerchief to dab the tears a bride is advised to shed at the altar by another wise old saw, which says that weeping before you are wed ensures no weeping afterwards. The something blue could be a satin ribbon threaded through the bride's obligatory garter, traditionally made of satin and lace. Another saying advises you to take care not to break anything on the wedding day lest you break the love between you.

The decision on dress for your attendants should be agreed between you. Discuss your preferences with them but try not to be dogmatic. Listen to their wishes, too, and do not finalise things until you feel they are completely happy with the colour, fabric and design. If your family is paying for the dresses, your bridesmaids should make every effort to comply with your wishes.

BRIDEGROOM

His attire is dependent on the formality of the bride's and will also dictate what other men in the party should wear. If she wears a long white gown, he should wear morning suit or black tie, depending on the time of day. (For definitions of appropriate dress, see pages 179–183.)

MOTHER OF THE BRIDE

Perhaps the most difficult person to dress is the mother of the bride, who must try to look distinguished and elegant and at the same time feel at ease in what she wears. A common mistake is to try too hard. Wear something consistent with your own character and style rather than what you feel a mother of the bride ought to turn out in. Remember that while people will certainly notice what you wear, their full attention will be on the bridal pair and their attendants. Now is not the time to experiment. Stick to a look that is tried and true.

GUESTS

It's a happy occasion, so guests should dress in optimistic colours and make an effort to look their best out of respect for the families. It is important also to remember that everyone there is part of a pageant to be immortalised in the photograph album and the video, so add to the spectacle by turning out in full finery. Women guests should not wear black, which is gloomy, or white, because nobody should be seen to compete with the bride. Some wedding guests believe they must wear new clothes, but that is not necessary, and certainly not practical if you are in an age group that receives wedding invitations regularly.

BRIDAL BOUQUET

If you dream of carrying lilac or lily-of-the-valley, don't plan an April wedding. You prefer gardenias? Better time it for December. As for hyacinths and tulips, their best time is winter, just as waterlilies bloom best in February. Here is a guide.

FLORAL CALENDAR IN AUSTRALIA

January	*Agapanthus, dahlia, daisy, frangipanni, fuchsia, gardenia, geranium, ginger, gymea lily, hollyhock, lily, lisianthus, magnolia, rose, snapdragon, sunflower, waterlily.*
February	*Allium, clematis, dahlia, frangipanni, gladiolus, honeysuckle, larkspur, lavender, lisianthus, lotus, rose, scotch thistle, sturt desert pea, tiger lily, tuberose, waterlily.*
March	*Convolvulus, daisy (everlasting), delphinium, hibiscus, tuberose.*
April	*Buddleia, chrysanthemum, cyclamen, ginger, hyacinth, iris, lavender, rosehip, wattle.*
May	*Arum, jasmine, jonquil, kangaroo paw, marigold, parrot tulip, rose, tulip.*
June	*Blushing bride, boradia, gumnut, lupin, magnolia (burgundy), snowdrop.*
July	*Crocus, cyclamen, daffodil, daphne, hyacinth, jonquil, orchid, poppy, ranunculus, snowbell, stock, tulip.*
August	*Azalea, camellia, freesia, fruit blossom, hellebore, jasmine, pansy, primrose, pussy willow, rhododendron, rosemary, stock.*
September	*Azalea, anemone, bluebell, citrus blossom, flannel flower, iris, japonica (quince blossom), jasmine, primrose, may, wattle, wisteria.*
October	*Amaryllis, bird of paradise, bottlebrush, bearded iris, dogwood, flannel flower, forget-me-not, gilderose, lilac, lily-of-the-valley, rose, wisteria, waratah.*
November	*Calla lily, foxglove, gerbera, hydrangea, jacaranda, lily, mock orange, peony, phalaenopsis orchid, rose, sweet pea.*
December	*Agapanthus, christmas bells, christmas bush, cornflower, violet, delphinium, gardenia, gloxinia, poinsettia, protea, rose, tuberose.*

What flowers signify

One charming tradition that remains from Victorian times is the language of flowers. The meaning bestowed on each flower was used as a way of sending secret messages during courtship. With the wonderful variety of modern flowers, not all have a meaning, so you won't find the floral calendar repeated here in full.

Acacia	*Secret love*
Allium	*Good fortune*
Amaryllis	*Pride*
Azalea	*Temperance*
Bird of paradise	*Wonder*
Bluebell	*Constancy*
Camellia (red)	*Unpretending excellence*
Camellia (white)	*Perfected loveliness*
Chrysanthemum (Chinese)	*Cheerfulness under adversity*
Chrysanthemum (red)	*I love*
Chrysanthemum (white)	*Truth*
Clematis	*Mental beauty*
Convolvulus (pink)	*Worth sustained by judicious and tender affection*
Cornflower	*Delicacy*
Crocus (spring)	*Youthful gladness*
Crocus (saffron)	*Mirth*
Cyclamen	*Diffidence*
Daffodil	*High regard; Chivalry*
Dahlia	*Instability*
Daisy	*Innocence*
Daisy (everlasting)	*Never-ceasing remembrance*
Daphne	*I would not have you otherwise*
Delphinium	*Swiftness and light*
Dogwood	*Endurance*
Forget-me-not	*True love; Remembrance*
Foxglove	*Insincerity*

Frangipanni	*Welcome*
Freesia	*Calm*
Fuchsia (scarlet)	*Taste*
Gardenia	*Grace*
Geranium (ivy)	*Bridal favour*
Geranium (rose-scented)	*Preference*
Gerbera	*Purity*
Gladiolus	*Natural grace*
Hibiscus	*Delicate beauty; Seize the moment*
Hollyhock	*Ambition; Fecundity*
Honeysuckle	*Generous and devoted affection*
Honeysuckle (French)	*Rustic beauty*
Hyacinth	*Young love; Play*
Hydrangea	*Boastfulness; Heartlessness*
Iris	*Message*
Iris (German)	*Flame*
Jasmine	*Good luck*
Jonquil	*I desire a return of affection*
Larkspur	*Lightness; Levity*
Lavender	*Distrust*
Lemon blossom	*Fidelity in love*
Lilac (purple)	*First emotions of love*
Lilac (white)	*Youthful innocence*
Lily (day – *hemerocallis*)	*Coquetry*
Lily (imperial)	*Majesty*
Lily (white)	*Purity; Sweetness*
Lily (yellow)	*Falsehood; Gaiety*
Lily-of-the-valley	*Return of happiness*
Lotus	*Estranged love; Truth and beauty*
Lupin	*Voraciousness; Imagination*
Magnolia	*Dignity*
Orange blossom	*Your purity equals your loveliness*
Orange flowers	*Chastity; Bridal festivities*
Orchid	*Ecstasy*

Pansy	*Thoughts*
Passion flower	*Religious superstition*
Peach blossom	*I am your captive*
Peony	*Secrets*
Poppy (red)	*Dreams*
Poppy (scarlet)	*Fantastic extravagance*
Primrose	*Early youth; Hope*
Protea	*Challenge*
Ranunculus	*You are radiant with charms*
Rhododendron	*Danger; Beware*
Rose (red)	*Love*
Rose (white)	*Purity and silence*
Rose (yellow)	*Jealousy*
Rosebud (red)	*Pure and lovely*
Rosebud (white)	*Girlhood*
Rosemary	*Remembrance*
Snapdragon	*Presumption*
Snowdrop	*Hope; Consolation*
Stock	*Lasting beauty*
Sunflower (dwarf)	*Adoration*
Sunflower (tall)	*Haughtiness; Power; Longevity*
Sweet pea	*Delicate pleasures*
Thistle (common)	*Austerity*
Thistle (Fuller's)	*Misanthropy*
Thistle (Scotch)	*Retaliation*
Tuberose	*Dangerous pleasures*
Tulip	*Fame*
Tulip (red)	*Declaration of love*
Tulip (variegated)	*Beautiful eyes*
Tulip (yellow)	*Hopeless love*
Violet	*Faithfulness*
Waterlily	*Purity of heart*
Wisteria	*Obedience*
Zinnia	*Thoughts of absent friends*

Who's invited?

The list of guests is divided evenly between the bride's family and the groom's, although there is no pressure on anybody to be strict about these numbers. It may be that somebody's nearest and dearest are on the other side of the world and may not be able to afford the time or the money to make the journey. On the other hand, they may arrive in force, creating a challenge of another sort: where to put them up and how to entertain them at this frantic time, is another issue (see Chapter 13). No matter how big or small the wedding, it is courteous to invite the person who conducts the service and partner, if appropriate, to the reception, although the invitation may not be accepted.

No matter how careful you are, be assured that somebody is going to be offended at not being invited. Even if you consider yourself a close friend of the bride or groom, don't be offended if you do not receive an invitation. Because a wedding is a major family event, members of both families may take precedence over friends of the bride and groom, their colleagues and neighbours. The bride and groom might want to limit the guest list to intimate family members only, or the budget might not be big enough to cover a large gathering.

If, as the bride or groom, you have a particularly disagreeable relative – drinks too much, criticises everything, wants to dominate, or whatever – don't put your parents in an embarrassing position by stubbornly refusing to have the dreaded cousin or grandparent on the list. The best way to handle it is to delegate responsibility for the troublemaker to a treasured person who is tolerant, kindly yet strong enough to measure up to the challenge of heading off potential problems.

FORMAL INVITATION AND ACCEPTANCE

Invitations should be sent out six weeks before the date of the wedding. Formal folded invitations are engraved in black ink using copperplate script or Roman type on white paper that folds to 140 mm by 178 mm. They are put into matching envelopes lined in tissue paper. The wording is in the third person and reciprocated in kind (see below).

RSVP stands for 'Répondez s'il vous plaît', the French way of saying 'Please reply'. These words are placed on the lower left-hand corner, above the address. On formal invitations a date by which replies are expected is not included because it is assumed that the respondent will be well mannered enough to reply as soon as possible. If you think this subtlety may be lost on some of your guests, include a date. A telephone number is likewise absent because it would not be appropriate to reply to a formal invitation by any means other than a handwritten letter.

Indication of dress appears in the bottom right-hand corner. In Britain, for a wedding at six or later in the evening, there would be no indication of dress on a formal invitation because you would be expected to know that it was black tie. In Australia, that is not widely understood so it is safer to specify dress to avoid confusion and possible embarrassment. The engraved invitation reads like this:

Mr and Mrs Adam Peerless
request the pleasure of the company of

(handwrite guest's name)

at the marriage of their daughter
Angela Jane to Mr William Standawfish
at St Joseph's Church, Cosmic Heights
on Saturday, 8th November, 2003
at 6.00 p.m.
and afterwards at Château Jacaranda, Cosmic Bay

RSVP   *Black tie*
1 Swans Way
Swankton Vic. 3142

Although the above is the format I prefer because I like the inclusion of a guest's name within the context of the wording rather than outside it, writing the guest's name at the top, to the left, is equally correct.

(handwrite guest's name)

Mr and Mrs Adam Peerless
request the pleasure of your company
at the marriage of their daughter . . .

In replying to a formal invitation, whether to accept or refuse – 'due to your absence from the country' or whatever the reason – it is important to follow the form of the invitation precisely on a sheet of plain white paper or your personal letterhead.

Acceptance

Mr and Mrs August Britsches
thank Mr and Mrs Adam Peerless
for their kind invitation to the marriage
of their daughter Angela Jane
to Mr William Standawfish
on Saturday, 8th November,
and have pleasure in accepting.

Inability to attend

Mr and Mrs August Britsches
thank Mr and Mrs Adam Peerless
for their kind invitation to the marriage
of their daughter Angela Jane
to Mr William Standawfish
but regret that they are unable to attend
due to a previous engagement.

When you receive an invitation addressed to you and 'friend', you should name that friend in your acceptance. For example, your reply comes from 'Mr Jason Argonopoulos and Ms Pru Merrimount'.

FAMILY COMPLICATIONS

The possibilities of wording on the invitation are endless. The important thing is to make it clear who is putting on the event so that guests know how to word their acceptances and who to thank for the hospitality.

If the bride's parents are divorced, her mother has not remarried and they are both hosting the wedding, the invitation should come from 'Mr Adam Peerless and Mrs Eva Peerless'.

If the bride's mother has remarried, then the invitation would read 'Mr Adam Peerless and Mrs Neville King'.

A widow hosting the wedding of her daughter would send an invitation from 'Mrs Adam Peerless'.

In the case of an acrimonious relationship between divorced parents who have each remarried, if they cannot be relied upon to be civil on the day, it's best if only one of them puts on the wedding. In that case, the invitation would come from either 'Mr Adam Peerless' or 'Mrs Neville King'.

Both sets of parents hosting the wedding happens increasingly in Australia. In such a case, the invitation would read 'Mr and Mrs Adam Peerless and Dr and Mrs Peter Standawfish request the pleasure of your company at the marriage of their respective children, Angela Jane and William . . .'

If the bride's parents are both dead and another couple, say an aunt and uncle, put on the wedding, the invitation would read 'Mr and Mrs Joshua Kirby request the pleasure of the company of . . . at the wedding of their niece, Angela Jane', etc.

The bride and groom might choose to put on their own wedding, in which case the invitation would begin 'Angela Peerless and William Standawfish request the pleasure of the company of . . . at their marriage', etc.

WEDDING PRESENTS

Opinions differ on whether or not it is appropriate for the bride to draw up a list of preferred wedding presents. I think it is a helpful thing to do. What matters is the way in which it is done. Make the list, taking care to include plenty of items that do not cost a lot of money. Lodge this at a store – more than one shop if you wish – that stocks the goods you want and also provides this kind of service. Most of the reputable department stores and many speciality shops do. (See Chapter 11 for suggestions for household presents.)

A word of caution about the store you choose. At some, the service is so popular, its telephone lines are constantly busy. I have waited twenty-five minutes for someone to answer my call to the bridal registry of one department store and all I wanted was the list. That's a good reason for lodging a list at one or two specialist shops, as well as a comprehensive one.

However, don't tell anyone about this list except your immediate family, your future mother-in-law and your attendants. It must not be used to put pressure on anybody. It is there in case a wedding guest asks for advice on what to give. And there will be plenty of those. Distant relations, particularly elderly ones, often have no idea what your heart is set on and welcome being relieved of the burden of trying to decide on a gift and risk bestowing something that will finish up in the 'monster' cupboard.

A PRESENT IS OBLIGATORY

It is the custom for each person, couple or family invited to the wedding to give a present whether or not they attend. It is also perfectly good form for several guests to pool their resources and buy one big present they know will be welcome. At a Christian wedding, presents should never be brought to the church or to the reception. That is an imposition on the bride's parents, who have to lug them home and

store them. Among some other faiths, bearing gifts is part of the ceremonial, but more of that later.

Gifts should be addressed to the bride and delivered to her house
during the week before the wedding. The gift card should include the
groom's name; for example, 'For Angela and William . . . ' The intended
newlyweds open presents at their discretion, but when they do unwrap
each one, it's a good idea to write a description on the back of its gift
card, to avoid slip-ups in the thank-you notes. If you have not sent your
gift before the wedding, send it afterwards so that it will be waiting
when the honeymooners return.

THE WEDDING DAY

Even if you are already living together, you might like to observe the
tradition of not seeing each other on the day until the groom is standing at the altar and the bride in her finery begins to advance down the
aisle to join him. This heightens the romance of this moment of truth.
If the reception is taking place at a hotel, as the bride you might choose
to stay in a suite with your attendants the night before and leave from
there for the ceremony next day. There's a lot to be said for not having
to bother with the household routine on this day of all days and to be
waited on hand and foot.

In any case, the bride's attendants gather around her, well ahead of
time, along with a professional make-up artist and hairdresser, if they
have been employed. Some members of the party might prefer to do
their own hair and make-up or to speed out early to a salon but, whatever happens, dressing should not be rushed. Every effort should be
made by everyone to stay calm and help the bride look and feel her best.
If required, the photographer and video operator arrive about an hour
before the party is due to leave for the ceremony.

Meanwhile, the best man and groomsmen should meet at the
bridegroom's home, although they need not necessarily dress there.

The best man must pocket the wedding ring, check that bow ties and buttonholes are in place, that the groom is immaculately turned out and generally take charge of things, including getting the party to the church in good time, about fifteen minutes before the ceremony is due to start.

Ushers should be the first members of the wedding to arrive at the church, about half an hour ahead of time. They should be willing to help anyone who seems to need it and to acquaint themselves with the immediate area so that, if necessary, they can direct cars to suitable parking spots.

THE CEREMONY

The first car to leave the bride's house for the church carries her mother and, if she prefers not to be alone, one or two close relatives or friends. The next car carries the bridesmaids; if they are numerous, another car may be necessary. The bride and her father, or the person who is to give her away, travel in the final car. They should aim to be in the vestibule of the church one minute after the appointed time.

We are all familiar with stories of the bride keeping everyone waiting, but being late is an inconsiderate practice, only forgiveable if there is a legitimate reason, such as an unforeseen traffic hold-up. Let's hope she hasn't changed her mind, like the leading female character in Anita Brookner's novel *Hotel du Lac* who, while genteel and sympathetic, is no model of good behaviour in leaving her intended waiting at the church.

What happens next varies widely from one religion to another but, whether exchanging beribboned crowns, sharing a cup of wine under a *chuppah* (canopy) or participating in a nuptial mass, the pair come out of it joined in wedlock. A shaft of sunlight touching the altar when the ceremony is in progress is regarded by the sentimental as a blessing. So is a sunshower.

As the congregation leaves the church, photographs are taken, greetings are exchanged and the newlyweds showered with confetti and rice, but only if it has been established that this ritual is acceptable on the doorstep of this particular church. Rose petals could be a diplomatic as well as romantic solution. The ushers should make sure that everyone has transport to the reception and, if necessary, find seats in cars or call taxis. Mobile telephones are very useful at this time, as long as everyone remembers to turn them off before entering the hallowed place.

THE RECEPTION

Throughout the entire day, the trickiest timing to get right is the length of the wait between the end of the ceremony and the beginning of the reception. Photography and moviemaking have now assumed such importance that they can tend to take over, leaving guests hanging around for hours like extras on a movie set as bride and groom are snapped in poses reminiscent of fashion pictures in glossy magazines and sequences in big-budget feature films.

The bridal party should not dillydally on the way to the reception and the photographs must be done as speedily as possible, but guests should feel free to dawdle without fear of missing out on the proceedings.

At a large formal wedding, there would normally be a receiving line so that every guest has at least one chance of meeting and greeting the bride and groom and their families. Since the queue can be lengthy and slow-moving, people joining it should be offered drinks, which must, however, be put aside before they reach the receiving line. The first couple to greet guests are the bride's parents, then the groom's parents, then the newlyweds, then the groomsmen and bridesmaids, if it is decided to include them.

As a guest, move quickly along the receiving line, pausing just long enough for formalities; this is not the time and place for lengthy chats or personal asides, no matter how well you know the people involved. You need not say more than your name and 'How do you do' to those you have not met before, although you might like to tell the bride how beautiful she looks and congratulate the groom.

Food served at a wedding does not have to be elaborate but it should be special, whether it is presented as finger food, a buffet or served at tables. It should also be something that most people are able to eat, whatever their dietary restrictions. For a sit-down occasion, melon, avocado or a manageable pasta with a light vegetable sauce is a good choice as a first course. If you serve red meat, there should be an alternative, such as salmon. There should be plenty of cooked vegetables, salads, fruit and bread.

When the main course has been brought and eaten and dishes taken away, it is usual for champagne flutes to be filled in anticipation of the speeches. Understandably, since a formal wedding doesn't happen often in most families, there is a temptation for speech-makers to hold the floor too long. This is to be avoided at all costs. Keep it short, sincere, loving and, if you can manage it, witty. Never be bawdy or suggestive.

A master of ceremonies announces the speeches. The first is made by someone who knows the bride well, often her father or other close relative or family friend, who finishes by proposing a toast to the bride and groom.

It is the bridegroom's turn to reply, although sometimes the bride has a few words to say, too. His speech is mainly a litany of thanks: to his new wife's parents for their daughter's hand, their acceptance of him into their family and for the splendid reception; to the wedding guests for their presence and presents; to the bridesmaids for looking beautiful and being so helpful to his bride. With that, he proposes a toast to the bridesmaids.

The best man gets to his feet to thank the groom on behalf of the bridesmaids and tell a few amusing but tactful home truths about him before he reads some or all of the written messages received from people not there in person.

Wedding cake

After the speeches, it is time for the ceremonial cutting of the cake, which is usually displayed in splendour on a table of its own, providing the

obligatory photo opportunity when the couple join hands on the beribboned knife and pierce the lower tier. The cake is taken away and cut into
as many pieces as there are people at the wedding but, as a symbol of fertility, the bride and groom should share the first piece. It is customary for
the bridesmaids to pass the slices around to guests. Since at this point
many of them might not be able to face another crumb, it is perfectly in
order to ask for a piece of cake to be wrapped in foil, so that it can be
taken home and placed under the pillow and slept on for good luck.

The traditional, tiered wedding cake is usually a rich fruit cake
with thick almond icing. If it has three tiers, the lower one is consumed
at the wedding, the second kept for the first wedding anniversary and
the top one brought out for the christening of the first child. In the
United States, a wedding cake may be an iced sponge (angel's food
cake) or chocolate cake. In France, it is usually a croquembouche.

If there is to be dancing, now is the time. The bride and groom take to
the floor first, usually in a waltz. The bride should then dance first with
her father-in-law, then with her father, while the groom dances with his
mother-in-law, then his mother. Everyone then joins in, encouraged by
the other members of the wedding party. The kind of dancing depends
greatly on the ethnic origins of the families. Orthodox Jews and strict
Muslims do not dance with the opposite sex.

Before long, all unmarried women should be urged to cluster
around the bride and groom, who should be elevated a little on a stair-
case or platform, for the throwing of the bouquet. Tradition has it that
the woman who catches it will be the next to marry. If the atmosphere
is frolicsome and high-spirited, all unmarried men, including those in
the wedding party, might then be asked to form a group in front of the
bride and groom. The groom removes the bride's garter and throws it to
the pack. The man who catches it is destined to be the next bridegroom.

After that, the bride and groom might disappear along with their
attendants to change into going-away outfits, although I notice that

contemporary brides are often so reluctant to part company with the wedding dress, they wear it to wherever they're spending the night. Even though they might want these special festivities never to finish, the newlyweds must consider their guests, whom custom decrees should not depart until after the bride and groom have left – unless they are Chinese, Japanese or German, in which case it's the guests who must leave first.

If the newlyweds were leaving immediately for their honeymoon, traditionally the best man would make sure that the couple's luggage, passports and other travel documents were present and their transport booked. He would watch out for pranksters, never be tempted to become one himself and head off any efforts to conceal confetti or other embarrassing things in the bags. He must always have the couple's best interests at heart.

Word should go out among the guests when the reappearance of the two is imminent so they can line up to say au revoir. At places that specialise in organising wedding receptions, guests are sometimes asked to stand in two lines facing each other, raise their arms and link their hands to form a tunnel through which the bride and groom make their getaway.

It is not a good idea for the newlyweds to drive themselves on their wedding night. Too much champagne and too much excitement might lead to too little responsibility on the road. It is up to the best man, along with the parents, to ensure that the loving pair are conveyed safely to their first-night love nest in a car driven by someone sober, preferably the professional driver of a hired car. While guests might like to stay for one more drink or a chat, they should not linger too long.

SECOND OR UMPTEENTH TIME AROUND

Unlike first-timers, people who remarry are free to make their own rules. Presumably they have been through one of the scenarios outlined above and their duty to the tribe has been despatched. However, if there are children of an earlier union, care must be taken to include them in the planning and to give them key roles on the day. If appropriate, they may become members of the wedding party although they should never be pressured if they do not want to take part. When children are involved, there's a lot to be said for the wedding being very low-key.

WHO PAYS?

No obligation falls on the bride's parents to pay for her second wedding. Usually, the happy couple foot all bills themselves, although family and friends might want to contribute.

CHURCH SERVICES

The wedding may take place on hallowed ground, if the faith it represents sanctions remarriage, or in a registry office with two witnesses. The Roman Catholic Church does not recognise divorce; once you marry in that church, you do so for life. While Protestant churches accept any divorce recognised by Australian law, not every minister will agree, without certain conditions, to marry people who have been divorced. For instance, a Presbyterian minister will need to be sure that the divorced person accepts some responsibility for the marital breakdown and is repentant and genuine in his or her determination to do better next time under the guidance of God.

An alternative to a church service is to have a celebrant perform a tailor-made ceremony in a venue that caters for weddings, in a private or public garden, in a house with enough space to take the numbers comfortably, or in just about any public place provided permission is given. Some couples prefer a service attended by only their nearest and dearest, followed by a reception for many more people somewhere else, such as in a hotel or restaurant.

What the bride chooses to wear depends on the formality and size of the wedding but the traditional, long white wedding frock is not appropriate. At a black-tie wedding in late afternoon or evening, you might wear an elegant evening dress, long or short, in any colour except white (virginal) or black (gloomy). At an informal wedding during the day, one of the most attractive and sophisticated looks is a beautifully tailored suit, with skirt or trousers, in cream or a pastel colour with matching pantihose and shoes and a small posy or corsage.

THE INVITATION

Make sure the invitation is consistent with the nature of the occasion. If the wedding is to be formal, follow the guidelines earlier in this chapter. If the wedding is to be small and informal, the most charming way to invite people is by handwritten letter:

> *Dear April and Robin,*
> *Ken and I hope you can be with us when we tie the nuptial knot in Aunt May's garden, 35 Hazelbank Close, Noosaville, at 5 p.m. on Saturday, 8th November.*
> *With love, Maggie*

For a larger wedding that is nevertheless informal, printed invitations might be necessary. For example, it might read something like this.

(handwrite name of guest here)

Ken Glover and Maggie Herriott
hope you can be with them when they marry
at 35 Hazelbank Close, Noosaville 4566
at 5 p.m. on Saturday, 8th November,
followed by an appropriate celebration.

RSVP

If a couple wish to be married privately, it is a good idea for them to send a card to friends and acquaintances afterwards.

Ken Glover and Maggie Herriott
are delighted to tell you
that their marriage took place
quietly in Noosaville last month.

100 Eden Grove
Hamilton 4007

ANNIVERSARIES

Behaving well at all times includes remembering special dates and choosing appropriate gifts to mark the occasion. Here are the traditional wedding anniversary presents.

First anniversary	*Paper or plastics*
Second	*Calico or cotton*
Third	*Leather*
Fourth	*Silk*
Fifth	*Wood*
Sixth	*Iron*
Seventh	*Copper or wool*
Eighth	*Electrical appliances*
Ninth	*Pottery*
Tenth	*Tin or aluminium*
Eleventh	*Steel*
Twelfth	*Linen (table, bed, etc.)*
Thirteenth	*Lace*
Fourteenth	*Ivory*
Fifteenth	*Crystal or glass*
Twentieth	*China*
Twenty-fifth	*Silver*

Thirtieth	*Pearls*
Thirty-fifth	*Coral or jade*
Fortieth	*Ruby*
Forty-fifth	*Sapphire*
Fiftieth	*Gold*
Fifty-fifth	*Emerald*
Sixtieth	*Diamond*

OUR VARIED TRADITIONS

Wedding customs and ceremonies among Australians today are wonderfully varied, drawn from many different religious beliefs and cultural traditions, and you will probably find that many people have borrowed bits and pieces from each other's rituals and pasted them onto their own. May the practice flourish, all the better to nourish our fledgling Australian identity as it grows and matures into something culturally rich, unique and inclusive.

THE CHINESE WEDDING

What happens today in Chinese weddings is a simplification of ancient practices that applied when marriages were arranged by the parents through a go-between and a series of letters. To begin with, the couple's times and dates of birth determined whether or not they should wed; if dates were incompatible, attempts at a union did not proceed. Even today, the advice of a fortune-teller is often sought to assess the suitability of the match and to settle on auspicious dates for the wedding, just as a master of feng shui (the Chinese art-and-science of placing people and things harmoniously within the universe) is consulted regarding the physical aspects of a house and the arrangements within it.

When the date is set, the groom's family send gifts of food and perhaps money to the bride's family. It is usual for the groom's family to pay for the entire cost of the wedding, although that may vary from one family to another. The bride's family provide the dowry (pots, pans, bed linen and so on), although the bed, preferably new, is supplied by the groom. Historically, a man deemed by the family to have a fortunate life was engaged to place the bed in a propitious position. A woman similarly well favoured would be chosen to make the bed with red sheets and leave lucky foods there for the bridal pair.

If they can afford it, the bride's parents often prefer to give their daughter expensive jewellery rather than money because they feel it's more likely to remain with her as a personal asset. If, as is usually the case, other members of the bride's family also give her jewellery, it's customary for her to wear all of it on her wedding day as a show of wealth. Sometimes the groom's family give the nuptial pair matching watches to symbolise a long life together. The Chinese value family connections, even those as remote as second cousins living on the other side of the world, and a wedding gives them an excellent reason for getting together.

Rituals on the day begin with the groom and his attendants taking decorated cars to the house of his intended parents-in-law, where he and the bride-to-be serve tea to her family. Because tea comes from an enduring plant, it holds great significance for the Chinese, who believe it symbolises fidelity and a long life. The couple pay their respects by kneeling before each person (except family members who are younger than them), starting with the most senior, and pouring tea for them. In return, each member of the family gives the pair a red envelope containing a gift, usually jewellery or money. Gifts that come in red envelopes are called 'lucky money' (*lai see* in Cantonese).

The couple and their attendants then visit the groom's family to serve tea and receive presents before everyone congregates at the church, registry office or wherever the ceremony is being performed. Although Buddhism is the traditional Chinese religion, it does not have a standard text for marriage ceremonies; the general message conveyed will emphasise the Buddhist belief in benevolence to all living

things. Christianity has also had an influence on many Chinese, particularly those from Hong Kong, so a Protestant ceremony may form
the blueprint for a Chinese marriage.

Red, symbolising power and good fortune, is the predominant
colour in dress and interior decoration at a Chinese wedding. As a guest,
you should never wear all-over black or white. Avoid cool, sombre
colours, such as dark blue and green. Wear warm, optimistic colours:
red, pink, orange and yellow.

Appropriate gifts are jewellery, brightly coloured homewares and
lai see, which is sometimes tied with gold ribbon. The amount of money
should be an even number, never odd, but avoid the number four,
which sounds like 'death' in Cantonese. Forty-four is equally bad. Eight
and eighty-eight are considered very good numbers. There is a rule of
thumb for how much *lai see* you should give. Because it is intended to
help meet the cost of the reception, the amount depends on the standard of the venue and is calculated on a per head basis. In other words,
couples pay twice as much as singles and what they contribute to a
reception at a five-star hotel would be greater than one at a more
modest place.

Be careful in your choice of a gift. Never give a clock, for instance.
The word for clock in Cantonese sounds like 'funeral', unlike 'watch',
which does not have negative connotations. Traditionally, it is customary to bring your present to the wedding banquet, although nowadays
presents are often sent to the bride's house ahead of time or, as one
modern Australian–Chinese bride told me, the money may be keyed
straight into a bank account! In presenting your gift in person, remember to hold it in both hands.

The most important part of the wedding day is the banquet, which
is as lavish as the family can afford and contains certain delicacies
believed to exert positive influences. There might be any number of
courses, ranging from eight to twelve. If there is roast suckling pig it
will be served first because it is a symbol of virginity. Because a dragon

represents the husband and a phoenix the wife, lobster (dragon shrimp) and chicken (phoenix) represent the perfect balance of yin and yang. Shark's fin soup stands for affluence, Peking duck happiness and, when presented whole, completeness. Rice signifies plenty. Pigeon and other small birds are a symbol of peace. Sea cucumber promotes goodwill. A whole fish stands for prosperity and accord, noodles mean longevity and sweet buns or dumplings filled with lotus paste indicate fertility. Tea is served, along with a selection of soft and alcoholic drinks, which might include a good cognac.

The seating is usually at round tables of ten. The newlyweds sit with their parents at a bridal table laid with a red cloth. During the banquet the newlyweds and their parents visit each of the other tables to show their appreciation and to see that their guests are enjoying themselves. As a guest, you should rise when they arrive at your table, raise your glass with both hands, wish them happiness and drink a toast.

After the banquet, don't wait for the bride and groom to depart before you do. It is the custom for them to wait until all the guests have left, so don't be tardy.

THE GREEK WEDDING

The Greeks regard marriage as a heaven-sent reason for joyous celebration. I know a family who started dancing at home on the day of their eldest son's marriage, hours before wedding crowns were to be placed on the heads of the nuptial pair in church.

By tradition, ceremonies start well before that date, although many of the rituals are now a thing of the past. First there was a get-together where the bride's entire trousseau was displayed and the bridal bed, a gift from the groom's family, was made with white sheets and a bedspread hand-embroidered by young virgins. The finishing touches were a scattering of sugared almonds and strings of cloves, and a baby was bounced up and down on the bed.

Sunday is the favoured day for a Greek wedding and, on the evening before, the groom-to-be and his family are feted at the home of the bride-to-be. Her parents used to give jewellery to all the members of his family; these days they usually give their future son-in-law a gold watch. The bride-to-be receives jewellery from her family and his.

On that Saturday night, the priest would come to perform a charming ritual of 'smoking' the clothes that were to be worn to the wedding by the bride, groom and best man. He would set fire to wild herbs such as oregano and marjoram laid out in the middle of a room and bless the clothes three times as the smoke permeated them with the scent.

In former times, the groom met the bride at the door of the church and led her down the aisle but the practice has in general been modified in Australia. It is now more usual for the bride to be on the arm of her father when she walks down the aisle to meet the groom at the altar. No music is played, although there is much chanting by the priest and the cantor in a church often richly decorated with gold mosaics and lit by candles.

The priest stands before a ceremonial table. On it have been placed the holy gospel, the precious cross, two candlesticks, a cup of wine, the wedding rings and the wedding crowns. The ceremony is twofold, first the betrothal followed by the marriage crowning service.

After the priest blesses the rings, he makes a sign of the cross with them over the couple's heads and pronounces them betrothed. The best man takes the bride's ring and places it on the groom's finger, and places the groom's ring on the bride's finger. He does this three times. The transfer of rings means that in marriage the weaknesses of one partner will be counterbalanced by the strengths of the other.

Prayers and blessings follow. Then the priest takes the crowns, which are linked by a ribbon symbolising the marriage bond, and places them on their heads. The best man exchanges the crowns three times. The crowns represent the noble characteristics of justice, wisdom and integrity the couple will bring to their rule over their own domain. When bride and groom drink from the common cup it means they will be equal participants in whatever happiness or sadness occurs in their life together.

Led by the priest and followed by their attendants, the bride and groom now take their first steps together as a married couple in what is known as the Dance of Isaiah. The group walks in a perfect circle around the lectern three times. This rite means that, since a circle has no end, it mirrors the endless love the couple should have for each other, around the central core of their life, which is Jesus Christ. The 'dance' also expresses the delight the church has in this marriage.

When the ceremony is over, the bridal party and close family form a receiving line facing the congregation, members of which step forward one by one to kiss and congratulate them, all this with great warmth and informality. The crowns given to the couple are destined to be hung above their bed; the ribbons must never be cut otherwise, according to the doomsayers, the marriage will be finished. Once the congregation is outside the church, bells ring, rose petals are scattered and the group moves off for feasting, speech-making and dancing à la Zorba.

It's quite a tradition for family and friends to pin money on the bride and groom during the festivities. Usually the oldest guest has the honour of going first. The sum you give depends on how well you know the couple.

THE INDIAN (HINDU) WEDDING

Hinduism is an accommodating religion. A Hindu is free to marry someone of a different faith without that person needing to convert to Hinduism. The Hindu priest determines the time and date of the wedding according to the birth dates of bride and groom.

The whole ritual can extend to three or four days but in Australia now, it is often pared down to about an hour without the essential elements being lost. There are variations in some procedures and practices between northern and southern India but the overall spirit is the same.

It is wonderfully colourful and entertaining, humorous rather than sombre, with all the guests participating in the play.

Wedding guests are often dressed in richly coloured silk saris with gold embroidery. White is considered funereal, the garb of widows, so if you are not a widow but you want to wear white, it should have a border or some other sort of coloured decoration. It is traditional for gifts to be brought to the wedding.

On the day before and on the wedding day, the bride is bathed and anointed with sesame oil scented with flowers. In some parts of India, elaborate designs are drawn with henna on the hands and feet of the bride and her attendants.

She wears a silk sari to the wedding, changes into a half-white (unbleached cotton) sari, signifying purity and simplicity, for the meaningful part of the ceremony, then changes one more time into a very elaborate and often expensive silk sari presented by the groom's family. This final sari will be kept and worn only on very special, formal occasions for the rest of her life. The groom often wears a turban.

The marriage takes place under a *mandapa*, a cloth canopy supported by a wooden frame hung with flowers. Inside it is a flame burning from a pure cotton wick in oil. At one time or another during the ceremony, bride and groom garland each other with flowers, tie their clothes together, walk around the *mandapa*, pray for health, fertility and prosperity, go outside to seek the blessing of a particular star, and pour rice over each other to symbolise providence.

The groom might entertain guests by pretending to change his mind about marriage and say he's going on a pilgrimage to Varanasi, before being persuaded by the bride's brother to come back. Three happily married women from the congregation might approach the pair to bless them. One of the most significant moments is when the groom ties a necklace called a *mangalasutra* (a *tali* in southern India) around the bride's neck; it is the Hindu equivalent of the Christian wedding ring.

At the close of the ceremony, a plate of camphor, an auspicious substance, is set alight and people put their hands to the flame, then to their eyes, as a form of worship.

Afterwards the newlyweds are feted with a feast, dancing and improvised songs that make fun of the participants. There are no speeches. It is traditional to have lots of food but no alcohol. Water and buttermilk are usually offered.

THE ISLAMIC WEDDING

There is no prescribed procedure for proposing marriage in Islam, but traditionally it is done by the suitor's parents or relatives. Once it's known that two people are interested in each other, the prospective husband or his family pay a visit to the girl's parents. Until they declare they are engaged, the pair continue to be free agents.

It is perfectly acceptable for a Muslim woman to take the lead in asking for the hand of a man in marriage. A precedent was set in the sixth century AD, when Mohammed worked for a rich widow named Khadija, fifteen years his senior. She proposed, he accepted, they had six children, were devoted to each other and he was heartbroken when she died.

Rituals surrounding the *nikah*, or marriage ceremony, and the reception vary depending on the culture in which they take place and the tastes and wishes of the family. The Islamic requirement of marriage is very simple. All that is needed is the consent of both parties, a dowry from the groom to the bride and two reliable adult witnesses. The dowry (*mahr*) is a symbol of the groom's commitment to taking care of his wife. The value of it depends on how well-off the groom and his family are, although the dowry is often only symbolic and not necessarily of great material worth.

As for what the bride and groom wear on the day, it will conform to the normal dress code for Muslim men and women. The prophet Mohammed referred to the face and the hands as being the only parts of a woman's body that should be shown in public. Everything else is to be concealed. Her dress should be loose-fitting so that it doesn't take on the shape of the body. It may be of any colour but it must not be transparent. It is not supposed to draw attention to her physical appearance at the expense of her personality and intelligence or to make her the target of unwanted advances. Dress for a Muslim man is based on similar principles. His clothing is loose, opaque and not flamboyant. He must always be covered from the waist to the knees.

After the marriage ceremony, men and women do not mingle. It is normal practice to have women-only celebrations that include the bride but not the groom.

THE JAPANESE WEDDING

Spring and autumn are the chosen seasons for Japanese weddings. Only immediate family and close relatives are invited to be present when two people are united in marriage at a traditional Shinto ceremony. This intimate affair, at which kimonos are worn, is quite short and usually takes place at a sanctuary specially set up in a hotel or at home. Guests gather afterwards at a reception that is often big and lavish.

Money is the usual gift. It should be in crisp, new banknotes in an uneven number: one or three, rather than two or four. An acceptable amount would be one hundred or three hundred dollars. Tuck it into a special red or red-and-white envelope, write the couple's names on the front of the envelope at the bottom, and the amount of money on the back at the bottom, and place it on a black lacquer tray on the table provided for such gifts at the reception. If you present this envelope to anybody – perhaps a receptionist supervising the gift table – hold it in both hands with the front of it facing the other person.

Bride and groom sit at their table and receive guests, who offer congratulations and may toast the couple in wine, beer or sake. It is inappropriate to mention anything negative, such as ill health.

The principal speakers have their say and the wedding cake is cut before the feast begins. Festive foods might include lobster, prawns, whole fish, beef, sashimi and, of course, rice. During the proceedings, the bride may disappear and return several times wearing something different each time. A white western wedding gown is a big favourite.

Now it is the turn of anyone who wants to say a few words of congratulation or sing a popular song to get up and do so. If you take a turn, be very careful not to use words that could serve as metaphors for misfortune, such as 'break', 'drop', 'crack', and so on. The brevity of the marriage ceremony is more than made up for by the possible length of the reception, once the speeches and the karaoke get under way. The father of the groom and the groom himself probably have the last word.

At the end of the evening, each guest receives a souvenir bag of small gifts, including a piece of wedding cake to take home.

THE JEWISH WEDDING

The Jewish Sabbath, lasting from sundown on Friday until sundown on Saturday, is a day of rest when the devout avoid writing, handling money, driving, travelling, using electricity, listening to music, watching television and playing computer games. They also avoid doing certain types of work related to the creation, as God rested on the Sabbath Day and commanded human beings to do the same.

Weddings may take place on any day except the Sabbath or certain other festival days of special significance, such as Rosh Hashanah (New Year), Yom Kippur (Day of Atonement), Pesach (Passover), Shavuot (God's gift of the Torah) and Sukkot (harvest festival). They are also forbidden to marry during the Omer, the period from Pesach to Shavuot, which is a traditional time of mourning.

On the Sabbath immediately before the wedding day, the couple and their families visit the synagogue. In Orthodox communities, the groom-to-be, in front of the whole community, has the honour of being called up to recite the blessings given before and after the reading of a portion of the Torah, the five books of Moses that are the basis of Judaic teaching. In Progressive communities, both bride and groom are called to the Torah to recite the blessings.

If the wedding is to occur in the morning or afternoon, the bride and groom begin to fast at sundown on the previous day. If it is an evening wedding, they begin their fast on the morning of the wedding day.

The wedding canopy known as a *chuppah* shelters the bride and groom when they exchange marriage vows, whether in a synagogue or elsewhere. This shelter symbolises the home the bride and groom will create together. In the Jewish tradition, the home is considered holy, a mini-sanctuary, and should be treated as such.

Traditionally, the procession down the aisle starts with the rabbi or cantor, followed by the groom's grandparents, the best man, then the groom and his parents, then the grandparents of the bride, then the bridesmaids, then the bride flanked by her parents. It is very much a family affair. They all remain in or around the *chuppah*.

At an Orthodox wedding, the bride circles the groom seven times to represent her responsibility and willingness to make a home for him. Often at Progressive Jewish weddings, the bride circles the groom three and a half times and he does the same to her to demonstrate their mutual commitment to creating a home for each other.

The marriage service involves the bridal pair sipping wine from the same cup and the groom placing a plain gold ring on the index finger of the bride's right hand. In ancient belief, the index finger was directly connected to the heart. After the ceremony, the ring is given its permanent place on the third finger of the left hand.

When the pair are pronounced husband and wife, the rabbi places a glass, usually in a decorative bag, under the groom's right foot, an invitation for him to stamp his foot and break the glass, a signal for the musicians to play. There are many theories on the symbolism of this dramatic gesture but, traditionally, the breaking of the glass reminds the couple of the destruction of the temple in Jerusalem, that even in good times they must remember the tragedies which have befallen

Jewish people. In modern weddings, it is the time when the rabbi often names the grandparents or significant people in the lives of the couple who have died and are not able to celebrate their special day with them. The pieces of glass are gathered and kept in the decorative bag or framed as a keepsake for the couple. Bride and groom lead the way down the aisle after the ceremony.

The two then disappear briefly to a private room for a tête-à-tête and something light to eat, usually traditional Jewish bread called *challah* and some hors d'oeuvres to break their fast, while the reception begins immediately with lots of food and wine for the guests. When the bride and groom reappear, they are applauded and escorted to their seats at the bridal table. There is much singing and dancing to traditional tunes. At ultra-Orthodox weddings, men and women dance separately but at most modern Orthodox as well as Progressive weddings, women and men dance together.

Chapter Eleven

YOUR HABITAT

Being serious about acquiring beautiful things to last a lifetime – well, at least a decade – can start at any age but it usually happens when you begin to realise you have definite likes and dislikes. Your taste has matured. You have become selective and you want to surround yourself with only the things that please you. Until then, be careful about investing a lot of money in objects that might bore you after a while. Here are some ideas on how to establish and maintain a well-run house.

EQUIPPING YOUR HOME

Starting from scratch to furnish the place where you live, you need something to sit on, a surface to eat off and a bed to sleep in. But, given our standard of living, not to mention our aspirations now, it's not as simple as that. Then come the designer pots and pans, food processors, juice extractors, lemon squeezers and chefs' knives, apart from furniture, furnishings and big-ticket essentials such as washing machine, dryer, vacuum cleaner, dishwasher and all the rest of it.

In any case, here's a basic list to start off a pair of newlyweds:

BEDROOM

Begin with at least three complete sets of bed linen, each comprising a fitted sheet, flat sheet and two pillowcases. If you choose colours or patterns, make sure the pieces can be interchanged. For example, if one set is plain pink, another plain white and the third is in pink-and-white candy stripes, the pieces can be switched around to create different looks. It's the same principle as your wardrobe. Have as many pillows as you like to sink into – that might mean more pillowcases. For the bed you'll need: two cotton blankets; two pure wool blankets; and an eiderdown or doona. If you choose a doona, it will need at least one cover that matches the rest of your bedding. To finish off the look you might have a bedspread and a few cushions that coordinate with it. A cashmere throw, if you can afford it, is total luxury across the end of the bed.

BATHROOM

Include three sets of towels, each comprising two bath towels, two hand towels, two face cloths and a bath mat. In deciding on colours, follow the same principle as you do with bed linen. It makes even more sense to be able to mix your towels because then it's clear which towels belong to which person. For guests you'll need an assortment of hand towels in terry, linen, huckaback or a combination of different kinds. Find two different kinds of soap: big tablets for the shower and bath; small ones for the hand basin. Two large towelling bath robes are a small indulgence; they're more comforting than a towel when you step from the shower.

TABLEWARE

It's sensible to have two different sets of plates, cutlery and glassware for the table: one set for every day and the other when you put on your best bib and tucker. Ideally think in dozens rather than smaller quantities because families do grow and china and glass tend to chip and break. That's why it's a good idea to select products that are replaceable piece by piece, not just as complete sets.

Everyday tables

It's long been my theory that the objects and utensils we use every day should be even better designed than the things we rarely see and touch. Don't go for second-best just because you're looking for something that can survive the dishwasher. Many utilitarian objects are superbly designed and made, so seek out the good ones.

Your dozen place settings do not necessarily have to match, although they should all be in character – for instance, ceramics or stoneware. You could choose them in jellybean colours and have mats and napkins to match. Alternatively, wonderful bargains in blue-and-white bowls and dishes are to be found in Chinatown; they always look good on the table and are replaceable for pin money. A dozen mugs of various sorts come in handy for holding anything from morning coffee to fresh herbs.

Stainless steel is best for knockabout knives, forks and spoons. You also need a dozen steak knives with serrated blades for grilled and roasted meats. The most practical serving dishes for hot food go from oven to table. The most practical ones for salad are wooden bowls and servers. Baskets are useful for bread, biscuits, fruit and breakfast pastries. A big wooden pepper mill needs to be refilled less often than a small one. Time-saving is something to bear in mind when you shop for items you'll be using regularly. Add to your list a dozen all-purpose wine glasses that are dishwasher-proof, a dozen pilsener glasses and a dozen tumblers for water and juices.

Best-dressed dinner table

For 'best', it's usual to choose fine bone china or porcelain from a reputable maker in a style that will not date. Plain white, or white with an elegant gold or silver rim, is hard to beat, although more ornate patterns are not to be dismissed because, unless you host formal dinners every night, these decorative designs should not be on the table often enough to become tiresome. Choose a style you can buy in pieces rather than be restricted to sets, so you can start with the essentials and add to them later.

Each place setting consists of: soup dish or coupé, bread-and-butter plate, appetiser plate, dinner plate and dessert plate or bowl. If you wish, the teacup and saucer and coffee cup and saucer may be of another style if they come as complete sets with pots, sugar bowls and milk jugs. Here are some other essentials for a stylish dinner setting.

- Soup tureen
- Serving platters in two different sizes
- Serving dishes, for vegetables and meat or fish dishes that come with sauces, in three different sizes
- Small pots, jugs and dishes for sauces and condiments, such as mustard and mint sauce, because a commercial package should never be placed on a formal table; its contents must be decanted into something more decorous
- Sterling silver, good silverplate or stainless steel settings for a dozen people in a style compatible with the china. Each comprises: soup spoon, dinner fork, dinner knife, butter knife, dessert fork, dessert spoon, teaspoon, coffee spoon
- Carving fork, knife and steel for sharpening
- Serving forks and spoons of various sizes (you cannot have too many serving spoons)
- Pepper mill, salt cellar and salt spoon. If you prefer a salt mill, try to find one that really works. Salt is so corrosive it can rust or blunt the cogs, and so absorbent it can become too damp to flow freely from the grinder
- Cheese knife
- Cake slice
- A dozen champagne flutes

- A dozen white wine glasses
- A dozen red wine glasses
- A dozen tumblers for water
- Champagne bucket
- If you are a wine buff, you'll need a crystal decanter
- Candlesticks and vases, which should be either very low or very tall so as not to obstruct people's view of each other across the table

If your table has a polished surface that's easily damaged, you need a thick felt pad to go underneath the tablecloth and insulation of a similar kind under linen table mats. As for how many cloths, mats and napkins you have, there is no limit, but start with at least two formal sets, which means two dozen napkins.

The most formal cloth is white damask but much depends on your own preferences and whether or not you have heirloom embroideries that you're not afraid to put on the table. For a dinner, don't settle for table napkins that are any smaller than forty centimetres square. Lunchtime napkins may be smaller. Cocktail napkins should be smaller still.

CARING FOR YOUR NEST

A home should impart a sense of wellbeing the minute you step across the threshhold. Creating a welcoming atmosphere can be as simple as buying fresh flowers every week and making sure the sofa cushions are plumped up, papers are put away and the kitchen is tidy. Whatever you do, a well-loved home is a sign of respect for yourself and for anyone you invite in.

TABLE AND BED LINEN
A linen cupboard stocked with pristine contents cheers the heart of a devoted homemaker. Many of today's fabrics are easy-care, which

means virtually no ironing, and that makes sense, particularly when both partners go out to work and there is little or no household help.

However, there is nothing quite like the touch of fine pure cotton or linen sheets, double-damask tablecloths and napkins or table mats finely embroidered by accomplished hands in Spain, Ireland, Madeira or Italy. These traditional female skills are fast disappearing and, along with them, the mother-to-daughter secrets of caring for fine linen properly.

BEDSHEETS   Sheets should always be folded lengthwise once, then lengthwise once again. This means that, when they are stacked in the cupboard, you can tell by the width which are king, queen, double or single size. It just makes sense.

DAMASK TABLECLOTH   To iron a tablecloth, fold it in half, lengthwise, with the wrong side outward. If it has not been starched in the laundering process, you'll need to wield the commercial spray to give it body and a perfectly smooth finish. Press the cloth on one side, making a sharp crease at the fold. Turn the whole folded cloth over completely and press it on the other side. Now fold the upper side back upon itself, until its edge touches the crease. Press that side, making a second deep crease. Flip the whole cloth over and turn the other side back upon itself. Press it, creating a third deep crease. This is known as screen-folding.

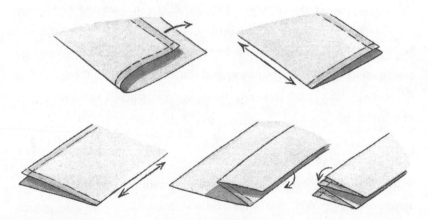

EMBROIDERY   Fine needlework rewards the person who looks after it properly. To emphasise it, always press embroidered linen on the wrong side. This helps to raise the pattern on the right side, throwing its beautiful fancywork into relief.

HAND-ROLLED EDGES   Handkerchiefs and table napkins that are hand-rolled should be ironed on the wrong side up to the rolled edge, but never over it, otherwise it will be flattened.

A STITCH IN TIME SAVES NINE   Darning and patching are thought to be very quirky by people who have never known the anguish of seeing a treasured piece of linen start to wear out. If you have not mastered these skills yourself, save your ancient linen by finding someone who has. They may be rare but they're still around. I have enormous respect for darns and patches. My favourite damask napkin has a darn that might not measure up to the work of the needlewomen of Ireland, but I am proud to have done it as neatly as I was able.

TEA TOWELS   The best are pure Irish linen, which is exceptionally absorbent, dries quickly and never leaves lint behind. They are expensive and not easy to find, particularly if you're looking for something without a pattern, but it's worth persevering. Some people iron tea towels but I prefer to dry them over a clothes horse so that they are flat but much crisper than they would be after ironing. If you dry your tea towels on the line in the sun, all the better.

STORAGE CUPBOARDS

To discourage moths and silverfish, put any combination of cloves, bay leaves, rosemary, lavender, sage, thyme or eucalyptus oil in cupboards where you store table linen and bed linen and make sure they are well aired and bone-dry.

Drawers may be lined in tissue paper, or with special scented paper made for the purpose. The drawers of the chests where I store silver and table linen are lined with hand-hemmed fabric, an idea that enraptured me when I first encountered it on a trip to France.

REMOVING STAINS

Planet earth is the only one we have. If we don't stop polluting it, it won't be capable of supporting us and we'll have nowhere to go but outer space, looking for another planet to muck up. Like charity and courtesy, being a friend of the earth begins at home, so before you reach for chemicals at the supermarket and hardware store, try some old-fashioned ingredients for cleaning and sterilising around the house.

With salt, lemon juice and a small scrubbing brush, you can make wooden chopping boards not only clean but sterilised, before you protect them with a few drops of vegetable oil. Lemon juice is a great whitener and salt a great antiseptic. Steel wool and pure soap are all you need to scrub a pot until it gleams. Baking soda (bicarb) is a harmless stain-remover and deodoriser. So is borax, although it is poisonous and must be kept out of reach of children. White vinegar has a great many purposes outside the salad bowl. Its acidity helps to cut grease in the wash and in general cleaning.

Unfortunately, I am easily seduced by convenience products so I cannot claim to be a complete do-gooding ally of the environment, but I am trying. I buy a citrus-based multi-purpose cleaner by the twenty-litre flagon and decant it for washing dishes, washing clothes and general cleaning. It is deliciously fragrant and environmentally safe.

However, there are times when a commercial product is the only truly effective thing I can find for a particular purpose. If you have greater success than me in being environmentally correct at all times, I dip the lid of my Napisan to you.

Treatment of some common stains

RED WINE If you can't pour salt over the stain as soon as it happens, soak it in cold soapy water before laundering in cold water. If the stain persists and the fabric is sturdy enough, rub salt and lemon juice into the stain or use a product formulated to clean, whiten and sterilise babies' nappies.

WHITE WINE Make a solution of 1 tablespoon of borax to 1 cup of hot water. Soak the stain for an hour before washing.

COFFEE AND TEA Soak and launder in cold water. For stains on teacups and coffee cups, soak in lemon juice or buy a bottle of solution used to sterilise babies' bottles and follow its instructions.

RUST Make a paste of lemon juice and salt and rub it into the mark. If that fails, use the excellent old-fashioned product Rustiban. If your supermarket doesn't stock it, try a pharmacy.

CANDLE WAX Cover it with ice. When it is hard, scrape what you can from the surface with a blunt knife. Place the wax mark between paper towels, brown paper or blotting paper and press with a warm iron. Keep changing the paper until greasy marks are negligible. To get rid of the last vestiges, rub with a pre-wash soaker. Launder in the usual way.

STONE FRUIT AND BERRIES Soak in a solution of white vinegar and water or borax and water.

BODY SECRETIONS AND EXCRETIONS Soak the garment in cold water until the stain is completely gone (this includes blood), then wash in the usual way. If soaking does not remove the mark entirely, launder in cold suds, or use a product made to clean babies' nappies.

WHITES THAT HAVE YELLOWED Soak in Napisan, or a similar product unless the linen is old, in which case it might be too fragile for modern treatments. Safest to leave it and pretend the colour is meant to be ecru.

MILDEW Soak in lemon juice and salt, wash in warm suds and dry in the sun.

CARING FOR SILVER

Always rinse and soak sterling or silverplated knives, forks and spoons immediately after they have been used. At a dinner party, keep a tub of hot soapy water in the kitchen for the purpose and wash and dry them properly as soon as possible.

The best way to wash silver is by hand. Dry it immediately with a linen towel in preference to letting it drain. Before you put it away, give it a light rub with a soft polishing cloth. If the object is silverplated take care not to rub too hard on the engraved moniker or you might rub it away. If you must put good silver in the dishwasher, make sure it is well separated from stainless steel.

Store it in a box with compartments lined in anti-tarnish felt, or put the pieces in the slots of a treated cloth, then roll it up and keep it in a dry place.

Take care in your choice of a silver polish. Some, particularly the dips on supermarket shelves, may be too harsh. Ask for recommended brands from a specialist, such as the shop where you bought your silver, or a trader who specialises in antique silver.

CARING FOR GLASS AND CRYSTAL

Remove the identifying labels from new glassware with eucalyptus oil, then hand-wash in warm suds and rinse in clear water. When you hand-wash stemmed glasses, hold them by the bowl rather than the stem, which is the weakest point.

To keep crystal glasses from going cloudy, wash them in hot water with a dash of vinegar. Then leave them to drip dry.

Chapter Twelve

EAT, DRINK AND BE CIVILISED

Nowhere is etiquette put to the test more tellingly than at the table. Whether formal or informal, eastern or western, the rituals that have grown up around the sharing of food and drink are aimed at civilising what in primitive terms is simply a means of survival. Good manners belong to everyday eating, to the three meals a day that sustain us, as well as to grand occasions. That is why it's just as important to eat a pie and chips in the staff canteen as neatly and ungreedily as you would a poached fillet of salmon in an expensive restaurant.

Nevertheless, there are very different rules and expectations attached to different sorts of occasions. You wouldn't hand around your finest embroidered linen napkins with the sauce at a backyard barbecue, any more than you'd put plastic plates on a formal table. Each occasion has its own set of guidelines. Let's start with the essentials and work our way up.

TABLE MANNERS

When the meal is placed in front of you, do not attempt to eat it until your hostess begins unless you are instructed to start eating the moment you are served. It is an insult to the cook to salt or season the food unless you have tasted it. If you need salt, don't fling it all over the meal, but spoon a little on to the side of your dinner plate and dip the food into it, as you need it. However, it is permissible to grind pepper over the entire dish.

Implements used for eating are not intended to be waved about like Simone Young conducting the Opera Australia Orchestra. Rest them on your plate, as explained below, while you chew your food with your mouth closed. If necessary, speed up or slow down your eating to match the pace of others.

It is perfectly good form to eat everything on your plate or to leave some of it. If you do not like any of the dishes or ingredients, on no account make a fuss. Accept everything, toy with what you don't want and leave it on the plate. Be sure to offer food, water and wine to everyone else before serving yourself.

HOW TO HOLD A KNIFE AND FORK

Hold your knife and fork lightly in your hands, with all four fingers curled around each one and the thumb steadying it. Never hold them like a pen. Use the fork, with tines pointing downward, to hold the food and the knife to cut it. Transfer the food to your mouth with the fork, never with the knife. The American habit is to cut up the food, put the knife down, transfer the fork to the right hand, turn it so the tines point upward and spear or scoop up the food.

Do not put too much food into your mouth at once. From time to time, rest the knife, with its blade inward, and fork with its tines pointing downward, on the plate at right angles to each other. Tines down indicates that you have not yet finished.

It is a breach of etiquette to turn your fork over while holding it in your left hand, in order to scoop up skittish vegetables, such as peas, although this is perfectly acceptable, indeed widely practised, in Germany. You may, however, put down your knife on the plate, transfer your fork to the right hand and, with its tines upward, use it to cradle the peas and bring them to your mouth.

When you have finished eating, place your knife and fork together, their handles pointing towards you or angled slightly to your right, with the tines of the fork pointing upward and the blade of the knife turned inward.

BREAKING OF BREAD

Whenever cut bread or rolls are offered to you, you should take one piece and place it on your bread-and-butter plate. If there is no bread-and-butter plate, place it on your dinner plate or on the upper left part of your table mat and don't worry about the crumbs. Never cut this bread with a knife. Break it in half, then into smaller pieces, which you butter (if you choose to use butter) as you need them, not all at once. If there is a small knife beside the butter dish, use it to slice off a portion of butter and transfer it to your bread-and-butter plate. If each person has been given an individual butter dish, there is no need for a communal butter knife, so you may dip in with your own. But be careful to put the butter on to your plate first, not directly on to the bread.

HOW TO EAT SOUP

If soup is served and it comes in a wide, fairly flat dish, scoop it up by pushing your spoon away from you rather than towards you. Bring the spoon sideways to your lips and sip from it without slurping. Elegant eaters take only a little at a time; it's safer that way. If consommé is served in a cup or a bowl with handles, use your spoon to consume what you can of it, then put the spoon on the saucer, concave side upwards. Pick up the cup or bowl by its handle/s and drink the rest.

COME TO OUR DINNER PARTY

Your sorties into society as a gracious host and hostess may vary in scale depending on the occasion; however, the basic principles are the same. In welcoming people into your private domain, your aim is to make them as comfortable and happy as possible. If you are wise you will not attempt anything beyond your capability and the potential of your house.

FORWARD PLANNING

Successful entertainers start planning well ahead of the date of the event. The work you put in ahead of time pays off on the day, leaving you relaxed and free enough from anxiety to enjoy your own party. If you don't nobody else will.

Write everything down: guest list, menu, shopping list, wine order. Check that you have enough plates, glasses, cutlery and chairs. Make sure the silver is shiny, glasses polished, pepper and salt mills filled and working. The linen should be impeccable and the napkins large and of an absorbent natural fibre such as linen or cotton. Have a stock of candles and back-up lightbulbs.

You'll need comfortable seating arranged for easy conversation in the living area and handy places for people to rest their pre-dinner drinks. Always include something non-alcoholic. It is perfectly correct to limit the choice of drinks; this is a private house, not the local public bar. On your checklist, put bottle opener, corkscrew and mixers, and remind yourself to get plenty of ice. Have on hand some suitable music, preferably on CD or long-playing tape, but keep it muted. Loud music is the conversation-killer of our time. To me, the civilised sounds of a chamber orchestra playing Bach, Haydn, Vivaldi or Telemann, or the piano concertos of Mozart, Beethoven and Brahms, are perfect dinner companions.

Keep the numbers manageable. Six or eight around the dinner

table is a good number for the relatively inexperienced. If you want more, then make sure you have a few close friends among them who are willing to give you a hand with serving and clearing away.

WHO'S INVITED?

The structure of the guest list will determine the pace and tone of the evening. You may choose people on the basis of their ability to help the party succeed even if you do not know them well. You may prefer to have a balance of talkers and listeners plus one or two surprises. Unless you want a cosy affair that never rises above shop talk, don't restrict the list to people who know each other well. By all means range over the age groups, but be cautious of mixing too many members of the same family or you might have to listen to carping or tiresome domestic stories.

Now that you've made your preferred list, add a couple of possibilities, just in case there are some refusals. The most sensible thing to do, before you settle on a final date, is to invite people by telephone. Do this two or three weeks ahead of time and be prepared to juggle the dates around to suit everyone. While you're at it, remember to ask if there are any foods they do not eat and make it easy for them to tell you of any dietary restrictions they might have, whether for health, religious or cultural reasons.

Having secured verbal agreement, you may wish to confirm it in writing, although it's not strictly necessary these days. Often a phone call or email confirming the time of arrival and dress is the most suitable option. It is sensible, though, particularly if you are entertaining guests from overseas, to send them a written reminder on an At Home card if you have them (see page 134), or a note on any writing paper or card you think is appropriate to the occasion. When in doubt, keep it simple.

If you do send a card, remember to cross out the RSVP and write 'To Remind' beside it because you have received the acceptance by telephone and therefore no written reply is expected.

Polly Feckleford and Ali bin Hussein
Angela and William Standawfish at Home
Dinner 8 o'clock, 4th March

RSVP To Remind
8 o'clock
32 Surf Drive
Couth Cove NSW 9496
Telephone 2928 3029

An alternative is to pen a note on regular writing paper.

32 Surf Drive
Couth Cove NSW 9496
Telephone 2928 3029

Dear Polly and Ali,

William and I are delighted that you can come to dinner on
4th March. It's very informal so please wear something comfortable.
We look forward to seeing you at around 8 o'clock.

Affectionately,
Angela

If the place where you live is hard to find, include a map. Remember, most
flats and many houses are hard to find. Some buildings have complicated
forms of security, so be clear about which buttons to press to get in.

WHO DOES WHAT?

In entertaining as a couple, divide the responsibilities between you.
Decide who will cook, be in charge of the drinks, tidy up the house, put
guest towels and fresh soap in the bathroom, set the table, light the
fire, serve the food and clear the table after each course. If you're doing
it single-handedly, ask a reliable guest to take charge of the drinks and
another to help you serve and clear away the dishes.

This kind of organisation means that you can enjoy yourself, too, and that is essential to the success of the evening.

THE MENU

Whatever the dishes you plan to serve, don't decide on anything you have never cooked before and bear in mind any dietary restrictions. Dinner guests should not be guinea pigs. Keep to something you know you can do well, even if it is just a stew. Think about a first course that doesn't have to be fussed over: smoked salmon, soup, prosciutto with melon, avocado, and a simple salad are stalwarts.

Never be afraid to serve the dishes of your heritage, even if they are not particularly fashionable. Australians are interested in food and willing to try new things, whether experimenting in their own kitchens or sitting down to try the yield of somebody else's. Be cautious, though, of ingredients that are sure to put some people off. Brains, liver, kidneys and tripe should be offered only if you know that everyone around the table has a passion for them.

Another thing to keep in mind is the appearance of the food on the plates you plan to use. White fish with mashed potatoes on a white plate does not look as appetising as it would on a coloured or patterned plate. If you love white plates – they are hard to better for a look of quality – then serve something colourful with the fish, such as spinach and sauté potatoes, or a sauce of sorrel or tomatoes.

When deciding on which wines to have with which courses, the suggested matches on pages 283–284 might be of interest.

THE TABLE SETTING

In setting the table, follow the general plan for a formal dinner (see pages 294–296) but feel free to use imagination in the choice of cloth, mats, colour, candles, china, cutlery, chopsticks, glassware, or whatever. If you do use a formal tablecloth, it's traditional to have an undercloth of felt to protect the surface of the table and to cushion noise; it should be big enough to hang about ten centimetres over all sides of the table and still be hidden beneath the tablecloth. If you are really going all out to impress, make sure the tablecloth has no creases whatsoever, which means it must be re-ironed when it has been put on the table before the rest of the setting is laid.

It is not necessary to make place cards for as small a number as eight. For ten people or more, though, it's a good idea if only to jog your memory at the last minute. It makes people feel special, too, as long as you don't misspell their names.

WHO SITS WHERE?

Always make a seating plan and take trouble over it. Don't seat two chatterboxes together or the entire table will be drowned out in their desperate desire to outdo each other. Never leave people undecided about where or with whom to sit. Letting people choose their places is like boarding an aircraft without a reserved seat: the pushy get the best ones and the polite find themselves sandwiched in the middle of the back row. They will blame you less for seating them beside someone they hate than for not bothering to seat them at all. Unless you are trying your hand at match-making, there is no need to alternate male and female, like neat and tidy couples about to enter the ark. Make a thumbnail sketch of the seating plan and keep it handy because a lapse of memory is common at the last minute for hosts with a lot on their minds.

When you've set the table, sit down at each setting to double-check that everything each person will need is to hand. Make sure your own chair gives you easy access to the heart of the kitchen so you can get up and down without disturbing anybody else.

ARRIVAL OF YOUR GUESTS

Your guests, if they are courteous, will arrive ten to fifteen minutes after the time appointed on the invitation. It is an entrenched Australian habit, and a generous one, to bring a bottle of wine to an informal dinner. Serve the wine if you wish or put it away for another occasion, unless the donor has brought something very special and there is enough for all of you.

If somebody brings flowers, of course you accept them graciously. But now is not the time to find the right kind of vase and fuss over the arrangement. Thoughtful guests do not arrive with flowers. They send them beforehand or as a thank you the next day.

OFFERING DRINKS

Take your guests' coats, scarves, hats or whatever outerwear they wish to shed and either hang them on a coatstand in the hall or put them on the bed in your bedroom. Lead them into the sitting room and offer them a drink. Instead of asking, 'What would you like to drink?', to which they might reply, 'A grasshopper' or some other concoction you have never heard of, give them a lead. Indicate the array on the side table and say, 'We're having martinis tonight or would you prefer some still or sparkling wine . . . ?' Lime juice or iced tea are good alternatives for people who do not want alcohol. Make them look special, with a slice of fresh lime, a twist of lemon peel or a sprig of mint.

Serve drinks from a tray on a side table where all the ingredients and implements are in place: bottles, glasses, bucket of ice, olives, lemons, mint, wine chilling in an ice bucket, champagne opener, corkscrew, napkins for mopping up drips, small linen mats to collect moisture from icy glasses.

Savoury titbits may be handed around but these should be very light, unless they are meant to be the first course.

WHEN'S DINNER?

Never leave your guests longer than an hour over drinks before sitting down to eat. The invitation has specified eight o'clock and guests have all arrived by 8.15, so the right time to sit down is between 8.45 and nine. Before they do, make sure they know where to find the toilet ('The loo is that way' or 'If anyone would like to wash their hands, there's a bathroom at the top of the stairs').

When you summon them to the table, the first course has been put out, your partner or volunteer sommelier is pouring the wine and bread is being offered. A nicety is to seat elderly people first, as they do in Asia. I like to see men stand until the women are seated, too. In any case, as a host or hostess, don't take your own seat until everybody else is properly settled, then pick up whatever implement/s you have laid out for the first course and tuck in. This is the signal for your guests to do the same.

Entertaining without professional help means that volunteers can always be put to work, unless you are confident of doing it all yourselves without getting into a tangle. Although wine bottles would never be put on the table at a formal dinner, it's quite okay to do so at an informal one. Glasses for water are virtually obligatory now as well, and you may fill them almost to the brim.

THE MAIN COURSE

Always warm plates on which hot food is to be served. You may choose to plate the food in the kitchen, or at a side table, although having serving dishes on the table is a guaranteed way of getting people to feel comfortable. The passing back and forth of dishes laden with delicious concoctions will help your guests get to know each other. There'll always be someone who can serve the salad with a fork and spoon in one hand. Any moment now he will admit to having worked as a waiter in order to put himself through university and that's a good conversation starter.

SPILLS AND OTHER MISHAPS

At some time, in every successful party, somebody's going to spill wine, break a glass or stumble over a priceless treasure. If it's your most precious possession, don't let it appear so. Dismiss it with a flippancy such as 'The party's started at last' or 'I've wanted to kick that pot myself for years.' And smile, though your heart is breaking. You can cry tomorrow.

TO SMOKE OR NOT

Then there is the question of smoking, not only cigarettes, pipes and cigars but illegal substances. What you do, or permit to be done, under your own roof is your own business. That being so, you dictate the rules. A guest should always ask permission before attempting to smoke tobacco in somebody else's house. Most smokers now have been made to feel such pariahs, they disappear outside automatically, even from smoker-friendly habitats. Unless the group is of one mind, nobody should seek to use illegal drugs in a social situation.

WANDERING HANDS

Unwanted advances under the table are a bit more difficult to handle decorously but a swift kick in the shins or the stab of a stiletto on the foot usually does the trick. If not, then a whispered 'I am about to embarrass you in front of your partner' should put an end to it. This threat should never become a reality. That would be too embarrassing for everyone.

TIME TO DEPART

When the table has been cleared after dessert, you have a choice of whether to stay there for tea or coffee or whether to move to another room. Shifting a group can break up a party so, if you want them to linger, stay put at the table. For a reasonably early night, try a change of territory. It's easier then to offer a nightcap or 'one for the road'.

A decent time for guests to begin to leave is twenty minutes after the dinner is finished but circumstances vary so much that your own instincts and powers of observation should be your guide. Being aware of the needs and feelings of others is a social skill of inestimable value. It's not difficult to master, if you really try.

Some people just won't go home and the worst offender is the one who has drunk too much. Handle this situation by tipping the tippler into a taxi or the back seat of a kind guest's car but never behind the wheel of any vehicle. For stayers of other kinds, these tried and true tricks are socially acceptable.

- Suggest one last drink before disappearing with the bottles.
- Look not too furtively at your watch.
- Say, 'It's been so pleasant having you here' and start tidying up.
- Collude with your partner for one of you to chide the other, very sweetly, for keeping everybody up.
- If you think you can carry it off, borrow an idea attributed to the American former talk-show host, Johnny Carson, and say, 'Would you mind very much dropping the kids off at school on your way home?'
- If all else fails, and there are no Wagnerians in the group, put on the 'Ride of the Valkyries' and say that, after that, you're going to play the whole of his weighty opera *Parsifal*. That should get them moving.

APPROPRIATE THANKS

The considerate guest will respond promptly with a thank you in the form of a telephone call, card, letter, fax or email. It doesn't matter which means you choose when the occasion has been informal, as long as you respond. To be strictly correct, you would send a card if the invitation was extended in the form of a card.

UNCORKING THE MYSTERIES OF WINE

There's an awful lot of pretentiousness and snobbery about wine and too many boring words have been written and spoken about it. By all means make a study of it, if you are so inclined, but be careful not to become a wine bore. In general, the true connoisseur never parades his or her knowledge because, for goodness sake, the purpose of wine is taste not talk. Savour in silence, as most continental Europeans do. The basic rules about wine are these.

The right temperature

Whether still or sparkling, white and rosé wines are served chilled, at a temperature of somewhere between six and eight degrees Centigrade. About six hours in the refrigerator should do. Never shock the wine by putting it in the freezer. An even better method is to chill it for half an hour in a bucket into which you have tipped a tray of ice cubes followed by a teacupful of cold water to swirl them about in. It is a mistake to serve it too cold because some of its subtlety will be lost. Put a folded napkin across the top of the bucket to keep the contents cool for as long as possible and use that napkin to collect drips from the bottle when you pick it up to pour.

Red wines, with the exception of certain light ones, such as those labelled pinot noir or beaujolais, are served at room temperature. The flavour of most decent reds is improved if they are opened an hour or so before they're to be drunk. A good red wine is likely to have sediment, which must be given time to sink to the bottom of the bottle and left virtually undisturbed until the wine is poured.

Food and wine

White wines are usually served with white meat and seafood. Sweet white wines are usually served with sweet foods. (A 'sticky' is Australian vernacular for a sweet wine.) Red wines are usually served with red meat and cheese. The word 'usually' is important here because so much depends on the intensity of flavours in the dish, which will influence the selection of the wine to go with it. Personal taste is also a crucial factor.

Traditionally, the only wine served with soup is sherry. It often accompanies pâté as a first course, too, although a good sweet wine also makes a good companion to pâté. In both cases, chill the bottle.

The respected wine writer Huon Hooke suggests the following pairings.

Most hors d'oeuvres	*Dry sparkling wine; champagne; dry sherry*
Raw oysters	*Young un-oaked semillon or sauvignon blanc; French chablis; champagne*
Crustaceans	*Various fresh dry whites, from riesling and semillon right through to chardonnay*
Crayfish/lobster	*Rich, full-bodied chardonnay*
White-fleshed fish	*Dry riesling*
Pink-fleshed fish	*Rosé; rosé champagne; light, soft red, such as a lighter pinot noir*
Chicken	*Wooded chardonnay*
Lamb	*Medium- to full-bodied red, especially cabernet or cabernet blend*
Beef	*Full-bodied red, especially shiraz or shiraz blend*
Feathered game	*Pinot noir; lighter grenache*
Furred game	*Lighter shiraz; grenache shiraz mourvèdre blends; Tuscan red/sangiovese*
Vegetable dishes	*Unwooded chardonnay; semillon; sauvignon blanc; riesling; rosé*
Cheese (hard, cooked and aged)	*Full-bodied reds, especially cabernet, shiraz and blends aged at least five years*
Cheese (blue-mould)	*Sweet whites, especially botrytis semillon and riesling; sauternes; port; dessert muscat; tokay*
Cheese (fresh and goat's)	*Young un-oaked sauvignon blanc and semillon sauvignon blanc*
Cheese (washed-rind)	*Rich traminer; pinot gris or viognier; light pinot noir; aged sparkling red*

Definition of champagne

Champagne and other sparkling wines are best served either before the meal or with the dessert. The term 'champagne' is often applied to sparkling wines regardless of their origins. That is very bad form. Only wines that come from the Champagne region of France are permitted to be described that way, no matter how good other sparklers may be and whether or not they are made by the *méthode champenoise*. Australia makes very good sparkling wines but they are not Champagne.

As an aperitif, champagne's best accompaniment is something salty: anything made with olives, anchovies or cheese is appropriate. Caviar is a natural. With dessert, beware of offering champagne with anything tasting strongly of chocolate because its subtle flavour will be overwhelmed.

Flute or flat champagne glass?

The saucer shape is said to have been developed because, originally, champagnes were very sweet and usually not drunk on their own but poured over cake or something else as part of a dessert. The compote shape was functional for this purpose, although the legend lingers that it was made in the form of Marie Antoinette's breast. A more likely possibility is that the compote shape was already in existence and the extravagant Queen of France, who was sent to the guillotine in 1793, wanted one tailor-made to her own shape. It was not until the early 1920s, when officers in England requested drier champagnes, that the flute was developed. It is still the shape most often used for dry sparkling wines.

How to open and pour a bottle of sparkling wine

- When the wine is at the correct temperature, wrap a napkin around the bottle and, holding the bottom of it in your right hand with your thumb in the indentation, undo the wire that holds down the cork and remove it.
- Grasp the cork with your thumb on top and turn the bottle, not the cork, easing the cork out gently and holding it back if you feel it is about to shoot out. Some corks are very stubborn, so it's

a good idea to buy a special implement that grips the cork more masterfully than most mortals can manage with one hand.

- As the cork is freed, it should make a soft purr, not a loud pop.
- Never use the bottle as a gun to shoot a cork at the ceiling; it is vulgar, dangerous and an offence to its delicious contents.
- Be prepared to catch overflowing foam with the napkin or a spare glass, particularly if the bottle has been moved around a bit.
- To pour, hold the bottle by its base, not its neck. Let the bubbles subside in the glass before you top it up to two-thirds full and try not to let any bubbles run down the side of the glass. If you are having a party, fill the glasses half-full a little before serving the drinks, then top them up just before serving. This 'damping down' stops the great rush of bubbles.

How to open and pour still white wine

Just like red wine, white wine develops tartrates during production that crystallise into sediment, but this is removed before the wine goes on to the market. Opening a bottle of white is simpler than opening a bottle of red because there is no need to be careful about moving it or to consider decanting.

- Cut the top off the metal or plastic sleeve that covers the neck of the bottle with a small, sharp knife or a special implement designed for this purpose.
- Draw the cork from the bottle.
- Wipe the opening with a clean cloth.
- Before you pour the wine into glasses, wrap a napkin around the bottle to collect moisture and be ready to catch random drips if necessary.
- Pour wine until the glass is two-thirds full, at most, turning the bottle and lifting it slightly as you finish so that nothing spills.
- At the table, don't wait for anyone's glass to be entirely empty before you offer more.

Opening and decanting red wine

There is no need to decant the wine unless you know there is sediment, or you want to show off a beautiful decanter that displays the wine's clarity to perfection. It's also a good idea to do it if the bottle is encrusted with grime from a life spent in a cellar. Some people believe that the flavour of a young wine improves by being in contact with air on its way into a decanter.

Wines are usually stored horizontally, in which case the sediment will have collected along one side of the bottle. Make sure you know exactly where it is and be careful to disturb it as little as possible when you bring it to the dining room – or wherever you plan to decant it – a few days ahead of time. Some people slide the bottle gently into a basket so that it sits in a kind of cannon-firing position but, unless you are a sommelier, it's not easy to draw the cork when a bottle is on its side. Stand it upright and leave it there for a few days to let the sediment collect in the bottom.

An hour before you plan to serve the wine, cut the covering from around the top of the cork, insert the corkscrew and pull, keeping the bottle as still as possible. Then light a candle behind the bottle so that as you pour the wine steadily into the decanter you can see the sediment and make sure you stop pouring before any of it finds its way into the decanter. There might be quite a bit of wine left behind in the bottle but it will be cloudy and taste of gravel. Pour it down the sink.

THE BUFFET

At informal lunches and suppers or when there are not enough helpers to serve large numbers of people at the table, a buffet is a sensible solution. However, the presentation of so many luscious-looking dishes sometimes tempts people into overloading their plates, a very bad habit.

It's not just that a huge plateful looks gross. It's also that individual flavours that somebody in the kitchen has slaved to perfect are lost in the muddle. How much better it is to take a little at a time and return to the buffet table, again and again if necessary, to savour the next tasty thing as it was intended to be eaten. That way you are paying due respect to the chef, your hosts and your fellow buffet-goers.

Thoughtful hosts make sure that delicacies likely to be very popular are also abundant. In any case, do not put all the food out at once. It's wise to hold back a quantity of each dish until the first lot has gone. That way the courteous, as well as the greedy, do not miss out and the food is not exposed for too long.

Perhaps the most important thing in presenting a buffet, apart from the food and wine, is providing enough tables and chairs for everyone to be seated comfortably, with room for their plates and glasses. It is tiresome to have to drift about clutching plate, cutlery, napkin and glass as you search for a perch, then use your lap as a table and fumble for a flat surface on which to put your glass. It is the perfect scenario for spills, breakages and embarrassment.

THE BARBY

The fun of this great Australian tradition is its simplicity. On no account attempt to turn it into something other than what it is. With ingredients of good quality – steaks, chops, sausages, fish, vegetables, fruit – little preparation is needed before they are put on the fire. The crucial part of the cooking is having the fire at the right glow and paying attention to timing.

However, only the method of cooking should be primitive. As with the buffet, which is the barbecue's refined cousin, have proper seating for people. Benches and a long trestle table are ideal for a barbecue and it is the one time in entertaining where stacks of paper napkins should be provided, along with cloth ones, because barbecued food is often finger food – that is part of the pleasure of it.

Homemade accompaniments are a special treat, although commercially bottled sauces and relishes are permissible as long as they are immaculate, with tops cleaned, when you put them on the table. Try to present them in a rustic and attractive way, each wrapped in a white paper napkin to collect the drips and perhaps stacked with the others in a big basket, with a clutch of spoons, if some are needed. Make sure there is also a vessel in which to plonk used spoons. A basket is easy to pass around so that everybody can see the full choice of condiments.

In fact, baskets are indispensable at a barbecue because they are practical, unpretentious and good-looking for bread, napkins, cutlery, fruit or whatever. Because wood is sturdy, unbreakable and more rustic than plastic, it is best for salad bowls and boards for cheese and even meat.

THE PICNIC

Experienced picnickers know that this form of entertaining is not as easy as it seems. In fact, it is one of the least controllable of all culinary occasions. Its success relies on an enormous amount of preparation and a stroke of luck with the weather. Only the brave would attempt it.

Never undertake an ambitious picnic without having chosen the spot ahead of time and make sure you have a contingency plan, just in case. Anyone who grew up in Australia knows the frustration of driving for hours without finding a place to spread the rug on the grass beside a babbling creek and instead settling at last for a layby off the freeway in mid-afternoon.

If the spot you have chosen is in a public park, ask for volunteers to get there early to claim and protect your patch and make it look inviting. Delegate responsibility: one person brings the ice, another the sandwiches, another the chicken legs, and so on. Spears of asparagus with dipping mayonnaise, spicy meat balls impaled on toothpicks, raw carrot and celery sticks with guacamole, figs wrapped in prosciutto, hummus with pita bread, homemade muffins and fruit tarts are good picnic staples. Just make sure that whatever food you bring travels well; tomato sandwiches are delicious but not after their juice has had time to saturate the bread. It's vital to make a truly comprehensive list of what to bring because once you're in the wild there won't be a corner shop. And don't bank on buying something farm-fresh beside the road; that will be the day when there is not a tomato-seller or an 'Eggs 4 Sale' sign in sight.

It should go without saying that picnic food must be capable of being eaten with fingers, not knives and forks, unless you are being trailed by a bevy of butlers and waiters. In that case, ignore the advice given here and bring on the Baccarat flutes, Villeroy & Boch plates, Cristofle forks and double-damask tablecloth.

AFTERNOON TEA

A nostalgic leftover from a more leisurely past when the English upper classes dressed for dinner at nine is tea wheeled into the drawing room on a traymobile at four or five in the afternoon. It was the quintessence of civility, involving doilies, fine bone china, polished silver, embroidered linen and that oddity known as the cake stand, three tiers of plates of different sizes to hold cucumber and watercress sandwiches, fairy cakes, diminutive pastries and homemade scones with strawberry jam and clotted cream. Cake forks? Why not! The more paraphernalia the better. There would also be a plain butter cake, just out of the oven, partially cut into delicate slices, and thin slices of buttered white bread, sometimes spread with a dark, savoury paste called Gentlemen's Relish. In winter, toasted crumpets dripping butter were very comforting.

The correct form was this. Seated beside the traymobile, as the hostess you picked up a cup and saucer, poured tea into the cup, then asked the first guest whether milk or a slice of lemon was preferred before adding anything. (Milk, as we know, must never be put in the cup first – it's not the done thing – and it must never, ever appear in its carton but in a china or silver jug.) You then asked if the guest would like sugar and, if so, how much before reaching for cubes with silver tongs. You handed the cup and saucer, with silver spoon on the side, to the guest, along with a bread-and-butter plate and a small, exquisite napkin. To avoid an ungainly juggling act, there would be a small table beside each guest to hold the teatime trappings. Think of something out of Oscar Wilde's *The Importance of Being Earnest* and you get the idea.

At least, that's the way it was done in Edwardian England where it was just called 'tea'. In Australia, we have translated that into 'afternoon tea' – a much less formal affair – which usually takes place at about four o'clock around the dinner table or outside in the garden. Delicacies from a traditional Australian afternoon tea include Anzac biscuits, neenish tarts, lamingtons and pumpkin scones. Now you're just as likely to find plump chicken sandwiches and a lemon cake, with lashings of tea and good coffee, or champagne.

THE COCKTAIL PARTY

The length of time for a pre-dinner drinks party is two hours, usually starting at 6 p.m. Because, unfortunately, some Australians are stayers, it is wise to put a finishing time on the invitation. This is easier to do in writing than verbally. Telephone the people first, establish that they are coming, then send a note or card of confirmation.

How many people you invite is up to you but make sure you have enough help to cope with the numbers. For twenty or more people, you'll need a bartender if you plan to serve mixed drinks such as fancy cocktails, and a waiter to serve them, clear away the glasses and hand around food. Well-meaning friends are a great asset but do not exploit their goodwill; they are guests, not hired help.

Determine what sort of simple finger food there'll be and whether you are going to offer mixed drinks or stick to still and sparkling wines. It is obvious which will be simpler but offering the wider choice does make the occasion special. There are some people who prefer scotch, vodka or beer to wine. In any case, always have something interesting in the way of non-alcoholic drinks – fresh lime juice or chilled fruit infusions – as well as water and present them just as attractively, with a slice of lime, twist of lemon or a sprig of mint.

If you are serving wines only, a generous calculation is a bottle per person, with a predominance of white. If you decide on mixed drinks, the basics are gin, scotch, vodka and, to a lesser extent, rum and brandy. Decide on which of the four hundred or so known cocktails you plan to offer. As a rule of thumb, four drinks per person is a reasonable amount.

Calculate about seventeen jiggers of spirits to the regular 750 ml bottle, which means seventeen gentle, dry martinis to a bottle of gin. For fifty drinks you'll need three bottles. (When in doubt, err on the generous side; a dry bar is an embarrassment.) You'll also need the mixers such as dry vermouth, soda and tonic waters; pitted green olives, lemon rind, and limes in season; a cocktail shaker, mixing glasses, jugs and plenty of ice. Provide at least two glasses for each guest: make them a mixture of stemmed martini glasses, champagne flutes, wine goblets and tumblers and hope for the best. Again, be lavish. Sometimes a certain drink can catch on like a bout of the latest flu: everybody wants the Pisco Sour from Chile, or an old-fashioned Pimm's. The time of year has something to do with what people choose to drink.

When you specify the finishing time on the invitation, make it half an hour earlier than you expect the last guest to be out the door because, no matter how clear you have been, you can bet there will be people who outstay their welcome. If this goes on too long, you may need to resort to drastic measures (see also page 282).

- Say you're meeting friends for dinner and start preparing to go out.
- Announce that you feel like a plate of pasta at the local bistro and ask if anyone would like to come. Cut short any suggestion of ordering food in by inventing a horror story about someone who was poisoned by a delivered pizza.

THE FORMAL DINNER

What happens when the Governor-General entertains at his official residence, Yarralumla, sets the standard for formal dinners throughout Australia, whether they are put on in private houses, clubs or public buildings, for social, business or political purposes. So whether you are the host or guest, this is the procedure.

For most of us, it doesn't happen very often, which is why an invitation to a formal dinner can set off a minor panic attack. Remain calm. Australia is a relaxed and unpretentious place and this is reflected in even the highest offices of government. There is no need to be nervous, even about an invitation to dine with the Governor-General. Respectful, yes. Awestruck, never. (For how to reply to a formal invitation, see page 237. For what to wear, see pages 179–182.)

YOUR ARRIVAL

The correct time to arrive is ten to fifteen minutes after the time specified on the invitation. Never bring a present, wine or flowers and never arrive early. If the invitation has specified 7.15 for eight o'clock, you should be there by 7.30 and you will sit down to dinner at eight.

You are greeted by a receiving line comprising the Governor-General, his wife and the guests of honour (if there are any) in the drawing room, diagonally opposite the main dining room. Do not dally but move swiftly along the receiving line to avoid causing a bottleneck. You should address both your host and hostess as 'Your Excellency' and any guests of honour by their formal titles, whether that means Mr and Mrs, or My Lord and Madam. As Australians we are tempted to use first names for everyone but do not presume to do so on formal occasions. When in doubt, always choose formality (see Chapter 20).

A range of soft and alcoholic drinks is offered and, during the next thirty minutes or so spent mingling and chatting, you are introduced to your dinner partner by a member of the Governor-General's personal staff and shown a copy of the seating plan.

SEATING FOR DINNER

When dinner is announced by the butler, the Governor-General leads the way into the dining room with the female guest of honour. The Governor-General's wife and the male guest of honour enter the dining room next and the rest of you follow with your designated dinner partners. Men should wait until the women are seated before they sit down.

Seating is arranged according to precedence. Place cards positioned to the top left of the settings indicate who is to sit where. Their Excellencies do not necessarily occupy opposite ends of the table – sometimes they are seated in the middle of it – but in all cases, the female guest of honour is seated to the right of the host and the next most important woman guest sits at his left. On the other side of the table, the hostess has the male guest of honour on her right and the next most important man on her left. Husbands and wives or other partners are not seated together.

THE TABLE SETTING

In front of you is a fine linen table mat (a white damask tablecloth would be equally correct). Upon it is a service plate, which will be taken away before the main course. The distance between the centre of this plate and the centre of the service plate at the next setting is exactly 60 centimetres. (The distance from the end of the table to the middle of the first service plate is precisely 46 centimetres.) A linen table napkin rests on the small plate to your left. Immediately you sit down, unfold this table napkin and place it across your lap. Keep your elbows off the table.

The menu determines the choice and positioning of the silver, but forks are lined up on the left, knives and spoons on the right, two to three centimetres from the edge of the table. The tines of forks point upward, the concave bowls of spoons also face the ceiling and blades of knives face left. Implements to be used first are placed furthest from the plate, so that you work through them from the outside in. For example, for a three-course menu of soup, a main course and dessert, working from the outside inwards, the implements to the right of your plate are soup spoon, dinner knife, dessert spoon; to the left of your plate are dinner fork and dessert fork.

Bread and butter are not usually served at a formal dinner at Government House but if they were, there would be a bread-and-butter knife at the far right of your setting – to the right of the soup spoon – which you would transfer to the small plate on your left on which your napkin was resting when you sat down. This is your bread-and-butter plate. Wait until grace is said before you touch any food or drink.

Menus on little silver stands are placed at the top left of every second setting, a considerate gesture so that you can pace yourself, knowing what's ahead. At the top of each place setting is a silver salt cellar and spoon and a silver peppermill.

While a table setting should be attractive, its decoration must never interfere with its true purpose. That is why the flowers on the table at formal dinners are low, or sprout from excessively tall, slender vases, so that people can see each other. The same applies to candles. In both cases, they are also unscented so as not to overwhelm the atmosphere. There should be plenty of space for food to be served from the left and taken away from the right, and for drinks to be poured and glasses removed from the right. Wine bottles are never placed on a formal table.

Glasses

Above the knives and spoons stands a group of glasses, lined up according to the order in which wines will be served. The largest one is for water and, because it will stay on the table for longer than the others, it is placed to the left of the other glasses or a little behind them.

Starting at the outside, there may be a small glass intended for sherry, to be served chilled with the consommé, or sauternes to be served with the pâté. It is taken away when that course is finished.

The next is a slightly larger glass, intended for the white wine, which may be served chilled with the fish or white meat course. A glass with chilled wine is held by the stem, not the bowl, so as not to warm the contents.

A larger glass still comes next and this is intended for the red wine served at room temperature with red meat or game. It is permissible to cup the goblet in the palm of your hand because warmth can do red wine no harm. Finally, only a champagne or sweet white wine glass remains, to be filled when dessert is served. A champagne glass may be a tall flute or a saucer-shaped one on a stem (see page 285).

THE FOOD

It is very unlikely that you would be given difficult-to-manage foods at a formal dinner, so don't worry beforehand that you may have to tackle an ungutted artichoke or behead and de-vein a prawn (see pages 298–307). Sometimes, if the main course is especially heavy or rich, a palate-cleansing sorbet will be served after that course. Eat it with the small spoon provided. The next course to be served is dessert, which is usually the final one at Government House although not necessarily so at formal dinners elsewhere. If cheese were served, it would appear after dessert. (At a French table, cheese would be served immediately after the main course and before anything sweet.) Port is sometimes put on the table with the cheese. According to English tradition, it must be passed around the table from left to right, never the other way.

The days of a great succession of courses are over at Yarralumla. At a typical dinner you would be given three courses, all of them easy to manage, and offered two or three different wines.

Dessert, pudding or sweet?

In England, 'sweets' are what we call 'lollies' and Americans call 'candy'; 'dessert' is fresh fruit; anything else that is sweet, sloppy, covered with pastry or firm like a cake, served after the main course and before the cheese, is called 'pudding'. This is too confusing for Australians who, like the French and Americans, feel more comfortable with 'dessert' as a term that covers anything sweet, whether pudding, ice cream or fruit, served at the end of a meal.

NEIGHBOURLY NICETIES

Apart from taking note of these niceties, you are also required to be charming to the people seated beside you. The old rule of devoting your attention to the person on one side of you for the first course, the person on your other side for the second course, and then whoever takes your fancy for the rest, is quite a good discipline, even though it should not be too obviously a calculated tactic. Don't attempt to raise your voice to communicate with someone across the table. That is very bad form, as is monopolising the conversation.

Polite subjects

The old taboos still apply at a formal dinner. Do not speak of politics, religion or ill-health. Safe subjects are the arts, travel, gardening, sport and any non-controversial events of the day. Usually the most successful ice-breaker of all is to encourage people to talk about themselves. They will leave with the conviction that you are the most intelligent conversationalist they have ever met.

LOYAL TOAST

After the main course, the table is cleared of salt cellars and pepper mills, and any crumbs removed discreetly. Glasses are then raised to Her Majesty, The Queen, in what is known as the Loyal Toast. Everyone should rise with the host, raise their glasses, repeat after him 'The Queen', and take a sip. It used to be the signal for smoking but, as in most places now, smoking is not permitted anywhere in Government House.

TAKING YOUR LEAVE

When dinner is finished, all guests leave the table and gather in the drawing room for coffee. After-dinner drinks are offered.

It is bad form to leave before the guests of honour and equally bad form to hang around for too long afterwards. Make sure you have transport waiting for you, either a car you have driven yourself or a pre-ordered limousine. Do not expect to prevail upon your hosts for assistance in getting a lift or a cab.

As a well-mannered person, you handwrite a thank-you letter promptly and post it within the next day or two. A fax, email or telephone call will not do. (See pages 137–138 for appropriate letters of thanks.)

HELP! WHAT'S THIS?

We are lucky in Australia with the wide variety of exotic foods we are able to find here. You may not have been brought up on snails or sushi, but don't let your trepidation of how to tackle them diminish your enjoyment or prevent you from sampling them. Here's an easy guide to looking like a pro at any dinner table.

All food intended to be eaten with fingers should be accompanied by an individual fingerbowl, half-filled with tepid water, perhaps with a thin slice of lime or lemon, or with weak rose tea or lemon-scented tea. Dip the tips of your fingers – don't dunk your whole hand – into the fingerbowl when you have finished eating and dry them on your napkin.

If the food is very messy – mud crab in its shell or mussels in soup, for example – hand around a basket of rolled-up damp face cloths before you clear away the dishes.

Whole globe artichoke

The best part of this glorious thistle is the bottom, which you have to work hard to reach. If the leaves of the artichoke have been trimmed so that only their edible tips remain and the choke – the bushy spikes that grow in the centre – has been removed, then everything that is left may be eaten with a knife and fork. If, however, the whole untrimmed artichoke, standing up on a plate, is presented to you with melted butter, vinaigrette or mayonnaise, this is what you do.

1   Starting at the outside, peel away the leaves, one at a time. Dip the tender end of each into the sauce and gently pull the leaf between your front teeth to detach the soft flesh. Place the leaves neatly on the edge of your plate or in an empty dish provided for the debris.

2   When you have worked your way to the centre, pick up your knife and, steadying the artichoke with the fingertips of your other hand, scrape the choke away from the bottom and place it on the edge of your plate. In a perfectly cooked artichoke, this will be easy; in an overcooked one, beware of losing half the delicious bottom; in an undercooked one, you're in for a

tussle. On no account eat the choke or you will find out why
it is so named.

3 Eat your reward with your knife and fork.

Asparagus

When only the tips are served they will be part of a composite dish so
use whatever implements are suitable for the whole dish. If whole
stems are served, the European way is to pick them up, one at a time,
by the straight end, dip the tip into whatever sauce is provided, and
consume it, bite by bite, until you reach the end or come to a stringy
part; then you simply place the remainder on the side of your plate.

Oysters on the shell

Detach the oyster from its shell with your oyster fork. The conventional
way to consume it is to spear it with the fork, dip it into the sauce provided and pop it into your mouth. If you are a purist, you might prefer
to pick up the shell, oyster and all, with your fingers, use the oyster fork
to cut through the connective muscle (known as the stump), throw
back your head, open your mouth, let the oyster and juice slide on to
your tongue and glide down your throat. It's the sort of thing you'd
imagine Horace Rumpole would do.

Mussels in soup

On restaurant menus, this is usually listed as *moules marinière*, a dish of
mussels opened up in a broth of white wine, garlic, thyme and bay leaf and
finished with cream. Separate the two halves of each mollusc with your fingers and use the clean half to scoop the mussel from the other half before
bringing it to your mouth. Finish the remaining juices with a soup spoon.

Rock lobster in the shell

Lobster is a misnomer for the creature found in Australian waters;
bereft of the big front claws of the true lobster, ours is a rock lobster,

known as crayfish in most states. Whatever its name, a crustacean of this type is usually halved so it is easy to detach the body from the shell with a knife and fork and cut slices crosswise from it. Pull off the legs with your fingers and break them in half; if the lobster is fresh and properly cooked, the flesh will spring out; give it a quiet suck to pull the rest out. If the flesh refuses to budge, give up.

Crabs and other clawed shellfish
A crab in its shell should be cracked before coming to the table. The decent host will provide implements to loosen the flesh; be uninhibited about putting them to work. Nobody who serves a dish such as this expects you to be exquisite in eating it.

Prawns in the shells
Let's hope these do not come drowned in sauce but pristine on the plate, with sauce served separately or, simpler still, with half a lemon. Pick up each prawn, take off its head and remove the tail by squeezing it. With your thumb, ease the shell from around the body, starting with the cluster of feet. The vein, which runs the length of the body and is really the digestive canal, usually has grit and waste in it, so it must be removed. Starting at the back of the neck, pull the vein out and down, bringing a little piece of flesh with it, until it is completely dislodged. The prawn is now ready to eat with your fingers or a fork.

Snails
This muscular gastropod seems to have disappeared from Australia's tables but in countries where tradition dies hard, snails are still savoured. They are usually served hot in a garlic butter with parsley in their shells, which are seated in a dish with indents or embedded in mashed potato to keep them from rolling about. You clutch the shell and hold it firmly with a pair of purpose-built tongs while you extract the body with a tiny fork. The butter, which is the most

delicious part, may be tipped on to broken bread. An easier way of serving them is without their shells in a terracotta dish made for the purpose with six pot-holes, each big enough to hold a snail and lots of garlic butter.

Fish on the bone

A whole fish can be messy to eat, so it's worth practising the technique before you tackle one in public. Run your knife along both edges of the fish to detach the spiky bits. Then cut along the middle of the back-bone before you begin to slice the first bite-sized portion. When the top side of the fish has been consumed, do not try to turn the fish over but ease your knife and fork underneath the backbone to loosen it and get at the rest of the flesh.

If you find yourself with a mouthful of bones, push them to the front of your mouth with your tongue, cup your hand, remove them as tidily as you can and put them on the side of your plate. Hold your nap-kin over your mouth if you think the whole operation might be unsightly. Mashed potato is often served with fish just in case it is needed to cushion stray bones on the way down. Bread should also be provided for this purpose.

Pasta

A fork is the only implement needed for pasta, unless it is served in broth, in which case you will need a spoon. A knife is never used. With long strips of pasta, such as spaghetti, tagliatelle and fettuccine, a spoon is sometimes provided in certain regions of Italy. If so, it is placed to the left of the plate, for it is intended to be used instead of the plate as the surface on which to twirl the long strands into manageable mouth-fuls. Straggly bits should be slurped up as cleanly and silently as possible or bitten off if they are too long. Instead of a spoon, a piece of torn crusty bread may be used as a buffer and to mop up the sauce when it is oily or creamy.

Quails and other small birds

Cut the breast down either side of the breast bone and, unless the flesh is very rare, it should come away easily. Except when the bird has been drenched in sauce, it is permissible to detach wings and legs, one at a time, with your fingers and hold them with one hand as you nibble delicately.

Lamb cutlets

When most of the flesh has been eaten with knife and fork, it is quite acceptable to pick up the cutlet by its rib to finish it off. They might even come with little white paper 'chefs' hats' to encourage you. The same applies to a rack of lamb but not to pork, veal or beef, whose bones are usually a bit too big to be gnawed elegantly in public. In any case, although you should not be excessively fastidious, it's equally important not to attack a bone with the enthusiasm of a terrier.

Bone marrow

Osso buco (a dish made from pieces of knuckle of veal, sawed through the bone) seems to be as popular in Australia as it is in Italy, where special spoons exist just for the purpose of removing the delicious marrow from the bones (coffee spoons are a possible substitute). Picking up the bones and sucking them is not recommended unless you are among people you are sure will not be offended. If in doubt, worry the marrow a bit with your knife and hope for the best.

Peas

The English require well-mannered people to carry peas to their mouths perilously on the most challenging side of the fork. This is why a soft root vegetable should be served with them, so that at least they have the chance to stick to something and not run all over the place. The only other option is to put down your knife and transfer the fork to the right hand, in which case the tines may be turned to point upward, all the better to scoop up a pile of peas. This is how the Americans handle it. In continental Europe, however, most notably Germany, it is perfectly acceptable to keep the fork in the left hand, turn the tines over so that they point upward, use the knife to round up the peas and cradle them on the fork.

Corn on the cob

This sunny vegetable is too messy to be appropriate at a dinner table but, if you do encounter it, steady it from both ends, try to keep your fingers fairly free of the butter and do not bite into the kernels so vigorously that bits get stuck between your teeth. The way to civilise fresh corn for the table is for the host to acquire special forks with knobs as handles and stick one into each end of the trimmed cob. Otherwise, take all the kernels off their cobs, put them in a serving dish and your guests can eat them as they would peas.

The modern salad

The traditional French side salad is eaten with a fork. If a knife is used, it is to help fold the leaves into manageable pieces, not to cut them. Today's Australian salads are trickier, usually presenting leaves so large and feathery they seem more appropriate as centrepieces for the table than as greens destined to be eaten. Depending on the company, it may be permissible to pick up individual pieces delicately with your fingertips – it's certainly the safest way to acquire a cherry tomato – but you'll probably find you need a knife as well as a fork to be able to manage the whole posy, dressing and all.

As the term implies, a side salad should be served on a side plate as an adjunct to a main course. At very formal dinners, you'll find this plate is often crescent-shaped to dovetail neatly with the dinner plate. In a more informal situation, use the serving spoon and fork to take some salad and put it on the same plate as your main course, or on your bread-and-butter plate, if it is clean.

Pistachios and peanuts in shells
The problem here is in the disposal of the shells. Never put shells back in the dish of whole nuts. It is a habit as bad as putting spent matches back into the box. If no receptacle is provided and there are no ashtrays, make yourself useful by finding something suitable, although not the vase on the mantel or the potted palm.

Quail eggs
They are sometimes served hard-boiled as an accompaniment to drinks. The shells are soft, speckled and fiddly to peel but once they are shed, you dip the eggs into salt or tapenade and eat them with fingers.

Sushi
Don't reach for the chopsticks. Sushi is meant to be picked up in the fingers and dipped in whatever sauce accompanies it before being eaten.

Pizza
This much-travestied Neapolitan invention was never meant to be more than a simple snack. Round and hot from a wood-fired oven, it was folded over into a half-moon before being eaten as a kind of pie. In Australian restaurants, pizzas are usually cut into wedges; the quantity of the topping and the company you are in might determine whether you eat with fingers or knives and forks.

Fruit at a formal dinner
Fresh fruit may be offered at formal dinners and is ubiquitous in many parts of continental Europe. In Australia now, it is usual for fruit to be cut up in the kitchen and ready to eat when it is offered to you at the table, sometimes with the cheese. It was not always so. Traditionally, small, pearl-handled knives and forks were provided with the whole fruit and gentlefolk were expected to know how to consume that piece of fruit in a neat and tidy way, often without it being touched by human hand.

The setting for it was brought to each place after everything but the candles and flowers had been cleared from the table. A fingerbowl and small lace mat arrived on a plate with a fruit knife and fork. You placed the fork at the left of the plate and the knife at the right. You then lifted the fingerbowl on its mat and placed it to the top left of the plate. A glass of port was offered and placed at the top right of your setting.

If unprepared fruit is offered to you, either take the coward's way and pass on it, or follow these guidelines to what is quite a nerve-wracking feat that has been known to putt a half-cut peach into an alien lap.

There are more ways than one to prepare an apple, pear or piece of stone fruit at table, but never bite into the whole fruit, as you would curled up with a book at home.

1 Stand the piece of fruit upright on your plate, spear it with your fork and cut it downwards into quarters. Remove the core or stone with the knife, while holding the quarter securely with the fork. Skin the fruit (if you dare) using the knife and fork. Cut the pieces with the knife and fork and eat them with your fork as you would a steak.

2 Alternatively, hold the piece of fruit in one hand, peel it with the knife, core it and cut it into manageable pieces and eat it with your fingers. Do this as decorously as possible.

3 If you are in a restaurant and you would prefer not to do either of the above, smile sweetly at the waiter and ask him if the chef would cut it up for you.

Take a handful of cherries and cut a cluster of grapes with the small scissors provided on the serving plate. Never pull individual grapes from a bunch on the serving plate. Ideally, the host should cut grapes into small bunches before serving. Pick up grapes and cherries with your fingers and use the palm of your hand to transfer pips and seeds from your mouth to your plate. Dates are eaten with fingers. If they have not been pitted, their stones should be disposed of in the same way as cherry pips.

Mango, one of the most loved summer fruits, has a large stone to which the flesh clings tenaciously. The best way to tackle it is to stand it, skin and all, on its side and take as big a slice as possible off each side. Then cut a deep, checked pattern in each slice, turn the skin from convex to concave and the checks will open up into chunks that are ready to be detached easily with a spoon. If no implements are provided, pick up the piece of skin and use your teeth to remove each chunk. Be careful: a good mango is very juicy.

Kiwi fruit may be peeled with a sharp knife, quartered or sliced crosswise and eaten with a fork. It may also be cut in half, each half cupped in the hand and the flesh eaten with a teaspoon. In France it is sometimes served unpeeled in an egg cup at breakfast. Figs are such a voluptuous fruit, it seems a shame to cut them into quarters or skin them but that is the polite way. The most sensual way of eating them, however, is to break them apart and tuck into the flesh and even the skin, if that takes your fancy.

Oranges are peeled with a knife in a circular movement around the fruit, taking care to remove most of the pith with the rind. Then the fruit may be cut in thin slices crosswise and eaten with a fork, or broken into natural segments and eaten with fingers. Mandarins, clementines, tangerines and tangelos are easy to peel with fingers and to break into segments.

Bottoms up!

As many designs for drinking vessels exist as there are imaginative designers and skilled craftspeople. But the best of them work within broad practical requirements that start with the type of drink the cup, glass, tankard, goblet, stein, chalice, beaker, mug or tumbler is meant to hold. The vessel should enhance the look, scent and flavour of its contents.

How you place wine glasses on the dinner table is largely a matter of good sense and personal preference, but a simple starting point is to position the glass for the wine you are serving with the main course immediately above the dinner knife. To the left of it, and slightly behind it, is the water glass. To the right of it, a little closer to the diner, is the glass for the wine you plan to serve with the first course, if it is going to be different. With consommé, for example, the traditional drink is sherry. With pâté, some people like to serve a good sweet white wine, such as sauternes. If different wines are to be served with later courses, place the basic group and then bring the appropriate glasses to the table when required. Avoid coloured glasses for alcoholic drinks, especially beer and wine, because they change the perceived colour of their contents and detract from the presentation.

STYLES AND USAGE

The best English teacups and saucers are made of delicate-looking but strong, fine bone china. The Chinese teacup has no handle and no saucer or teaspoon either, because milk or sugar are not meant to be added. To pick it up, grasp the rim with the thumb and forefinger of your right hand and hold it steady it from underneath with your left fingers while you sip. Hold the Japanese teacup in the same way as the Chinese, never with one hand only. The breakfast coffee cup and saucer are often sturdier than a teacup although the best are just as precious, in porcelain or stoneware. The demi-tasse is for black coffee. (The word means 'half-cup' in French.) For iced coffee or tea, a tall glass in a decorative metal holder is usually served on a saucer with a paper doily to stop it rattling. The ubiquitous tumbler is for water and other soft drinks. Beer glasses usually come in three sizes: the small pony or glass, the medium-sized middy or pot, and the large, tall schooner or pint. The tankard or stein is made of metal, such as pewter, or ceramic with a handle, for beer or ale. The whisky glass is ideal for whisky, gin or vodka, straight or on the rocks. It's also suitable for cocktails with ice such as Whisky Sour and Gimlet, Pimm's and

English teacup	*Chinese teacup*	*Japanese teacup*	*Breakfast coffee cup*
Demi-tasse	*Iced coffee or tea*	*Tumbler*	*Pony or glass*
Middy or pot	*Schooner or pint*	*Tankard or stein*	*Whisky*
Martini	*Champagne*	*Sherry*	*Dry white wine*
Red wine	*Sweet white wine*	*Port*	*Sake*

Vermouth. The martini glass is for true cocktails. The champagne flute is the most common these days. The sherry glass will appear on a formal table if there's consommé to start. Hold a white wine glass by the stem as chilled wines should not be held by the bowl. For red wine glasses, the bowl is a little larger than that of a white wine glass. Sweet white wine and port glasses are placed on the table only if required. A sake cup should be picked up and held in the same way as a Japanese teacup.

WHAT TO SAY WHEN YOU RAISE YOUR GLASS

Arabic countries	*Fi sihitaek*
Australia	*Good health*
Austria	*Prosit or Zum Wohl*
China	*Ganbei*
Denmark	*Skaal*
Finland	*Kippis*
France	*Chin-chin or Salut or A votre santé (or Santé)*
Germany	*Prosit or Zum Wohl*
Great Britain	*Good health (Cheers is thought to be common)*
Greece	*Steniyasas*
Ireland	*Sláinte*
Israel	*L'Chayim*
Italy	*Salute (noble Italians say nothing)*
Japan	*Kanpai*
Korea	*Gunbae*
Netherlands	*Proost*
Norway	*Skøl*
Poland	*Na zdrowie*
Portugal	*Sáude*
Russia	*Na zdorov'e*
Spain	*Salud (or 'Salud, pesetas y tiempo para gasarlas', which means 'Health, money and the time to enjoy them')*
Sweden	*Skøl*
Turkey	*Şerefe*
United States	*Good health or Here's looking at you*

The rich diversity of Australia's tables

Ask people of different religious and ethnic backgrounds how they place knives, forks, spoons and plates on the table and you get some very interesting and often conflicting answers. The correct form varies not only from one nation to another but often from one social or geographic group to another within that country, not to mention the different sets of social niceties surrounding the shared table. When you ditch the cutlery altogether or replace it with chopsticks, the etiquette changes yet again.

Dishes that many Australians now prepare and eat at home incorporate influences from the cuisines of many cultures. Look into our shopping baskets and kitchen cupboards and see how commonplace are lemongrass, ginger, soy sauces, mirin, couscous, burghul, tofu and coriander. You have only to watch a bit of television to see that stirfrying has become so ubiquitous that manufacturers of packaged food have devised products specifically for this method of cooking which, a generation ago, was not seen outside Asian restaurants.

The table settings most of us grew up with are not always appropriate to the foods we eat regularly now. Table settings have to evolve to cope with Vietnamese noodles, Moroccan tagine, Indian rogan josh, Japanese suki yaki, Italian fettuccine, Chinese suckling pig and the fusion known as modern Australian cooking.

Since, as far as I know, no higher authority has yet laid down the ten commandments of contemporary Australian table etiquette, let's make up our own from some of the following.

THE AMERICAN TABLE

An American table is set in much the same way as an Australian one, except that the bread-and-butter plate is placed directly above the forks instead of beside them. Diagonally across it rests a butter knife with its blade facing the diner. If oysters are to be served, the fork for them is placed to the right of the knives. Disregarding the oyster fork and the butter knife, there should be no more than three sets of implements on the table at one time. If there are to be more courses, the silver is brought with them when they are served. Glasses are grouped according to size, not the order in which wine is to be served. What we call 'cutlery' and the English call 'silver', Americans call 'flatware'.

When Americans use a knife and fork for a dish, they cut the food as we do but the knife is then put down, the fork transferred to the right hand and turned over, tines facing upward, to pick up the piece to be eaten. It is not good form to cut up a lot of pieces at a time, as you would for a child; a piece should be cut and eaten before the next is cut. Knife and fork (tines up) are placed together on the plate diagonally from top left to bottom right to indicate that you have finished.

Salad is often served as a first course at informal lunches and dinners. This habit has the singular advantage of ensuring that every leaf is likely to be eaten because the edge hasn't yet been taken off people's appetites by more substantial courses. Americans refer to their main course as the 'entrée', the term we use for an earlier course.

THE CHINESE TABLE

The Asian table with which Australians have long been familiar is that of the Chinese who have been here in sizeable numbers for at least 150 years. For generations, every suburb and town throughout the land had a Chinese restaurant, although plenty of their dishes – curried prawns and rice, chicken with almonds – had been adapted to the local taste, so they bore little resemblance to either their provinces of origin or the choice we have now.

Chopsticks are placed on a ceramic rest, at the right-hand side of the table setting, where we would place the dinner knife in a western setting. If you are uncomfortable with chopsticks, don't hesitate to ask for a spoon and fork. Knives are never used at a Chinese setting. Each setting has a bowl for rice on the left, a small plate that is flat like a bread-and-butter plate and a teacup at the top right.

It is discourteous to refuse a drink when it is offered. Similarly, you should be willing to taste every dish offered to you. The correct way to hold a cup of tea or wine is to pick it up with the forefinger and thumb of your right hand around the rim and steady it from underneath with the fingers of your left hand.

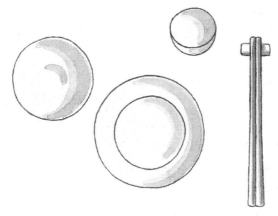

The Chinese share their dishes and, except at a banquet, everything is put on the table, or on a rotating lazy Susan, at the same time. Separate chopsticks or spoons should be provided for each serving dish. If they are not, turn your own chopsticks around when you help yourself from the common bowl. Wait until your host invites you to eat before you take any food. Unless you are the guest of honour, it is courteous to wait until people your senior have helped themselves.

As with Japanese meals, it is customary to pay homage to the rice by eating a little of it before anything else and then to eat it spasmodically throughout the meal. Pick up the bowl, then your chopsticks, hold the bowl close to your mouth and gather up the rice with your chopsticks. If you finish the rice and you'd like more, pick up the bowl with both hands.

While rice and noodles are symbolic at a banquet, they are generally considered to be fillers. When you are a guest in a private house or a restaurant, it is not polite to each too much rice because it suggests that there are not enough dishes to satisfy your appetite so you need to fill up on rice.

Try not to drop your chopsticks as it's considered bad luck. Don't cross them like swords. Don't suck them either. If you take a lengthy pause between mouthfuls, put your chopsticks down with their points on the rest, if one is provided, or on the small dish that holds your individual portion of soy sauce. You may also rest them side by side across your rice bowl but never stick them into the rice.

Food that is runny with sauce may be spooned over the rice in your bowl. Any foods that are not sloppy can be picked out of the serving dish with chopsticks and placed on your flat plate. Make sure you do not take too much. It's not considered polite in a private house to leave food on your plate. At the end of the meal, if you use a toothpick, cover your mouth with your free hand.

At yum cha (also known as dim sum), when lots of small dishes in bamboo steamers are wheeled by on trolleys, it is not good form to put more than one piece of food on your plate at a time. It is permissible to pick up buns and custard tarts and eat them with your fingers. Young people pour tea for their elders, never the other way around. To acknowledge the gesture of tea having been poured for you, cup your right hand and tap the table lightly with the nail of your middle finger; it means thank you.

There is an interesting tale associated with the origins of this gesture. Once upon a time, there was an emperor who wished to be incognito when he travelled around the country. His attendants had the dilemma of wanting to acknowledge his status without compromising his anonymity so, instead of bowing to him as they normally would, they signalled their respect by tapping their fingers on the table.

In general, be unassuming about yourself and your accomplishments in the company of Chinese people. If someone pays you a compliment, accept it modestly and protest that you do not deserve it.

Showing off is not well regarded by the Chinese, who keep a low profile because, as their wise saying goes, 'a tall tree catches the wind'.

Gifts for your host

It is polite to give a small present to your hosts if you are being entertained at home, but choose your offering very carefully. Chinese delicacies from overseas are highly prized but, unless you are a connoisseur of all things Chinese, you risk choosing the wrong thing. Fresh fruit is a good choice, as long as it's not a melon, certainly not a watermelon, because the word for it in Cantonese sounds like the word for death. Give an even number of things, although don't bring anything in fours; to the Cantonese and Hokkien people, four is an unlucky number because it sounds like death, too. Six is good, so is eight. An acceptable gift would be six or eight apples, oranges or, better still, mandarins, which symbolise good luck.

THE FRENCH TABLE

When the French set the table, they turn the forks and spoons the other way around from the direction Australians do – that is, with the tines (prongs) of the forks and the bowls of the spoons facing down. (Some say that this is to show the hallmarks or the moniker on the silver, but I'd take that with a grain of salt.) The dinner knife, with its blade facing left, may rest on a *porte-couteau*, a little silver bar that lifts it off the table; at informal family or country dinners in France you may be asked to keep your knife and fork for the next course, in which case you rest both on the *porte-couteau* between courses.

Unlike in England, where you must keep your hands off the table and in your lap, in France you must keep your hands on the table, otherwise who knows what they might be up to under the table?

Another difference is the order of courses. The French serve cheese before the dessert; the English serve it afterwards. For a simple lunch or dinner in France the order of courses goes like this: hors d'oeuvres, main course, salad, cheese, dessert. The hors d'oeuvres will probably be on the table before you are seated; the other courses are presented on serving dishes. Don't start to eat until your host or hostess begins. 'Bon appetit' should be said once only, just before the first mouthful is taken, and not repeated.

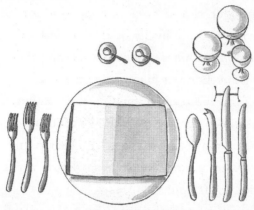

When a course is placed in front of you, it is very bad form to touch the plate, to turn it around or, in the case of a soup plate, to tilt it away from you to scoop up the last drops. If soup is served it will be eaten with a pointed spoon, shaped like an oversized dessert spoon. Do not sip from the side of it but from the point.

Well-brought-up French children are taught never to use a fork as a spoon, but to use it to steady food that is being cut and to spear the food to pick it up. They are also taught that if the meat you are eating belongs to a creature that can fly, you may eat it with your fingers, although it is not considered *comme il faut* (proper) at a formal dinner to eat any food with your fingers except for asparagus and bread, which must be broken, never cut. You break off a small piece and eat it before you break off the next. If you want to finish the sauce on your plate, spear a small piece of bread at a time with your fork and mop it up that way, but only if you see your host doing it. Always take the lead from your host.

More than one wine is likely to be served, beginning with the lightest and gradually becoming more full-bodied as the courses progress. When the French raise their glasses they say 'Chin-chin' or 'Santé' (health). The host first pours a little of the wine for himself to taste. Having established that it is satisfactory in temperature and flavour, he then serves the women first, starting with the one on his right. No matter what the level of formality or who the guests are, women are always served first with food and wine.

If there is meat to be carved, it is up to the man of the house to do it. The French pay particular attention to the presentation of food and find any dish that is not good-looking to be suspect.

At a very formal dinner in France, there are often additional courses, including an entrée, served after the hors d'oeuvres. It may be followed by a lemon sorbet and a glass of calvados (the palate-cleansing apple brandy of Normandy), which is said to stimulate the appetite for the main course.

In expensive restaurants, a small delicacy sometimes precedes the meal. This is called an *amuse-bouche* or, more vulgarly, an *amuse-gueule*.

Salad, served on a fresh plate, may be eaten with knife and fork but it must never be cut. If the leaves are too big to go into your mouth with decorum, you may fold them with your knife and fork.

When you have finished a course, leave a little on your plate to indicate that you have eaten well, and place your knife and fork together with handles pointing to the right, the tines of the fork pointing upward and the sharp edge of the knife facing the fork. If you've seen French people leave their fork and knife spreadeagled across the plate, do not imitate them. It is simply not done in polite circles.

Cheese, which is eaten with a knife and fork, is served on a platter that must pass around the table only once before being taken back to the kitchen. Since you will not be offered a second helping, take as much as you want while you can. One theory behind this practice is that, because French cheese is often deliciously whiffy, it could be overpowering if it stays too long in the dining room. When you cut the cheese, leave its shape intact; for instance, if it's a piece of brie or camembert, slice off a wedge-shaped sliver, don't hack off the best bit at the end.

If whole fruit is served at the end of the dinner, you will be held in high esteem if you render it edible with a knife and fork instead of fingers (see also pages 305–307). Never ask for milk with your coffee. The French, like the Italians, believe milk belongs in the nursery and, for adults, at breakfast only.

Gifts for your host

Gifts of any kind are inappropriate at a formal dinner, and if you are thinking of taking a bunch of flowers to your hosts on a less formal occasion, don't. Send them on the morning before or the day after. Take care in choosing them. The superstitious in France believe that carnations bring bad luck, yellow flowers point to infidelity and chrysanthemums mean death.

THE INDIAN TABLE

Beside the front door of a house in India there is sometimes a pot of water. Before going inside, you take off your shoes and wash your feet. It is still the custom to take off your shoes before entering a Hindu house, no matter where it is. Hinduism, encompassing innumerable sects, is the predominant religion in India and many people who practise it are vegetarians. Even those who are carnivorous do not eat beef or veal.

Food is not eaten with implements other than the fingers of the right hand (never the left hand, which is associated with the body's nether regions). Before they eat, Hindus pick up a small portion of rice and put it aside in gratitude for the food.

THE ISLAMIC TABLE

Take off your shoes before you enter a Muslim house. You will be warmly greeted. It is an Islamic practice for Muslims to greet each other with the words 'Peace be with you'. The golden rule when greeting is not to offer your hand to a Muslim of the opposite sex unless you know it will be accepted because physical contact between people of the other gender is not allowed unless they are members of the immediate family. It is important to behave in a reserved manner when in the presence of Muslims. Take note of your body language and be careful not to show the soles of your feet when you are seated because it is considered offensive to people of some cultures.

Bringing a present is quite acceptable as long as it does not contain alcohol, gelatine or pork; if it's meat, make sure it is labelled 'halal'. The term halal refers to the Islamic procedure applied to ensure that the animal is slaughtered quickly with minimum pain and suffering, and that the name of God is invoked at the beginning of the procedure. Islam forbids the consumption of pig meat and any derivative. It also forbids the use of any kind of intoxicating drink. The consumption of healthy food and a healthy lifestyle are seen as an integral part of Islamic beliefs.

Before eating, grace is said: 'In the name of God, Thank you God for the food you have given us.' Food may be eaten with the fingers of the right hand (not the left) or with spoons, forks and knives. When they have finished eating, Muslims say 'Thank God'.

THE ITALIAN TABLE

Like some other countries in continental Europe, Italy is more a collection of highly individualistic communities than a homogeneous whole. Different regions have their own specialities and local customs die hard.

Given the choice, Italians prefer their own regional produce to anything imported – even if it's just from a neighbouring province – and are happy to pay a premium for something grown virtually in their own backyards. As with the Chinese, freshness is an obsession, which is why most of their cuisine is seasonal. In a proper Italian kitchen, the only permissible tinned foods are anchovies and tomatoes.

A useful thing to know about Italians is that a person's appearance is extremely important. If you are stylishly dressed and well groomed – good presentation is known as *la bella figura* – you will be given respect, admiration and, in an authentic Italian restaurant, excellent service. Taking pride in your appearance is a national imperative, as you cannot fail to notice in the streets of Rome and Milan.

In everyday settings, Italians do not clutter the table, so implements are often not laid all at once but brought with their relevant courses, as they are needed. Spoon (and sometimes a fork) for the dessert are placed at the top of each place setting. A typical menu goes like this: antipasto, pasta, main course (meat or fish), salad, dessert.

Pasta must be eaten with a fork, which is placed at the right-hand side of the plate. Italians never twirl their spaghetti in the bowl of a spoon although sometimes they place a soup spoon to the left of the plate for the convenience of a foreigner whom they think might not be able to manage lengthy strands of pasta with a fork in the Italian way. Use it only if you must. Never cut pasta with a knife or you will be considered barbaric.

If pasta is served with a seafood sauce, never add cheese. (For guidelines on how to eat spaghetti, see page 302.) Salad is served with the main course but a separate salad plate for it is provided for each person.

When you have finished, lay forks on the plate with their tines pointing down. Not so in Greece, though. The Greeks cross knife and fork, with the knife underneath and the prongs of the fork facing down to indicate that they have finished.

THE JAPANESE TABLE

In a traditional Japanese restaurant or at a private house, take off your shoes at the door, leave your socks on and use the slippers provided. When you are invited to the table, you may be seated on a chair, or on a cushion on the floor with your legs underneath you or to one side. Men usually sit with their legs crossed in the lotus position. Allowances are made for Australians who are not used to sitting in a cramped position for an extended period of time, so manoeuvre yourself into a position that is dignified but comfortable. Sometimes there's a shallow hole under the table so that the floor acts as a ledge; you perch there with your legs in the hole.

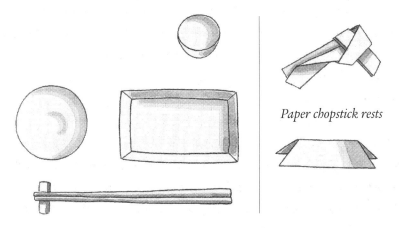

Paper chopstick rests

Table napkins are not provided. Instead, you are offered a moist terry-towelling cloth before and after the meal. Japanese carry handkerchiefs – often fine and decorative – which are not intended for blowing the nose, something regarded as so offensive that no Japanese would ever do it in public, much less at the table. They may use one to mop their faces or wipe their hands. It is perfectly acceptable to lay a clean handkerchief in your lap at the table and use it as you would a regular table napkin.

Chopsticks, which in Japanese are called *ohashi*, are placed on the table horizontally immediately in front of you with the narrow ends facing left and resting on a little stone or ceramic stand, which is called a *hashioki*. There are also two bowls. The one on the left is for rice. The one on the right, usually lidded, is for soup. A teacup, glass or sake cup is placed at top right.

It is bad form to pour sake for yourself. When your host or somebody else is about to pour sake into your cup, pick it up, hold it in your right hand, support it with your left hand, bow, say thank you, sip the sake and put the cup down. It is then up to you to pour a drink for your host and remember to fill the cup completely. *Kanpai* is the Japanese word for 'cheers'. Your host will make sure that your cup is never empty.

Courses may be served individually on a series of different plates and bowls chosen to complement the particular food they bear. Frequently, though, a complete meal for each person is served at once on a square or oblong lacquered tray, often with divisions in it for individual foods.

Sometimes the two *ohashi* are joined together and sticking half out of a paper sleeve. Take them out of the sleeve and separate them by pulling them apart. This should be done discreetly and delicately. If there is no *hashioki* on which to rest the chopsticks, take the paper sleeve, tie a loose knot in it and use it as a rest. To manipulate the chopsticks, pick them up in your right hand (unless you are left-handed) and, holding them at the thick end, keep one resting firmly in the curve between your thumb and forefinger and the other loosely held between the forefinger and the middle finger, so that you can move it up and down. Use them like pincers to pick up food with the tips.

When the host indicates that it is time to eat, the guests respond with 'Itadakimasu', meaning 'thank you'. Sometimes the host says it too, out of habit or as a kind of thanks to otherworldly powers. It is customary to eat a little rice, the staple food of the Japanese diet, before you touch anything else on offer. Pick up the bowl and tilt it slightly towards you, bringing it close to your chin, then you eat a little with your *ohashi*.

Then take the lid off the soup bowl and place it upside down on the table or tray. Pick up the bowl with two hands, then cup it in your left hand and single out solid pieces – tofu, seaweed, bits of vegetable – with your *ohashi*. To consume the soup, steady the side of the bowl with your right hand, and drink some of it. Take a little more rice. After that, choose whatever you want from the food set before you. Eat morsels from several dishes in succession, including the rice and soup bowls, rather than stick to one dish at a time, so that you finish them all at about the same time. Make sure you eat all the rice because it is considered discourteous to leave any.

Making a slurping noise when you eat noodles in soup is acceptable in Japan but in Australia some people might find it offensive if you slurp excessively. If pieces of food are too big, they should be worried apart with your *ohashi* (it's often not easy, with the obligatory one hand) rather than picked up whole and bitten in half; you should never take a bite of food and put the rest of it back on your plate.

A man often eats sushi with his fingers, but a woman would normally use *ohashi*. Check this with your host before you start. If the sushi has raw fish on one side, that is the side to dip into the sauce. Never spear food with your *ohashi*, or procrastinate with them hovering over the food, a practice the Japanese call 'dithering'. Pickles, which are used as a palate cleanser always appear among the main dishes.

If there are no serving chopsticks or spoons and you want to help yourself to more food from a communal bowl, turn your chopsticks around so that the thicker ends touch the food and not the thin ones that have been in your mouth. Transfer the food to your bowl or plate, but not to your rice bowl, which should remain pristine, and never straight to your mouth.

Never use chopsticks to drag a bowl closer to you. Never stand chopsticks upright in a bowl of rice; that's what offerings for the dead look like at Buddhist shrines. Never touch or hold anything with your *ohashi* that someone else is touching with theirs; this is the way families pick up the bones of their loved ones from the ashes of the cremated body. Lay them neatly side by side in front of the bowl with the thin ends pointing left and resting on the *hashioki* or the knotted paper sleeve. If you stick the *ohashi* through the knot it signals that you have finished eating. If a stand has not been provided, rest them across your rice bowl but not flat on the surface of the table. At the end of the meal put any lids back on their bowls.

You will endear yourself to your hosts afterwards if you bow a little and say, 'Go-chiso-samadeshita' to acknowledge your appreciation of their hospitality.

Going to the toilet

When you go to the toilet in a private house, you may find another set of slippers outside the door to it. Step out of the slippers you are wearing and step into these other slippers because they are meant to be worn in the loo. If you are confronted by a Japanese-style toilet, face the hooded end and squat there. When you leave the room, put your own slippers on again to go back to the table, leaving the loo slippers where you found them.

Gifts for your host

The Japanese are forever giving presents so it is very important to reciprocate but with caution. Avoid giving four of anything because that number is associated with death. A box of chocolates or a bottle of scotch is usually welcome. Anything small and delicate will be received with delight. The packaging is almost as important as the gift itself, and while few of us can hope to match the exquisite wrappings that materialise from nimble Japanese fingers, your efforts will be noted and appreciated.

Other Asian tables

A spoon and fork replace chopsticks on the Thai table; the fork is used to prod food into the spoon, which then takes it to the mouth. A typical Thai repast is made up of soup, a fragrant curry or spicy salad and fried fish with dipping sauces. All dishes, except desserts, are served at once. Some Koreans prefer to eat with a spoon and fork rather than chopsticks because it's thought to be neater and tidier. Vietnamese settings, rules and taboos at the table are similar to Chinese.

Chapter Thirteen

HOUSE GUESTS

Regardless of the scale of your accommodation for people staying a night, a weekend or longer, there are certain basic obligations for hosts and guests. When you are the host, it's your overall responsibility to set the house rules and make them clear. When you are the guest, it's up to you not only to accept those rules willingly but to be sensitive to the ones that are unspoken, such as leaving shower walls and bath tubs clean and dry, knowing how to make yourself useful and not outstaying your welcome.

DOES YOUR HOUSE MEASURE UP?

Before you ask anyone to stay, cast a cold eye over your abode to determine whether or not it can accommodate overnight guests with relative ease. A lot depends on your age group and the character of the guests. If you are students, then bunking down on sofas or in sleeping bags all over the place and queuing up for the solitary bathroom can be great fun. Not so once you reach the age of reason. The need for privacy and comfort grows with age and privilege. Mentally match up the people you plan to ask with quarters you have to offer and make sure they are compatible before you extend an invitation. For each couple, or each single guest, the ideal arrangement is a room with its own bathroom.

EQUIPPING THE GUEST ROOM

The bed must be comfortable – no making do with sunken springs and a cast-off mattress – and for each guest there should be a choice of at least two pillows, one firm, one soft. Sheets and pillowcases should be fine and pale because vivid colours and patterns are not to everybody's taste. Be generous with the blankets; better too many than too few.

Don't clutter the surfaces of tables, benches or chests of drawers with useless ornaments and dried floral arrangements. Your guests will find much greater charm – in fact, bliss – in a clean surface on which to put their personal items. They will also appreciate a luggage rack or somewhere to stow their bags so they're not falling over them all the time.

Three essentials are a light perfectly positioned for reading in bed, a full-length mirror and an easy chair. Replace any wire coathangers with proper ones in the wardrobe, which must otherwise be empty, and make sure drawers are clean and lined with fresh paper. A thoughtful optional extra, depending on the size of the room, is a table near the window with a notepad, pen and pencil. If you have writing paper printed with your address, add that too, along with envelopes; it's fun to write letters from somebody else's address and, often, there's more time to pen something than there would be at home. If the bathroom has to be shared, put a little wooden clothes horse in the bedroom on which damp towels can dry.

Added comforts

Useful extras include a small pile of suitable reading matter, such as magazines, volumes of short stories and coffee-table books. Add a vase of fresh flowers from your garden and if there is room for them, a bottle or jug of water, a glass, a bowl of fruit and a tin of homemade biscuits. It's unlikely that there'd be a blackout, but who knows? Just in case, provide a candle and matches, so they won't be groping around in the dark. If the weather is warm, better include insect repellent. If the weather is cold, there's nothing as comforting or homey as a hotwater bottle, as well as room heating.

Guest bathroom

Provide each guest with a bath towel, hand towel, face cloth, bath mat and, if you really want to spoil them, a big towelling robe. A good magnifying mirror and a powerful hair dryer will be gratefully received. Don't forget the waste basket and the dunny brush. Put a selection of soaps, a box of tissues, toothpaste, spare toothbrushes, mugs, cotton balls, shampoo, body lotion, bath foam and headache pills in a basket on the bench or in the cupboard above the basin. Under the basin, stack lavatory paper and back-up tissues.

WEEKEND HOUSE PARTIES

First, choose the group carefully. While assembling people with diverse opinions might make for a stimulating dinner party, it's not a good idea to have them in close proximity for any length of time. People who are full of wit and humour at dinner might be disagreeable next morning and that can be unpleasant. Although they need not necessarily have met each other before, they should have some interests and beliefs in common.

Unmarried couples

Even if you know that a man and a woman, or a man and a man, or a woman and a woman, share a bed at home, don't assume they will want the same arrangement in somebody else's house, where there may be people they have never met before. Since you must know them quite well if you've invited them for the weekend, ask them openly. If possible, give them a choice of sleeping in one bed, separate beds, or in separate rooms, if they'd prefer.

EXTENDING AN INVITATION

Be clear and specific when you invite people on the telephone or in writing. In fact, to avoid any misunderstanding, it's best to call them first to secure a commitment, then follow it up in writing with all the details, including any planned activities, so they know what to pack. Do it a few weeks ahead of time and be prepared to suggest more than one possible date if you have hand-picked a group on the basis of compatability, so as not to risk anyone being otherwise engaged. Remember these points.

- Be specific about the length of stay by telling them when they are expected to arrive and to leave. For instance, 'We'll expect you for supper on Friday and that means two full nights before you leave after lunch on Sunday.'
- Tell them who else is coming and briefly give the background of anyone they have not met before.
- Make sure they know how to get to your house, or where you plan to meet them. Put it all in writing, together with a map, so there can be no mistaking the time, date and place.
- If you are laying on bath robes, hair dryers, beach towels and sun hats, let them know. They'll be grateful not to have to pack them.

A GUEST'S RESPONSE

- If, for any reason, you are not sure whether you can make it or not, turn down the invitation straightaway. It's inconsiderate to wait until the last minute to confirm because, if you pull out then, it's too late for your host to fill the gap.

- Once you do accept, on no account change your mind.
- Don't expect others to provide transport. If it is offered, accept graciously. If not, then find your own way there and home again.
- Make sure you know the degree of formality to expect and any social events your host has planned and pack appropriately. Make sure you don't forget anything. Borrowing a jacket and tie from your host, or pantihose and dressy shoes from your hostess or anybody else, is an imposition.
- Take a gift and don't leave the choice to pot luck on the way. Rather than give them a decorative object for the house that may not suit their taste, make it something that's both luxurious and useful during the time you'll be there. Good presents include new books, videos, CDs, flowers, wine, soaps and fancy foods. Most people like smoked salmon, exotic cheeses and seasonal fruit, such as mangoes, peaches and cherries. Be generous with the food and wine so there's plenty for everyone.
- This is one time when a mobile telephone is very useful because, if you do have to make a telephone call, you don't need to bother your hosts. However, turn it off for the rest of the time. If you must check your voice mail, disappear into the garden or somewhere out of sight, once a day, to retrieve messages. Make any calls while you're at it, then turn it off and put it away.

ARRIVAL OF YOUR GUESTS

Make sure you are home and well organised by the time your guests are due on Friday night. Allow for flexibility in their arrival times because traffic is unpredictable and, no matter how carefully you have briefed everybody on how to find your house, somebody is likely to get lost on the way. Therefore, whatever you've planned to serve should be capable of waiting without spoiling. Keep it to one course, plus cheese and something sweet. Salads are good in summer. Casseroles and thick farmhouse soups are the way to go in winter.

HOUSE RULES

Give people time to unpack, settle in and have a drink before you sit down to eat. Over supper, explain the house rules. If you have staff to run the place or day help coming in to prepare meals, make beds and tidy up, briefing your guests will be simple. Tell them where and when meals will be, and whether or not breakfast may be brought to the room if any guest prefers it.

The easiest, and perhaps the most satisfactory, way to serve breakfast is to put all the fixings on a bench in the kitchen – basket of breads and pastries, toaster, butter, jams, cereals, fruit, milk, coffee and tea – and let everyone help themselves. Unless you are in snow country, a cooked breakfast should not be necessary. If it's icy, fill them up with porridge.

If there are any idiosyncracies in your house that could cause embarrassment – a tricky flushing system in a bathroom, a stubborn lock on the door, a window that gets stuck – tell everyone about them and fix reminder messages on the trouble spots so that nobody makes a mistake.

A good host would always invite guests to make themselves at home, which includes helping themselves to tea and coffee, fruit from the fruitbowl and making telephone calls whenever they want; however, a good guest would always ask permission first. Asking people to make their own beds should also tell them they are expected to keep their rooms tidy and their bathrooms sweet-smelling, spick and span.

WEEKEND ACTIVITIES

Don't be too bossy about organising your extended family. Give them time to themselves, especially if you are at the beach or in the bush where just being with nature is a pleasure in itself, especially for city people or visitors from abroad. In general, arrangements for daytime should be left loose – unless the purpose is picnic races or some other sporting event – so that evening becomes the time when everyone gets together to talk about the day's doings.

As host, you must take responsibility for providing meals but that doesn't mean you have to do everything yourself. Delegate. Good house guests know how to make themselves useful without getting in the way. Put them to work on specific tasks: one to set the table, another to prepare the salad, someone to be in charge of the drinks, and so on. If someone in the group is an especially accomplished cook, a smart host will make sure this skill is applied at some time during the weekend. Guests love to feel they are useful. It gives them a sense of belonging.

THE WELCOME GUEST

Be punctual, sociable, look your best and obey the house rules.

- Offer to help and do whatever is asked of you readily and cheerfully.
- Some people hate having others around when they are working in the kitchen. If your host says your presence is not required there, make yourself scarce.
- Strike a careful balance between relentless affability and silence. People who talk all the time are exhausting. Those who say nothing are a burden.
- Be self-motivating. Don't hang around waiting for someone else to find something for you to do.
- Keep your room tidy and make your bed every morning.
- If you have to share a bathroom, don't monopolise it. Always leave it immaculate, whether or not you found it that way.
- Heavy make-up and jewellery are not appropriate at the breakfast table. Neither is a dressing gown.
- If there are pets in the family, respect the house rules about whether or not they should be inside and never feed them from the table.
- Never outstay your welcome. Leave at the agreed time.
- On the morning of your last day, if there is no household help, ask your host what you should do with the bed sheets and towels.

- If there is help in the house, ask your host if you should give them a financial token of appreciation for the extra work they've had to do because of your stay and, if so, how much.
- When you pack up to leave, make sure you have all your belongings. It's tiresome for your host to have to find a way of getting your leftovers back to you.

The final gesture by the well-mannered house guest is a letter of thanks. Do it promptly after you get home while the memory is still fresh enough for your words to be warm and pertinent. (See pages 137–138 for ideas on how to word letters of thanks.) It is a privilege to be asked to stay in someone's house and it often leads to a more intimate friendship than existed before. You have learned more about each other by being under the same roof for a few nights than is possible even after years of working together or sharing dinners now and again. If you liked what you experienced, keep up the momentum by returning the hospitality. If you can't accommodate people overnight, repay them by treating them to some special event, such as a concert or play in which you share an interest, and dinner beforehand or supper afterwards.

Chapter Fourteen

GROWN-UP GRACES

The French call it savoir-faire, the Americans say savvy. Social tease is not something we inherit, although some people acquire it more readily than others. It takes practice, experience and a level of self-possession that stays put, even under siege. In fact, one of the saving graces of growing older is self-assurance and the ability to put things into perspective. As you sail into the upper echelons of civility and refinement, think of yourself as a leading player in a comedy of manners. That way, you'll keep a sense of humour and never be at a loss for the right words at the right time. Remember, it's only a game waiting to be mastered.

THE ART OF CHAT

We have all felt dismay on entering a room – say, for a cocktail party or reception of some sort – and not seeing a single familiar face. Your host should be well mannered enough to introduce you to at least one group of people but that doesn't always happen, particularly at big gatherings where you're left to fend for yourself. The fear that you might stand like a wallflower all night with a glass in your hand and an unconvincing smile fixed on your face should be enough to goad you into being brave. Sally forth and say something to somebody. Yes, but what and to whom?

Turning to the person next to you is a better idea than charging across the room in an obvious way to a particular target. The impact of rejection is diminished if you appear not to have made a great effort. Crashing a group and interrupting someone in mid-sentence is also not a good idea. Take it easy. Emanate a sense of calm. Catch the person's eye and smile before you say something.

OPENING GAMBITS

There are any number of approaches and the trick is to pick one that suits your personality, your target and the situation in which you find yourselves. You could try the dramatic approach: 'I thought I'd never get here tonight. Did you run into that demonstration in Cook Street?' 'I heard on the radio just before I left home that a hailstorm is on the way.' 'I've been stuck on the bridge for an hour. The traffic in this city is getting worse by the day.' Be careful, though, not to let the conversation deteriorate into an endless grumble about life in general.

People who make themselves useful are welcome in any group: 'I'm about to get a drink, can I freshen yours up?' 'I didn't realise, did you, that the parking lot closes at ten?' Volunteering inside information is also a good way of endearing yourself to others: 'Our host is a good painter but he's very modest about it. That's one of his pictures.' Or you could try collusion: 'Oops, just remembered to turn off my mobile. Have you done yours?' 'I wonder if you know the man standing beside the potted palm. I've met him but do you think I can remember his name?'

Don't make your opening remark too personal ('I noticed you the moment I walked in') or your victim might assume you're making a pass, although that depends on gender and age. (If you are making a pass, ignore this advice and good luck.)

Everybody loves a compliment. 'Love your hairstyle' is an effective one, as long as it's genuine, and not directed at someone who is clearly having a bad-hair day. 'Let me guess what you do: I bet you're a film-maker' (or barrister, doctor, vintner, dancer or any other role generally thought to be glamorous or powerful); flagrantly flattering though it sounds, it can be very effective, particularly to someone with a mundane job and an uneventful life. Come to think of it, if your guess was correct you'll be credited with being remarkably astute.

Praising your host is a convincing way of presenting yourself as a kind and courteous person. 'I was just thinking how cleverly June has decorated this room.' 'I always enjoy Diana's parties. She's a born host-ess.' 'Aren't the flowers brilliant? Margôt is a genius at that.'

Helplessness is not to be recommended unless you are young, in which case somebody is likely to target you before you need to make the first move. If they don't, then 'My name's Jack, I'm from up north and I don't know a soul here' should work wonders.

Storytelling is a good idea but only if the tale is clean, preferably topi-cal and neither politically partial, religious, racist nor sexist. That doesn't leave too many amusing subjects, does it, but they do exist. You could preface your narration with 'I just heard this from a taxi driver . . .'

If you do know lots of people at the party it's up to you to be gen-erous in rescuing those who do not. Whether or not you are hosting the party, go out of your way to make others feel at ease, newcomers as well as people you know.

SUSTAINING A CONVERSATION

Whenever you are with a group of people, an unwritten code of eti-quette determines that nobody should hog the conversation, parade their knowledge of some esoteric subject that is of no interest to anybody else, be dogmatic in expressing opinions, ridicule those with a different view, repeat stories everybody has heard many times before, whisper asides to another person or make a habit of interrupting people in mid-sentence.

Name dropping is an indication of insecurity. So is the awful habit of trapping somebody and intruding on their space, so they have to ease back until they're cornered and desperate. If you see this happening to someone else, speed to the scene. Excuse yourself and say to the captive, 'I believe you're wanted on the telephone' or 'We need your advice in the kitchen' or 'Ziggy wants a word with you before he leaves.'

It is impertinent to ask personal questions of people you do not know well. And never use a social event as a convenient occasion on which to have a free consultation with a doctor, lawyer or travel agent. That is a dreadful imposition. Colleagues may talk shop but not in the company of others. Don't go on endlessly about someone the others do not know and don't indulge in malicious gossip. Tittle-tattle about celebrities is inevitable and usually harmless, since being talked about is an essential ingredient in their success.

Not every social event runs smoothly. Animosity can develop between people who have differing viewpoints or longstanding grievances, or who antagonise each other for no obvious reason. The ability to defuse a potentially explosive situation is a great social skill and when you see it in action it is awe-inspiring. It is not done by a head-on tackle, but by distraction, changing the subject, charming and disarming one or both protagonists and, if possible, spiriting one away in a calm and reasonable manner on some petty excuse, such as to look at a painting or help open a bottle. Any pretext will do. If a fight is inevitable, let it be after the party, far away.

GOSSIP

We all do it. Shame on us! All we can do to exonerate ourselves is to make sure it's not malicious or destructive and that we're not gullible enough to believe everything we hear. Or say, for that matter. The childish chant

'Sticks and stones may break my bones but names will never hurt me' is not accurate. Whispering campaigns can destroy people's reputations and their livelihoods. Think about the consequences before you are tempted to pass on a choice piece of gossip. If a friend entrusts you with a secret, do not violate that trust or you deserve to lose your friend.

DINING OUT

If you are hosting a lunch or dinner in a restaurant, you are responsible for booking the table, determining who sits where, ordering the food, choosing the wine and paying the bill. As a guest of such a person, your role is to go along happily with your host's decisions. If you need anything, such as a glass of water or more bread, ask your host, not the waiter.

The correct thing for a host to do before ordering the wine is to ask each guest which sort is preferred, red or white, then take into account the dishes ordered before making a final choice. If you are not familiar with the wines on the list, ask your guests or the sommelier (wine waiter) for advice. If as a guest you have been asked to choose the wine, go for something neither too expensive nor too cheap, but in the mid-price range. Much depends on how well-off or generous your host is. If you sense that the budget is limited, it is perfectly in order to say something like 'Why don't we settle on the house red? I believe it's very good here.'

Make things as straightforward as possible for the people who wait on your table. When a waiter comes to explain the specials of the day, pay attention. Ask questions about a particular dish, if you want to know more about what goes into it or how it is cooked, but don't expect to have the whole delivery repeated because you were too busy gasbagging to your neighbour to listen properly.

To be absolutely correct, the guests should tell the host what they have chosen from the menu so that the host can convey this to the waiter. But it's usually more practical for the waiter to take the orders directly from each person. There's less chance of something going wrong.

TASTING THE WINE

When the sommelier brings the bottle to the table, he or she should show you the label, to confirm that this is the wine you ordered, before opening it in front of you. Unless you have ordered house wine in a carafe, never accept a bottle that has been opened before it got to your table. The sommelier will expect to pour a little of the wine into your glass to make sure it is satisfactory. This ritual is performed primarily for you to check its temperature rather than its quality, although if a wine has gone off, this is your chance to send it back. If you are confident that the wine will be satisfactory, particularly if it is a modest one, you might forego the tasting and just ask for it to be poured. If you have brought your own wine and the restaurant is a very casual one, you might be expected to do the pouring yourself. Always remember to pour wine for the others before you fill or refill your own glass.

SHARING THE COST

Often when several people go together to a restaurant there is an understanding that the cost will be shared. To avoid fuss and confusion, make sure that when the bill comes it is given to someone with mathematical expertise to add a suitable tip and divide the total into equal or appropriate portions. It is petty to quibble over a few dollars' difference between the cost of what one person consumed versus another. On the other hand, if someone orders crayfish and another settles for spaghetti bolognese, or one person drinks wine and another does not, there'll be a big difference in the cost and it is only fair to take that into account when it's time to divvy up the bill.

HOW TO COMPLAIN

Australians are not good at sending food back if it is either improperly cooked or not what they had expected because they feel they don't want to make a scene or embarrass their guests. Restaurateurs would far rather you complained to them than to a whole lot of your friends and colleagues afterwards. If your complaint is made courteously and with goodwill, it should be accepted in the same manner, even if the mistake was yours or your guest's. If you say, 'I am so sorry, I have ordered the wrong thing . . . ' the waiter should offer something else that can be brought quickly without fuss and without charge. The important thing is to remain cool. It is both sad and embarrassing to see someone lose his temper or be rude to a waiter because it's an unfair contest. The waiter cannot retaliate without risking his job and the patron shows himself to be an insensitive bully.

If the service has been too slow or the staff have a bad attitude, the most effective way to retaliate is to take your business elsewhere. If you feel you must complain, do it in person to the restaurant manager, or put it in a letter afterwards.

THE ARTS

To the outside world Australians are sports-lovers (with a climate like ours, it would be surprising if we weren't) but it is interesting that more of us attend cultural than sporting events. That does not mean we necessarily go in for highfalutin intellectual pursuits, since statistics on things 'cultural' include rock concerts and all movies, even the seriously dreadful ones. But we are very proud of our symphony orchestras, our opera, ballet and theatre companies, our spirited dance groups and our galleries, although they are rarely given the front page newspaper coverage that sports heroes regularly command.

CONCERT HALL VS STADIUM

What must be remembered is the big difference between the way you behave as a spectator at a stadium and what you do as a member of the audience at a theatre. Eating, drinking, talking, yelling and waving your arms around sit comfortably with most games but not with the performing arts. Even at the movies, it is not seemly for adults to crackle cellophane wrappers as their fingers fumble for lollies when others are trying to concentrate on the screen. If you must eat, unwrap the package before the lights go out and eat as silently as you can. While you may eat whatever takes your fancy in front of television at home, in a public place you must be considerate of other people. At a live performance in the theatre or concert hall, even a matinee, do not eat anything when you are seated in the auditorium. Wait until interval and go into the lobby to consume whatever it is you want.

ENTERTAINMENT VS ART

A distinction must also be made between entertainment and art. A musical is entertainment that lifts your spirits while you are watching, but doesn't leave too many imponderables afterwards. The performance of the work of a serious playwright, whether comedy or tragedy, takes greater effort from the audience and leaves a lot to think about afterwards. It is not appropriate to refer to serious theatre as 'a show'. 'Dinner and a show', that favourite Aussie description of an outing, should be used judiciously, if at all. 'How did you enjoy the show?' is another clanger in the lobby after a performance of Chekhov, Verdi or Bach.

THE PERFORMING ARTS

When the lights dim and the curtain rises or the conductor lifts his baton, good manners are put to their supreme test. In most venues, there's not much room between rows or between seats, so what people do has an immediate effect on their neighbours and often on the performers. People who wear overpowering scent, fidget, conduct the orchestra, hum along with the music, take up all the room on the armrests, tell their neighbours in stage whispers what happens next, lean forward in their seats even though they are tall, check the time on their watches, talk, yawn, snore, make no attempt to pull their feet in when others try to pass or arrive late and expect to be seated in the middle of a row belong in a stadium, not a theatre. If you are so bored that you can't sit still, wait until interval to leave your seat and don't come back.

One civilised practice that we are yet to see in Australia's performing arts venues is the facility to pre-order and pre-pay drinks and have them waiting at interval. If you have been to the theatre in London you might have noticed how well this works. Instead of fighting for the bartender's eye in a six-deep mob at the bar, you find your drinks placed on a chit with your name on it at a pre-determined place. It is a refinement that must please staff as much as patrons and it adds to the quality of the evening.

Basic manners

Switch off your mobile telephone and still the alarm on your digital watch before you enter any theatre. Dress appropriately. Making an effort to look glamorous is as much a mark of respect for the performers as it is for the rest of the audience. Think of yourself as part of the occasion and help make it special for others as well as yourself. Shorts and sneakers are fine at the football but not at the Opera House.

Leave any accoutrements, such as umbrella and coat, at the cloakroom. As you move along a row of people to find your seat, smile and say, 'Excuse me' before advancing, with your back half-turned towards them. There is disagreement among some people about which way you should face as you sidle along a row but, if some part of the intimate anatomy has to be level with my face when I am sitting in an auditorium, I prefer a bottom to a crotch. Either way, as the one already seated, swing your legs sideways and pull your feet in to let others pass, otherwise you deserve to be stepped on. If the space between rows is very narrow, stand up willingly, push your seat back and smile as though it's no effort at all.

Don't clap at the wrong time

If you must cough or sneeze during the performance, muffle it with your handkerchief. In any case, do your best to save it for a noisy bit of music or a boisterous crowd scene and hope it will be drowned out.

Applauding between movements of a concerto or a symphony is a definite no-no, although Karl Haas, a pianist and gifted teacher who is respected wherever in the world his radio broadcasts are syndicated, has said more than once that he sees no reason why you shouldn't applaud if a performance of the first movement has been particularly inspiring. Usually only the erudite are confident enough to get away with breaking such iron-clad rules. The rest of us are advised to remain silent.

The end of the performance

In the misbegotten assumption that it will please the performers (or perhaps in an effort to draw attention to themselves), some people have the very irritating habit of applauding before the last note of music has died away. Do not emulate them. Prolong your appreciation and show respect by waiting before being as demonstrative as you wish. It is perfectly permissible to stamp your feet, give voice to your praise and pay the artists the great compliment of rising (this is known as a standing ovation), but do sit down again if you are blocking the view of people who are not as nimble as you are.

'Bravo' is not always correct

If you are moved to yell 'Bravo', get the terminology right. The word is Italian in origin. 'Bravo' and 'bravissimo' refer to a man. 'Brava' and 'bravissima' refer to a woman. 'Bravi' and 'Bravissimi' mean everybody. Worrying about vowels may seem unnecessarily picky in Australia until you remember how many foreign-born artists perform here. They are well aware of the distinction and are likely to mistake the object of your praise if you use the wrong suffix.

PUBLIC ART GALLERIES

While you are not expected to be as quiet as you would be in a library, it's important not to disturb others by airing your opinions in a loud voice unless you are a child, in which case spontaneous observations are to be encouraged, not inhibited. Take care not to monopolise a picture by standing closely in front of it if there are others trying to look at it too.

It helps appreciation if you know something about the painter's time and place, so sit down for a few minutes with the catalogue or do some swotting in the library or on the Internet (there are wonderfully informative sites on the web) before the visit.

It is also important to realise that each of us responds in different ways to painters and paintings and that you don't have to like something just because others do. Neither do you have to look at every painting in the gallery, especially if it is as big as, say, the Metropolitan Museum of Art in New York, the Prado in Madrid or Tate Modern in London. Don't try to consume too much at once or you'll suffer cultural indigestion. Be satisfied with a little and do it justice by giving yourself time for contemplation rather than hit and run. Aim for quality rather than quantity.

PRIVATE ART GALLERIES

To a novice at the opening of an art exhibition, the purpose of this reception seems to have more to do with hobnobbing than with art since more attention is paid to who is there than what is on the walls. An art opening is indeed a social get-together whose main purpose is to generate publicity and reinforce the credentials of the gallery by the calibre of names it attracts, both exhibitors and viewers. Serious buyers go to previews, sometimes private ones. The pictures they choose to buy acquire the red spots that signify the works have been sold by the time the exhibition opens officially.

Have your best small talk ready for these occasions and make sure you know enough about the artist to say something relevant, though not pedantic, about the works. Otherwise, keep silent and bear the following in mind.

Do's and don'ts at an art opening

Don't ask, 'What does that red spot mean?' If a picture has a red spot, don't ask 'Who bought it?' If a picture has a red spot, don't say, 'I would have bought that.' or ask, 'Have they paid for it yet?' If ten pictures out of a show of thirty have been sold, don't complain that 'Everything is sold!' After an overview of the show, don't ask, 'Why are they so expensive?' Never sidle up to the gallery assistant and ask for the artist's telephone number. Never ask if the frame is included. Never tell the gallery assistant that the frames are hideous, even if they are. The artist probably chose them. Never ask, 'Are the paintings less expensive if they don't sell at the exhibition?' Before you ask where the loo is, try to look as though you're interested in what is hanging on the walls. Don't touch the works, even if they are temptingly tactile. Don't ask, 'Are these originals?' Don't say, 'My twelve-year-old could have done that.' Take care where you sit. It might be a work of art.

THE ART AUCTION

Because an auction of any kind is a public event rather than a deal clinched in private, it's a fair way of establishing the true market value of any object at a given time. A decade or two ago, auction rooms were mainly clearing houses for deceased estates and dealers were the main bidders. Today, with better access to information, collectors as well as dealers enjoy bidding and buying at auction.

Your first acquisition

If you are just starting out as a collector, don't buy too many art works at once, even if you can afford them. Do your homework by reading and researching. This will help you define your taste and preferred styles. Great collections are built judiciously over time. If you are buying for financial investment, it's better to buy one good thing than two mediocre ones. Also bear in mind that works of art, like everything else, are subject to fashion. A period or style that's unfashionable and moderately priced now could well be highly desirable and expensive in a decade's time.

The first step is to have your name put on the mailing lists of the leading reputable auction houses. Check the daily newspapers for announcements of forthcoming auctions. If you fancy certain artists, find out who their dealers are and let them know of your interest. Enrol in a series of lectures, such as the Art History and Appreciation Diploma courses run by the Art Gallery of New South Wales and sponsored by Sotheby's. Most galleries around Australia offer varied and interesting programs. Acquiring knowledge usually becomes automatic once you own something of artistic merit because curiosity leads you to study other works by the same artist, or of the same period, and soon you're on the way to being a connoisseur.

Previews

A week or two before a major sale, an auction house will hold an invitation-only client preview, followed by a few days of open house, when the works are on view and beautifully produced catalogues, with illustrations and estimated prices, are distributed. Experts are there to answer any questions about particular works.

Even in these refined and cultivated realms, not everybody behaves as well as they should. Beware of shysters. One pathetic tactic is to run down a painting at the preview with the aim of trying to limit its value, and then to bid on it at auction. Sometimes someone will remove the lot number from a particular piece hoping that people will be confused and not bid. In one case, a brass handle disappeared from a valuable piece of furniture just before it was auctioned. Justice was served when the culprit, who was an unsuccessful bidder, was tracked down and made to return the stolen trophy.

Bidding

If you are interested in bidding on a piece but you can't be there on the day or evening of the auction, you can either place a bid, specifying your upper limit, with the auctioneer, or prearrange to do it by telephone during the bidding. Or you could appoint a dealer to bid for you.

When you attend an auction in person with the aim of buying, you are given a number and a bidding paddle when you register. Unless you are known to the auction house, you may be asked for identification. Techniques for bidding range from touching the nose or winking, to standing up and waving the arms about flamboyantly. Neither extreme is satisfactory because the first may be so discreet it is missed by the auctioneer and the second is unduly ostentatious. The best way is somewhere between the two, so that your wishes are clear without being overplayed. A bidder who chooses to remain anonymous is often represented by a dealer.

Successful bidders are usually expected to pay for the goods and take possession of them within two days of the sale.

ABORIGINAL AND TORRES STRAIT ISLANDER (ATSI) ART

The history of art as we know it shows a succession of movements that are linked, as in a chain, with one developing out of another, each dependent on what went before and crucial to what comes next. Learning from artists of the past, borrowing and building on their techniques, is a legitimate pursuit of an artist.

With tribal artists, the images they produce in various media today are still inextricably linked to the ancient art of their ancestors. Just as non-ATSI artists use written language to record and impart information, indigenous peope use pictorial symbols to communicate and much of their art is spiritual and sacred because it contains traditional ritual knowledge. To imitate these works is considered a serious offence which amounts to theft of someone else's land. In addition, the Trade Practices Act forbids false claims being made about any saleable goods, including works of art.

It's imperative that we respect and protect this art as an important part of tribal lore and of Australia's heritage. Whether knowingly or not, non-Aboriginal people sometimes take advantage of Aboriginal artists. Even when a non-indigenous person has spent time with an Aboriginal or Torres Strait Islander community and been accepted – say, as a 'brother' or other family relation, once outside the community that privilege no longer exists. The outsider has no right to exploit any connections with individual artists, or use acquired knowledge of artistic styles or methods in any way, such as by claiming the right to assist an artist with a traditional painting or to produce art using the clan's designs, on the basis of having been 'adopted' by the community.

Ensuring authenticity

Think twice before you buy anything with an Aboriginal motif on it, whether it's a T-shirt or a painted boomerang from a souvenir shop. Always go to a reputable source to buy an ATSI work of art or craft and make sure you know its provenance. Fakes are not rare. Because the artists live and work in isolated communities, a long way from the cities in which much of their work is sold, they are often not aware of rip-offs being traded as the real thing.

TRÈS SNOB

One of the reasons why 'etiquette' seems a severe word is because it has so often been a means of separating people rather than bringing them together. It smacks of snobbery, a mark of the insecure, where differences in speech, dress and behaviour are used to classify people as 'them' or 'us'. Such divisions do no credit to any society, certainly not ours, whose character is still being formed. For better or worse, we are now more influenced by the United States than we are by the United Kingdom because we are part of the new world, not the old one. Like the United States, our country has striven to be egalitarian, a word we translate to mean 'a fair go' and the only barriers that exist between one person and another in Australia are those that individuals put up themselves.

Although we don't carry a lot of baggage, there are still vestiges here of the old colonial days when the British way was the standard by which we lived. The class system in Britain has been upheld brilliantly by language. Nothing is more effective than the spoken word in keeping apart the uppers, middles, lowers and their various subdivisions (explained with acuity by Jilly Cooper in her wickedly witty book *Class*). The differences exist not just in accent but, just as tellingly, in terminology.

English upper classes (referred to as U, as opposed to non-U) would never call a table napkin a serviette, the telephone a phone or use a complicated word if there is a simple one for it. For instance, they would never call jam a preserve. Long words, particularly euphemisms, are the domain of Americans. They love words such as 'amelioration', whereas the English would use 'betterment'. One of the most damning of snobbish terms is 'She's frightfully milk-in-first.' This refers to the non-U habit of putting milk in the teacup before the tea. What you're supposed to do is pour the tea, then add milk, or a slice of lemon or nothing at all (see pages 290–291).

The word 'toilet' has become a tricky one. In 1960, it was definitely non-U. The upper-class word was 'lavatory'. As time went by, U people realised that this knowledge had broken rank and infiltrated other classes. So when everybody else started calling it lavatory, they started saying toilet. Toilet seems to have become gentrified just as lavatory has slipped on the social scale. Who knows for how long? There are plenty of other terms, although some – little girls' room, little boys' room, powder room – are too twee to be mouthed other than in irony. Loo, john, toot, bathroom, bog, it (as in 'where is it?'), ladies', gents', men's, women's are passable. I myself prefer dunny, such a no-nonsense Australian country term.

However anachronistic and quaint some of these terms and habits now seem, it's still good to be aware of them. Here are some guidelines to help you navigate tricky social channels in Great Britain if you want to move among people cheeky Cockneys would describe as la-di-da.

U-TERM	NON-U TERM
Drawing room/Sitting room	*Lounge room*
Curtains	*Drapes*
Tea	*Afternoon tea*
Sofa	*Couch or lounge suite*
Sink	*Vanity*
Flat	*Apartment or unit*
Pudding	*Sweet*
Lavatory paper	*Toilet tissue*
Riding	*Horseback riding*
How do you do	*Pleased to meet you*
What?	*Pardon?*
Rich	*Wealthy*
Vegetables	*Greens*
Bike/bicycle	*Cycle*
Lunch	*Dinner*
Dinner	*Tea*
Spectacles	*Glasses*
Looking-glass	*Mirror*
House	*Home*
Sick (for nauseous)	*Ill (for nauseous)*
Mad	*Mental*
Writing paper	*Notepaper*
Goodbye	*Bye-bye*
English	*British*
Children	*Kiddies*
Bag	*Handbag*
Scent	*Perfume or fragrance*
Valet (pronounced val-ette)	*Valet (pronounced val-ay)*

Top marks if you can pick the non-U terms in this playful poem by Barbara Cartland.

THE SOCIAL CODE

Society through the centuries
Has evolved a social code
Not written down but handed down
From the time we all wore woad.

For those who think they have blue blood
There are rules of what to do;
The penalty of ignoring them
Is to be told – 'you're just non-u'.

So don't say 'cheers' when you have a drink
Or hold your knife like a pen,
'Pardon's a word which should never be heard
'Perfume' does not entice men.

Never 'phone' for a taxi
'To take you up to town'.
Don't put clean wine glasses
On a cocktail tray – upside down.

Don't eat asparagus with a fork
Or put the milk in first,
Don't ask your guest to 'have a gin'
When he has a thirst.

Don't write to me on 'notepaper'
Or send me a 'photo', please.
Don't put 'née' in the births and deaths
Or use pretty lace doilies.

Don't ask the way to 'the toilet', dear,
Or use a 'serviette'.
Men don't enter a restaurant first
Or perspire at the bill they get.

Don't have a 'lounge' in your lovely 'home'
Or open the 'bubbly' with glee.
Don't have gold-tipped party cards
Or use little forks at tea.

You can do all these things if you wish,
And it doesn't matter a damn,
But they label you neatly as what you are
Like a pickled-herring can.

Chapter Fifteen

BON VOYAGE

lthough travel is one of the world's great privileges it is also one of the world's great challenges. Going somewhere far away is not always as glamorous in reality as it is in anticipation. The bewildering size of airports, unwieldly baggage, delays, missed connections, skittish computers, traffic congestion, touts and pickpockets, language barriers, culture shock and the awareness that you are just another tourist among millions can all conspire to diminish you, taking the edge off your enjoyment and eroding your good manners. To lengthen the odds of having a great time and put class back into travel, find an exceptional travel agent, plan ahead carefully and never lose your temper.

CHOOSING A DESTINATION

Not everyone shares the same affinity with a particular place, so just because you know someone who had an unforgettable time in Munich,

Phuket, Glasgow, Palermo, Boston, Fez, Shanghai or Buenos Aires doesn't mean that you will. Follow your own dream in making decisions and then take a few other things into account.

By all means read travel guides but beware of fantasy. Something that enthralled you in a book or a movie is not necessarily going to be like that when you get there. Fiction and biography set in exotic places are often about times long gone or written by people who have lived there, so their experiences are impossible for someone on a two-week visit to emulate. Clever moviemakers involve us by idealising a subject, planting very beautiful people there and romanticising it all with camera, sound and editing techniques that take it right out of reality. Don't expect travel to be like the movies.

Be ruthlessly analytical about yourself. If you'd rather be on a beach than in museums and concert halls, you're better off in Hawaii than St Petersburg.

Let the climate determine your timing. There's no point in planning to loll about on a beach in the monsoon season.

If your time is short – say, a week – try not to choose a place that takes twenty-four hours, or several changes of aircraft, to get to. A tedious return journey can cancel out much of the good a holiday has done for you.

Ten countries in as many days is a fine way of not seeing anything. Don't cram too much into your itinerary. You experience much more when you unpack your bags and stay in one place for as long as possible.

ALONE OR WITH OTHERS?

Many a friendship, or marriage for that matter, has foundered on the rocky shore of a shared journey. Make sure you're compatible before you choose to take a lengthy trip with an old friend, a new lover, or whomever. Try a weekend away and see how it feels before you suggest anything more ambitious.

Travelling alone is not as daunting as it might seem, but that depends on your character and circumstances. Although you pay more as a single traveller because you do not share a room, you have a better chance of meeting the locals than you would as a couple or in a group, which usually moves as an impenetrable pack. If you get lonely you can always book yourself on a day tour to see the sights without being locked into a group full-time.

Preparing for a trip

The success of a trip abroad is not necessarily equal to the financial investment put into it, but money does help. If you can arrange for a car to meet your flights, wherever they happen to touch down, and you can afford to shell out money for porters and other bearers it's a good start, although if you can limit your baggage to a size and weight you can manage yourself, you're well ahead.

Better still, if you can live out of a carry-on bag that fits under an airline seat, you're never likely to be a candidate for lost luggage and you'll be through Customs before anyone else on the flight. It can be done. The trick is not so much to pack wisely as to buy wisely, because if you don't have the right clothes, how can you pack them (see also pages 112–115)? Think about this next time you shop: how well will that garment travel?

YOUR LUGGAGE

The more experienced a traveller you are, the more likely you are to travel light. Who wants to be weighed down like a beast of burden? Unless your luggage has wheels, limit yourself to two small, lightweight bags rather than one large one, so you balance the load evenly; it's less of a strain on your back. Invest in good luggage, not for its label but for its quality. The last thing you want is a bag that falls apart in transit, so don't buy something cheap and risk it bursting apart under the strain. There is no substitute for a travel bag that is lightweight, easy to manage, tough enough to be treated roughly by baggage handlers and does not scream 'Steal me, I'm expensive'.

There's a lot to be said for something that stands out on the carousel because it's an unconventional colour or pattern. You can identify it quickly and it's too conspicuous to tempt a thief. In any case, always mark your bag in some way to distinguish it from the rest. Luggage tags are essential but they are removable; to be on the safe side, also attach a sticker that's difficult to budge. My trick is to give each of my bags a permanent 'tattoo' with a thick felt pen.

If the bags do not have their own locks, buy small padlocks. Keep the keys on your keyring in your handbag or pocket. Each bag, whether you check it in or carry it aboard the plane, should have identification inside as well. Before you put anything into your bags, identify them, inside and out, with the labels supplied with your airline ticket. If there aren't enough labels, improvise with your own. The important thing is to make it clear that this is your property.

A practical wallet

The three most important items in your possession when you travel are your passport, your tickets and your money, in one form or another, so choose your travel wallet carefully. It's convenient to have them all in one place, although some cautious travellers keep them in different places so that all is not lost if the wallet vanishes. The only problem with that is it can leave you fumbling at the wrong moment when you forget precisely where you put those crucial papers.

Many wallets are too small to carry an airline ticket and that's a nuisance. For me, the ideal one is lengthy enough for the ticket, has a pocket for each charge card and separate compartments for passport and at least two kinds of currency: Australian dollars and whatever notes are legal tender in the country of first destination. I always carry some US dollars, too, which are recognised and accepted universally, other than in countries antagonistic to the west.

It's up to you whether you rely on traveller's cheques, charge cards, cards that enable you to draw cash from ATMs – or all three – but don't carry too much cash. If it's lost, it's gone forever, whereas there are numbers you can ring to report the loss of cards or cheques to have them invalidated and new ones issued. Keep those numbers in more than one place. Relying on ATMs alone is risky. What happens if you land penniless on foreign soil and the machine at the airport is out of action?

WHAT TO TAKE IN-FLIGHT

For a woman

You'll need a smart handbag with a shoulder strap in which you put: your wallet with your passport, airline ticket, credit cards, traveller's cheques and cash; house keys, luggage keys, itinerary, hotel vouchers if applicable, small address book and ballpoint pen (sometimes necessary for filling out forms in duplicate). A fountain pen that is your pride and joy might leak under cabin pressure so, if you must take it on a flight, shroud it in bubble wrap.

You can also carry onto the plane a small holdall with a shoulder strap that contains: cleanser, toner and moisturiser in miniature containers (make sure their lids are firm enough to prevent leaks, otherwise wrap them in bubble plastic); toothbrush and toothpaste; small mirror; eye drops; comb and brush; tissues; make-up; miniature fragrance; a change of underpants, although a satisfactory alternative is a few panty liners; something to read and any papers you plan to deal with on the wing; a sweater if what you are wearing might be too chilly at a high altitude; mobile telephone if necessary, switched off; camera, if applicable.

For a man

If you feel comfortable with a small shoulder bag of the style Italian men carry, it's a sensible travelling companion. If not, keep your wallet somewhere on your person at all times and put your house keys, luggage keys, itinerary, hotel vouchers if applicable, pen and small address book in a zippered side pocket of your ovenight bag.

Your overnight bag should also contain your shaving kit, tooth-brush and toothpaste, comb, eye drops, moisturiser, change of underpants, a sweater, something to read, any papers you plan to deal with during the flight, your mobile telephone if necessary (switched off) and your camera.

WHAT TO PACK

If you've been guided by the principles of building a basic wardrobe (see Chapter 8), you'll already have the pieces. It's just a matter of choosing which ones to take, depending on the purpose of your journey and the climate at your destination. Don't pack too much; I used to travel heavy until I disciplined myself because too often clothes I'd lugged around the world returned home unworn. The few that worked were so adaptable, I wore them all the time.

When you are on the move, you can do with fewer outfits because the people you meet don't realise you've been wearing the same thing again and again. The downside is your own boredom with what you've got on every day but that is a small price to pay for light luggage and swift unpacking and repacking in hotel rooms. Besides, unless you're trekking in the Gobi Desert or scaling Everest, there are shops at the other end. You don't have to take absolutely everything with you. Restock there, as you need to. For some of us, one of the great joys of travel is shopping.

Here are some invaluable fellow travellers to Europe or North America in spring or autumn: a raincoat, preferably with a warm, detachable lining; a large wool or cashmere wrap; a collapsible umbrella; a beret or beanie for the cold. The weather can be tempera-mental at the change of a season. If you're travelling in summer or winter at least you know the temperatures at the other end are likely to be consistent, so you can pack accordingly.

Leave your precious jewellery in a safe place at home or in a bank vault.

HOW TO PACK

If you want to travel in absolute style, have on hand a great swag of tissue paper. Line the suitcase with it and be lavish in spreading it between layers, stuffing it into sleeves and between the folds of individual garments.

- Start with the shoes. Fill them with small items, such as jewellery wrapped in tissue, film, pantihose, socks and gloves.
- Pack the shoes and any other heavy items, such as toiletry bag, manicure set, books, presents in boxes, and place them so they'll sit at the base of the bag, once it's in its usual carrying position.
- Lay trousers, long skirts, dresses and stoles flat along the bottom of the suitcase, with the ends left dangling over one side.
- Turn jackets inside out and tuck layers of tissue in and across the back before you fold them once and lay them over the flat garments.
- Add short skirts, shirts, scarves and other items, each of them interleaved with tissue paper.
- Before you pack your underwear, place it in a drawstring bag made for the purpose, or put it in a scarf, tied like a hobo's bundle, so that it's easy to find.
- When all the items have been packed, fold the ends that still protrude back over the top and cover with more tissue paper.
- If there is still room in the case and you want to prevent things from moving around and turning into a crumpled mess, a smart trick is to blow up balloons and use them to load the space without adding weight. Deflate them once your bag starts to fill with papers, clothes or souvenirs on the way.

LEAVE YOUR HOUSE IN ORDER

Apart from the guidelines set out in Chapter 5, make the following arrangements, unless there will be someone staying at your place and handling all your affairs while you are away.

- Make sure your insurance policies are paid up.

- Arrange for any bills that are due while you are away to be paid by your bank or a reliable friend or relative.
- Ask someone to collect your mail.
- Any domestic pets should be boarded in a kennel or cattery, or sent to stay with a friend or relative. Cats may be left at home as long as the trip is not lengthy and a reliable person with whom they are familiar comes twice a day to feed them, give them fresh water and change their litter.
- Cancel newspapers and any other regular deliveries unless you know somebody nearby would appreciate them and can be trusted to pick them up every day.
- If your immediate neighbours are trustworthy, tell them how long you plan to be away. Watchful eyes next door are a great form of security.
- Leave a house key and a copy of your itinerary with someone you trust.
- Consider having some house lights operated by an automatic system that switches them on each evening and off again at the time when you normally go to bed. Houses that look uninhabited can be targets for burglary.
- Remember to bring back small tokens of appreciation for the people who have done favours for you.

PRESENTS FROM ABROAD

While bringing back presents is a charming gesture on the part of the traveller, it should not be expected by those who stayed at home. The same branded goods blanket the world now and there are few bargains, except in isolated communities that western ways are yet to infiltrate. Trying to find something suitable and affordable for a number of family members, friends and colleagues is time-consuming, often frustrating and usually costly in the long run. It also sets a precedent the traveller might regret.

On the subject of trophies from abroad, avoid offering to buy things requested by other people. There'll be no end to it, and you might find yourself wasting days looking for the elusive object. If you are the one staying at home, don't ask the traveller to buy something for you unless you are an immediate loved one. It's an awful imposition.

To give a polite no to a request such as this, you could say that Australian Customs impose a limit to the amount of overseas goods you can bring in without paying duty and you can't risk exceeding it. This is a valid point and should be readily understood. Other useful excuses: you are planning to top up your shoe collection on this trip and you're afraid of overweight luggage; you are travelling with one carry-on bag and you won't be able to fit another item in it; because this trip is part business, paperwork is going to stretch your luggage to its limits.

SAFE TRAVELLING

Be prepared for tight security, long queues, sniffer dogs and spot checks at airports, particularly when you travel internationally. Give yourself plenty of time to check in and always carry something to read in case of delays. Anything that might be construed as a weapon – nail file or scissors, corkscrew, multi-purpose knife – will be confiscated if you try to carry it on board, so either leave it at home or pack it in the bag that will be stowed as cargo.

Be wary of bags that have been left alone at airports and never leave yours unattended. Never agree to carry a bag, post a letter or put a parcel into your own luggage for anybody else, particularly someone you do not know. Crooks lurk around airports waiting to importune the gullible to become unwitting couriers of illegal goods or substances. However plausible the argument from a man or a woman, never fall for it. The correct action is to refuse politely and report the incident to the airport security office or to somebody else in authority. (For other aspects of safety abroad, see pages 115–116.)

IN-FLIGHT SECURITY

There is no need to go through the elaborate security precaution of strapping your essentials to your body when you're travelling by plane unless this is your first trip overseas (see page 105). It's too inconvenient because you have to reach for them so often during the journey. Save that for when you're walking around the streets of a big city and on overnight trains. However, on the plane, never leave your seat without your passport, tickets and money (or its equivalent), no matter whether you are going to the cockpit or just to the washroom. A friend of mine, on a trip to London first class, didn't notice until she disembarked at Heathrow that all her cash had disappeared from her bag during the flight. It's a good idea for a man as well as a woman to carry a small handbag with a shoulder strap. Take it with you at all times.

YOUR ATTITUDE ON BOARD

Smile and say 'please' to the flight attendants when you ask them to do anything, such as hang your coat, and 'thank you' when you accept something offered to you.

Don't carry too much on board. It's a bore for you and unfair to everyone else trying to find a place for their things in an overstuffed overhead locker. I never put anything up there. I prefer to tuck my bag under the seat in front of me, so I can reach it at any time without disturbing anybody else. That's a particularly good idea when you're down the back of the plane because the bag doubles as a footrest.

Once you get to your seat, don't hold up the other passengers by blocking the aisle as you shove your chattels in the overhead locker, take off your jacket and grope for your laptop. Pause to let people pass.

Don't make a fuss if you find yourself seated beside a mother with a baby or young children. Some are very well organised and not every infant is a screamer. If you are travelling with young children, don't let them bother other travellers by jabbing them with sticky fingers, kicking the seat in front or galloping up and down the aisles. Always change a baby's nappy in the washroom equipped with a changing table, never on the seat beside you.

Be pleasant to your neighbours but don't intrude on them. Limit your small talk to mealtimes unless you are sure your chat is welcome. (It's true that love has been kindled in the hearts of two strangers on a plane, although it happens more often in the movies than in real life.)

If your neighbour is talkative and won't let up, stick your nose in a book and say, 'I don't mean to be rude, but I cannot put this down, it's so totally engrossing' or take out your notebook or papers, sigh and say, 'Work time, no rest for the wicked.' If all else fails, pretend to take a pill (or really take one) and say, 'Must get my beauty sleep, nighty-night' before you close your eyes and turn away.

People spoiling for a fight, sometimes prompted by too much alcohol, make very uncomfortable fellow passengers. If you are being pestered by one, don't enter into a direct discussion. Ask the flight services director to deal with it and hope the flight is empty enough for one of you to be moved.

If the person beside you is unfamiliar with the workings of the seat and its apparatus, be helpful without being patronising. As you show how it works, say something like 'You need a university degree, these days, to operate these complicated things.'

When seats are narrow, as they are in economy class, take care not to commandeer both armrests. If you must open your laptop, be sensitive to others when you use it. Don't disturb them unnecessarily by flailing about as you set up your complicated apparatus and dismantle it again when the dinner trolley rolls along. When the whole plane is in darkness and everyone else is trying to sleep, a spotlit work station can be very intrusive.

If your flight is delayed in taking off and you are worried about missing a connection with another flight, tell the flight attendant so that ground staff at the other end can be alerted and you can be hurried off the plane as soon as it lands.

Don't dally in the washroom and make sure it's clean and tidy when you leave it.

After you've landed and the 'fasten seat belts' sign has been switched off, there's not much point in scrambling to your feet and cluttering up the aisle. It impedes passengers who may need to be given priority to make connections with other flights. Sit still and let them pass. The proper procedure for leaving the plane is for passengers in first class to go first, followed by those in business class. Passengers in the first row of economy class should go next, then those in the second row, and so on. If you're in the back row, bad luck. People with babies and young children, or those who need wheelchairs, may be ushered out first or asked to wait until everyone else has gone, depending on circumstances and the airline's regulations.

As you leave the plane, always have a smile and a few words of thanks for the crew members who have looked after you.

CONDUCT IN A STRANGE LAND

Given that the main reason for choosing to visit a foreign country is to experience its culture first hand, it's surprising how many travellers do not open their minds to values and beliefs that are different from their own. No matter where they are, they seem never to have left home, so you wonder why they bother to travel at all. It's pointless and tiresome to make comparisons that invariably favour the homeland. Besides, you miss out on so much if you let preconceptions obscure the reality of what is going on around you.

Every Australian who travels is an ambassador for this country and that is a serious role. The way you look, what you say, how you say it and your general demeanour can confirm or change other people's opinions of Australians in general. Stereotypes are easily reinforced. Ugly behaviour reflects on us all even more powerfully than its opposite. Being polite is important at all times but never more so than when you are among people of another land.

HOTELS

Hotels come in all shapes, sizes, degrees of comfort and levels of luxury and, although they are rated according to a star system, it is not a reliable guide to anything more than physical attributes, such as whether there's a swimming pool or a hook for a robe behind the bathroom door. The star system also varies from one country to another, so that a hotel that is given a six-star rating in one country might only merit four and a half in another.

As experienced travellers know, hotels are a lot more than just buildings. There is no rating for tender loving care. That is why word of mouth is a far more credible recommendation than an advertisement or in some cases even editorial coverage, provided the person who gives you the word is someone whose judgement you trust. A good travel agent will offer sound advice, but bear in mind that not all hotels give agent discounts, particularly those affordable little charmers that do excellent business without the need to promote themselves. In a case like that, it's natural enough for the agent to try to steer you to one that does. Whether or not you heed that advice is up to you.

Top-scale hotels around the world now fall into two broad categories.

TRADITIONAL GRAND HOTELS

The glorious old piles, such as Hotel de Crillon, The Ritz Hotel and Hotel Le Bristol in Paris, the Dorchester, Claridge's and The Savoy in London, Hotel Imperial in Vienna, the Baur au Lac in Zurich and others elsewhere in Europe still operate in much the same way as they always did. Their decoration is richly embellished, usually reflecting a former era of perceived glory. Staff wear black tie, service is formal and the division between guest and staff is never breached.

When you stay in this sort of hotel, you are expected to behave and dress somewhat like the lord and lady of the manor. You should be charming to the staff, remember the names of the people who serve you and thank them for what they do, but remain at a distance. In this kind of hotel you will not earn respect by trying to be on equal terms with the duty manager, concierge, head waiter or any of the staff. You, as well as they, are expected to know your place.

If you lunch or dine in the restaurants of such hotels, do dress for it: a man in jacket and tie, a woman in her most chic finery and both of you shod and accesssorised to the nines. Some of these places, such as Les Ambassadeurs at the Crillon in Paris and the gloriously decorated Restaurant at The Ritz in London, are unforgettably grand. Others are so understated you wonder what made them famous, until you see the names of people who've frequented them; The Savoy Grill's list reads like a who's who of the twentieth century.

A bidet is not a loo

A note here about that delightfully foreign invention, the bidet. The first encounter many Australians have with a bidet is in France where bidets are de rigueur, even in modest establishments. The sole purpose of this piece of plumbing, which the uninitiated may think resembles a lavatory, is not for washing your socks (although it is very useful for that) but for washing your bottom. You sit on it and, depending on its design, it either squirts water at your nether region, or you fill it with water and wash yourself in the regular way. It means you can be nice and clean down under without having a bath or shower – handy when you're in a hurry to change and go out, and after amorous encounters.

STAFF AND SERVICES

In the hierarchy of hotels there are two broad divisions of pecking order under the overall responsibility of the general manager. In one there are management people, and they include administrators, receptionists, cashiers and executives in sales and marketing. In the other are the people who look after you. That category is subdivided into three: front-of-house, housekeeping, food and beverage.

Concierge

For a guest, one of the most important people is the concierge, or hall porter, as he (almost invariably a man) is known in Great Britain. His value lies in his connections. A good concierge can get you tickets to performances and restaurants that are booked out. He can unlock doors that are closed to the general public. He knows the best florist, bookshop, boutiques, hire-car services. He's in with the airlines. Seasoned travellers on the grand scale know how to make the most of a good concierge. The concierge is boss of the front-of-house department that includes porters, doormen and messengers.

Housekeeping

The chief housekeeper is usually a woman, often one you will never meet, although in a grand hotel she or one of her deputies inspects your room every day to make sure it has been cleaned properly and suitably arranged. If a lamp doesn't work, you'd like more towels or you need your suit pressed in a hurry, you call housekeeping.

A word about sending anything fragile or precious to be dry-cleaned. Even at some very grand hotels, dry-cleaning can be risky. Try to make do until you can hand your treasured clothes to your trusty dry-cleaner at home.

Food and beverage

If you'd like the minibar restocked or you want to order food and drinks sent to your room, you call the food and beverage department, usually listed in the directory under 'room service'. This division also runs all restaurants and bars in the hotel.

Butler

In cases where you have the services of a butler, he or she will expect to be your go-between not only with the other staff but with the outside world. The way to handle this is to summon your butler each morning, go through the activities of the day and then delegate responsibility for arranging meetings, changing or confirming your flights, booking tables in restaurants, sending flowers, buying theatre tickets. Once you get used to it, you'll wonder how you lived without one. But these services do not come cheaply; for details on tipping see pages 368–380.

MODERN HIP HOTELS

Apart from being ambitious in contemporary design, these are geared to attract those people who are more comfortable with current style and informality than with the decorum of the traditional grands. Firmdale Hotels (The Covent Garden, The Pelham and others) in London, the Royalton, Morgans and Paramount in New York, the Buci Latin in Paris, the Mondrian in Los Angeles, Art'Hotel and Hotel Bleibtreu in Berlin exemplify this kind of property. In Melbourne, such hotels include Hotel Lindrum and the Hatton; in Sydney, Regents Court, Establishment Hotel, the Kirketon and W Sydney.

Black tie is virtually unknown in most of them. Staff wear something of the moment, perhaps by a famous designer, and while they'll be efficient, they will not be subservient but more like your equal. In this kind of hotel, there are likely to be guest relations people who look after the needs of all patrons but usually in a less personal way than the butlers mentioned above. The staff-to-guest ratio is not nearly as great as it is in traditional hotels. It's all supposed to make you feel as relaxed and comfortable as you would be at home. Be pleasant and as informal as you choose to be, although in many of these hotels being cool is the expected attitude, just as groove is the right kind of look.

CHAIN HOTELS AND MOTELS

Then there are the countless chain hotels that fall into the upper, middle and lower ranges where you get what you pay for and, in many of them, that can be very good. At the top end are Four Seasons, Park Hyatt, Ritz-Carlton, Inter-Continental, Sheraton, Meridien, Regent,

Sofitel, Westin, and so forth, polished places that lay on the works in service and amenities.

A step down, at a more affordable level, are chain hotels such as Novotel and Travelodge. Then there are the motels that can usually be found around Australia and the rest of the world; they are no-nonsense places where you can park the car and find a clean bed and bathroom for the night. It is important not to let your level of expectation exceed that of the hotel's status. A motel is not The Ritz. Don't expect a porter, fancy toiletries or towelling robes. While properties in the lower ranks are not known for lavishing attention on their patrons, it is still important to smile and be courteous to everyone who works there.

BED AND BREAKFAST

This is a good choice if you prefer company to being anonymous, although the procedure varies from one B&B to another, depending on the dimensions and facilities of the house and the preferences of its owners. Apart from a room of your own, with a private or shared bathroom, you sometimes have a sitting room that you share with other guests. A good breakfast is the only meal provided although, in some places, other meals may be ordered ahead of time.

As the host of a B&B, take care to make the house rules clear and don't encroach on the privacy of your guests unless you are invited to do so. Similarly, as a guest, don't intrude on your host in their own territory. Because there is usually no staff, except perhaps for someone who makes the beds and cleans your room, be considerate in arriving when you say you will so as not to inconvenience your host by having them hang around waiting for you (see also Chapter 13). Try not to make a last-minute cancellation because, unless you give them plenty of warning, they will be unlikely to find a replacement; the loss of income can hurt when there are only a few rooms to let.

Be punctual at breakfast and make sure you let your host know your broad plans for the day, including when you are likely to return.

By all means seek their advice on local sights and other distractions but don't expect them to pamper you, or cause them to go to a lot of trouble to find things out for you. If you need to reconfirm your flight don't ask for the number, reach for the telephone directory. Be friendly but self-sufficient. Don't forget your key otherwise you'll risk waking up the whole house in the middle of the night to get in.

Unforeseen changes

The best of all possible flights are those that are uneventful and depart and arrive on time. It is not always so. When schedules are disrupted, or you lose something as crucial as your passport or traveller's cheques, you realise the necessity of always having the right papers and contact numbers with you. As we've already mentioned, all your travel documents should be duplicated and the second set kept somewhere quite apart from the first; say, one set in your shoulder bag, the other in the pocket of your suitcase.

No matter where you are, you should know how to call home, your office, travel agent, bank, insurance company, the outfit that issued your traveller's cheques and charge cards, the airlines on which you are travelling and the places you are booked to stay in. Efficiency of this kind can't stop unwelcome things happening but it does ease the stress when they do. Being in control of the situation and yourself is a reassuring feeling, especially when you're a long way from your own backyard.

Global guide to tipping

NB When dollars are mentioned here, they are US dollars, except in the context of Australia. For other countries, convert US dollars into local currency.

Opinions differ as to where and when the word 'tip' originated but I believe it started in the coffee houses of London in the early eighteenth century when patrons paid a little extra 'to insure promptness' and its acronym went into common use.

When authorities on the subject of tipping hand out advice in books and magazines, you can bet your last euro that most will reassure you the practice is discretionary, not obligatory. Don't believe it. In North and South America, Europe, Africa and most countries in the Asia–Pacific region, you are expected to hand over some cash to the people who serve you and you will be made to feel uncomfortable if you don't.

There are exceptions but they are few. It is a breach of etiquette to offer a tip to anyone in Japan. Korea had no heritage of tipping until after the Seoul Olympic Games in 1988, although it is largely limited to hotels and restaurants that cater to westerners. With the exception of Hong Kong, tipping is officially illegal in China. However, the arrival of big international hotels has brought western practices and this one has been adopted willingly. Some hotels in Chinese cities make a point of telling clients when a service charge is included in the tariff. Government policy in Singapore specifies that tipping is not necessary but leaves it up to the discretion of the individual to reward exceptional service.

Australians abroad are not known for their generosity. This seems to me to be out of character with our general outlook on life and I can only think that some kind of deep-seated egalitarianism makes us resist master and servant roles. Tipping might be an antiquated custom of which you do not approve, but that is no excuse for being seen as a tightwad. In the United States, where fifteen to twenty per cent of a restaurant bill is the normal gratuity, a waiter's or bartender's pay is not enough to live on; tips are necessary to bring it up to a reasonable level. Compounding the problem, his or her tax is calculated on what the government estimates was received in the form of tips. That means they have to pay tax on the tip whether you gave one or not.

This is why Americans seem to be so ruthless in their expectation of a handout. If I am in any doubt about how much or who to tip in America, I go for broke. In that country service is directly related to fiscal gain. Las Vegas taught me my greatest lesson in tipping. I had a package for the public relations manager of the hotel where I was staying so I left it with one of the concierges. He looked expectant but I had no change so I thought I'd square up when I checked out. The package never reached its destination, two floors up.

Next day, when I got to the airport, there was curbside check-in, that wonderful all-American practice (perhaps now obsolete, with security measures so stringent) that means you hand over your bags and receive your boarding pass the moment you step out of the cab. Having conferred largesse on the taxi driver and received his heartfelt blessings for a wonderful trip, I then peeled off greenbacks for the beaming porter and the check-in man. As I stood there basking in their approval, a backpacker under a huge load approached. The porter eyed him, knew there would be no tip and waved him in the direction of the distant counters inside. This is the American way. When I'm in America, it's my way, too.

Italy is another shocker for the Aussie innocent. While the technique is more subtle there than in the New World, the expectation of a little present is just as strong and the revenge when it is denied is equally clear. One wild winter night, I had to get someone to fix the dishwasher. When it was done, I paid him what he requested, self-righteously deciding not to hand over any extra cash, and asked for a receipt for my landlord. He said, 'Si, signora' and sat down willingly at the table to write it. He then wished me 'Buona sera' politely before he disappeared into the night and I closed the door after him. The receipt was gone. So was my umbrella. After that I gave the equivalent of ten dollars to any tradesman who crossed my threshold. How often do the wise words 'When in Rome do as the Romans do' have to be hammered home?

Most of us who grew up in Australia haven't a clue about the subtleties of tipping because it's not generally part of everyday life. I have even had a chambermaid turn down a tip, some years ago in a hotel, because she felt there was something not quite right in taking it. Taxi drivers are not likely to abuse us, as they do in London and New York, if we don't reward them with something extra. But when we travel it is churlish or naive not to conform to the customs of the countries we visit.

AT AIRPORTS

At civilised airports, luggage carts that you push yourself are usually free. You simply help yourself to one when you arrive, and pick up another when you disembark from your aircraft at your destination. At other airports, you must put money into a slot machine before you can release a trolley. This is an irritating imposition, especially if you don't have the right change in local currency. At Australian airports, trolleys at departure terminals have to be paid for, but at least when you arrive from somewhere the use of trolleys at international terminals is free.

There are times when you have lots of luggage, or you're particularly tired, or you just need someone to take a load off your mind as well as your body and steer you through Customs or speed your time at check-in. That is what porters are for. At US airports they are called sky-caps. Often they operate at a fixed rate and that's a big help, although it can be quite expensive at airports such as Heathrow in London. If there is no fixed rate, offer one or two dollars for each bag. In Australia, a dollar per bag is adequate.

IN TAXIS AND LIMOUSINES

Add ten per cent to the fare in most countries and fifteen per cent in the US (with a two-dollar minimum) but just round out the amount to the nearest dollar in Australia. Don't hesitate to ask for a receipt from any of them. If you don't speak the local tongue, communicate in sign language. In some instances, there might be a flat rate for a journey rather than one calculated by a meter. Find out before you enter a cab which method is used, and if it is the former, agree on a fare before you start. Add a tip at the end of the journey if you have been happy with it.

Limousines vary, from a cushy vehicle you have to yourself to a mini-bus shared with others. Tip accordingly. Add the same percentage to the driver of a private limo as you would for a taxi. Give a token amount of one or two dollars to the driver of the mini-bus.

ON TOUR BUSES

At the end of a half-day or a day tour with a large group, it is customary for each person to give the guide and the driver one or two dollars each. If the tour lasts for several days or weeks, still calculate on one or two dollars each a day.

IN HOTELS

It might be simplest to start with the people whose palms you do not have to grease. You do not tip receptionists, cashiers and the people who run the business side of things. Having said that, I see nothing wrong with sending flowers or giving a present to a receptionist or secretary who has been particularly helpful, but money is not appropriate.

In the other division are the people who provide the services, at the front of house and behind the scenes. They are there to look after you and it is important for you to understand your role as well as theirs. They expect you to know how to use them and how to reward them.

Before you even get to the hotel, make sure you have the appropriate change in your pocket for the porter (bellhop in America) who takes your bags to your room. If you don't, get some from the cashier when you check in. Give one or two dollars a bag. In the United States, don't be pressured into handing over more just because he shows you how the room works. On the other hand, if a porter seems genuinely to have your comfort and not his own venality in mind, feel free to add a subsidy. In my experience, it is rare for a porter to place a bag in the proper position for unpacking – say, on a collapsible rest near the wardrobe or on a bench provided in a dressingroom. Sometimes a porter puts the bag in the right spot but fails to notice when it is upside down. When a porter gets it right, I have been known to spray dollars around like confetti at a wedding.

In a foreign country, don't leave tips in Australian currency unless it is freely acceptable in that country; the assumption that the other person should take the trouble to change the money is patronising. In my experience, the only foreign currency that is almost universally acceptable is the US dollar, but not in the Arab world, where it is astute to use local currency. Whenever you travel to poorer countries, such as India, it is a good idea to take a swag of single American dollars and give one to each and every person who does anything for you in the hotel. However, do not make the mistake of adopting the same practice in the streets or you'll be besieged.

Think ahead and be prepared for the unexpected, such as two porters (divide the tip between them or give the money to one and say it is intended for both) or the delivery of flowers or a written message to your room. Always have the equivalent of a few single dollars handy so that you don't have to fumble or make a production out of finding the right coins or notes. Don't tip the porter until the bags get to your room; it's an incentive for them to materialise swiftly. In some hotels, a guest relations person or duty manager will show you to your room and point out how certain things there work. Do not tip this person. He or she is part of management.

Butler

If you are provided with the services of a butler, that person should introduce himself or herself within minutes of your arrival. Remember your butler's name and, ideally, think of something he or she can do: unpack your bag, bring some herbal tea, take something to be pressed. As a gesture of goodwill, and to ensure that you will be well looked after, you might press a note or two into your butler's hand straightaway.

A smooth way of doing this is to shake hands, slipping the money into the other's hand as you do so. A fair tip for your butler would be ten dollars a day; more, if you are relentless with your requests.

Room attendant

A person often neglected because rarely seen is the one who cleans your room. It is not the world's most inspiring job, neither is it well paid, so an extra dollar or two a day is money well spent. When I check out, I usually leave the money in an envelope, inscribed with 'Many thanks' and my signature, under the pillow of my unmade bed. That way I'm confident it will get to the right person. I used to leave loose money under the pillow each morning until the time when I found it on the bedside table after the room had been serviced. That gesture reminded me that anyone who services your room is vulnerable and needs to be sure any money left out is intended for him or her and not something that fell out of a pocket by mistake. This precaution is not altogether altruistic. If you have forgotten something in your haste to pack, it's more likely to be returned if you have been generous.

Room service

If you order food on room service – breakfast, for example – and you don't have cash, the simplest thing to do is add the tip to the bill, as you would in a restaurant, before you sign it. Make sure, though, that a percentage has not already been added. Leave what you would normally in a restaurant. If you are not wide awake enough first thing in the morning to cope with money, leave it under the table napkin when you have finished breakfast.

Concierge

There is no need to tip the concierge unless you ask him or her to do something for you, such as give directions, book a tour, buy theatre tickets, recommend and book restaurants, or whatever, in which case five or ten dollars is adequate. However, if you ask a big favour, such as good seats at the hottest play in town, or the best table at the most famous restaurant, think upwards of twenty dollars. Don't be too concerned if the one who fulfilled your wishes is not at the desk when you leave. Tips usually go into a common fund to be shared.

If the doorman makes an effort to find you a cab, give him a dollar. Give a dollar or two to the attendant who brings your car from the car park.

RESTAURANTS

Ten per cent of the total bill (excluding the tax, if applicable) is usual in restaurants throughout the world. The figure can creep up to fifteen per cent in expensive restaurants in the United Kingdom, France and Germany but it is usually added to the bill as 'service', which means you don't need to do anything, except be prepared for it. However, feel free to reward attitude and service if they have been exceptional.

In the United States, fifteen to twenty per cent is expected. This amount is not usually on the bill when you receive it so you are meant to add it yourself. The percentage is easy to calculate in New York City, where tax on dining is 8.5 per cent and it should be itemised clearly on the bill; you just double the tax to make a perfectly acceptable 17 per cent of the pre-tax total. You do the same in Los Angeles, where the tax on dining is 7.5 per cent. You may write the tip on the bill or pay it in cash.

If it's a particularly smart restaurant with a captain or maître d', it is advisable to pass money to him when you shake hands on departing, particularly if you plan to come back and you want a good table and the best of care. Ten dollars should merit solicitous attention next time. If, when you first arrive at a restaurant, whoever is in charge takes you in ahead of the queue, that deserves a reward of five or ten dollars, but not if it's the owner.

A dollar per person to any cloakroom attendant and fifty cents to the person who hands you a towel in the washroom is enough.

BARS AND NIGHTCLUBS

In glamorous bars all over the world, such as those in deluxe international hotels, tip fifteen per cent, the standard gratuity for all bars in the US. If you request a special song from a pianist or disc jockey at a nightclub, one dollar should do, unless you want the song played immediately, in which case be prepared to splurge with five or ten dollars.

In British pubs, you don't tip at the bar but you would leave around ten per cent for service in a lounge. It is not usual to tip at the bar in Australian pubs but you might leave the small change on the counter.

HAIR AND BEAUTY SALONS

Do not tip the owner of the business – even if he or she attends to your hair, face or body – but when you settle your bill do tip any others who wait on you. Once you are familiar with a salon, its people and its charges, you can be confident of tipping as you go along. If the operator's hands are busy attending to another customer, slip the money into the pocket of his or her overall. If this uniform has a pocket in the top of the sleeve, you don't have to try too hard to guess what it's for.

Don't be put off if you don't have the right change. Be straightforward and ask the cashier for the denominations you need. Give a couple of dollars to the person who shampoos your hair or prepares you for a facial or massage. Give the main operator – hairdresser, masseur, manicurist or pedicurist – between ten and twenty per cent of the fee charged for that particular service. For example, if you are presented with one bill that covers hair styling, facial and manicure, calculate tips on the charges for individual items rather than on the sum total or you may find yourself spending more on tips than on your own beautification. If this is too complicated, just give the total tip to the manager and ask for it to be distributed to the right people. Carry it all off with a smile and aplomb because the whole thing should seem to be a pleasure not the pain in the neck it sometimes becomes for many of us.

CRUISE SHIPS

The practice dies hard on the high seas although some cruise lines now include tips in the fare. If gratuities are expected, there will be a guide in your cabin suggesting suitable amounts for cabin and dining-room stewards. As with the butler in a grand hotel, it is a good idea to give your cabin steward something in advance as encouragement and reassurance that you understand the correct form. Shipboard gratuities are quite hefty and can increase the overall cost of a journey by as much as ten to fifteen per cent so it's important to scan the literature before you finalise the booking to find out whether or not they have been included in the quoted fare. On no account think that a prettily wrapped gift with a thank-you card can ever be a substitute for money in these circumstances. That is totally out of order.

On a superior cruise ship, if tips have not been included in the fare, appropriate amounts would be: cabin steward three dollars, dining-room steward three dollars, maître d' one dollar fifty and busboy one dollar fifty, from each person for each day of the voyage. In other words, on a fourteen-day cruise, a cabin steward should be given forty-two dollars from each person attended. The maître d' would receive twenty-one dollars from each person, a tidy sum when you think of the number of tables in his realm. At the bar, fifteen per cent is usually added automatically to the bill, as it is to the tab for drinks from the wine steward in the dining room.

PRIVATE HOUSES

In lofty circles, especially overseas, you might be invited to spend a night or more as a guest in a private household that has permanent or part-time staff. It is customary to tip anyone who has more work to do because of your presence – that is, the people who tidy your room, make your bed and handle your laundry (see page 333). The chauffeur who picks up your shopping and the groom who washes your car as a special favour also deserve a token of appreciation in the form of cash.

How much you give is up to you but, if you know your hosts well, it is a good idea to ask their advice on what is acceptable in that particular house. Within their guidelines, give as much as you can afford. If you are not comfortable about asking, then a general rule is to give ten dollars a day, or thirty dollars for a weekend, to each person. It is appropriate to give your maid the same as you'd give the butler because, as one butler told me, 'the private nature of her service compensates for her being lower in the household hierarchy'. In a very grand spread with a sizeable staff, you tip only the people who have looked after you. If the household staff numbers fewer than five, you tip them all.

It is customary to bestow this in cash just before you leave. In a vast stately home with many willing hands, you could ring from your bedroom for the housekeeping staff who have served you and give each folded notes – in an envelope, if you wish – with a warm smile, a thank you and a few pleasantries. If you plan to tip the butler, do so in the hall on your way out. Tip the chauffeur in the car.

If you don't know who has been attending to your needs, or if you are nervous or embarrassed about tipping, it is best to put the total amount into an envelope, give it to the butler and ask him to apportion it. In fact, that is the simplest and safest solution of all because some butlers, particularly those in charge of a very large staff, might be so well paid that a top-up from a house guest could be offensive unless it is a very handsome one for some service beyond the call of duty. On the other hand, a butler whose responsibilities are not so great probably expects to be tipped. There are no strict rules to follow because each household is different and no two are managed in the same way. Listen to your own instincts. On no account ask the butler what is appropriate or you will be thought not quite up to the circumstances in which you find yourself. If you need guidance, ask another guest or, as mentioned earlier, your host.

In a smaller house, if you can't find the staff in the public rooms just before you finally leave, go into the kitchen to reward and thank everyone, including the cook.

CASINOS

Tipping is forbidden in all casinos in Australia. However, that's not the case elsewhere in the world. In Austria, France and Germany, for example, if you are gambling fairly large amounts it's common to give three to five per cent of your winnings to the dealer at games such as roulette, blackjack, craps and poker. Small-time punters and slot-machine players are not expected to tip. All these tips, supplemented by a certain percentage of takings from slot machines, go into the pool from which casino employees are paid. In other words, tips are their primary source of income.

If you strike it rich in the casinos of Macau, Asia's traditional gambling mecca, you are expected to leave between one and three per cent of your winnings in gratitude for your good fortune. If you don't win, think how lucky you are not to have to leave anything.

Las Vegas, gambling capital of the world, is as good a place as any to give examples of appropriate tips in the US. There you might give a dollar to the cocktail waitress at a casino for every free drink you take from her, and a dollar a round to the bartender if you are seated at the bar. Tip the dealer at a gaming table by placing a bet next to your own often during play and finish with something extra, depending on how much you won and how generous you feel.

When you buy a ticket to a show in Las Vegas, drinks are usually included and may be served at your table; check to see if service has also been added, in which case you are not expected to leave anything in addition. If you have to go to a bar for the drinks, leave a dollar or two for the bartender.

PRESENTS AT CHRISTMAS IN AUSTRALIA

If you have someone who cleans your house regularly, it is customary to give an extra week's wages as a bonus at Christmas plus a special present of some kind, possibly boxed crystallised fruits, glacé chestnuts, chocolates or fragrant toiletries. Be mindful not to give anything containing alcohol to someone whose religion forbids it.

It is appropriate but not obligatory in Australia to give a Christmas gift of money, a bottle of wine or a few cans of beer to anyone who consistently delivers groceries, liquor or anything else to your house. Give the same to a regular handyman. The tradition of giving something to the garbage collectors and posties seems to have died out.

If an apartment building with a company title employs a full-time superintendent, concierge, gardener or handyman, the body corporate might give a Christmas bonus in the form of a week's wages – or more, depending on the services performed – plus a case of beer or wine. Individual apartment-dwellers might choose to give something on top of that, particularly if the employee has been especially helpful to them during the year.

OTHERS

In the United States, you give: one to five dollars for takeaway food delivery; five to ten dollars per person for delivery of furniture or heavy appliances; two to five dollars for delivery of flowers; five to ten dollars for delivery of a large plant; fifteen per cent of the bill for dog grooming and dog walking; and fifty cents to one dollar per party to the usher at a sports venue. In any other country, if ever you're unsure of the tipping protocol, just ask someone reliable what's customary.

Chapter Sixteen

CALENDAR OF AUSTRALIAN FESTIVITIES

C ollective celebrations have been an important part of human life since people first started living in tribes. We all share the need for joyous release and the wondrously varied and creative ways in which we choose to express ourselves is a clear demonstration of the limitless scope of human faith, hope, imagination, gravity and irreverence.

Of all the special days in an Australian year, several stand out for their particular significance. Some arise from religious belief. Some commemorate important times in history. Some are just for fun and embrace superstitions and practices from pagan times. The degree of importance they hold for each of us depends on who we are and where we have come from. The beliefs and traditions of others, whether or not we share them, must be respected. We should always be sensitive to friends, colleagues and acquaintances who are going through periods of self-discipline, such as fasting, and not tease them, try to weaken their resolve, put them under pressure or regard them as curiosities. Bringing the traditions of our former homelands far away gives all of us a sense of continuity, keeping alive positive cultural links that add to the richness of Australian society as a whole.

JANUARY

After midnight on 31 December, many Scots take a bottle of whisky and perhaps some shortbread and make house calls in what is known as 'first footing', which means being the first person to put a foot over the threshold of the houses of friends and neighbours. If the first person to visit your house is a tall, dark stranger, you'll have a lucky year, according to a custom that's believed to date back to the Viking invasion when a blond Nordic type would not have been welcome.

EPIPHANY

On 6 January, the Christian holy day of Epiphany commemorates the coming of the Magi, the three wise men, to acknowledge the baby Jesus as the son of God. It is also known as Twelfth Night, the date by which all Christmas decorations should have been taken down and put away. Certain Christian groups, including Armenians, Greeks, Russians and some Central and South Americans, celebrate Christmas on this date instead of 25 December.

PILGRIMAGE TO MECCA

Depending on the year, the Muslim holy day of Eid al-Adha may occur this month, commemorating Ibrahim's (Abraham's) offer to sacrifice his son as an act of devotion to Allah (God). A sheep is killed and the meat shared among family, friends and the poor. The festival coincides with the hajj, the pilgrimage that a believer who can afford it is expected to take at least once during his or her lifetime, to Mecca in Saudi Arabia, birthplace of Islam.

FAMILY HOLIDAYS

For many of us, January is a lazy month of heat, holidays, the cricket and the Australian Open, the beach and the barby. Its finale occurs on 26 January, Australia Day, which commemorates the arrival of the First Fleet in 1788.

FEBRUARY AND MARCH

Various important events fall on different dates from one year to the next due to the fact that not all societies and religions use the same method of calculating time. In any case, it seems that none of these methods is entirely accurate so compensations have to be made to make sure festivals do not drift into inappropriate seasons.

CHINESE NEW YEAR

This falls on the second new moon after the summer solstice (about 22 December) so it usually takes place in February. In preparation, the house is cleaned throughout, cupboards and everything, and all debts are settled. Sweets are exchanged, a hangover from times when people believed in a kitchen god, who watched over the household and reported on its doings once a year to the Jade Emperor; sweets were used to influence him to 'sweeten' his report. Sharp instruments must not be used in preparing feasts because they might cut the good luck. There are usually lively street parades and festivities in cities where there's a strong Chinese population.

Anybody who is unmarried is given 'lucky money' in red packages and the amount you give depends on how close you are to that person; what's important is not the sum but the gesture. You are not supposed to sweep the floor for three days because you might sweep away the luck and the money. You're not supposed to chastise anybody either, not even your children. You wish everyone good luck, prosperity, good health and happiness.

BE MY VALENTINE

When we send long-stemmed red roses to a beloved on 14 February, who among us pauses to wonder who Valentine was? Poor St Valentine literally lost his head for being a Chistian in Rome in the year 270 and later was made patron saint of lovers. And why red roses? According to a Persian legend, the white rose represented the ultimate in flowers until its thorns drew blood from a lovesick nightingale, which stained it red.

MARRY ME

Every four years, February has twenty-nine days and according to tradition that bonus day gives a woman the opportunity to propose marriage to a man instead of the other way around. I wonder if she has to buy him an engagement ring and ask his mother for his hand?

DAYS OF REJOICING

In the days or weeks preceding Ash Wednesday, which signals the beginning of Lent, mardi gras is staged enthusiastically in Europe and Latin America. Sydney's Gay and Lesbian Mardi Gras spans a month and culminates in a graphic and uninhibited parade along Oxford Street to Centennial Park. Whether these events occur in February or March depends on the date of Easter; the timing of Ash Wednesday is set at forty days before Holy Week, which ushers in Easter.

Sometime in March at a date determined by the lunar calendar, the Jews have a day of celebration called Purim to mark the triumphant defeat of a plot to destroy their forebears in ancient Persia.

SOBRIETY FOR LENT

The day before Lent is called Shrove Tuesday, also known as Pancake Day, when sins are supposed to be absolved. An old-fashioned tradition is to celebrate by cooking, flipping and eating pancakes. From Ash Wednesday until Easter, good Christians are expected to show discipline and fortitude by giving up something they like and it's usually food or drink. Some people give up meat, sweets or rich ingredients, such as butter, oil and cream. Some give up alcohol. Some people eat only one meal a day.

WEARING OF THE GREEN

On 17 March, anyone with a drop of Irish blood (and many without any ties to Ireland) wears something green as a tribute to St Patrick, patron saint of Ireland, and pubs do grand business. Although there is at least one pub in Victoria that sells green beer, I have never seen a green bagel such as Jewish bakers sell in New York on St Patrick's Day.

EASTER

The significance of Easter for Christians is sorrow for the crucifixion on Good Friday and joy in the resurrection on Easter Sunday. Traditional foods for Good Friday are smoked fish and hot cross buns. On Easter Sunday, painted or chocolate eggs are exchanged, or hidden in the garden by the Easter Bunny for children to find. There has been a move in Australia to replace the bunny (rabbits not being a welcome species here) with the bilby, a native bandicoot with rabbit-like ears.

ORTHODOX CHRISTIANS

Greek Easter usually falls on a different date from the one set by Catholic and Protestant churches because the Orthodox church works to a different calendar. It is a very important festival for the Greeks, many of whom attend church on Friday, Saturday and Sunday. A floral 'tomb' with the figure of Christ inside is the centrepiece in the church. On Friday evening it is brought out for a street procession in which each person in the congregation carries a lit candle.

On Saturday, people start entering the church from about nine p.m. At midnight it is plunged into darkness before the priest lights a candle from the holy light within the altar. His act symbolises the resurrection of Christ. That candle ignites all the candles held by the congregation.

People greet each other by saying 'Cristos anesti' (Christ has arisen) and go home to break their fast on a supper of special breads, biscuits, boiled eggs in red-dyed shells, and other light foods, such as egg-and-lemon soup and fish. Sunday is the day of abundance and generosity when lamb is roasted on the spit and a proper feast gets under way to celebrate the resurrection.

PESACH (PASSOVER)

This is an important eight-day Jewish remembrance of the Israelites' redemption from slavery in Egypt. Pesach is centred in the family and revolves around the story of Exodus in ritualised tellings called *seders* in synagogues and temples and at the family table. Since a Jewish day begins and ends at sundown, any event dates from sundown on the previous day.

During this time it is forbidden to eat, or to have in the house, any food containing barley, millet, oats, rye or wheat, except for matzo, a crisp unleavened bread. Food and drinks that contain any of these grains, which are known as *hametz*, include bread, pastries, cakes, biscuits, pasta, beer and whisky. Some Jews also abstain from eating other grains and legumes, such as rice, corn, peas and beans.

When the Pesach table is set for the highly ritualised *seder*, particular foods are presented on the *seder* plate for their symbolic significance. They include a roasted shank bone (sacrificial offering), green vegetable (spring), salt water (tears), horseradish (bitterness) and hard-boiled egg (rebirth). Gefilte fish, chicken soup, matzo balls, salmon, beef, roast veal, turkey, mushrooms, carrots and chocolate are favourite foods for the feast.

APRIL

Unless Easter falls during this month, the most important date is 25 April, Anzac Day, when many people congregate at the cenotaph of their nearest city for a dawn service to commemorate Australians who have participated and died in war. The date was chosen because on 25 April 1915, Australian soldiers were involved in a bungled allied attack on Turkey. Thousands of them lost their lives, primarily because the troops were landed on the wrong beach, which made them vulnerable to a well-equipped force led by Mustafa Kemal, who ultimately became Atatürk, founder and hero of modern Turkey. After the service, crowds cheer as servicemen and women, some wearing uniform and decorations, march in the streets. Celebrations continue all day.

May, June, July and August

Public holidays of various kinds are declared in certain states and not others during these months. The first Monday in May is May Day in the Northern Territory and Labour Day in Queensland. South Australia has the third Monday in May off for Adelaide Cup Day and Western Australia does the same on the first Monday in June for Foundation Day. The second Monday in June marks the Queen's Birthday in all states except Western Australia, which dips its lid to HM on the Monday nearest 30 September. The winter solstice falls around 21 June, which is a good time for a 'winter' Christmas dinner. The first Monday in August is Picnic Day in the Northern Territory. Brisbane Royal Show Day is on the Wednesday in the second week of August.

September

Sometime in September or October, depending on the lunar calendar, the Jewish New Year begins with the celebration of Rosh Hashanah, the anniversary of God's creation of the world. It lasts two days and ushers in eight days of atonement that finish with Yom Kippur, the final day of reckoning, when people fast for twenty-five hours. In religious services a *shophar* (a trumpet made from the curved horn of a ram) is sounded to arouse spiritual awareness. On celebratory tables, the head of a fish is sometimes presented, symbolising the wish to be at the forefront of the coming year. *Challah*, a bread made with yeast and eggs, is always served. So is honey, to represent sweetness in life, and other festive foods.

OCTOBER AND NOVEMBER

New South Wales, the Australian Capital Territory and South Australia take their Labour Day holiday on the first Monday in October. Hobart Show Day falls on the Thursday after 17 October and its Recreation Day on the first Monday in November. One of the world's most famous racing events, the Melbourne Cup, falls on the first Tuesday in November.

WITCHES' NIGHT OUT

Although Halloween on the night of 31 October is not celebrated as widely in Australia as it is in the USA, it gives children a thrill to think that ghosts and goblins are about. They enjoy dressing up as witches and warlocks to knock on doors and cry 'trick or treat', which translates as 'give us some sweets or we'll play a trick on you', a threat it's not customary to exercise. The contemporary world being what it is, it's wise for a couple of parents to be hovering when their children and friends embark on these adventures.

THANKSGIVING

To Americans, the fourth Thursday in November is one of the most important dates in the calendar, when thanks are given for the yield of the harvest with a feast that has its origins with the Puritans of New England in the early seventeenth century. Although the kind of food that is put on the table varies from one state to another, its traditional centrepiece is turkey with cranberry sauce and lots of trimmings, such as corn, sweet potato, squash and beans followed by pumpkin and pecan pie. It is a family time of gratitude for privilege and plenty.

RAMADAN

The month-long celebration of Ramadan is of great significance to Muslims because it commemorates the month when Allah, through the archangel Gabriel, revealed the first verses of the Qur'an to Mohammed. Because its date is dictated by the lunar calendar, Ramadan moves on by eleven days each year. In 2002 it begins at sundown on 5 November so, to calculate when it falls in 2003, subtract eleven days from that date.

For the entire month of Ramadan, Muslims have nothing to eat or drink between dawn and sunset. Tobacco is also forbidden. Most of them rise before dawn for prayers and breakfast. The next meal they have will be when the sun disappears over the horizon. Meanwhile, they go about their normal duties. Muslims believe that fasting purifies the spirit and builds self-discipline, a sense of fellowship and empathy with the privation of those less privileged. People who can afford it donate 2.5 per cent of their year's financial gains to the poor.

A sighting of the next new moon signals the end of Ramadan and the beginning of the Festival of Breaking the Fast (Eid al-Fitr), when Muslims dress in their finest to congregate for prayers, confer holiday blessings on each other, sit down to a great feast and enjoy two or three days of goodwill and get-togethers, similar to the way Christians celebrate Christmas.

DECEMBER

In or around December, Jewish people celebrate Hanukkah, the Festival of Lights, which commemorates a victory by the Israelites over the Hellenic Syrians. For eight nights prayers are said and a candle or a wick dipped in oil is placed in a nine-branch candelabra called a Hanukkah *menorah*. These candles are lit from the central candle, called a *shamash*. The ritual pays tribute to the immediate aftermath of the victory when the Jews reclaiming their Temple found only a day's worth of oil to light the *menorah*. Miraculously, it lasted for eight days. Certain foods cooked in olive oil are standard fare at this time. They include potato latkes and *sufganiyot*, an oddly shaped jam doughnut dusted with sugar. A game is played for sweets or coins using a spinning top called a *dreidel*.

THE FESTIVE SEASON

The most widely celebrated and commercialised holiday in any Australian year is Christmas Day, 25 December, and the build-up to it starts weeks ahead. As leaders of the church are fond of reminding us, it is a religious holiday, although it's fair to say that for a great many Australians it is nothing more than a chance to be with family and friends, no matter what their beliefs, to exchange gifts and over-indulge in good food and wine. While the traditions of Christmas as we know it have their origins in the northern European winter, incongruities in their relocation to an Australian summer seem to go unnoticed. Home cooks slave over the preparation of puddings, Santas sweat in their arctic outfits and families hang fake icicles, cottonwool snow, electric candles and plastic holly on felled pine trees that wilt in the heat. But that's Christmas.

SOME EUROPEAN TRADITIONS

The Austrians and Germans begin their rituals on the first weekend of December with an Advent wreath made of pine branches with room for four candles, one of which will be placed there and lit on each of the four Sundays until Christmas. There is also a special Advent calendar for children; behind the date of each day leading up to 24 December is a little treat, usually a chocolate.

On the night of 5 December, children put their shoes out hoping that St Nicholas, who arrives next day to assess their behaviour over the past year, will fill them with chocolates, oranges and other gifts. He is often accompanied by the sinister Knecht Ruprecht, who has a sack containing naughty children (their rag doll legs sticking out), a persuasive reason for being good.

The Italians have a similar character called La Befana, a kind of witch who arrives overnight on Christmas Eve. If the children have been good, she fills their shoes with toys and other goodies. If they were bad, she fills them with coal.

Finnish children are the luckiest in the world on Christmas Eve because Father Christmas, played by daddy or a family friend, visits them in person and they dress as his little helpers in anticipation of the visit. Before opening his sack he asks, 'Are there any good children here?' and you can guess the reply.

CHRISTMAS EVE IN AUSTRALIA

December 24 is the time for having a drink with colleagues from the office. Whether or not you exchange presents with them depends on your level of friendship and on company culture (see pages 170–172). It's also time to deck the Christmas tree, wrap the presents and, if you feel inclined and have the voice for it, to go carol singing with friends. While 'Jingle Bells', 'White Christmas' and 'Rudolph the Red-nosed Reindeer' seem to be ubiquitous, particularly in shopping malls, the great time-honoured carols are the ones serious carollers should learn.

One of the most interesting is 'The Twelve Days of Christmas', because its delightfully fanciful lyrics are not as innocent as they seem. Between 1558 and 1829, Catholics were forbidden to practise their religion in England. The carol is said to have been written in code as a learning tool for children.

Its words start like this: 'On the first day of Christmas, my true love gave to me a partridge in a pear tree. On the second day of Christmas, my true love gave to me two turtledoves and a partridge in a pear tree' and so on, through three French hens, four calling birds, five gold rings, six geese a-laying, seven swans a-swimming, eight maids a-milking, nine ladies dancing, ten lords a-leaping, eleven pipers piping and twelve drummers drumming.

The 'true love' is God, who gives 'me', the baptised person, all these presents: a partridge (Jesus), two turtledoves (Old and New Testaments), three hens (faith, hope and charity), four birds (the evangelists), five gold rings (the first five books of the Old Testament), six geese (six days of creation), seven swans (the sacraments), eight maids (beatitudes), nine ladies (fruits of the Holy Spirit), ten lords (ten commandments), eleven pipers (faithful apostles) and twelve drummers (twelve points of the Apostles' Creed).

CHRISTMAS DAY

Since this day is a family time, it's important to establish well ahead of December who is going to host the occasion. As children grow to adulthood and acquire partners and children of their own, a subtle change of roles begins to take place; grandparents start to seem more like dependants as their children take on more responsibility within the family.

It's a delicate time. As the older person, you might welcome being relieved of the burden of having everyone at your place. Or you might not. Either way, be flexible and gracious. As a younger person who is anxious to demonstrate how brilliant the day can be, don't push it too far if you sense real resistance. Remember that such a shift might indicate a loss of capability to an older person. It's a confirmation of creeping old age, so be thoughtful, kind and inclusive.

If there is competition between siblings for the right to host the day, the best solution is to make it a movable feast each year. No matter who is host in any given year, everyone else should rise to the occasion and be useful in any way they can. That way everyone feels part of it. Since it's an expensive time, family members might offer beforehand to contribute something practical: a box of cherries, a case of wine, a salad, the dessert or simply the willingness to fetch and carry or be the chauffeur on a shopping expedition.

It's also a time to be generous and inclusive of people who are without their families. The presence of stranger or two at the Christmas table often prompts others to make more effort at conversation and charm than they might do with a group of family members who are all too familiar, and lift the level of chat above domestic detail and family doings.

Bring good humour and goodwill to the day and be prepared to head off potential ructions. Not all members of an extended family adore each other and some might be there under sufferance. Alcohol has a way of dissolving inhibitions and loosening tongues and that sometimes leads to behaviour that might be regretted tomorrow. It's a pity to spoil the day for everyone else, so do the heroic deed of defusing anything that looks explosive.

The groaning table

As other traditions now influence the ones that formed the basis of an Australian Christmas, we have become more realistic and relaxed about the foods we cook and serve. All manner of shellfish, smoked salmon, salads and ice cream are the new mainstays, although turkey, ham and steamed pudding die hard in some households. No matter what you serve, make the table look welcoming and festive with your best plates, glasses and cutlery, and plenty of Christmas crackers. Beautiful presentation adds to the merriment, the quality of the day and the taste of the food. Be as generous as your means allow. It's not a time to be stingy.

BOXING DAY

December 26 is a day for leisure when entertaining is rarely more formal than being barefoot in the garden, eating delicacies left over from yesterday. Sales in the stores immediately after the holiday lure some people to town but others prefer to disappear to holiday houses or just enjoy being at home.

NEW YEAR'S EVE

Big crowds, displays of fireworks, the popping of champagne corks, hooting, revelry and the singing of 'Auld Lang Syne' seems to be the global way of greeting a new calendar year. Making a noise has pagan origins; it was done to ward off evil spirits. The Japanese eat buckwheat noodles, which symbolise long life, and make sure the house is clean and tidy and all matters have been finalised by the end of the old year. The Italians toss unwanted pots and pans into the street from their balconies along with money, for good luck, and sup on *zampone* (pork sausage) with lentils, which symbolise money. The Germans fling little spoonfuls of molten lead into cold water and, when it solidifies, the shape it takes is supposed to indicate what the new year will bring. The Scots put their houses in order and clear all debts before midnight.

As we raise our glasses and exchange kisses on the stroke of midnight, we are sincere in making resolutions to be better human beings in the year about to start. Wouldn't it be wonderful if we could keep them?

Chapter Seventeen

THERE GOES
THE MARRIAGE

How could it happen to you? Your mother is distraught, your father is stony-faced, your best friend is tearful, your spouse is not the person you married. The whole world is talking about it. And they're all saying you were such a lovely couple. Even if you know your marriage was far from perfect, even if there is someone else in whose arms you are blissfully happy and whether or not you were the one to force the break, the shock of separation is profound, particularly if you have children.

AVOIDING ACRIMONY

One reason why these things often start out calmly and finish up acrimoniously is because there is nothing like a divorce to make even the most civilised people forget their manners. So much is at stake and it's not just material. There's hurt pride, anger, a feeling of failure, a sense of loss, the need to apportion blame, dread of what other people are saying about you and fear of the future.

If you have children, they will want and need reassurance. Belittling the other parent is totally inappropriate, no matter how much you feel it is deserved. While demeaning the other person may give you some transient pleasure, it is likely to do far more harm than good to your relationship with your children in the long run.

DIVORCE

To apply for a divorce under Australian law you or your partner needs to establish that you have sufficient ties to Australia, such as having lived here for the past twelve months, or that one of you is an Australian citizen. To instigate divorce proceedings, you also need to establish that there is no hope of a reconciliation between the two of you, which must be evidenced by your having been separated for twelve months. You can lodge the application at either the Family Court or with the Federal Magistrates Service, which has considerably cheaper filing fees.

Obtaining a divorce is a totally different procedure from working out arrangements for the children and dividing property. A divorce is simply the dissolution of your marriage and is quite separate from the settling of parenting and property issues. You do not have to wait for twelve months from the date of separation before resolving your parenting or property disputes; an application in relation to those issues may be lodged as soon as you separate. Again, such applications may be lodged with either the Family Court or the Federal Magistrates Service, in certain circumstances. By all means lodge the application on your own behalf but, at this time of high emotion, engaging a solicitor who practises in family law might be the better option.

The big choices are who will take the children, the house, the furniture and other assets and who will pay the bills. The best outcome is the one you reach by yourselves or with the help of a counsellor – say, from a body such as Relationships Australia, which used to be called Marriage Guidance. It is prudent to have the agreement checked by a solicitor to ensure that you are receiving what you are entitled to, and that all issues have been covered. A solicitor can also put the agreement into proper legal form and have it lodged at the Family Court.

CHILDREN COME FIRST

Every effort should be made to avoid a bitter public wrangle over who gains residence (formerly called 'custody') of a child. It is not only the antithesis of good manners but an indication of immaturity and self-ishness on the part of one of the parents, or both. If the parties engaging in this kind of battle truly considered the wellbeing of the child, they would surely recognise what damage their zeal is likely to inflict on the object of their hopes and desires. And all in the name of love, which is a word people often use to mask possessiveness. When courtesy is jettisoned under stress, barbarism takes its place. Whatever the outcome, nobody wins.

Research by Relationships Australia into which aspect of divorce has the most negative effect on children – the separation itself, or the attitude of the parents to each other afterwards – acrimonious behaviour turned out to be the culprit. Children of parents who were amiable and cooperative with each other were less affected by the divorce than the children of antagonistic parents. A side issue, and an important one, is that a child who loses contact with one parent often also loses that parent's extended family – the grandparents, aunts, uncles, cousins – and is left with only half the family to which she or he is entitled.

When you tell your children that you plan to divorce, do it as a couple, not separately, and predetermine the party line to make sure your stories are consistent. Unless they are adults, ask yourself if they need to know what happens in court or, indeed, whether they have to know the court is involved at all. The judiciary take a dim view of children being subjected to the sordid details of what goes on in court. If the divorce is likely to be fodder for the media, it's best to explain to your children what is happening beforehand rather than put them through the shock of watching it on television, reading it in a newspaper or hearing about it at school. Do that as calmly as you can. Try not to exaggerate its importance by seeming to be upset by it, even if you are.

PARENTAL RESPONSIBILITY

Regardless of whether you live together, are separated or are divorced, each of you has responsibility for your children until they turn eighteen years of age. If it is impossible for you to find a mutually agreeable solution regarding the children, the court can make the decision for you. It will set down orders that outline the responsibilities of each parent in relation to each child. The interests of the child will be paramount in deciding who will be given residence, the degree of contact (formerly called 'access') given to the other parent and where financial support will come from. According to the law, parents' rights to spend time with their children are secondary to a child's rights to be in touch with both parents.

Needless to say, the less you need to prevail on the court for solutions the better. In Australia, about 95 per cent of disputes intended for the Family Court and the Federal Magistrates Service are settled before they get there. The age of the children is crucial to any decisions about who lives where. For example, a very young child's needs will be best served by the primary carer, whereas an older child might be happy spending every second week with the other parent, if that household can cope and it's not too far away. Arrangements need to be flexible to keep pace with children's needs as they grow.

The best possible outcome is for both parents to make a supreme effort to put their children's wellbeing before any other consideration. You need to reassure them that they are loved, that they don't have to choose between you because it's all right to love you both, and that they are in no way to blame for the split. You need to be in touch with them constantly, even if it has to be by telephone or email or letter for a lot of the time, and take a keen interest in their schooling and all their other activities. It's important to keep your word when you promise a visit or an outing. Don't let them down.

While their thoughts and feelings must be taken into account, they should not be given the responsibility of choosing which parent they will live with for most of the time; that is a decision for grown-ups and should be made jointly. Another good reason why the two of you as parents must keep in touch directly with each other is to avoid being manipulated by impish little angels who are tempted to play off one parent against the other.

The Family Court of Australia produces a series of easy-to-understand leaflets on many aspects of separation and divorce and they are available gratis at the court's offices. It also conducts information sessions, each lasting about an hour and also free of charge, to explain off the record what a court case involves and to help you make decisions about your children and property without going through the legal process. The court also has the means to protect you if you fear for your safety.

TELLING OTHER PEOPLE

Once you are separated and you know that a divorce is inevitable, let your family, friends and colleagues know about it. It's only fair to them and it will be much easier on you once word gets around. People are fascinated by the unknown and find speculation irresistible but they tire of it quickly once everything is out in the open. If your partner abandoned you for someone else, remember those words of comfort, said to be an old Spanish proverb, 'Living well is the best revenge'. Smile. Look confident. Buy something new to wear. Spoil yourself. Spend time with people who make you feel good and avoid those who don't.

Keeping your feelings under control in a dignified way for the sake of the children could affect your physical and psychological wellbeing unless you have some kind of outlet. Vigorous physical exercise, meditation and participation in support groups work for some people. Sympathetic family members or trustworthy friends can keep you sane by listening to your outpourings and distracting you from them when necessary. There is nothing like a dependable shoulder to cry on in a crisis and a sense of humour to help you see the absurdity of it all afterwards.

SUPPORTIVE FRIENDS

If you are a close relation or friend of someone going through a divorce, watch your step. Many's the poor duffer who sympathised deeply with the aggrieved and villified the other party only to be mortified when the two kissed and made up. Being the soul of tact is very tricky. Your best bet is to hold your tongue and listen. Never offer advice unless it is sought and then be cautious and diplomatic, especially if you are asked to mediate.

The well-mannered person is not the one who says, 'Saw your ex with a gorgeous girl last night' or 'I've never seen Angela looking so radiant.' Like the three wise monkeys, courteous people see, hear and speak no evil and do not meddle in other people's affairs.

After their divorce, you may want to stay friends with both parties or you may not. Your friendship with a married couple does not necessarily mean you like both people equally; you might have a strong bond with one of them but not with the other. If that is so and they divorce, don't force an association if it does not happen naturally. Let time determine the viability of a close friendship with each party.

On the other hand, if you love both parties equally, their split-up will be devastating for you. Keeping faith with both of them is a challenge for your tact, optimism and clear-headedness. Try to avoid talking negatively with either about the other and, if intimate stories are told of obnoxious behaviour, close your ears to them or at least try to forget them as quickly as possible or they could poison your feelings for the other person. Do not repeat any confidences. Except in extreme cases, resentment usually mellows with time as people find new partners and new pursuits.

Unlike a widow, who may continue to be addressed by her full married name – Mrs William Standawfish – a divorcée who wants to keep her married name drops her ex-husband's first name, to become Mrs Angela Standawfish.

LIVING ALONE

In cultures where resources are scarce and opportunities for outside experience are limited, human beings are virtually never alone. They sleep, eat, work and play in family and tribal groups. In cities as affluent and populous as ours, many people live alone either from choice or necessity. As our standard of living rises, the extended family starts to break down unless there are strong religious or cultural reasons for it to be maintained.

Financial independence gives us a big say in how, when, where and with whom we live. The relaxation of society's attitudes to marriage, divorce and informal sexual liaisons means we can romp in and out of partnerships at will. Marriage that unites two people for life until they walk into the sunset together is rare and becoming more so.

Medical advances and better nutrition are keeping us healthy and alive for longer than our parents and, for many of us, that will mean living alone for a lot of that time. In Australia in 1996, the expected life span of a man was 75.2 years, for a woman 81.1 years. By the year 2041, a man can expect to live to be eighty-one, and a woman to reach the grand old age of eighty-five.

AVOIDING LONELINESS

All this points to the wisdom of developing self-reliance. Self-sufficient we can never be, neither is it desirable or practical to try. But to be comfortable enough to enjoy, say, a weekend in solitude without longing for company is an accomplishment. Lots of people do it and would have it no other way. Some people confuse solitude with loneliness, although the two are very different. We all know how lonely we can be with the wrong person.

People who live alone successfully do not feel guilty about pampering themselves with small luxuries. They are resourceful, with plenty of interests within their domain and outside it. They have to be optimistic enough not to feel let down if nobody calls. They cannot afford to feel sorry for themselves because that is self-destructive. They pull their weight. They count their blessings. They overcome any shyness they might have and take initiative. That's the key: action. If you wait around for someone else to act, you could wait forever.

DEALING WITH DOWN TIMES

There are certain times of day when most of us have low spots. It's important to find distractions at those times, whether it's having friends in, calling them for a chat, working on some project, walking the dog, going to the movies, digging the garden, shopping, cooking a dish that takes time and concentration, or whatever. If you have a friend you know feels blue at certain times, a telephone call or a suggested outing, even if it's just buying supplies together at the supermarket or having a cup of coffee, can give an enormous lift to the spirits.

Entertaining at home is one of the most rewarding experiences for someone who likes to cook and it usually generates invitations in return. If you don't like to cook, get professionals to cater (they need not be there when your guests arrive, unless you want them), shop for pre-prepared dishes or host people at a restaurant. These events need not be elaborate. Midweek, a one-pot dinner for a small group of friends on their way home from work is a marvellous way of sharing your table and making sure everyone still has an early night.

TRUSTY FRIENDS

What would we do without our friends, especially in tough times? When you find yourself newly single after a death, a divorce or just a failed love affair, friends, particularly those in a similar situation, are your mainstays. Find one or two you can trust when you need to share the experience after a frustrating or triumphant day at the office. Trading confidences with someone you can count on is terribly important if you are to keep a healthy outlook and not become paranoid, too introspective or anti-social.

Make sure it's give and take, though, not just one-sided, or the intimacy may not endure. Whether we recognise it or not, each transaction must be satisfactory on both sides. I don't know how to put it without it sounding calculated or commercial, but each of us must receive something from a relationship with another person and it could be as simple as feeling good in their company or having interests in common. There is no point in being with someone who makes us feel unhappy, resentful, frustrated or bored. Self-sacrifice might be the way to sainthood, but who among us is a saint?

VOLUNTEERING

If you have the time and empathy with certain groups or causes, doing good can be very satisfying, whether you join a committee to raise money for medical research, spend time helping an underprivileged social group or become a guide at a public art gallery. Choose something you feel can benefit from your particular talent and skill. It's a fine way to meet people and to feel that you are achieving something worthwhile. If you want to get down to grassroots, try your local council for schemes aimed at helping those who need it in your own neighbourhood.

BRIEF ENCOUNTERS

Looking for the ideal partner has been, and always will be, a subject of endless fascination, not only to the population at large but to authors of books and makers of movies. We may or may not find the object of our dreams and desires but we can have an interesting time trying, even though our encounters don't always have a happy ending. It makes the successful ones that much more exhilarating.

With the easing of strictures on dating and how far to go with someone you barely know, I think it is a matter of personal choice. You know yourself, your needs, the world and its dangers. If you take risks make sure they are calculated ones and that you can live with the consequences if things go wrong.

That doesn't mean that when a casual paramour with no strings attached comes through the door, manners should go out the window. Respect the other person before, during and after the liaison. If the sex is disappointing, it's not necessarily the fault of the other party; you're probably incompatible. Be kind. What's the point of being destructive?

Making the first move

How does a woman who lives alone ask a man she barely knows but finds attractive home to dinner? Simple. Having first established that he is a free agent, make it a party of six, preferably all singles. Then any ulterior motive is disguised, at least at the start. Plan it as you would a normal dinner. Seating him beside you is a good idea but at your left, rather than your right, which is where a guest of honour would normally be seated; put an old friend in that privileged spot.

On the evening, do not be obvious in expressing your feelings, yet don't be so distant that the chosen one imagines you have no interest in him. If he offers to help, say yes, and give him the wine to open. How the evening progresses is anybody's guess but don't expect too much and don't look as though you do. You might frighten him off. If he's attracted to you, you'll be hearing from him. If he finds somebody else at the table more attractive, she (or he) will be hearing from him. Don't take it to heart. That's life. Better luck next time.

Another way of making the first move is to call the chosen one to say that you and a few friends are planning to go to the play, musical, movie or concert that's the latest smash-hit and would he like to join you? Tell him the price of the tickets so he knows he'll be paying for himself and therefore is not committed to being your partner but just one of the group.

Easing the way by having other people around might seem to be overly cautious but it lessens any awkwardness that might result from a premature attempt at intimacy. That might scare him off and disappoint you. A comfortable get-together rather than a standard date can give him the chance to size you up in unpressured circumstances. Leave the next move to him.

Chapter Eighteen

PLAYING THE GAME

In her *Etiquette for Australians*, published in 1945, Noreen Routledge writes, 'on any playing field do learn to play the game, to acquire the spirit of sportsmanship which helps you rejoice in the other side winning'. How quaint that idea seems in an era when winning is all.

She then goes on to set standards that tell us how much our attitude to sport has changed since the middle of the twentieth century: 'Never lose your temper – no matter how bad the provocation. Never rejoice when an opponent makes a bad slip anywhere. Never be annoyed when your partner makes a bad move. Never take an unfair advantage of your partner or opponent. Never bawl at the top of your voice or make vulgar gestures. Never criticise players or their games. Indulgence in any of the above "nevers" shows not only bad sportsmanship, but bad breeding.' By these criteria, there's a lot of bad breeding evident on the playing fields and waterways of Australia today.

Not everybody is a bad sport. It's just that those players who do behave badly are conspicuous, especially when caught on television, which puts us in the front line of the game. When a famous sportsperson lapses, standards are lowered for idealistic youngsters watching and admiring. No wonder they imagine that losing your temper, letting down a partner, demeaning an opponent, turning on a tantrum and cheating, just a little bit, are the legitimate rules of the game.

A good sport is a person who does not brag about winning, whinge or brood about losing, or exaggerate trivial bruises and scratches. A good sport gives the other player the benefit of any doubt, never plays the second-rate game of one-upmanship, and thanks and shakes hands with fellow players before heading home.

Spectators also have an obligation to conduct themselves in a civilised way. A home crowd that is grudging about a foreign team winning is an embarrassment. Hooligans who go on a rampage and a crowd that gets out of hand are chilling examples of what happens when lack of self-control makes people degenerate into bullies who rely on packs to give them a sense of power.

That's the opposite of sportsmanship, fair play and joy in the game. Sport is supposed to be fun. Wouldn't it be great if everybody thought so?

AT THE BEACH

The beach is our playground with official and unofficial rules of conduct, in and out of the water. In stripping off to your Speedos, make sure you don't drop your manners along with your shorts and T-shirt. To make the beach a pleasure for everyone (and to help save a great natural resource from degradation), follow these few simple rules.

- Don't shake sand over your neighbours when shaking out your towel.
- Anchor your beach umbrella securely so it doesn't take off and injure someone.

- Do not remove creatures or plants from rockpools or gather shells of any kind, whether or not they are inhabited. Empty shells are often used as homes by various forms of life on the beach.
- Don't damage sand dunes and the plants that grow on them. Stick to existing tracks.
- Take all your rubbish home and put it in your own garbage bin. Even if there is room in open public litter bins, don't tempt birds and animals to rummage there by dumping food in them.
- Find out the regulations about fishing at any waterway where you're thinking of casting a line. Don't take more fish than you need and throw the undersized ones back immediately.
- Stay away from burrows dug for shelter by birds or animals in the dunes.
- Never displace middens, stones or rock art at Aboriginal sites.
- As a spectator, never get in the way of a rescue by lifesavers but be willing to help if necessary.
- Abide by the rules of the surf club responsible for the beach where you happen to be.
- Horseplay does not belong on a crowded beach. If you want to play ball games or throw a frisbee, find an isolated spot to do it.

IN THE WATER

By behaving selfishly or recklessly in the water you risk not only your own skin but the lives of others, primarily the professional and volunteer lifesavers who start the day by assessing the safest spot to plant their flags and spend the rest of it watching over the safety of everyone who swims between them.

Holidaymakers often make the mistake of thinking that a glorious empty beach is as benevolent as it looks. The invitation to take a dip is irresistible, until you remember the risks involved in unseen hazards such as undertows, sharks and, in the far north, other lethal marine creatures during certain seasons. Never forget that the sea is unpredictable and uncontrollable and it's easy to get out of your depth. That can prove fatal if there is nobody around to rescue you.

- Swim only on a beach patrolled by lifesavers.
- Never swim outside the red-and-yellow flags.
- Don't go into the water straight after a meal or when you've been drinking alcohol or taking drugs of any other kind.
- Don't take a running dive into the surf, even if you think you know the beach well. The sea is volatile and depth can change very quickly.
- When you venture into the water, single out a landmark so that you can tell if you begin to drift too far.
- To avoid cramp, leave the water the moment you begin to feel too cold.
- Most surf rescues occur when a swimmer is caught in a rip, a powerful current that drags them out to sea. If you get caught in one, don't exhaust yourself by fighting it. Go with the flow and raise your arm to signal distress. If you are a powerful enough swimmer, cut across the current diagonally until you reach the place where the wave breaks, then swim ashore or raise your arm for help.
- Never panic if you get into trouble of any kind. Raise your arm and float until help arrives.
- As soon as you hear a shark alarm, get out of the water.
- If a beach is declared closed because of treacherous conditions, on no account attempt to go in the water. It's closed for safety reasons and it's selfish to presume that you'll be fine. Other people will then be morally obliged to risk their lives in trying to save yours.

SURFING

Regular surfers in a beach break – the term for that part of the beach where they always surf – feel territorial about their patch, particularly against novices and tourists who want to share it. Surf rage occurs when a surfer is frustrated by too many other people in the same spot. The other guy becomes a convenient target. The beach belongs to everyone. Forbearance and mutual respect are imperative in controlling anger and resentment if surfers as a group are to be self-regulating. The alternative is for surf breaks to be patrolled, as they are on the west coast of the United States, by undercover police officers. It would be sad if we had to resort to such drastic action for civility to rule our waves.

In the early days, when a surfboard was a plank, ten or twelve feet long, a group of riders could share a wave because they all rode in straight to the shore.

Many contemporary boards have three fins and are shorter (usually around six to six and a half feet long), therefore they are more manoeuvrable. Surfers are able to ride more of the wave and perform daring and unpredictable feats of balance and coordination in more than one direction. That means that a wave can no longer be shared.

There have to be guidelines so there's no confusion about whose turn it is to take the next wave.

Basic rules

- Never ride between the red-and-yellow flags. That area is staked out for body surfers.
- While it might seem to be an individual undertaking, surfing is often a group activity and each surfer must be aware of the position, actions and rights of others.
- When you paddle out, steer clear of the boards that were there before yours.
- The next wave belongs to the person nearest the breaking face of the wave, or to the person who has been waiting longest.
- 'Dropping in', which means cutting in, on a wave that somebody

else has taken is a serious violation, as is 'snaking' – sneaking around the person who has right of way to catch that person's wave. These practices are often the cause of serious confrontations and physical abuse.

- Novices should be content to practise on small waves and leave the best for skilled riders.
- A surfboard is classified as a dangerous weapon. Stay with your board at all times. Never let go of it in the water or someone could get badly hurt.

CRICKET

This sport of gentlemen – played by two teams of eleven players each – has always been so strongly associated with impeccable conduct on the field that *The Macquarie Dictionary* gives one definition of cricket as 'fair play'. The term 'it's not cricket' is in common use to decry conduct that's not up to scratch. More recently, though, the sport's admirable ideals have not always been met. Aggressive, disrespectful and intimidating behaviour by players against umpires is a cause of concern for the New South Wales Cricket Board and its counterparts in other states. Suspicions of games being rigged have also undermined the credibility of cricket as a last bastion of sportsmanship.

However, its code of ethics dies hard and most cricketers seem prepared to honour it. Let's hope they influence the batsmen and bowlers of tomorrow.

- The umpire has the ultimate authority in any decision. If it is genuinely believed he has made a mistake, his decision may be questioned but he must not be abused or harassed.
- The captain has responsibility for the general behaviour of his team although each individual must police his own conduct.
- No player should use physical or verbal violence, or crude gestures, against any person on or off the field.

- Any behaviour that demeans the game is unacceptable.
- Breach of the code of ethics could result in a player being summoned to appear before a tribunal empowered to impose penalties, such as a fine, suspension or disqualification.

SPECTATORS

A few cans of beer in the Esky may still be acceptable at a match at your local cricket ground, but you are not permitted to take alcohol into the big arenas, such as the Brisbane Cricket Ground at Wolloongabba (better known as the Gabba), although there are bars inside where alcohol is served. Strict rules apply at the gate and everyone entering must be prepared to have their bags searched if requested.

- Guns or other objects that could be used as weapons are forbidden, as are seats, stools and musical instruments, pizza cartons, streamers, confetti, tickertape or any other items destined to be thrown or scattered.
- All belongings, including Eskys, prams, pushers and other paraphernalia, must be compact enough to fit underneath your seat.
- Smoking, if it is permitted at all, is limited to special zones on the outside concourses.
- It is forbidden to raise umbrellas during play because they impede the view of other people and drip water on them. Take a raincoat with a hood in bad weather.
- Caterers are not permitted to deliver to spectators inside the ground. You must go to the food stands to order and collect meals.

MEMBERS AND THEIR GUESTS

Club membership carries with it other responsibilities that the people outside on the hill don't have to worry about. One of them is dress and this applies to anyone who is invited into the Members' Reserve.

- Scruffy or skimpy clothes, boxer shorts, singlets, collarless T-shirts, swimsuits and thongs are not permitted. Children under twelve years and women may wear T-shirts.
- As long as they are clean and in good nick, sneakers are acceptable.
- Socks are optional.
- Be cautious of wearing shirts with messages on them. Anything considered offensive will not pass the test.

A few further general rules for members and their guests ought to be observed by all spectators, regardless of their seating.

- Sit still and watch the game respectfully rather than move about too much, particularly during an over.
- Unless you listen to it with an earpiece, turn off your transistor radio so as not to distract players and annoy other people.
- Don't obstruct the sight lines or passage of others by parking yourself in aisles or on stairways.

GOLF

Whether it is played competitively or just for fun, golf is a game of great precision and concentration but preoccupation with your own performance should not be at the expense of others. Being considerate of the players within your own group and those ahead of and behind you is important etiquette on the course.

As with all sports, uncivilised behaviour is competely out of line. Never lose your temper, shout, toss your club, swear, put other players off their game, litter the course or damage it. As a spectator, be as self-effacing as you can.

Membership at some clubs is very exclusive and, as is the case with all private clubs, sporting or otherwise, you must wait to be invited to join. To ask to be nominated for membership is completely unacceptable, therefore a guarantee that you'll never make it.

DRESS FOR PLAYERS

Golfers are snappy but conservative dressers. Although the dress code may vary from one club to another, here are some general guidelines. As a guest, it's particularly important to know the precise club rules on dress beforehand. Make a telephone call to enquire; clubs are very happy to oblige because that's far better for them than the embarrassment of having to turn anyone away for not conforming to the dress code.

- Tailored trousers or shorts, long socks, a shirt with a collar, a peaked cap (worn the right way round, needless to say) and shoes with non-metal spikes should be acceptable in any club. In many clubs now, short socks are acceptable.
- On most courses, metal spikes on shoes are banned because, unlike non-metal spikes, they cause too much damage. Always clean your golf shoes after you have played.
- Garments that are forbidden include football or tennis shorts, tracksuits, T-shirts, jeans and anything with a blatant advertising message or symbol.
- In the clubhouse, change out of your golf shoes, unless their spikes are short and made of a softer substance than metal, but do not go about wearing socks without shoes.
- At certain times in certain clubs, the dress code is jacket, collar and tie.

READY FOR PLAY

- You must have your own set of clubs, even if you hire them at the course.
- Leave your mobile telephone at home.
- If you have an old-fashioned golf buggy with narrow wheels, don't wheel it across greens, tees or bunkers. Some clubs – not all – allow buggies with wider wheels on the green. Check the rules before you play.

- If you drive a golf cart, you must stick to specific tracks, drive smoothly and park at a distance from all areas of play.
- Be punctual in teeing off and ready to play whenever it is your turn.
- Take only one practice swing and move along quickly between shots. If you are delayed – say, by a lost ball – let the group behind you go ahead until you have found the ball or decided to play with another one.
- Make sure the group in front of you is well ahead before you play a shot.
- Shout 'fore' as loudly as possible if your ball is likely to hit anyone.
- Do not distract or crowd a player who is about to play a stroke and never walk in front of the hole when a player is preparing to putt.
- Check the rules relating to the priorities of single players and groups. Some are entitled to take precedence.
- Leave each area of the course the way you found it: rake sand over your footprints in the bunker; repair any divots (holes) you make in the turf; when you take the ball from the hole on the green, don't lean on the flag stick or your putter; take care not to damage the hole or the fragile surface of the green. Courteous golfers do these things automatically.

By skill or just luck, some golfers achieve a hole in one. That means that they manage to get the ball directly from the tee into the hole on the green in one stroke. If that happens to you, remember you'll be expected to buy drinks for everyone at the nineteenth hole. (Golf courses usually have eighteen holes; the ninteenth is the bar in the clubhouse.)

YACHTING

When you own a motor yacht or a sailing yacht, the first essential is to familiarise yourself with the International Regulations for Preventing

Collisions at Sea, aka 'Coll Regs'. They tell you which vessels take priority in given circumstances, define various signals, outline pitfalls, specify minimum distances between vessels, give guidelines for the procedures for mooring, and other matters.

In general, sailing yachts have priority over motor yachts but both must give way to commercial ferries that display a certain symbol. With sailing yachts, the one on the starboard tack (which means, the wind is coming across its starboard side) has right of way over the yacht on the port tack. If two motor yachts approach each other head on, each must change course to starboard (right), so that they pass on the port (left) side of each other. Violations are usually caused by people who have not bothered to learn the rules.

PREPARING TO SAIL

Before you set off from the shore, every detail of the vessel must be checked so that it is totally seaworthy and there is enough fuel, food and water for the planned journey, plus extra in case of emergencies. Unless you are a qualified mechanic, leave the servicing of your boat to someone who is. Check the weather forecast so that you know what to expect if you up anchor; err on the side of caution if you have any doubts about the safety of your crew and passengers.

A yacht is not considered 'dressed' unless it flies three flags. The traditional red ensign of Australia or, alternatively, the Australian national flag should be flown from the stern and should be at least as large as, or larger than, any other flag you fly on board. Fly the emblem of your city at the bow of the yacht and the burgee of your club from the highest position on board. Flags must be in immaculate condition, never frayed, faded or grubby.

GUIDE FOR GUESTS ON BOARD

- Wear appropriate clothes. Be smart but comfortable. Be prepared for changes in the weather by making sure you have something warm and waterproof to put on if necessary, particularly on a sailing yacht.

- Wear soft-soled shoes, preferably deck shoes with non-slip soles. Never wear spiky heels, which can pit the deck and are wildly unstable at sea. In any case, before you board always ask, 'Do you mind shoes or should I take them off?' and go barefoot if your footwear is not appropriate.
- Take a hat and anchor it to your collar or buttonhole with a lanyard so that no matter how stiff the wind, it won't end up overboard.
- In boarding a small boat, hold on to something or someone and try to step into the middle of it. Don't jump into it and don't straddle the gap between ship and shore.
- Turn backwards to climb down narrow stairs.
- Remember that the captain is the person in authority, absolute master of the ship and all who sail in her, so show respect.
- Do not throw anything overboard. Keep all litter until you get back to shore. Put it in a lidded public litter bin, otherwise take it home and put it in your own garbage bin.
- As an overnight guest on a private yacht, remember that space will probably be scarce so pack accordingly. Limit yourself to one soft-sided bag, such as a duffel or the kind of thing you'd carry on board a plane. Don't forget the seasickness remedy, just in case.
- Don't waste water.
- When you go ashore, remember to take off your hat before you enter the bar in a yacht club, otherwise you'll be expected to buy drinks for everybody there.

Shipboard terms

You do not speak of the front and the back of the ship, but of the 'bow' and 'stern'. The words for ahead and behind are 'fore' and 'aft'.

'Port' is the word for left and 'starboard' is the word for right, as you stand on deck facing the bow. The signal colour for port is red and the signal colour for starboard is green. An old salt's way of remembering is the saying 'a little port left in the bottle and it's red'. You do not refer to something as being 'to port' or 'to starboard' of you. You say it's on your 'port hand' or your 'starboard hand'.

The place where food is prepared is not a kitchen, it's a 'galley'. You do not go downstairs, you go 'below'. You do not go upstairs, you go on 'deck'. A map is called a 'chart', a bed is a 'bunk', the window is a 'porthole' and the steering wheel is the 'helm'. A seat in a dinghy is not a seat, it's a 'thwart', because it runs athwartships (across the boat). Don't ask where the toilet, loo or WC is because aboard it's called the 'head'; after you have used it, make sure all valves are returned to where they were, otherwise you'll sink the boat.

If there's a ship to the side, it's on 'our beam to port' or 'our beam to starboard'. If it's towards the back, it's on 'our port quarter' or 'our starboard quarter'. If it's behind, it's 'astern of us'. Ahead, it's 'off our port bow' or 'off our starboard bow'.

Cardinal marks

These are signs stuck in the water to show the navigator in which direction the deepest water lies. The way sailors remember them is to start with the sign that indicates west. It consists of two triangles, one pointing upward and the one above it pointing downward, so that their points meet, making a kind of hourglass shape. Tars remember that it means west by calling it 'lady's waist'. When both triangles point upward, it means north. When they point downward, it means south. The fourth cardinal mark of one triangle pointing up and the other pointing down has to mean east because that's the only cardinal point left. It's a good idea, although not essential, to familiarise yourself with these marks before going aboard.

FOOTBALL

Contests between two groups of people, each trying to force a ball into the territory of the other, has been around a long time. The Chinese, Greeks and Romans were all doing it before the birth of Christ and there is good reason to believe the Romans introduced it into England soon after. Football is on record as having been played in Derby on Shrove Tuesday, 217 AD, to cheer a populace that had ousted a troop of Romans. By 1200, a soccer match was held on Shrove Tuesday every year.

Mobs in mediaeval Europe played a game called a 'mêlée' using a blown-up animal bladder as a football. The fact that this rough and tumble game was banned by Richard II didn't make much difference to its popularity. Order was a long time coming. It began in England's great public schools such as Eton in the seventeenth century in games of football between the young gentlemen of different houses of residence. In 1843 Cambridge University standardised the rules.

Kicking a ball with the foot rather than touching it with the hands was what football meant until 1823 when William Webb Ellis, a student at Rugby School, picked up the ball in a match and carried it instead of kicking. The idea took hold and gave rise to the English Rugby Union in 1871. The game was split into Rugby Union and Rugby League in 1895 after a dispute about whether or not players should be paid.

Australian Rules is also known as AFL or simply footy and Melbourne, where it was born in 1896, is still its heartland. You will feel like a social outcast in that city in winter if you do not support a local footy team.

SOCCER

Without touching it with their hands, each team of eleven players attempts to get the ball into the other team's goal by fancy footwork and urging it along with other parts of the body, such as the head or the shoulder. Only the goalkeeper is permitted to put his hands on the ball. The game, which is also known simply as football or association football (from which the name soccer is derived), requires a high degree of agility and skill.

RUGBY

There are two kinds, Rugby Union and Rugby League, summarised in this wise old saying: 'Union is a thugs' game played by gentlemen. League is a gentlemen's game played by thugs.' In Union there are fifteen players to a side; in League there are thirteen. Handling the ball is permissible, as is kicking or passing it to another player.

Union prides itself on sportsmanship and camaraderie. In fact, when children play, it is usual for each team to applaud the other at the end of the match. Players are required to measure up to a code of conduct that includes never betting on or fixing a match, not accepting bribes and reporting any that may be offered. They must never be physically or verbally aggressive, exhibit racism or do anything to discredit the game.

AUSTRALIAN FOOTBALL LEAGUE

There are eighteen players in each team, plus four more on the bench, and the play is fast and spectacular. The game starts when the ball is bounced in the middle of the ground and each side tries to get it to within about fifty metres of the other side's goal so it can be kicked between the posts. It may be hand-passed (held in one hand and punched with the other) or kicked. When a player kicks the ball, others try to catch it and if someone does, that is called a mark. It's an advantage to be tall if you play this game.

Misdemeanours, such as pushing someone in the back, grabbing him around the neck, running more than ten metres with the ball without bouncing it on the ground, earn a free kick for the other side.

Spectators

All team sports attract enthusiastic supporters, but AFL in Melbourne draws them from all social levels and all age groups. Although passion for a chosen team can border on the fanatical, certain standards are expected of a footy crowd.

- Racism and swearing are unacceptable.
- It is bad form to cheer when the other team makes a mistake.
- Singing the club song is essential to spur on your winning team.
- When an injured player is carried off the field, everybody should get to their feet as a gesture of respect.
- It is very much a family game with young children being given team jerseys at an early age.
- It is a nicety to indulge in friendly banter with supporters of the other team but, particularly when the game has been won and lost, this rivalry should not be allowed to turn ugly.
- Obligatory food is a pie and sauce.

The crowd is quick to pick up any indication of the rules being infringed and to voice its opinion. These are some favourites yelled by the crowd.

- 'Ball!' (A player is holding the ball too long.)
- 'In the back!' (A player has pushed an opponent in the back.)
- 'Carn the mighty Blues (or Bombers or Tigers, or whatever)' ('Carn' means 'come on'.)
- 'Get rid of it!' (The player with the ball should kick it or pass it on.)
- 'He's got a paddock!' (The player with the ball has lots of space to run with it.)
- 'You wanna kick for them, ump?' (The umpire is thought to be favouring the other team.)

YOUNG FOOTBALLERS

Parents and other adults at children's matches may barrack to spur the budding heroes on, but they must remember that this is supposed to be fun. Shouted terms such as 'kill him' are out of line, not just because they are ugly on the day but because children will grow up thinking not only that such language is appropriate, but that they must win at any cost, by fair means or foul.

LOCKER-ROOM ETIQUETTE

Except for very small outfits, there are always separate locker rooms for the two teams in a match and neither will go near the other before the game. In the warm-up beforehand, no outsiders should enter either room because it's a sensitive time and nobody should do anything that might take the players' focus away from the game. Even when an official comes to summon the team on to the field, he knocks on the door but does not enter.

Referees and touch judges also have their own dressing room. They never mingle with the players because they must be impartial, although they do inspect equipment, primarily the boots to make sure there are no attachments, such as studs, that could injure another player. The referee summons both captains for the toss that determines which team starts the game.

The atmosphere is usually more relaxed after the game. Sometimes the home team will provide a case of beer for the visiting team and some may even join them for a glass after they have showered.

In small venues, where facilities are limited and there is only one set of showers, it is courteous for the home team to let the visitors use them first.

LAWN BOWLING

Bowling greens began to appear in Sydney as early as 1845, but the first bowling club was formed in Melbourne in 1864. By 1900, there were clubs in all states and bowling never seems to have looked back. In its 'Participate in Sport and Physical Activity Report' for 1999-2000, the Australian

Bureau of Statistics ranked lawn bowls as Australia's third favourite organised activity, after aerobic/fitness and golf, and before tennis and cricket.

The game centres around a white ball called a jack. The aim is to get your bowl (never call it a ball) closer to the jack than your opponent does. Its popularity is largely due to the fact that it is not as complicated or physically demanding as many other sports so you are almost never too young or too old to play, socially or competitively. It is also a flexible game in that it can be played solo or with various numbers of people of either sex or in mixed groups.

To outsiders, its main distinguishing feature is the uniform its club members are required to wear. With the exception of a blazer, brown shoes, a hat band and perhaps a bit of trimming, the overall colour is white or cream. This long ago prompted women bowlers to be called 'white leghorns', a breed of white-plumed domestic fowls.

Over the years, there has been little modification of the dress code for members, although the guidelines may vary from club to club, or state to state. In Victoria, for example, navy blue para silk or gabardine slack suits are an option. In Queensland, the skirt of a dress must be at least eight centimetres below the crease at the back of the knee and a white slip underneath is obligatory. Decorous coverage is required. Fabrics must not be transparent or too tight, shirts must have collars and shorts must never rise above the knee.

TENNIS

Brat-like behaviour some years ago by a certain American tennis player and his imitators might sadden us but it should not lead us into thinking that the general standard of this noble sport is on the decline. Most tennis players, whether they are competing for the Davis Cup or having a social game on a Saturday afternoon, have the good sense and the good grace to be fair and just in play. In a tournament or competition the umpire's word is law.

Players must be fleet-footed and quick-witted to be good at tennis and these qualities make it a mesmerising game to watch. Spectators must do what they can to avoid distracting or irritating players by too much movement or noise. Quiet please, as your head swings back and forth in unison with others in the stand.

DRESS FOR PLAYERS

Professionals must conform to a stringent dress code and their garb in a modified form is also appropriate for all tennis players. Combinations of colours are often worn but the overall look is clean and simple. On the grass courts of Wimbledon, the only shoes allowed are those with rubber soles and no heels, ribs, studs or coverings; among unacceptable garments are sweatshirts, gym shorts and T-shirts, and there are strict regulations about the size and placement of logos.

Non-professional players having a social game on a private or public tennis court should wear shorts or skirts and tops that allow for unrestricted movement on the court. Men should never go without a top. White is a dashing colour on the court and it suits most people. All garments must be clean and well-pressed, at least at the start. Always wear tennis shoes.

There are also people, usually children, whose role it is to fetch balls. However, on private and public tennis courts where games are played for fun, there are not always people to perform these tasks, so the players must do it themselves.

NON-UMPIRED MATCHES

- You must make all the calls relating to your side of the court. If you have any doubt whether the ball is in or out, the point should be given to the other player.
- Make any call of 'out', 'let' or 'fault' immediately and loudly enough to be clearly audible.
- Traditionally on a clay court, if you call 'out' and you realise it is

incorrect, you lose the point. On all other court surfaces, if you call 'out' and you realise it is incorrect, the point should be played again. If you repeat the error, you lose the point because that could be construed as deliberate hindrance.

- Pick up all balls that fall on your side of the net and return them to the server.
- Do not return the first service if it is an obvious fault.
- No spectators should be invited to decide on anything that happens on the court.
- To be clear about the score, you should announce the game score before you start another game. Similarly, announce the point score before you serve for the next point.
- Don't be a bad sport and don't be tricky. Never indulge in psychological tactics aimed at undermining the concentration or confidence of your opponent.
- If your ball goes into another court, wait until the players there finish the point before fetching it. In fact, never walk behind a court where a match is being played until there is a pause between points or games.

POLO

A rudimentary form of polo was played three thousand years ago in Persia, where nobles on horseback whacked around the head of an animal instead of a ball. The Mogul emperors took the game to India where, centuries later, the British Raj adopted it as an excellent and enjoyable way for their cavalry riders to train. It spread throughout the British Empire and to North and South America, where its greatest stronghold is in Argentina. There the terrain is flat, people still use horses for tasks on the farm that motorbikes and helicopters have taken over in other countries, and there are plenty of gauchos to train and care for polo ponies.

Polo is a kind of hockey on horseback. Wearing white trousers, long boots, kneeguards and helmets, two teams, each with four players, tear down a playing area about nine times the size of a football field, wielding mallets made of bamboo or poly resins. During hectic seven-minute periods called chukkas, the aim is to bat the ball between the opposing team's goal posts without endangering horses or riders.

Two kinds of polo are played on horseback in Australia: polo and bush polo. Banjo Paterson, a polo player himself, described the difference graphically in these first two verses of his poem 'The Geebung Polo Club', published in *Antipodean* in 1893.

It was somewhere up the country, in a land of rock and scrub,
That they formed an institution called the Geebung Polo Club.
There were long and wiry natives from the rugged mountain side,
And the horse was never saddled that the Geebungs couldn't ride;
But their style of playing polo was irregular and rash –
They had mighty little science, but a mighty lot of dash:
And they played on mountain ponies that were muscular and strong,
Though their coats were quite unpolished, and their manes and tails were long.
And they used to train those ponies wheeling cattle in the scrub;
They were demons, were the members of the Geebung Polo Club.

It was somewhere down the country, in a city's smoke and steam,
That a polo club existed, called the 'Cuff and Collar Team'.
As a social institution 'twas a marvellous success,
For the members were distinguished by exclusiveness and dress.
They had natty little ponies that were nice, and smooth and sleek,
For their cultivated owners only rode 'em once a week.
So they started up the country in pursuit of sport and fame,
For they meant to show the Geebungs how they ought to play the game;
And they took their valets with them – just to give their boots a rub
Ere they started operations on the Geebung Polo Club.

The bush polo players on today's sheep and cattle stations are not quite as colourful as the Geebungs. They respect the rules just as much as players in the more refined polo matches put on at international equestrian tournaments and as social events in aid of charity. Their horses are probably stock horses, bred from thoroughbreds crossed with hardy Arab and maybe a touch of quarter-horse, and trained in the course of mustering. While they might not be as decorative as their beribboned and glossy counterparts, they'll be well fed and well looked after.

GOOD RIDERS AND PONIES

According to the experts, the rules are simple but the application of them is complex. For example, a player who has right of way in the line of the ball can lose it in a moment when the ball takes off in another direction. Because a polo player's means of transport is another living creature with a mind and will of its own, it requires subtle handling to avoid collisions and other entanglements. Good polo ponies are not too big or leggy because they have to be nimble and agile enough to pull up and change direction quickly. Their legs must be bandaged to protect their fetlocks. Their manes and tails are secured, often with plaiting and ribbons. Strength, muscle tone, an eye for the ball and a sensitivity to horses are the characteristics of a good polo player. Build is not so important, although the lighter the player, the faster the horse can go, and that can be anything up to sixty kilometres an hour.

COURTESY AMONG PLAYERS

As in most sports, the umpire's word is law and should not be questioned. Although traditional niceties associated with playing polo, such as saying 'bad luck, old chap' when a fellow player misses the ball, are becoming rare, it is still not good etiquette for a player to make disparaging remarks to an opponent during play. It is equally crass for an experienced player to take advantage of a newcomer instead of helping and encouraging him or her to learn the rules and tactics. Unfortunately, it does happen, so beginner players should be wary of being led deliberately into committing a foul.

SPECTATORS

- Don't forget your binoculars.
- Pick a possy at least ten metres from the side of the field, not at either end, because horses and riders often exceed the boundaries and that can endanger anyone too close to the game.
- Keep dogs on a leash.
- Because the action covers a lot of ground and is sometimes virtually out of sight, children can become bored and restless. Bring something to amuse them and keep them at your side.
- Don't attempt to put a player off by yelling something negative when, for instance, he or she is about to take a penalty and needs to concentrate.

DRESS FOR SPECTATORS

Find out what level the tournament will be because that will determine the right kind of dress.

At a big charity day, wear what you would to picnic races. A blazer, with or without a tie, is acceptable attire for a man. For a woman, those elegant weekend looks you see in Ralph Lauren advertisements are an ideal worth aiming for, with trousers or a skirt. If you wear a hat it should be functional, to shade you from the sun, and not just decorative. Very high heels are not appropriate. If you are working with the horses, forget the formality. Wear very practical clothes and shoes that start out being neat and clean and won't be ruined by horse manure.

There is no dress code for bush polo, although you would look awfully out of place in garden-party dress. Wear something comfortable and tough enough to withstand rough ground and mud or dust. This is one place where denim is almost de rigueur.

Chapter Nineteen

IN THE LIMELIGHT

Fame. It could happen to anyone and let's say it happens to you. Never mind why. Could be that, as a successful exporter of noodles to Japan, you win the Most Enterprising Business Person of the Year Award. Perhaps you've come up through the ranks to become CEO of a huge and politically sensitive corporation. Or maybe you've saved somebody's life or written a song that tops the charts or had a date with the world's most eligible superstar. Overnight, you are in the spotlight. Everybody, from *The Australian Financial Review* to *Women's Weekly* to SBS, wants to interview you. Even Oprah's on the line. Help!

GETTING IT INTO PERSPECTIVE

The first thing to realise is that you don't owe the media anything. If you do not want to be interviewed, just say no. Don't be dissuaded by arguments such as 'the public has a right to know'. Often, it is not the public's business. Remember that it is not always the public interest the publication or channel serves but the interests of shareholders in the company. They are after a story that will sell newspapers or increase ratings. If it is in your own interests to seek publicity, that's a different matter. Go for it.

The second thing is to seek advice on how to handle it. From which source depends on the level of your newfound celebrity. Maybe you have friends who have been in front of television cameras and journalists' tape recorders. If your attraction is likely to be ongoing, or the publicity generated could be negative, you are well advised to appoint an agent to handle the media or somebody the entrepreneur, Harry M. Miller, would describe as a 'media bodyguard'. In any case, you must be fully prepared. Make a plan and get some media training.

IMAGE MINDERS

Just as there are experts you trust to manage your money, your legal affairs and your ailments, there are now people qualified to school you in handling the media and minding your image.

They encourage you to start with a kind of marketing plan, with yourself as the product. This means deciding which audience you want to reach, targeting the publications and programs that appeal to that audience and eliminating those that don't. Then when a photographer approaches you at a social event, you can ask yourself, 'Do I want my face in that publication?' Be selective. One of the big dangers of celebrity is that it makes media junkies of the unwary who'll do anything for publicity regardless of its relevance. Don't be the one who wants to be the bride at every wedding and the corpse at every funeral because fame is fickle. Here today, gone tomorrow. Think of it as a game and nothing to do with real life.

DO YOUR HOMEWORK

Once you know your audience, perceive what's in their minds and understand their needs and wants, you can work on the best way of persuading them to your point of view. Knowing what makes news and how to reconcile what's important to the audience with what's important to you are challenges that few amateurs can meet without professional guidance.

Preparation is crucial but just as important as knowing your subject thoroughly is being able to present it clearly and convincingly, even when tricky questions are shot at you. This is where on-camera role-playing beforehand with a professional journalist is invaluable. The playback is the moment of truth. Apart from assessing the performance, you might see mannerisms you never knew you had.

One expert in the field told me, 'A live media interview is not a good time for an original thought.' Stick to what you have prepared, although be careful not to be so rigid as to sound like a robot. Time on television is limited, so it's wise to prepare some pithy statements that make sense by themselves, especially if they are being pre-recorded for news bulletins. You must also be clear about what action you want your audience to take as a result of seeing, hearing or reading an interview with you.

Knowing precisely what you want to get across means you may be able to take liberties with the rehearsed words without losing your way, all the better to sound spontaneous and genuine. But if you're not good at thinking on your feet, stick to the script.

GOING IT ALONE

If the circumstances are not controversial or your fame is likely to be short-lived you might feel comfortable about dealing with the media yourself without outside help. In that case, be aware of a few pitfalls.

In the case of print media, make sure you know the name of the newspaper or magazine journalist who has requested an interview, familiarise yourself with the publication and try to get hold of some of the journalist's published work. Some writers, especially those who cover celebrities, might enjoy being provocative at your expense. Remember that, no matter how ethical they may be, all journalists look for an 'angle' to a story, a hook on which to hang it. They want news. The aim is often, although not always, to sensationalise it in order to sell the publication rather than do you justice. In all cases, they will be seeking information about you that nobody else knows and making assumptions.

Be cautious of photography by someone whose work you do not know. The camera can lie and when it does, make sure it's in your favour. It is worthwhile paying a good professional photographer and make-up artist to do a series of pictures that you own and can hand out to the press. That way, you control what is shown. If, however, the publication is a very glamorous one, on no account turn down the chance to be dressed by a fashion stylist for the lens of one of the world's top photographers. But always make sure you are happy with the clothes selected for you and with the make-up and hairstyle you are given.

With television, watch a few episodes of the show to get a feel for it and what will be expected of you. Find out if the interview will go to air live or be prerecorded and edited for showing at a later date. Ask for a copy of the questions, or at least be aware of the line of questioning, so that you can think about your answers beforehand.

LOOKING YOUR BEST ON TV

Television is a very searching medium in which the subject has no control over the lighting or camera angles. It requires special make-up, which should be provided by a professional at the channel. If it is not, think seriously about hiring a good make-up artist yourself. Remember the fundamental lessons your mother taught you about grooming: clean hair, immaculate hands and nails, shiny shoes.

In what you wear, avoid solid black (too dense) and patterns that can dance a tarantella on camera. Plain colours are best. Not too much white because it reflects. Avoid checks and stripes (too busy) and red-hot red that can 'bleed'. By all means study the latest in fashion but beware of being a copycat. Not everybody looks good in the same kinds of clothes and it's crucial to feel comfortable and to be true to yourself in what you wear.

The other thing to be aware of in dressing is that it must be appropriate to audience perceptions of you and your purpose in being there. Responsible people in management and the professions are expected to dress in a businesslike way. On the other hand, sportspeople should be kitted out in the outfits of champions. It is as obligatory for an artist to dress like a free spirit as it is for a fashion designer to wear something drop-dead stylish. A friend of mine, touched by newspaper reports about a brave widow of a murdered policeman, was shocked when the young woman appeared on television wearing spiky heels and looking as sleek and confident as a television newsreader; it didn't fit audience preconceptions because, true or false, it made her seem superficial, concerned more with looking like a fashionplate than being the grieving widow with young children.

Make sure your outfit looks good when you sit down. A mini-skirt may not be the answer. Television tends to widen the face and figure, so keep the line as elongated as possible. If you wear trousers, put on tights or knee-length socks underneath so that if you cross your legs there will be no ugly gap that usually results from short socks. Keep jewellery to a minimum and do not wear things that bob about or rattle, like drop earrings and jangly bracelets.

Try to like the person interviewing you and take your time in answering questions. Be true to who and what you are because anything false or inconsistent will be apparent to viewers. You might have noticed some politicians at press conferences making the mistake of addressing the assembled journalists and forgetting the unseen millions watching. An even worse mistake for a politician is to brush the camera aside arrogantly, forgetting that it's not just a camera but a big slice of the voting public.

Don't speak too quickly and keep any nervous twitches or

mannerisms under control. By all means use your hands expressively but keep them away from your face. Don't frown or look grim or suspicious. Keep a sense of humour and a pleasant expression on your face without it being inane. It's a tall order, isn't it? Now you know why smart people get professional help.

COURTESY TO THE FILM CREW

If the interview is in a studio, be on time, say please and thank you and take the trouble to be agreeable and cooperative with the crew. Your fate is in their hands. In some ways, they are even more important than the journalist because, in a visual medium such as television, how you look often dominates what you say. Recently, I watched an episode of 'The Late Show' with David Letterman. Calista Flockhart (Ally McBeal) was a guest and the camera made sure the shot was wide enough for us all to see her right leg rocking up and down nervously over the left one, through the whole interview. It was an unkind distraction. Now, why would a producer permit that? We can only guess.

On your own home ground, be as hospitable and courteous to the camera crew as you would with anybody else. Offer them a cup of tea or coffee. Point out where the loo is. As one media bodyguard told me, 'It's not going to change the outcome, but it changes the dynamics.' The crew are human, too. Better that they like and respect you than otherwise. Make it as pleasant an experience as possible all round. Be willing to let them choose the most appropriate backdrop and to reposition furniture and other objects. Although it's an almost impossible achievement for the inexperienced, try not to be too aware of the camera. One good trick is to imagine your best friend is in the room giving you moral support as you face an interviewer. Another is to remind yourself that, however big the total viewing audience, you are talking one to one to someone at home. I believe that some people gain confidence by visualising everybody else in the room as naked, but that might just put you off or send you into hysterics.

REACTING TO PUBLICITY

Remember to thank people afterwards for the coverage. Make a telephone call or write a letter. Not everybody does it, so the gesture will be appreciated. If you are very pleased, write to the journalist's boss as well. If the interview goes wrong, don't hold a grudge or seek revenge. Regard it as a lesson in not believing your own publicity, good or bad. In the case of print, the writer has little, if any, say in the headlines; sub-editors are employed to write them and to cut the text if necessary to fit the available space. Sometimes a minor point buried in the copy is taken out of context and enlarged to attract readers, even though it distorts the essence of the story. Accept all this philosophically, take some responsibility for it (you slipped up, or you were gullible, or you allowed yourself to be vulnerable) and move on. Take the view that tomorrow your news will be stale and somebody else's story will be making headlines.

FEET ON THE GROUND

However brief or lengthy your fame turns out to be, take care not to become permanently bedazzled. Keep people around who, although they share your enjoyment, remind you that fame is not to be taken to heart. These allies usually turn out to be your family and close friends. They'll still be there when the fair-weather friends and hangers-on are fawning over somebody else.

The other aid to long-term sanity is not to fall into the trap of believing that everyone knows who you are. When you enter a room full of strangers, don't stand there waiting for all heads to turn towards you. Introduce yourself to those nearest you and join the conversation on equal terms, without airs or affectation. Most celebrities are known only within a certain group and outside that coterie they are just another face in the crowd. The wise take note of this little couplet from the American journalist Ambrose Bierce: 'Mark how my fame rings out from zone to zone: A thousand critics shouting, "He's unknown!"'

TRUE FRIENDS

Through fame you quickly find out who your friends are because not everybody celebrates the good fortune of somebody else. Envy gets in the way. If you are a true friend of the one in the limelight, be supportive at all times, no matter what other people are saying. It's your duty to stand by your friend and be positive in any remarks you make. Beware of using the word 'but', which is often a mask for envy: 'I am so proud of Bobby, but I think he's got a bit above himself' or 'Only I can say this because I love her so much, but I think she's lost it in her latest exhibition' or 'I admire what she's done so much, but didn't you feel that speech was a bit dull?' To a loyal friend there are no ifs or buts.

FACE TO FACE WITH THE FAMOUS

Inside every celebrity is a human being, just like you and me. If you recognise someone well known in a restaurant, in the street, in a department store or in the supermarket, don't stare. If you must say something – and think very carefully before you do – make it short and complimentary and don't hover. Never use the encounter to raise some controversial issue or behave as though the two of you are intimate friends. This illustrious person might be almost as familiar to you as members of your own family but, remember, it's not the same in reverse: you are a complete stranger.

The time for autographs is at the stage door with your program after a performance, not when your idol is trying to go about anonymously. One of the greatest sacrifices for someone famous is the loss of privacy. Put your admiration into a fan letter instead.

It's different if the luminary is making a special appearance – say an artist at the opening of her exhibition, a writer at a book-signing, an actor at a fund-raiser – because they are prepared for the public. They are on show. The purpose is to attract people and the more the merrier.

AUSTRALIAN HONOURS

A person who serves the community, the country or all humanity in some special way is sometimes given recognition in the form of an official award under what is known as the Australian Honours System. It replaced the British Imperial Awards when it was established in February 1975.

There are many awards and they fall into various categories but perhaps the best known is the Order of Australia, which has four tiers: Companion of the Order of Australia (AC), for eminent achievement and merit of highest degree in service to Australia or to humanity at large; Officer of the Order of Australia (AO), for distinguished service of a high degree in Australia or to humanity at large; Member of the Order of Australia (AM), for service in a particular locality or field of activity or to a particular group; and Medal of the Order of Australia (OAM), for service worthy of particular recognition.

Awards are made twice a year and a new Honours List is published in the daily newspapers on Australia Day, 26 January, and on the Queen's Birthday official holiday in June. Those newly honoured are invited to an awards ceremony at the Government House in their home state or territory. These investitures take place at some time in spring and autumn.

THE INVESTITURE

If you are being honoured in this way, you will receive an invitation from the Governor. If you live in the ACT the invitation will come from the Governor-General. It will carry a form that you are asked to fill in and return. You may accept on behalf of yourself and up to four guests. A confirmation card will then be sent to you. You'll also be given written instructions on all relevant details, including what to wear: lounge suit for men, day wear for women and smart casual for anyone under sixteen (see pages 182–183). No decorations may be worn. Interesting how times have changed. In the past, women would have been expected to wear some kind of elegant hat to such a formal occasion at Government House, Canberra. Now they are requested not to because they might obstruct the view of others seated in the drawing room to watch the awards being given.

To keep the numbers manageable, one ceremony takes place in the morning and another in the afternoon of the same day. Each lasts about an hour and a half, including time spent with drinks and nibbles on the terrace afterwards.

HOW TO NOMINATE SOMEONE

If you know someone you feel deserves an award, you may apply to the Council of the Order of Australia, an independent advisory body which assesses all nominations and makes recommendations to the Governor-General, who is responsible for the administration. For nomination forms and guidelines, log on to www.itsanhonour.gov.au. Or write to the Secretary, Order of Australia, Government House, Canberra ACT 2600. Or telephone toll free (1800) 552 275.

Chapter Twenty

FORMS OF ADDRESS

O Lord! How *do* you address the wife of the second son of a duke? What on earth do you say to introduce the Prime Minister of the Hashemite Kingdom of Jordan? And how should you start a letter to the Chancellor or the Vice Chancellor of the university where you hope to gain a place? Few of us have to face these dilemmas very often, but it's tricky when we do. Even knowing the right form of address for the local priest is challenge enough.

WE ALL HAVE TITLES

Guidelines have been laid down but, as with everything else in life, there are exceptions. Rules must adapt to changing needs and circumstances. A lot of it turns out to be plain commonsense, once familiarity gives you a working knowledge of the right form.

Everybody has a title of some kind although, for most of us, it is no grander than Mr or Mrs. Nevertheless, it's very important to get it right, particularly now that personal preference prevails among women about how they wish to be addressed. There is no blanket rule any more. It should go without saying that care must be taken to spell a person's name correctly but, as those of us with unusual names know, this is so rare an occurrence that anyone who gets it right is remembered with gratitude and admiration.

RESPECT PERSONAL PREFERENCES

I don't know why the term Ms antagonises so many people. It's a sensible title, particularly in business, where a woman's marital status is as irrelevant as a man's. Just as all that Mr tells us is that the person is a man, Ms denotes a woman and that's that. Married or not, a woman may use Ms if she wishes. Some people have the curious habit of using Ms only for a single woman, which defeats the whole purpose. The best thing is to find out how someone wishes to be addressed, socially and in business, and abide by it.

CORRECT TITLES

Traditionally, a girl is called Miss until she marries. If she never marries, she is known as Miss all her life, unless she becomes a doctor or professor or earns some other title. In the context of the theatre, Miss sometimes also precedes the name of a distinguished actress (actor, to be politically correct), such as Miss Maggie Smith.

A schoolboy used to be called Master until he reached adulthood but the practice is rare or non-existent in Australia now. At the age of consent, sixteen to eighteen years, a boy may be called Mister, always abbreviated to Mr, the designation he retains for life unless a more hifalutin title is conferred on him.

The correct address on the envelope of a business letter to a man is Mr. Although it is now antiquated, the correct address on the envelope of a personal letter to a gentleman is not Mr but Esq., which stands for

Esquire. It is placed after the name: Ned Kelly, Esq. I'm fond of that term and sorry it's fallen from favour. It reminds me of those wonderfully flamboyant addresses sometimes used on correspondence in Italy: *Gentile Signore* (kind gentleman); *Gentilissima Signora* (kindest lady); *Egrigio Professore* (distinguished professor), and so on.

When a woman marries, she is usually known by her husband's full name – that is, Mrs Ned Kelly (although by law she may keep her maiden name, if she chooses). If she is widowed, she continues to be addressed as Mrs Ned Kelly. However, if they are divorced, and let's say her given name is Sheila, she becomes Mrs Sheila Kelly.

That is the traditional way but there are endless variations, particularly now that so many Australians are not of British or Irish descent. The best way to find out is to ask a person directly. Don't rely on hearsay. It's so often wrong.

Australian Parliament

PRIME MINISTER

Envelope:	*The Hon. Ned Kelly, MP, Prime Minister of Australia*
Formal letter opening:	*Dear Prime Minister*
Formal letter closing:	*Yours faithfully*
Social letter opening:	*Dear Mr Kelly*
Social letter closing:	*Yours sincerely*
Verbal reference:	*The Prime Minister*
Verbal introduction:	*The Prime Minister or The Prime Minister of Australia*
Verbal address:	*Mr Prime Minister or Sir*
Place card:	*The Prime Minister*

The Prime Minister's wife is addressed in the same way as a normal citizen, except that you may refer to her verbally as the First Lady. She should be addressed as Mrs Kelly in conversation unless you are an intimate friend. (If the PM were a woman known by her married name, her husband would be addressed as Mr Kelly.)

MINISTER IN THE HOUSE OF REPRESENTATIVES

Envelope:	*The Hon. Ned Kelly, Minister for Finance*
Formal letter opening:	*Dear Minister*
Formal letter closing:	*Yours faithfully*
Social letter opening:	*Dear Mr Kelly*
Social letter closing:	*Yours sincerely*
Verbal reference:	*Mr Kelly*
Verbal introduction:	*The Honourable Ned Kelly, Minister for Finance*
Verbal address:	*Minister or Mr Kelly*
Place card:	*Minister for Finance*

MINISTER IN THE SENATE

Envelope:	*Senator the Hon. Ned Kelly, Minister for Energy*
Formal letter opening:	*Dear Minister*
Formal letter closing:	*Yours faithfully*
Social letter opening:	*Dear Senator Kelly*
Social letter closing:	*Yours sincerely*

Verbal reference:	*Senator Kelly*
Verbal introduction:	*Senator Kelly, Minister for Energy*
Verbal address:	*Minister, Senator or Mr Kelly*
Place card:	*Minister for Energy*

STATE PREMIER

Envelope:	*The Hon. Ned Kelly, Premier of South Australia*
Formal letter opening:	*Dear Premier*
Formal letter closing:	*Yours faithfully*
Social letter opening:	*Dear Mr Kelly*
Social letter closing:	*Yours sincerely*
Verbal reference:	*The Premier*
Verbal introduction:	*The Premier of South Australia*
Verbal address:	*Premier or Sir*
Place card:	*Premier of South Australia*

STATE GOVERNMENT MINISTER

Envelope:	*The Hon. Ned Kelly, (MLA, MLC or MP), Minister for Health*
Formal letter opening:	*Dear Minister*
Formal letter closing:	*Yours faithfully*
Social letter opening:	*Dear Mr Kelly*
Social letter closing:	*Yours sincerely*
Verbal reference:	*Mr Kelly*
Verbal introduction:	*The Minister for Health*
Verbal address:	*Mr Kelly*
Place card:	*Minister for Health*

SPEAKER OF THE FEDERAL HOUSE OF REPRESENTATIVES

Envelope:	*The Hon. Ned Kelly, MP, Speaker of the House of Representatives*
Formal letter opening:	*Dear Mr Speaker*
Formal letter closing:	*Yours faithfully*
Social letter opening:	*Dear Mr Kelly*
Social letter closing:	*Yours sincerely*
Verbal reference:	*Mr Kelly*

Verbal introduction:	*The Speaker of the House of Representatives*
Verbal address:	*Mr Speaker*
Place card:	*The Speaker of the House of Representatives*

MEMBERS OF THE FEDERAL HOUSE OF REPRESENTATIVES

Envelope:	*Mr the Hon. Ned Kelly, MP*
Formal letter opening:	*Dear Sir*
Formal letter closing:	*Yours faithfully*
Social letter opening:	*Dear Mr Kelly*
Social letter closing:	*Yours sincerely*
Verbal reference:	*Mr Kelly*
Verbal introduction:	*The Honourable Ned Kelly*
Verbal address:	*Mr Kelly*
Place card:	*The Hon. Ned Kelly*

MEMBERS OF THE SENATE

Envelope:	*Senator (or the Hon.) Ned Kelly*
Formal letter opening:	*Dear Senator*
Formal letter closing:	*Yours faithfully*
Social letter opening:	*Dear Senator Kelly*
Social letter closing:	*Yours sincerely*
Verbal reference:	*Senator Kelly*
Verbal introduction:	*Senator Ned Kelly*
Verbal address:	*Senator Kelly*
Place card:	*Senator Kelly*

SENATOR-ELECT

Envelope:	*Senator-Elect Ned Kelly*
Formal letter opening:	*Dear Sir*
Formal letter closing:	*Yours faithfully*
Social letter opening:	*Dear Senator-Elect Kelly*
Social letter closing:	*Yours sincerely*
Verbal reference:	*The Senator-Elect*
Verbal introduction:	*Senator-Elect Ned Kelly*
Verbal address:	*Mr Kelly*
Place card:	*Senator-Elect Ned Kelly*

MEMBER OF THE LEGISLATIVE ASSEMBLY, STATE PARLIAMENT

Envelope:	*Mr Ned Kelly, MLA*
Formal letter opening:	*Dear Sir*
Formal letter closing:	*Yours faithfully*
Social letter opening:	*Dear Mr Kelly*
Social letter closing:	*Yours sincerely*
Verbal reference:	*Mr Kelly*
Verbal introduction:	*Mr Ned Kelly*
Verbal address:	*Mr Kelly*
Place card:	*Mr Ned Kelly*

PRESIDENT OF THE LEGISLATIVE COUNCIL

Envelope:	*The Hon. Ned Kelly, MLC, President of the Legislative Council*
Formal letter opening:	*Dear Mr President*
Formal letter closing:	*Yours faithfully*
Social letter opening:	*Dear Mr Kelly*
Social letter closing:	*Yours sincerely*
Verbal reference:	*Mr Kelly*
Verbal introduction:	*The President of the Legislative Council*
Verbal address:	*Mr Kelly*
Place card:	*President of the Legislative Council*

Diplomatic

AMBASSADOR OR HIGH COMMISSIONER

Envelope:	*His Excellency Mr Ned Kelly, Ambassador of (or High Commissioner for) Rainbowland*
Formal letter opening:	*Your Excellency*
Formal letter closing:	*Yours faithfully*
Social letter opening:	*Dear Ambassador Kelly*
Social letter closing:	*Yours sincerely*
Verbal reference:	*His Excellency*
Verbal introduction:	*His Excellency the Ambassador of (or High Commissioner for) Rainbowland*
Verbal address:	*Your Excellency*
Place card:	*The Ambassador of Rainbowland*

WIFE OF AMBASSADOR OR HIGH COMMISSIONER

She may be called Her Excellency, although it is equally correct to refer to her as Mrs Kelly. If the Ambassador or High Commissioner is a woman, her husband is not entitled to be called His Excellency.

CHIEF MINISTER, AUSTRALIAN CAPITAL TERRITORY

Envelope:	*Mr Ned Kelly, MLA, Chief Minister of the ACT*
Formal letter opening:	*Dear Chief Minister*
Formal letter closing:	*Yours faithfully*
Social letter opening:	*Dear Mr Kelly*
Social letter closing:	*Yours sincerely*
Verbal reference:	*Mr Kelly*
Verbal introduction	*The Chief Minister of the ACT*
Verbal address:	*Mr Kelly*
Place card:	*Chief Minister of the ACT*

MINISTER, AUSTRALIAN CAPITAL TERRITORY

Envelope:	*Mr Ned Kelly, MLA, Minister for the Environment*
Formal letter opening:	*Dear Minister*
Formal letter closing:	*Yours faithfully*
Social letter opening:	*Dear Mr Kelly*
Social letter closing:	*Yours sincerely*
Verbal reference:	*Mr Kelly*
Verbal introduction:	*The Minister for the Environment*
Verbal address:	*Mr Kelly*
Place card:	*ACT Minister for the Environment*

MEMBER, AUSTRALIAN CAPITAL TERRITORY

Envelope:	*Mr Ned Kelly, MLA*
Letter opening:	*Dear Mr Kelly*
Letter closing:	*Yours sincerely*
Place card:	*Mr Ned Kelly*

ADMINISTRATOR OF THE NORTHERN TERRITORY

Envelope:	*His Honour the Administrator Mr Ned Kelly*
Formal letter opening:	*Your Honour*
Formal letter closing:	*Yours faithfully*
Social letter opening:	*Dear Administrator*
Social letter closing:	*Yours sincerely*
Verbal reference:	*Mr Kelly*
Verbal introduction:	*His Honour the Administrator*
Verbal address:	*Mr Kelly*
Place card:	*Administrator of the Northern Territory*

CHIEF MINISTER, NORTHERN TERRITORY

Envelope:	*The Hon. Ned Kelly, MLA, Chief Minister for the Northern Territory*
Formal letter opening:	*Dear Chief Minister*
Formal letter closing:	*Yours faithfully*
Social letter opening:	*Dear Mr Kelly*
Social letter closing:	*Yours sincerely*
Verbal reference:	*Mr Kelly*
Verbal introduction:	*The Chief Minister for the Northern Territory*
Verbal address:	*Mr Kelly*
Place card:	*Chief Minister for the Northern Territory*

SPEAKER, NORTHERN TERRITORY

Envelope:	*The Hon. Ned Kelly, MLA, Speaker of the Legislative Assembly of the Northern Territory*
Formal letter opening:	*Dear Mr Speaker*
Formal letter closing:	*Yours faithfully*
Social letter opening:	*Dear Mr Kelly*
Social letter closing:	*Yours sincerely*
Verbal reference:	*Mr Kelly*
Verbal introduction:	*The Speaker of the Legislative Assembly*
Verbal address:	*Mr Speaker*
Place card:	*Speaker of the Legislative Assembly of the Northern Territory*

MEMBERS OF THE EXECUTIVE COUNCIL AND MINISTERS OF THE NORTHERN TERRITORY

Envelope:	*The Hon. Ned Kelly, MLA, Minister for Housing*
Formal letter opening:	*Dear Minister*
Formal letter closing:	*Yours faithfully*
Social letter opening:	*Dear Mr Kelly*
Social letter closing:	*Yours sincerely*
Verbal reference:	*Mr Kelly*
Verbal introduction:	*The Minister for Housing*
Verbal address:	*Mr Kelly*
Place card:	*Minister for Housing for the Northern Territory*

LEADER OF THE OPPOSITION, NORTHERN TERRITORY

Envelope:	*Mr Ned Kelly, MLA, Leader of the Opposition*
Formal letter opening:	*Dear Sir*
Formal letter closing:	*Yours faithfully*
Social letter opening:	*Dear Mr Kelly*
Social letter closing:	*Yours sincerely*
Verbal reference:	*Mr Kelly*
Verbal introduction:	*Mr Kelly, the Leader of the Opposition*
Verbal address:	*Mr Kelly*
Place card:	*Leader of the Opposition, Northern Territory*

MEMBERS OF THE LEGISLATIVE ASSEMBLY, NORTHERN TERRITORY

Envelope:	*Mr Ned Kelly, MLA, Member for Port Darwin*
Formal letter opening:	*Dear Sir*
Formal letter closing:	*Yours faithfully*
Social letter opening:	*Dear Mr Kelly*
Social letter closing:	*Yours sincerely*
Verbal reference:	*Mr Kelly*
Verbal introduction:	*Mr Kelly the Member for Port Darwin*
Verbal address:	*Mr Kelly*
Place card:	*Member for Port Darwin*

LORD MAYOR

(In cities other than Geelong the form of address is the same for a woman Lord Mayor as for a man, except that she is addressed as Her Worship.)

. . . OF ADELAIDE, BRISBANE, HOBART, MELBOURNE, PERTH AND SYDNEY

Envelope:	*The Right Hon. the Lord Mayor of (city), Mr Ned Kelly*
Formal letter opening:	*My Lord Mayor*
Formal letter closing:	*Yours faithfully*
Social letter opening:	*Dear (Councillor, Alderman, or Mr) Kelly*
Social letter closing:	*Yours sincerely*
Verbal reference:	*The Lord Mayor*
Verbal introduction:	*The Lord Mayor (of city), Mr Kelly*
Verbal address:	*Mr Mayor or Sir*
Place card:	*Lord Mayor of (city)*

. . . OF DARWIN, NEWCASTLE AND WOLLONGONG

Envelope:	*The Right Worshipful the Lord Mayor of (city)*
Formal letter opening:	*My Lord Mayor*
Formal letter closing:	*Yours faithfully*

Social letter opening:	*Dear (Councillor, Alderman or Mr) Kelly*
Social letter closing:	*Yours sincerely*
Verbal reference:	*The Lord Mayor*
Verbal introduction:	*The Lord Mayor of (city)*
Verbal address:	*Mr Mayor or Sir*
Place card:	*Lord Mayor of (city)*

WIFE OF THE LORD MAYOR OF DARWIN, NEWCASTLE AND WOLLONGONG

Envelope:	*The Lady Mayoress of (city), Mrs Kelly*
Formal letter opening:	*My Lady Mayoress*
Formal letter closing:	*Yours faithfully*
Social letter opening:	*Dear Mrs Kelly*
Social letter closing:	*Yours sincerely*
Verbal reference:	*Mrs Kelly*
Verbal introduction:	*Mrs Kelly, the Lady Mayoress*
Verbal address:	*Mrs Kelly or Ma'am*
Place card:	*Lady Mayoress*

. . . OF GEELONG

Envelope:	*The Right Worshipful the Mayor of Geelong Alderman Ned Kelly*
Formal letter opening:	*Mr Mayor*
Formal letter closing:	*Yours faithfully*
Social letter opening:	*Dear Alderman Kelly*
Social letter closing:	*Yours sincerely*
Verbal reference:	*The Mayor*
Verbal introduction:	*Alderman Kelly, the Mayor of Geelong*
Verbal address:	*Mr Mayor or Sir*
Place card:	*Mayor of Geelong*

. . . OF OTHER CITIES IN AUSTRALIA

Envelope:	*His Worship the Mayor of (city), Mr Ned Kelly*
Formal letter opening:	*Mr Mayor*
Formal letter closing:	*Yours faithfully*
Social letter opening:	*Dear Alderman Kelly*
Social letter closing:	*Yours sincerely*
Verbal reference:	*The Mayor*

Verbal introduction:	*Mr Ned Kelly, the Mayor (of city, if appropriate)*
Verbal address:	*Mr Mayor or Sir*
Place card:	*Mayor of (city)*

WIFE OF A MAYOR OF ANY CITY OTHER THAN DARWIN, NEWCASTLE AND WOLLONGONG

Envelope:	*The Mayoress of (city) Mrs Ned Kelly*
Formal letter opening:	*Madam Mayoress*
Formal letter closing:	*Yours faithfully*
Social letter opening:	*Dear Mrs Kelly*
Social letter closing:	*Yours sincerely*
Verbal reference:	*Mrs Kelly*
Verbal introduction:	*Mrs Kelly, the Mayoress (of city, if appropriate)*
Verbal address:	*Mrs Kelly or Madam Mayoress*
Place card:	*Mayoress of (city)*

SHIRE PRESIDENT

Envelope:	*The Shire President, Councillor (or Mr) Ned Kelly*
Formal letter opening:	*Dear President*
Formal letter closing:	*Yours faithfully*
Social letter opening:	*Dear Councillor (or Mr) Kelly*
Social letter closing:	*Yours sincerely*
Verbal reference:	*Mr Kelly*
Verbal introduction:	*Councillor Ned Kelly, the Shire President*
Verbal address:	*Mr President or Sir*
Place card:	*The Shire President*

ALDERMAN (OF EITHER SEX)

Envelope:	*Alderman Ned Kelly*
Formal letter opening:	*Dear Alderman*
Formal letter closing:	*Yours faithfully*
Social letter opening:	*Dear Alderman Kelly*
Social letter closing:	*Yours sincerely*
Verbal reference:	*Alderman Kelly*
Verbal introduction:	*Alderman Kelly*

Verbal address:	*Alderman*
Place card:	*Alderman Kelly*

COUNCILLOR

Envelope:	*Councillor Ned Kelly*
Formal letter opening:	*Dear Councillor*
Formal letter closing:	*Yours faithfully*
Social letter opening:	*Dear Councillor Kelly*
Social letter closing:	*Yours sincerely*
Verbal reference:	*Councillor Kelly*
Verbal introduction:	*Councillor Kelly*
Verbal address:	*Councillor*
Place card:	*Councillor Kelly*

The law

CHIEF JUSTICE OF THE HIGH COURT OF AUSTRALIA

Envelope:	*The Hon. Justice Kelly (or, if appropriate, The Hon. Sir Ned Kelly) Chief Justice of Australia*
Formal letter opening:	*Dear Sir*
Formal letter closing:	*Yours faithfully*
Social letter opening:	*Dear Chief Justice Kelly*
Social letter closing:	*Yours sincerely*
Verbal reference:	*The Chief Justice*
Verbal introduction:	*Justice Kelly, Chief Justice of the High Court of Australia*
Verbal address:	*Chief Justice or Sir*
Place card:	*The Chief Justice of the High Court*

JUSTICE OF THE HIGH COURT OF AUSTRALIA

Envelope:	*The Hon. Justice Ned Kelly, High Court of Australia*
Formal letter opening:	*Your honour*
Formal letter closing:	*Yours faithfully*
Social letter opening:	*Dear Justice Kelly*
Social letter closing:	*Yours sincerely*
Verbal reference:	*Justice Kelly*

Verbal introduction:	*Justice Ned Kelly of the High Court of Australia*
Verbal address:	*Justice Kelly or Sir*
Place card:	*Justice Kelly*

CHIEF JUSTICE OF THE FEDERAL COURT OF AUSTRALIA

Envelope:	*The Hon. Justice Kelly, Chief Justice, Federal Court of Australia*
Formal letter opening:	*Your Honour*
Formal letter closing:	*Yours faithfully*
Social letter opening:	*Dear Chief Justice Kelly*
Social letter closing:	*Yours sincerely*
Verbal reference:	*Chief Justice Kelly*
Verbal introduction:	*The Chief Justice of the Federal Court of Australia*
Verbal address:	*Chief Justice or Sir*
Place card:	*The Chief Justice of the Federal Court*

JUSTICE OF THE FEDERAL COURT OF AUSTRALIA

Envelope:	*The Hon. Justice Kelly, Federal Court of Australia*
Formal letter opening:	*Your Honour*
Formal letter closing:	*Yours faithfully*
Social letter opening:	*Dear Justice Kelly*
Social letter closing:	*Yours sincerely*
Verbal reference:	*Justice Kelly*
Verbal introduction:	*The Honourable Justice Kelly*
Verbal address:	*Justice Kelly*
Place card:	*Justice Kelly*

PRESIDENT OF THE INDUSTRIAL RELATIONS COMMISSION

Envelope:	*The Hon. Justice Kelly, President, Australian Industrial Relations Commission*
Formal letter opening:	*Your Honour*
Formal letter closing:	*Yours faithfully*

Social letter opening:	*Dear Justice Kelly*
Social letter closing:	*Yours sincerely*
Verbal reference:	*Justice Kelly*
Verbal introduction:	*Justice Kelly, President of the Industrial Relations Commission*
Verbal address:	*Mr President or Sir*
Place card:	*President, Industrial Relations Commission*

DEPUTY PRESIDENT OF THE INDUSTRIAL RELATIONS COMMISSION

Envelope:	*The Hon. Justice Kelly, Deputy President, Australian Industrial Relations Commission*
Formal letter opening:	*Your Honour*
Formal letter closing:	*Yours faithfully*
Social letter opening:	*Dear Justice Kelly*
Social letter closing:	*Yours sincerely*
Verbal reference:	*Justice Kelly*
Verbal introduction:	*Justice Kelly, Deputy President of the Industrial Relations Commission*
Verbal address:	*Justice Kelly or Sir*
Place card:	*Deputy President, Industrial Relations Commission*

COMMISSIONER OF THE INDUSTRIAL RELATIONS COMMISSION

Envelope:	*Commissioner Kelly, Australian Industrial Relations Commission*
Formal letter opening:	*Commissioner*
Formal letter closing:	*Yours faithfully*
Social letter opening:	*Dear Commissioner Kelly*
Social letter closing:	*Yours sincerely*
Verbal reference:	*Commissioner Kelly*
Verbal introduction:	*Commissioner Kelly of the Industrial Relations Commission*
Verbal address:	*Commissioner or Sir*
Place card:	*Commissioner Kelly*

CHIEF JUSTICE OF THE FAMILY COURT OF AUSTRALIA

Envelope:	*The Hon. Justice Kelly, Chief Justice, Family Court of Australia*
Formal letter opening:	*Your Honour*
Formal letter closing:	*Yours faithfully*
Social letter opening:	*Dear Chief Justice Kelly*
Social letter closing:	*Yours sincerely*
Verbal reference:	*Chief Justice Kelly*
Verbal introduction:	*The Chief Justice of the Family Court of Australia*
Verbal address:	*Chief Justice or Sir*
Place card:	*The Chief Justice, Family Court of Australia*

JUSTICE OF THE FAMILY COURT OF AUSTRALIA

Envelope:	*The Hon. Justice Kelly, Family Court of Australia*
Formal letter opening:	*Your Honour*
Formal letter closing:	*Yours faithfully*
Social letter opening:	*Dear Justice Kelly*
Social letter closing:	*Yours sincerely*
Verbal reference:	*Justice Kelly*
Verbal introduction:	*Justice Kelly of the Family Court of Australia*
Verbal address:	*Justice Kelly or Sir*
Place card:	*Justice Kelly*

CHIEF JUSTICE OF A SUPREME COURT

Envelope:	*The Hon. Justice Kelly, Chief Justice, Supreme Court of (state or territory)*
Formal letter opening:	*Your Honour*
Formal letter closing:	*Yours faithfully*
Social letter opening:	*Dear Chief Justice Kelly*
Social letter closing:	*Yours sincerely*
Verbal reference:	*Chief Justice Kelly*
Verbal introduction:	*Chief Justice Kelly of the Supreme Court of (state or territory)*
Verbal address:	*Chief Justice or Sir*
Place card:	*Chief Justice, Supreme Court of (state or territory)*

JUSTICE OF A SUPREME COURT

Envelope:	*The Hon. Justice Kelly, Supreme Court of (state or territory)*
Formal letter opening:	*Your Honour*
Formal letter closing:	*Yours faithfully*
Social letter opening:	*Dear Justice Kelly*
Social letter closing:	*Yours sincerely*
Verbal reference:	*Justice Kelly*
Verbal introduction:	*Justice Kelly of the Supreme Court of (state or territory)*
Verbal address:	*Justice Kelly or Sir*
Place card:	*Justice Kelly*

CHIEF JUDGE OF A DISTRICT OR COUNTY COURT

Envelope:	*His Honour Judge Ned Kelly, Chief Judge, District (or County) Court of (place)*
Formal letter opening:	*Your Honour*
Formal letter closing:	*Yours faithfully*
Social letter opening:	*Dear Chief Judge Kelly*
Social letter closing:	*Yours sincerely*
Verbal reference:	*Chief Judge Kelly*
Verbal introduction:	*Chief Judge Ned Kelly of the District (or County) Court of (place)*
Verbal address:	*Chief Judge or Sir*
Place card:	*Chief Judge, District (or County) Court of (place)*

JUDGE OF A DISTRICT OR COUNTY COURT

Envelope:	*His Honour Judge Ned Kelly, District (or County) Court of (place)*
Formal letter opening:	*Your Honour*
Formal letter closing:	*Yours faithfully*

Social letter opening: *Dear Judge Kelly*
Social letter closing: *Yours sincerely*
Verbal reference: *Judge Kelly*
Verbal introduction: *Judge Ned Kelly*
Verbal address: *Judge or Judge Kelly*
Place card: *Judge Kelly*

STIPENDIARY MAGISTRATE OR POLICE MAGISTRATE

Envelope: *Mr Ned Kelly, Magistrate*
Formal letter opening: *Dear Sir*
Formal letter closing: *Yours faithfully*
Social letter opening: *Dear Mr Kelly*
Social letter closing: *Yours sincerely*
Verbal reference: *Mr Kelly*
Verbal introduction: *Ned Kelly (or Mr Ned Kelly)*
Verbal address: *Mr Kelly*
Place card: *Magistrate Kelly*

JUSTICE OF THE PEACE

Envelope: *Mr Ned Kelly, JP*
Formal letter opening: *Dear Sir*
Formal letter closing: *Yours faithfully*
Social letter opening: *Dear Mr Kelly*
Social letter closing: *Yours sincerely*
Verbal reference: *Mr Kelly*
Verbal introduction: *Ned Kelly (or Mr Ned Kelly)*
Verbal address: *Your Worship, if in court, otherwise Mr Kelly*
Place card: *Mr Ned Kelly*

Universities and the professions

Medical and dental practitioners are known as Doctor. Traditionally, male surgeons are referred to as Mr but this practice seems to be in decline in Australia.

Doctor may be shortened to Dr if it precedes a person's name, but it must be spelled in full if no name is added. Unless the doctorate refers to

medicine or dentistry, it is not normally used socially. If a doctor is knighted, he swaps the title for Sir and his qualifications appear after his surname; for example, Sir Ned Kelly, KT, LLD.

Professor is a title that should not be shortened.

Initials denoting academic degrees are placed after the person's name but only when they are relevant – for example, in official correspondence. They should be written in capital letters, such as FRACP (Fellow of the Royal Australasian College of Physicians) and punctuation used only to separate two or more qualifications. A Master's or Bachelor's degree is rarely used in correspondence.

UNIVERSITY CHANCELLOR

Envelope: *Mr Ned Kelly, Chancellor of the University of (place)*
Formal letter opening: *Chancellor*
Formal letter closing: *Yours faithfully*
Social letter opening: *Dear Mr Kelly*
Social letter closing: *Yours sincerely*
Verbal reference: *The Chancellor*
Verbal introduction: *Mr Ned Kelly, Chancellor of the University of (place)*
Verbal address: *Chancellor or Sir*
Place card: *Chancellor, University of (place)*

UNIVERSITY VICE CHANCELLOR

Envelope: *Mr Ned Kelly, Vice Chancellor of the University of (place)*
Formal letter opening: *Vice Chancellor*
Formal letter closing: *Yours faithfully*
Social letter opening: *Dear Mr Kelly*
Social letter closing: *Yours sincerely*
Verbal reference: *The Vice Chancellor*
Verbal introduction: *Mr Ned Kelly, Vice Chancellor of the University of (place)*
Verbal address: *Vice Chancellor or Sir*
Place card: *Vice Chancellor, University of (place)*

DEAN OF A COLLEGE

Envelope:	*Professor Ned Kelly, Dean of Ormond College, Melbourne University*
Formal letter opening:	*Dean*
Formal letter closing:	*Yours faithfully*
Social letter opening:	*Dear Professor Kelly*
Social letter closing:	*Yours sincerely*
Verbal reference:	*The Dean*
Verbal introduction:	*Professor Ned Kelly, Dean of Ormond College at Melbourne University*
Verbal address:	*Professor Kelly or Sir*
Place card:	*Professor Kelly*

British royalty, lords and ladies

ELIZABETH THE SECOND, BY THE GRACE OF GOD QUEEN OF AUSTRALIA AND HER OTHER REALMS AND TERRITORIES, HEAD OF THE COMMONWEALTH

Envelope:	*Private Secretary to Her Majesty The Queen*
Letter opening:	*Dear Madam; by name in subsequent correspondence*
Letter closing:	*I have the honour to remain, Madam, Her Majesty's most humble and obedient servant*
Verbal reference:	*Her Majesty and thereafter The Queen*
Verbal introduction:	*Her Majesty The Queen*
Verbal address:	*Your Majesty, then Ma'am*
Place card:	*HM The Queen*

Direct questions should never be asked of any member of the royal family. For example, never ask, 'Do you . . . ?' or 'Have You . . . ?' It is acceptable to turn the question into a statement, with the royal's name in the third person: 'I trust Her Majesty enjoyed the performance.'

THE QUEEN'S HUSBAND, HIS ROYAL HIGHNESS PRINCE PHILIP, THE DUKE OF EDINBURGH

Envelope:	*Private Secretary to HRH The Duke of Edinburgh*
Letter opening:	*Dear Sir; by name in subsequent correspondence*
Letter closing:	*I have he honour to be, Sir, Your Royal Highness's most humble and obedient servant*
Verbal reference:	*His Royal Highness, then Prince Philip or The Duke of Edinburgh*
Verbal introduction:	*His Royal Highness, The Duke of Edinburgh*
Verbal address:	*Your Royal Highness, then Sir*
Place card:	*HRH The Duke of Edinburgh*

THE QUEEN MOTHER

Envelope:	*Private Secretary to Her Majesty Queen Elizabeth The Queen Mother*
Letter opening:	*Dear Madam; by name in subsequent correspondence*
Letter closing:	*I have the honour to remain, Madam, Her Majesty's most humble and obedient servant*
Verbal reference:	*Her Majesty or Queen Elizabeth or The Queen Mother*
Verbal introduction:	*Her Majesty Queen Elizabeth The Queen Mother*
Verbal address:	*Your Majesty, then Ma'am*
Place card:	*HM Queen Elizabeth The Queen Mother*

PRINCE CHARLES, THE PRINCE OF WALES

Envelope:	*Private Secretary to HRH The Prince of Wales*
Letter opening:	*Dear Sir; by name in subsequent correspondence*
Letter closing:	*I have the honour to remain, Sir, His Royal Highness's most humble and obedient servant*
Verbal reference:	*His Royal Highness The Prince of Wales or Prince Charles*
Verbal introduction:	*His Royal Highness The Prince of Wales*
Verbal address:	*Your Royal Highness, then Sir*
Place card:	*HRH The Prince of Wales*

If Prince Charles were married, his wife would be referred to as the Princess of Wales, not Princess (her first name).

Only princes and princesses who belong to the immediate family of the monarch have their titles preceded by 'the'.

CHILDREN OF THE HEIR APPARENT

Envelope:	*Private Secretary to HRH The Prince William*
Letter opening:	*Dear Sir; by name in subsequent correspondence*
Letter closing:	*I have the honour to remain, Sir, His Royal Highness's most humble and obedient servant*
Verbal reference:	*His Royal Highness or Prince William*
Verbal introduction:	*His Royal Highness Prince William*
Verbal address:	*Your Royal Highness*
Place card:	*HRH Prince William*

Prince Harry should be addressed in the same way as Prince William.

PRINCE ANDREW, SECOND SON OF THE MONARCH

Envelope:	*Private Secretary to HRH The Duke of York*
Letter opening:	*Dear Sir; by name in subsequent correspondence*
Letter closing:	*I have the honour to remain, Sir, His Royal Highness's most humble and obedient servant*
Verbal reference:	*His Royal Highness or the Duke of York*
Verbal introduction:	*His Royal Highness the Duke of York*
Verbal address:	*Your Royal Highness, then Sir*
Place card:	*HRH The Duke of York*

PRINCE EDWARD, THIRD SON OF THE MONARCH

Envelope:	*Private Secretary to HRH The Earl of Wessex*
Letter opening:	*as for Prince Andrew*
Letter closing:	*as for Prince Andrew*
Verbal reference:	*His Royal Highness or The Earl of Wessex*
Verbal introduction:	*His Royal Highness The Earl of Wessex*
Verbal address:	*Your Royal Highness, then Sir*
Place card:	*HRH The Earl of Wessex*

PRINCESS ANNE, DAUGHTER OF THE MONARCH

Envelope:	*Private Secretary to HRH The Princess Royal*
Letter opening:	*Dear Madam; by name in subsequent correspondence*
Letter closing:	*I have the honour to remain, Madam, Her Royal Highness's most humble and obedient servant*

Verbal reference:	*Her Royal Highness or The Princess Royal*
Verbal introduction:	*Her Royal Highness The Princess Royal*
Verbal address:	*Your Royal Highness, then Ma'am*
Place card:	*HRH The Princess Royal*

PRINCESS MARGARET, SISTER OF THE MONARCH

Envelope:	*Private Secretary to HRH The Princess Margaret Countess of Snowdon*
Letter opening:	*as for Princess Anne*
Letter closing:	*as for Princess Anne*
Verbal reference:	*Her Royal Highness or Princess Margaret or the Countess of Snowdon*
Verbal introduction:	*Her Royal Highness the Princess Margaret, Countess of Snowdon*
Verbal address:	*Your Royal Highness, then Ma'am*
Place card:	*HRH The Princess Margaret, Countess of Snowdon*

The peerage

The British peerage is a system of titles that may be inherited or conferred. In descending order of importance, they rank as follows: Duke and Duchess, Marquess and Marchioness, Earl and Countess, Viscount and Viscountess, Baron and Baroness.

HEREDITARY PEERESS (DAUGHTER OF A NOBLEMAN)

Envelope:	*The Countess of Albion*
Formal letter opening:	*Madam*
Formal letter closing:	*Yours faithfully*
Social letter opening:	*Dear Lady Albion*
Social letter closing:	*Yours sincerely*
Verbal reference:	*Lady Albion*

Verbal introduction:	*The Countess of Albion*
Verbal address:	*Lady Albion*
Place card:	*Lady Albion*

DUKE

Envelope:	*His Grace the Duke of Albion*
Formal letter opening:	*My Lord Duke*
Formal letter closing:	*Yours faithfully*
Social letter opening:	*Dear Duke*
Social letter closing:	*Yours sincerely*
Verbal reference:	*The Duke of Albion*
Verbal introduction:	*His Grace the Duke of Albion*
Verbal address:	*Your Grace, or Duke*
Place card:	*Duke of Albion*

DUCHESS

Envelope:	*Her Grace the Duchess of Albion*
Formal letter opening:	*Madam*
Formal letter closing:	*Yours faithfully*
Social letter opening:	*Dear Duchess*
Social letter closing:	*Yours sincerely*
Verbal reference:	*The Duchess of Albion*
Verbal introduction:	*Her Grace the Duchess of Albion*
Verbal address:	*Your Grace, or Duchess*
Place card:	*Duchess of Albion*

DOWAGER DUCHESS

Envelope:	*The Dowager Duchess of Albion, or Duchess of Albion*
Formal letter opening:	*Madam*
Formal letter closing:	*Yours faithfully*
Social letter opening:	*Dear Duchess*
Social letter closing:	*Yours sincerely*
Verbal reference:	*The Duchess of Albion*
Verbal introduction:	*Her Grace the Dowager Duchess of Albion*
Verbal address:	*Your Grace, or Duchess*
Place card:	*Dowager Duchess of Albion*

DUKE'S ELDEST SON

Envelope:	*The Marquess of Tooting (father's second title)*
Formal letter opening:	*My Lord*
Formal letter closing:	*Yours faithfully*
Social letter opening:	*Dear Lord Tooting*
Social letter closing:	*Yours sincerely*
Verbal reference:	*Lord Tooting*
Verbal introduction:	*Marquess of Tooting*
Verbal address:	*My Lord, or Lord Tooting*
Place card:	*Lord Tooting*

DUKE'S ELDEST SON'S WIFE

Envelope:	*The Marchioness of Tooting*
Formal letter opening:	*Madam*
Formal letter closing:	*Yours faithfully*
Social letter opening:	*Dear Lady Tooting*
Social letter closing:	*Yours sincerely*
Verbal reference:	*Lady Tooting*
Verbal introduction:	*Marchioness of Tooting*
Verbal address:	*Lady Tooting*
Place card:	*Lady Tooting*

DUKE'S YOUNGER SON

Envelope:	*The Lord William Awesbury (family name)*
Formal letter opening:	*My Lord*
Formal letter closing:	*Yours faithfully*
Social letter opening:	*Dear Lord William*
Social letter closing:	*Yours sincerely*
Verbal reference:	*Lord William*
Verbal introduction:	*The Lord William Awesbury*
Verbal address:	*Lord William*
Place card:	*Lord William Awesbury*

DUKE'S YOUNGER SON'S WIFE

Envelope:	*The Lady William Awesbury*
Formal letter opening:	*Madam*
Formal letter closing:	*Yours faithfully*
Social letter opening:	*Dear Lady William*
Social letter closing:	*Yours sincerely*
Verbal reference:	*Lady William*
Verbal introduction:	*The Lady William Awesbury*
Verbal address:	*Lady William*
Place card:	*Lady William Awesbury*

DUKE'S DAUGHTER

Envelope:	*The Lady Caroline Awesbury*
Formal letter opening:	*Madam*
Formal letter closing:	*Yours faithfully*
Social letter opening:	*Dear Lady Caroline*
Social letter closing:	*Yours sincerely*
Verbal reference:	*Lady Caroline*
Verbal introduction:	*The Lady Caroline Awesbury*
Verbal address:	*Lady Caroline*
Place card:	*Lady Caroline Awesbury*

DUKE'S ELDEST SON'S ELDEST SON

Envelope:	*The Earl of Picton (his grandfather's third title) or Lord Picton*
Formal letter opening:	*My Lord*
Formal letter closing:	*Yours faithfully*
Social letter opening:	*Dear Lord Picton*
Social letter closing:	*Yours sincerely*
Verbal reference:	*Lord Picton*
Verbal introduction:	*Lord Picton*
Verbal address:	*My Lord or Lord Picton*
Place card:	*Lord Picton*

MARQUESS (ALSO SPELT MARQUIS)

Envelope:	*The Most Hon. the Marquess of Albion or The Marquess of Albion*
Formal letter opening:	*My Lord Marquess*
Formal letter closing:	*Yours faithfully*
Social letter opening:	*Dear Lord Albion*
Social letter closing:	*Yours sincerely*
Verbal reference:	*Lord Albion*
Verbal introduction:	*The Marquess of Albion*
Verbal address:	*My Lord, or Lord Albion*
Place card:	*Lord Albion*

MARCHIONESS (PRONOUNCED 'MARSHIONESS')

Envelope:	*The Most Hon. the Marchioness of Albion or The Marchioness of Albion*
Formal letter opening:	*Madam*
Formal letter closing:	*Yours faithfully*
Social letter opening:	*Dear Lady Albion*
Social letter closing:	*Yours sincerely*
Verbal reference:	*Lady Albion*
Verbal introduction:	*The Marchioness of Albion*
Verbal address:	*Madam or Lady Albion*
Place card:	*Lady Albion*

MARQUESS'S ELDEST SON

Envelope:	*Viscount Tooting*
Formal letter opening:	*My Lord*
Formal letter closing:	*Yours faithfully*
Social letter opening:	*Dear Lord Tooting*
Social letter closing:	*Yours sincerely*
Verbal reference:	*Lord Tooting*
Verbal introduction:	*Lord Tooting*
Verbal address:	*My Lord or Lord Tooting*
Place card:	*Lord Tooting*

MARQUESS'S YOUNGER SON

Envelope:	*Lord Scott*
Formal letter opening:	*My Lord*
Formal letter closing:	*Yours faithfully*
Social letter opening:	*Dear Lord*
Social letter closing:	*Yours sincerely*
Verbal reference:	*Lord Scott*
Verbal introduction:	*Lord Scott*
Verbal address:	*My Lord or Lord Scott*
Place card:	*Lord Scott*

MARQUESS'S DAUGHTER

Envelope:	*The Lady Caroline Awesbury*
Formal letter opening:	*Madam*
Formal letter closing:	*Yours faithfully*
Social letter opening:	*Dear Lady Caroline*
Social letter closing:	*Yours sincerely*
Verbal reference:	*Lady Caroline*
Verbal introduction:	*The Lady Caroline Awesbury*
Verbal address:	*Madam, or Lady Caroline*
Place card:	*Lady Caroline Awesbury*

MARQUESS'S ELDEST SON'S ELDEST SON

Envelope:	*Viscount Picton (his grandfather's third title) or Lord Picton*
Formal letter opening:	*My Lord*
Formal letter closing:	*Yours faithfully*
Social letter opening:	*Dear Lord Picton*
Social letter closing:	*Yours sincerely*
Verbal reference:	*Lord Picton*
Verbal introduction:	*Lord Picton*
Verbal address:	*My Lord, or Lord Picton*
Place card:	*Lord Picton*

EARL

Envelope:	*The Right Hon. the Earl of Albion or The Earl of Albion*
Formal letter opening:	*My Lord*
Formal letter closing:	*Yours faithfully*
Social letter opening:	*Dear Lord Albion*
Social letter closing:	*Yours sincerely*
Verbal reference:	*Lord Albion*
Verbal introduction:	*Lord Albion*
Verbal address:	*My Lord, or Lord Albion*
Place card:	*Lord Albion*

COUNTESS

Envelope:	*The Right Hon. the Countess of Albion or The Countess of Albion*
Formal letter opening:	*Madam*
Formal letter closing:	*Yours faithfully*
Social letter opening:	*Dear Lady Albion*
Social letter closing:	*Yours sincerely*
Verbal reference:	*Lady Albion*
Verbal introduction:	*The Countess of Albion*
Verbal address:	*Lady Albion*
Place card:	*Lady Albion*

EARL'S ELDEST SON

Envelope:	*Viscount Tooting (father's second title)*
Formal letter opening:	*My Lord*
Formal letter closing:	*Yours faithfully*
Social letter opening:	*Dear Lord Tooting*
Social letter closing:	*Yours sincerely*
Verbal reference:	*Lord Tooting*
Verbal introduction:	*Viscount Tooting*
Verbal address:	*Lord Tooting*
Place card:	*Lord Tooting*

EARL'S YOUNGER SON

Envelope:	*The Hon. William Awesbury (family name)*
Letter opening:	*Dear Mr Awesbury*
Business letter closing:	*Yours faithfully*
Social letter closing:	*Yours sincerely*
Verbal reference:	*William Awesbury*
Verbal introduction:	*The Hon. William Awesbury*
Verbal address:	*Mr Awesbury*
Place card:	*Mr William Awesbury*

EARL'S YOUNGER SON'S WIFE

Envelope:	*The Hon. Mrs William Awesbury*
Letter opening:	*Dear Mrs Awesbury*
Business letter closing:	*Yours faithfully*
Social letter closing:	*Yours sincerely*
Verbal reference:	*Mrs William Awesbury*
Verbal introduction:	*The Hon. Mrs William Awesbury*
Verbal address:	*Mrs Awesbury*
Place card:	*Mrs William Awesbury*

EARL'S DAUGHTER

Envelope:	*The Lady Caroline Awesbury*
Letter opening:	*Dear Lady Caroline*
Business letter closing:	*Yours faithfully*
Social letter closing:	*Yours sincerely*
Verbal reference:	*Lady Caroline*
Verbal introduction:	*The Lady Caroline Awesbury*
Verbal address:	*Lady Caroline*
Place card:	*Lady Caroline Awesbury*

VISCOUNT

Envelope:	*The Right Hon. the Viscount Albion*
Formal letter opening:	*My Lord*
Formal letter closing:	*Yours faithfully*
Social letter opening:	*Dear Lord Albion*
Social letter closing:	*Yours sincerely*
Verbal reference:	*Lord Albion*
Verbal introduction:	*The Viscount Albion*
Verbal address:	*Lord Albion*
Place card:	*Lord Albion*

VISCOUNTESS

Envelope:	*The Right Hon. the Viscountess Albion*
Formal letter opening:	*Madam*
Formal letter closing:	*Yours faithfully*
Social letter opening:	*Dear Lady Albion*
Social letter closing:	*Yours sincerely*
Verbal reference:	*Lady Albion*
Verbal introduction:	*The Viscountess Albion*
Verbal address:	*Lady Albion*
Place card:	*Lady Albion*

VISCOUNT'S SON

Envelope:	*The Hon. William Awesbury*
Letter opening:	*Dear Mr Awesbury*
Business letter closing:	*Yours faithfully*
Social letter closing:	*Yours sincerely*
Verbal reference:	*William Awesbury*
Verbal introduction:	*The Honourable William Awesbury*
Verbal address:	*Mr Awesbury*
Place card:	*Mr William Awesbury*

VISCOUNT'S SON'S WIFE

Envelope:	*The Hon. Mrs William Awesbury*
Letter opening:	*Dear Mrs Awesbury*
Business letter closing:	*Yours faithfully*
Social letter closing:	*Yours sincerely*
Verbal reference:	*Mrs William Awesbury*
Verbal introduction:	*The Honourable Mrs William Awesbury*
Verbal address:	*Mrs Awesbury*
Place card:	*Mrs William Awesbury*

VISCOUNT'S DAUGHTER

Envelope:	*The Hon. Caroline Awesbury*
Letter opening:	*Dear Miss Awesbury*
Business letter closing:	*Yours faithfully*
Social letter closing:	*Yours sincerely*
Verbal reference:	*Caroline Awesbury*
Verbal introduction:	*The Honourable Caroline Awesbury*
Verbal address:	*Miss Awesbury*
Place card:	*Miss Caroline Awesbury*

BARON

Envelope:	*The Right Hon. Lord Albion*
Formal letter opening:	*My Lord*
Formal letter closing:	*Yours faithfully*
Social letter opening:	*Dear Lord Albion*
Social letter closing:	*Yours sincerely*
Verbal reference:	*Lord Albion*
Verbal introduction:	*The Lord Albion*
Verbal address:	*Lord Albion*
Place card:	*Lord Albion*

BARONESS

Envelope:	*The Right Hon. Lady Albion*
Formal letter opening:	*Madam*
Formal letter closing:	*Yours faithfully*
Social letter opening:	*Dear Lady Albion*
Social letter closing:	*Yours sincerely*

Verbal reference:	*Lady Albion*
Verbal introduction:	*The Lady Albion*
Verbal address:	*Lady Albion*
Place card:	*Lady Albion*

A baron's children are addressed in the same way as a Viscount's.

WIDOW OF A HEREDITARY PEER

Traditionally, she is called The Dowager Duchess (Marchioness, Baroness or whatever) unless that role is occupied, in which case she would be referred to by her first name: Caroline, Duchess Albion. However, if her son who has inherited the title is unmarried, she is not required to include 'Dowager' in her title. According to Debrett's, lots of dowagers resist the term and prefer to use their first names, so it is advisable to find out how they wish to be addressed.

EX-WIFE OF A HEREDITARY PEER

Envelope:	*Caroline, Viscountess of Albion*
Formal letter opening:	*Madam*
Formal letter closing:	*Yours faithfully*
Social letter opening:	*Lady Albion*
Social letter closing:	*Yours sincerely*
Verbal reference:	*Lady Albion*
Verbal introduction:	*Caroline, Viscountess of Albion*
Verbal address:	*Lady Albion*
Place card:	*Lady Albion*

BARONET

Envelope:	*Sir William Awesbury, Bt*
Formal letter opening:	*Sir*
Formal letter closing:	*Yours faithfully*
Social letter opening:	*Dear Sir William*
Social letter closing:	*Yours sincerely*
Verbal reference:	*Sir William*
Verbal introduction:	*Sir William Awesbury*
Verbal address:	*Sir William*
Place card:	*Sir William Awesbury*

BARONET'S WIFE

Envelope:	*Lady Awesbury*
Formal letter opening:	*Madam*
Formal letter closing:	*Yours faithfully*
Social letter opening:	*Dear Lady Awesbury*
Social letter closing:	*Yours sincerely*
Verbal reference:	*Lady Awesbury*
Verbal introduction:	*Lady Awesbury*
Verbal address:	*Lady Awesbury*
Place card:	*Lady Awesbury*

A Baronet's children do not have titles.

WIDOW OF A BARONET

Envelope:	*Dowager Lady Awesbury*
Formal letter opening:	*Madam*
Formal letter closing:	*Yours faithfully*
Social letter opening:	*Dear Lady Awesbury*
Social letter closing:	*Yours sincerely*
Verbal reference:	*Lady Awesbury*
Verbal introduction:	*Dowager Lady Awesbury*
Verbal address:	*Lady Awesbury*
Place card:	*Dowager Lady Awesbury*

LIFE PEER

Envelope:	*The Lord Awesbury of Albion*
Letter opening:	*Dear Lord Awesbury*
Formal letter closing:	*Yours faithfully*
Social letter closing:	*Yours sincerely*
Verbal reference:	*Lord Awesbury*
Verbal introduction:	*The Lord Awesbury of Albion*
Verbal address:	*Lord Awesbury*
Place card:	*Lord Awesbury*

LIFE PEER'S WIFE

Envelope:	*The Lady Awesbury of Albion*
Letter opening:	*Dear Lady Awesbury*
Formal letter closing:	*Yours faithfully*
Social letter closing:	*Yours sincerely*
Verbal reference:	*Lady Awesbury*
Verbal introduction:	*The Lady Awesbury of Albion*
Verbal address:	*Lady Awesbury*
Place card:	*Lady Awesbury*

LIFE PEER'S SON

Envelope:	*The Hon. William Awesbury*
Letter opening:	*Dear Mr Awesbury*
Formal letter closing:	*Yours faithfully*
Social letter closing:	*Yours sincerely*
Verbal reference:	*William Awesbury*
Verbal introduction:	*The Honourable William Awesbury*
Verbal address:	*Mr Awesbury*
Place card:	*Mr William Awesbury*

LIFE PEER'S DAUGHTER

Envelope:	*The Hon. Caroline Awesbury*
Letter opening:	*Dear Miss Awesbury*
Formal letter closing:	*Yours faithfully*
Social letter closing:	*Yours sincerely*
Verbal reference:	*Caroline Awesbury*
Verbal introduction:	*The Honourable Caroline Awesbury*
Verbal address:	*Miss Awesbury*
Place card:	*Miss Caroline Awesbury*

LIFE PEERESS

Envelope:	*The Baroness Awesbury of Albion*
Formal letter opening:	*Madam*
Formal letter closing:	*Yours faithfully*
Social letter opening:	*Dear Lady Awesbury*
Social letter closing:	*Yours sincerely*
Verbal reference:	*Lady Awesbury*
Verbal introduction:	*The Baroness Awesbury of Albion*
Verbal address:	*Lady Awesbury*
Place card:	*Lady Awesbury*

KNIGHTHOOD

The orders of British knighthood and their initials are:

Knight (or Dame) Grand Cross of the Order of the Bath (GCB)

Knight of the Garter (KG)

Knight of the Thistle (KT)

Knight (or Dame) Grand Cross of the Order of St Michael and St George (GCMG)

Knight (or Dame) Grand Cross of the Order of the British Empire (GBE)

Knight Commander of the Order of the Bath (KCB)

Dame Commander of the Order of the Bath (DCB)

Knight Commander of the Order of St Michael and St George (KCMG)

Dame Commander of the Order of St Michael and St George (DCMG)

Knight Commander of the Royal Victorian Order (KCVO)

Dame Commander of the Royal Victorian Order (DCVO)

Knight Commander of the Order of the British Empire (KBE)

Dame Commander of the Order of the British Empire (DBE)

Knight Bachelor confers the title of 'Sir' but no initials are placed after the name.

KNIGHTS

Envelope:	*Sir William Awesbury, KG, KCMG*
Formal letter opening:	*Sir*
Formal letter closing:	*Yours faithfully*
Social letter opening:	*Dear Sir William*
Social letter closing:	*Yours sincerely*
Verbal reference:	*Sir William*
Verbal introduction:	*Sir William Awesbury*
Verbal address:	*Sir William*
Place card:	*Sir William Awesbury*

KNIGHT'S WIFE

Envelope:	*Lady Awesbury*
Formal letter opening:	*Madam*
Formal letter closing:	*Yours faithfully*
Social letter opening:	*Dear Lady Awesbury*
Social letter closing:	*Yours sincerely*
Verbal reference:	*Lady Awesbury*
Verbal introduction:	*Lady Awesbury*
Verbal address:	*Lady Awesbury*
Place card:	*Lady Awesbury*

The first name of the wife of a man who as been knighted should never be included in her title, for example Lady Caroline Awesbury, because that would mean she has inherited that title. This is a common mistake in Australia.

If there are two knights with the same surname, then it is permissible to make the distinction by inserting the first names of the men in their wives' titles. For example, Lady (William) Awesbury and Lady (Michael) Awesbury.

When knighthood has been conferred on a woman, she is known as Dame.

DAME

Envelope:	*Dame Caroline Awesbury*
Formal letter opening:	*Madam*
Formal letter closing:	*Yours faithfully*
Social letter opening:	*Dear Dame Caroline*
Social letter closing:	*Yours sincerely*
Verbal reference:	*Dame Caroline*
Verbal introduction:	*Dame Caroline Awesbury*
Verbal address:	*Dame Caroline*
Place card:	*Dame Caroline Awesbury*

Particular Scottish titles

ELDEST SON OF PEER

Envelope:	*The Master of Loch Lomond*
Letter opening:	*Dear Master of Loch Lomond*

Formal letter closing:	*Yours faithfully*
Social letter closing:	*Yours sincerely*
Verbal reference:	*Master Loch Lomond*
Verbal introduction:	*The Master of Loch Lomond*
Verbal address:	*Master Loch Lomond*
Place card:	*Master of Loch Lomond*

ELDEST SON OF HEREDITARY PEERESS

Envelope:	*Lord Loch Lomond*
Letter opening:	*Dear Lord Loch Lomond*
Formal letter closing:	*Yours faithfully*
Social letter closing:	*Yours sincerely*
Verbal reference:	*Lord Loch Lomond*
Verbal introduction:	*Lord Loch Lomond*
Verbal address:	*Lord Loch Lomond*
Place card:	*Lord Loch Lomond*

CHIEF OR CHIEFTAIN

Envelope:	*The MacGlen of MacGlen*
Letter opening:	*Dear MacGlen of MacGlen*
Formal letter closing:	*Yours faithfully*
Social letter closing:	*Yours sincerely*
Verbal reference:	*MacGlen of MacGlen*
Verbal introduction:	*The MacGlen of MacGlen*
Verbal address:	*MacGlen of MacGlen*
Place card:	*The MacGlen of MacGlen*

WOMAN CHIEF OR WIFE OF THE CHIEF

Envelope:	*Madam or Mrs MacGlen of MacGlen*
Letter opening:	*Dear Madam or Mrs MacGlen of MacGlen*
Formal letter closing:	*Yours faithfully*
Social letter closing:	*Yours sincerely*
Verbal reference, introduction, address and place card:	*Madam (or Mrs) MacGlen of MacGlen*

CHIEF'S ELDEST SON

Envelope:	*Duncan MacGlen of MacGlen, yr*
Letter opening:	*Dear MacGlen of MacGlen, yr*
Formal letter closing:	*Yours faithfully*
Social letter closing:	*Yours sincerely*
Verbal reference, introduction, address and place card:	*MacGlen of MacGlen, yr*

CHIEF'S OTHER CHILDREN

Sons do not have titles. The eldest daughter is called Miss MacGlen of MacGlen. All other daughters include their first names; that is, Miss Fiona MacGlen of MacGlen.

Particular Irish titles

HEREDITARY KNIGHT

Envelope:	*The Knight of Gaeil*
Letter opening:	*Dear Knight*
Formal letter closing:	*Yours faithfully*
Social letter closing:	*Yours sincerely*
Verbal reference:	*The Knight*
Verbal introduction:	*The Knight of Gaeil*
Verbal address:	*Knight*
Place card:	*Knight of Gaeil*

HEREDITARY KNIGHT'S WIFE

Envelope:	*Madam Gaeil*
Letter opening:	*Dear Madam Gaeil*
Formal letter closing:	*Yours faithfully*
Social letter closing:	*Yours sincerely*
Verbal reference, introduction, address and place card:	*Madam Gaeil*

CHIEFTAIN

Envelope:	*The Kelly of the Ballyderry*
Letter opening:	*Dear Kelly*
Formal letter closing:	*Yours faithfully*
Social letter closing:	*Yours sincerely*
Verbal reference:	*Kelly*
Verbal introduction:	*The Kelly of the Ballyderry*
Verbal address:	*Kelly*
Place card:	*The Kelly of the Ballyderry*

CHIEFTAIN'S WIFE

Envelope:	*Madam Kelly of the Ballyderry*
Letter opening:	*Dear Madam Kelly*
Formal letter closing:	*Yours faithfully*
Social letter closing:	*Yours sincerely*
Verbal reference:	*Madam Kelly*
Verbal introduction:	*Madam Kelly of the Ballyderry*
Verbal address:	*Madam Kelly*
Place card:	*Madam Kelly of the Ballyderry*

Viceroyalty

GOVERNOR-GENERAL

Envelope:	*His Excellency the Hon. Ned Kelly Governor-General of the Commonwealth of Australia (the term 'His Excellency' always precedes any other title, such as Sir, Dr or Professor)*
Formal letter opening:	*Your Excellency*
Formal letter closing:	*Yours faithfully*
Social letter opening:	*Dear Governor-General*
Social letter closing:	*Yours sincerely*
Verbal reference:	*His Excellency*
Verbal introduction:	*His Excellency the Governor-General*
Verbal address:	*Your Excellency*
Place card:	*His Excellency the Governor-General*

GOVERNOR-GENERAL'S WIFE

Envelope:	*Her Excellency Mrs Kelly*
Formal letter opening:	*Your Excellency*
Formal letter closing:	*Yours faithfully*
Social letter opening:	*Dear Mrs Kelly*
Social letter closing:	*Yours sincerely*
Verbal reference:	*Her Excellency*
Verbal introduction:	*Her Excellency Mrs Kelly*
Verbal address:	*Your Excellency*
Place card:	*Her Excellency Mrs Kelly*

A state Governor is addressed in the same way as the Governor-General. However, the Governor's spouse is not given any special honour beyond what he or she has already.

Ecclesiastics

In the Christian religion, the title conferred by the church takes precedence over any other title. For example, The Very Reverend Sir George English, or The Reverend Monsignor Dr Franco Sabatini.

Reverend may be shortened to Rev. or Rev'd, except for Reverend Sir.

If the person's name is used after Reverend, it must include the first name, or initials, with the surname.

Roman Catholic Church

THE POPE

Envelope:	*His Holiness The Pope*
Letter opening:	*Your Holiness, or Most Holy Father*
Letter closing:	*Yours faithfully*
Verbal reference:	*His Holiness*
Verbal introduction:	*His Holiness the Pope*
Verbal address:	*Your Holiness*
Place card:	*His Holiness The Pope*

CARDINAL

Envelope:	*His Eminence Cardinal Sabatini Archbishop of Melbourne*
Formal letter opening:	*Eminence*
Formal letter closing:	*Yours faithfully*
Social letter opening:	*Dear Cardinal Sabatini*
Social letter closing:	*Yours sincerely*
Verbal reference:	*His Eminence*
Verbal introduction:	*His Eminence Cardinal Wilson, Archbishop of Melbourne*
Verbal address:	*Your Eminence*
Place card:	*Cardinal Wilson*

ARCHBISHOP

Envelope:	*His Grace the Most Rev. Franco Sabatini, Archbishop of Melbourne*
Formal letter opening:	*Your Grace*
Formal letter closing:	*Yours faithfully*
Social letter opening:	*Dear Archbishop Sabatini*
Social letter closing:	*Yours sincerely*
Verbal reference:	*His Grace*
Verbal introduction:	*His Grace the most Reverend Franco Sabatini, Archbishop of Melbourne*
Verbal address:	*Archbishop Sabatini, or Your Grace*
Place card:	*Archbishop Sabatini*

In the United Kingdom and the United States, a Roman Catholic Archbishop is addressed as 'His Excellency'.

BISHOP

Envelope:	*His Lordship the Most Rev. Franco Sabatini, Bishop of Melbourne*
Formal letter opening:	*Dear Bishop*
Formal letter closing:	*Yours faithfully*
Social letter opening:	*Dear Bishop Sabatini*
Social letter closing:	*Yours sincerely*
Verbal reference:	*Bishop Sabatini*
Verbal introduction:	*His Lordship the Most Reverend Franco Sabatini, Bishop of Melbourne*
Verbal address:	*Bishop Sabatini, or Bishop*
Place card:	*Bishop Sabatini*

A bishop may also be addressed as 'The Right Reverend' without 'His Lordship'.

MONSIGNOR

Envelope:	*The Rev. Monsignor Franco Sabatini (or, depending on rank, The Right Rev. or The Very Rev.)*
Formal letter opening:	*Right Reverend Sir, or Dear Monsignor*
Formal letter closing:	*Yours faithfully*
Social letter opening:	*Dear Monsignor Sabatini*
Social letter closing:	*Yours sincerely*
Verbal reference:	*Monsignor Sabatini*
Verbal introduction:	*The Reverend Monsignor Franco Sabatini*
Verbal address:	*Monsignor Sabatini, or Monsignor*
Place card:	*Monsignor Sabatini*

PRIEST

Envelope:	*The Reverend Father Franco Sabatini (or the Very Reverend Father, in some religious orders)*
Formal letter opening:	*Dear Reverend Father*
Formal letter closing:	*Yours faithfully*
Social letter opening:	*Dear Father Sabatini*
Social letter closing:	*Yours sincerely*
Verbal reference:	*Father Sabatini*
Verbal introduction:	*The Reverend Father Francesco Sabatini*
Verbal address:	*Father, or Father Sabatini*
Place card:	*Father Sabatini*

BROTHER

Envelope:	*Brother Franco Sabatini*
Letter opening:	*Dear Brother Franco*
Formal letter closing:	*Yours faithfully*
Social letter closing:	*Yours sincerely*
Verbal reference:	*Brother Franco*
Verbal introduction:	*Brother Franco Sabatini*
Verbal address:	*Brother Franco, or Brother Sabatini*
Place card:	*Brother Franco Sabatini*

SISTER

Envelope:	*Sister Mary O'Brien*
Letter opening:	*Dear Sister Mary O'Brien*
Formal letter closing:	*Yours faithfully*
Social letter closing:	*Yours sincerely*
Verbal reference, introduction, address and place card:	*Sister Mary O'Brien*

Anglican Church

If a priest in the Anglican Church has received a knighthood, he uses the relevant abbreviated letters after his name instead of Sir before it. The preferred abbreviation for Reverend in the Anglican Church is Rev'd, although Rev. is acceptable in other Christian churches.

The correct written address for a clergyman and his wife is The Rev. George English and Mrs English. If you are writing to a woman member of the clergy and her husband, the address is The Rev. Jane English and Mr English.

ARCHBISHOP OF CANTERBURY (OR YORK)

Envelope:	*The Most Reverend and Right Honourable The Lord Archbishop of Canterbury*
Letter opening:	*Your Grace*
Formal letter closing:	*Yours faithfully*
Social letter closing:	*Yours sincerely*
Verbal reference:	*His Grace or The Lord Archbishop*
Verbal introduction:	*The Most Reverend and Right Honourable The Lord Archbishop of Canterbury*
Verbal address:	*Your Grace or My Lord Archbishop*
Place card:	*The Archbishop of Canterbury*

PRIMATE (ARCHBISHOP)

Envelope:	*The Most Rev'd George English, Archbishop of Adelaide, Primate of Australia*
Formal letter opening:	*Your Grace*
Formal letter closing:	*Yours faithfully*
Social letter opening:	*Dear Archbishop English*
Social letter closing:	*Yours sincerely*
Verbal reference:	*The Archbishop*
Verbal introduction:	*The Most Reverend George English, Archbishop of Adelaide and Primate of Australia*
Verbal address:	*Your Grace or Archbishop*
Place card:	*Archbishop English, Primate of Australia*

PRIMATE (DIOCESAN BISHOP)

Envelope:	*The Right Rev'd George English, Bishop of Adelaide, Primate of Australia*
Formal letter opening:	*Dear Bishop*
Formal letter closing:	*Yours faithfully*
Social letter opening:	*Dear Bishop English*
Social letter closing:	*Yours sincerely*
Verbal reference:	*The Bishop*
Verbal introduction:	*The Right Reverend George English, Bishop of Adelaide and Primate of Australia*
Verbal address:	*Bishop*
Place card:	*Bishop English, Primate of Australia*

ARCHBISHOP

Envelope:	*The Most Rev'd George English, Archbishop of Adelaide*
Formal letter opening:	*Your Grace*
Formal letter closing:	*Yours faithfully*
Social letter opening:	*Dear Archbishop English*
Social letter closing:	*Yours sincerely*
Verbal reference:	*The Archbishop*
Verbal introduction:	*The Most Reverend George English, Archbishop of Adelaide*
Verbal address:	*Your Grace or Archbishop*
Place card:	*Archbishop English*

BISHOP OF A DIOCESE

Envelope:	*The Right Rev'd George English, Bishop of Adelaide*
Formal letter opening:	*Dear Bishop*
Formal letter closing:	*Yours faithfully*
Social letter opening:	*Dear Bishop English*
Social letter closing:	*Yours sincerely*
Verbal reference:	*The Bishop*
Verbal introduction:	*The Right Reverend George English, Bishop of Adelaide*
Verbal address:	*Bishop*
Place card:	*Bishop English*

BISHOP (ASSISTANT OR COADJUTOR)

Same as the bishop above, minus the title 'Bishop of Adelaide'.

DEAN

Envelope:	*The Very Reverend George English, Dean of Adelaide*
Formal letter opening:	*Dear Mr Dean*
Formal letter closing:	*Yours faithfully*
Social letter opening:	*Dear Dean English*
Social letter closing:	*Yours sincerely*
Verbal reference:	*The Dean*
Verbal introduction:	*The Very Reverend George English, Dean of Adelaide*
Verbal address:	*Dean*
Place card:	*Dean English*

ARCHDEACON

Envelope:	*The Venerable George English, Archdeacon of Adelaide*
Formal letter opening:	*Dear Mr Archdeacon*
Formal letter closing:	*Yours faithfully*
Social letter opening:	*Dear Archdeacon English*
Social letter closing:	*Yours sincerely*
Verbal reference:	*The Archdeacon*
Verbal introduction:	*The Venerable George English, Archdeacon of Adelaide*
Verbal address:	*Archdeacon*
Place card:	*Archdeacon English*

CANON

Envelope:	*The Reverend Canon George English*
Formal letter opening:	*Dear Mr Canon*
Formal letter closing:	*Yours faithfully*
Social letter opening:	*Dear Canon English*
Social letter closing:	*Yours sincerely*
Verbal reference:	*Canon English*
Verbal introduction:	*The Reverend Canon George English*
Verbal address:	*Canon or Canon English*
Place card:	*Canon English*

PRIEST

Envelope:	*The Rev'd George English*
Formal letter opening:	*Reverend Sir*
Formal letter closing:	*Yours faithfully*
Social letter opening:	*Dear Mr English*
Social letter closing:	*Yours sincerely*
Verbal reference:	*Mr English*
Verbal introduction:	*The Reverend George English*
Verbal address:	*Mr English*
Place card:	*Reverend English*

Uniting Church in Australia

Formed in 1977, the Uniting Church in Australia comprises all Methodists, two-thirds of Australia's Presbyterians and two-thirds of Congregationalists. Women, as well as men, may be office-bearers.

PRESIDENT

Envelope:	*The Reverend Sarah Wellesley, President of the Uniting Church*
Formal letter opening:	*Dear President*
Formal letter closing:	*Yours faithfully*
Social letter opening:	*Dear Ms (or Miss or Mrs) Wellesley*
Social letter closing:	*Yours sincerely*
Verbal reference:	*Ms Wellesley*
Verbal introduction:	*The Reverend Sarah Wellesley, President of the Uniting Church*
Verbal address:	*Ms Wellesley*
Place card:	*Ms Wellesley*

MODERATOR (STATE SYNOD)

Envelope:	*The Reverend Sarah Wellesley, Moderator of Queensland*
Formal letter opening:	*Dear Moderator*
Formal letter closing:	*Yours faithfully*
Social letter opening:	*Dear Ms Wellesley*
Social letter closing:	*Yours sincerely*
Verbal reference:	*Ms Wellesley*
Verbal introduction:	*The Reverend Sarah Wellesley, Moderator of Queensland*
Verbal address:	*Ms Wellesley*
Place card:	*Ms Wellesley*

CHAIRPERSON (PRESBYTERY)

Envelope:	*The Reverend Sarah Wellesley, Chairperson, Presbytery of Brisbane*
Formal letter opening:	*Dear Chairperson*
Formal letter closing:	*Yours faithfully*

Social letter opening:	*Dear Ms Wellesley*
Social letter closing:	*Yours sincerely*
Verbal reference:	*Ms Wellesley*
Verbal introduction:	*The Reverend Sarah Wellesley, Chairperson of the Presbytery of Brisbane*
Verbal address:	*Ms Wellesley*
Place card:	*Ms Wellesley*

MINISTER

Envelope:	*The Rev. Sarah Wellesley*
Formal letter opening:	*Dear Madam*
Formal letter closing:	*Yours faithfully*
Social letter opening:	*Dear Ms Wellesley*
Social letter closing:	*Yours sincerely*
Verbal reference:	*Ms Wellesley*
Verbal introduction:	*The Reverend Sarah Wellesley*
Verbal address:	*Ms Wellesley*
Place card:	*Ms Sarah Wellesley*

Baptist Union of Australia

PRESIDENT-GENERAL

Envelope (clergyman):	*The Reverend John Hollander*
Envelope (layman):	*Mr John Hollander*
Formal letter opening:	*Dear Sir*
Formal letter closing:	*Yours faithfully*
Social letter opening:	*Dear Mr Hollander*
Social letter closing:	*Yours sincerely*
Verbal reference:	*Mr Hollander*
Verbal introduction:	*The Reverend John Hollander (or Mr John Hollander), President-General of the Baptist Union of Australia*
Verbal address:	*Mr Hollander*
Place card:	*Mr John Hollander*

Greek Orthodox Church in Australia and New Zealand

With some modifications, the following also applies to Armenian, Serbian and Russian Orthodox Churches.

PATRIARCH

Envelope:	*His All Holiness Patriarch Spiro*
Letter opening:	*Your All Holiness*
Formal letter closing:	*Yours faithfully*
Social letter closing:	*Yours sincerely*
Verbal reference:	*His All Holiness*
Verbal introduction:	*His All Holiness Patriarch Spiro*
Verbal address:	*Your All Holiness*
Place card:	*His All Holiness Patriarch Spiro*

ARCHBISHOP

Envelope:	*His Eminence the Most Rev. Archbishop Spiro*
Formal letter opening:	*Your Eminence*
Formal letter closing:	*Yours faithfully*
Social letter opening:	*Dear Archbishop Spiro*
Social letter closing:	*Yours sincerely*
Verbal reference:	*Archbishop Spiro*
Verbal introduction:	*His Eminence the Most Reverend Archbishop Spiro*
Verbal address:	*Your Eminence*
Place card:	*Archbishop Spiro*

PRIEST

Envelope (unmarried):	*The Very Reverend Father Spiro Papadopoulos*
Envelope (married):	*The Reverend Father Spiro Papadopoulos*
Formal letter opening:	*Your Reverence*
Formal letter closing:	*Yours faithfully*
Social letter opening:	*Dear Father Spiro*
Social letter closing:	*Yours sincerely*
Verbal reference:	*Father Spiro*
Verbal introduction (unmarried priest):	*The Very Reverend Father Spiro Papadopoulos*
Verbal introduction (married priest):	*The Reverend Father Spiro Papadopoulos*
Verbal address:	*Father Spiro*
Place card:	*Father Spiro*

Presbyterian Church

MODERATOR-GENERAL

Envelope:	*The Right Rev. James Stern*
Formal letter opening:	*Dear Moderator-General*
Formal letter closing:	*Yours faithfully*
Social letter opening:	*Dear Mr Stern*
Social letter closing:	*Yours sincerely*
Verbal reference:	*Mr Stern (Reverend Stern is incorrect)*
Verbal introduction:	*The Right Reverend James Stern*
Verbal address:	*Mr Stern*
Place card:	*Mr Stern*

MODERATOR (STATE ASSEMBLY)

Envelope:	*The Right Rev. James Stern*
Formal letter opening:	*Dear Moderator*
Formal letter closing:	*Yours faithfully*
Social letter opening:	*Dear Mr Stern*
Social letter closing:	*Yours sincerely*
Verbal reference:	*Mr Stern*
Verbal introduction:	*The Right Reverend James Stern*
Verbal address:	*Mr Stern*
Place card:	*Mr Stern*

MINISTER

Envelope:	*The Rev. James Stern*
Letter opening:	*Dear Mr Stern*
Formal letter closing:	*Yours faithfully*
Social letter closing:	*Yours sincerely*
Verbal reference:	*Mr Stern*
Verbal introduction:	*The Reverend James Stern*

Verbal address:	*Mr Stern*
Place card:	*Mr Stern*

Lutheran Church of Australia

GENERAL PRESIDENT

Envelope:	*Pastor Axel Martin, General President, Lutheran Church of Australia*
Formal letter opening:	*Dear Pastor*
Formal letter closing:	*Yours faithfully*
Social letter opening:	*Dear Pastor Martin*
Social letter closing:	*Yours sincerely*
Verbal reference:	*Pastor Martin*
Verbal introduction:	*Pastor Axel Martin, General President of the Lutheran Church of Australia*
Verbal address:	*Pastor Martin*
Place card:	*Pastor Martin*

PARISH PASTOR

Envelope:	*Pastor Axel Martin*
Formal letter opening:	*Dear Pastor*
Formal letter closing:	*Yours faithfully*
Social letter opening:	*Dear Pastor Martin*
Social letter closing:	*Yours sincerely*
Verbal reference:	*Pastor Martin*
Verbal introduction:	*Pastor Axel Martin*
Verbal address:	*Pastor Martin*
Place card:	*Pastor Martin*

Seventh Day Adventist Church

PASTOR

Envelope:	*Pastor Rupert Cumming*
Formal letter opening:	*Dear Pastor*
Formal letter closing:	*Yours faithfully*
Social letter opening:	*Dear Pastor Cumming*

Social letter closing:	*Yours sincerely*
Verbal reference:	*Pastor Cumming*
Verbal introduction:	*Pastor Rupert Cumming*
Verbal address:	*Pastor Cumming*
Place card:	*Pastor Cumming*

Salvation Army

COMMISSIONER

Envelope:	*Commissioner Robert Carey*
Formal letter opening:	*Dear Commissioner*
Formal letter closing:	*Yours faithfully*
Social letter opening:	*Dear Commissioner Carey*
Social letter closing:	*Yours sincerely*
Verbal reference:	*Commissioner Carey*
Verbal introduction:	*Commissioner Robert Carey*
Verbal address:	*Commissioner Carey*
Place card:	*Commissioner Carey*

Other ranks in the Salvation Army, whether Lieutenant-Commissioner, Colonel, Lieutenant Colonel, Senior Major, Major, Senior Captain, Captain or Lieutenant, are addressed in the following way:

Envelope:	*Colonel Robert Carey*
Letter opening:	*Dear Colonel Robert Carey*
Formal letter closing:	*Yours faithfully*
Social letter closing:	*Yours sincerely*
Verbal reference:	*Colonel Carey*
Verbal introduction:	*Colonel Robert Carey*
Verbal address:	*Colonel Carey*
Place card:	*Colonel Carey*

COPTIC POPE

Envelope:	*His Holiness Pope John IV, Pope of Alexandria, Patriarch of the See of St Mark*
Letter opening:	*Your Holiness*
Formal letter closing:	*Yours faithfully*
Social letter closing:	*Yours sincerely*

Verbal reference: *His Holiness*
Verbal introduction: *His Holiness Pope John the fourth, Pope of Alexandria, Patriarch of the See of St Mark*
Verbal address: *Your Holiness*
Place card: *His Holiness Pope John IV*

Judaism

CHIEF RABBI

Envelope: *The Chief Rabbi Benjamin Steiner*
Formal letter opening: *Reverend and dear Sir*
Formal letter closing: *Yours faithfully*
Social letter opening: *Dear Chief Rabbi Steiner*
Social letter closing: *Yours sincerely*
Verbal reference: *Chief Rabbi Steiner*
Verbal introduction: *The Chief Rabbi Benjamin Steiner*
Verbal address: *Chief Rabbi Steiner*
Place card: *Chief Rabbi Steiner*

RABBI

Envelope: *The Rabbi Benjamin Steiner*
Formal letter opening: *Reverend and dear Sir*
Formal letter closing: *Yours faithfully*
Social letter opening: *Dear Rabbi Steiner*
Social letter closing: *Yours sincerely*
Verbal reference: *Rabbi Steiner*
Verbal introduction: *The Rabbi Benjamin Steiner*
Verbal address: *Rabbi Steiner*
Place card: *Rabbi Steiner*

CANTOR

Envelope: *Cantor Benjamin Steiner*
Letter opening: *Dear Cantor Steiner*
Formal letter closing: *Yours faithfully*
Social letter closing: *Yours sincerely*
Verbal reference: *Cantor Steiner*
Verbal introduction: *Cantor Benjamin Steiner*

Verbal address: *Cantor Steiner*
Place card: *Cantor Steiner*

Islam

GRAND MUFTI

Envelope: *His Eminence Abdullah Al-Aziz, The Grand Mufti of Jerusalem*
Letter opening: *Your Eminence*
Formal letter closing: *Yours faithfully*
Social letter closing: *Yours sincerely*
Verbal reference: *His Eminence*
Verbal introduction: *His Eminence the Grand Mufti of Jerusalem*
Verbal address: *Your Eminence*
Place card: *The Grand Mufti of Jerusalem*

IMAM

Envelope: *Imam Abdullah Al-Aziz*
Letter opening: *Dear Imam Al-Aziz*
Formal letter closing: *Yours faithfully*
Social letter closing: *Yours sincerely*
Verbal reference: *Imam Al-Aziz*
Verbal introduction: *Abdullah Al-Aziz, Imam of (name of mosque)*
Verbal address: *Imam Al-Aziz*
Place card: *Imam Al-Aziz*

Buddhism

DALAI LAMA

Envelope: *His Holiness The Dalai Lama*
Letter opening: *Your Holiness*
Formal letter closing: *Yours faithfully*
Social letter closing: *Yours sincerely*
Verbal reference: *His Holiness*

Verbal introduction: *His Holiness, The Dalai Lama*
Verbal address: *Your Holiness*
Place card: *His Holiness The Dalai Lama*

Although forms of address for Buddhist nuns and monks depend on where they are and to which tradition they belong, it's usually acceptable to put 'Venerable' before the name and to address them in a letter as Dear Reverend Sir or Dear Reverend Madam. Better still is to find out precisely how the individual concerned wishes to be addressed.

Hinduism

There is no hierarchy among the Hindu clergy so you address them as you would other citizens.

Armed forces

Ranks of commissioned men and women officers in the services, in descending order of importance, are as follows.

ARMY

Field Marshal
General
Lieutenant General
Major General
Brigadier
Colonel
Lieutenant Colonel
Major
Captain
Lieutenant
Second Lieutenant

NAVY

Admiral of the Fleet
Admiral
Vice Admiral
Rear Admiral
Commodore
Captain
Commander
Lieutenant Commander
Lieutenant
Sub Lieutenant

AIR FORCE

Marshal of the Air Force
Air Chief Marshal
Air Marshal
Air Vice Marshal
Air Commodore
Group Captain
Wing Commander
Squadron Leader
Flight Lieutenant
Flying Officer
Pilot Officer

OFFICIAL CORRESPONDENCE

Officers are addressed by rank, first name or initials, and surname. For example: Major General James Warren. If the officer has another title, it comes after the military one: Lieutenant Colonel Dame Jennifer Warren. Non-commissioned officers are addressed by rank and surname without the first name or initials.

Initials indicating any awards or honours are placed immediately after the surname, followed by those indicating the regiment or service. For example: Squadron Leader James Warren, SC, DFM, RAAF.

After retirement, former full-time officers are addressed by their full rank, followed by (Rtd). For example: Rear Admiral James Warren, DCM, RAN (Rtd).

TO AN OFFICER OF OR ABOVE THE RANK OF LIEUTENANT COLONEL, COMMANDER OR GROUP CAPTAIN

Formal letter opening: *Air Commodore*
Formal letter closing: *Yours faithfully*

Less formal letter
opening: *Dear Air Commodore Warren*

Less formal letter
closing: *Yours sincerely*

Air Chief Marshal:	*Air Marshal*
Air Vice Marshal:	*Air Marshal*
Lieutenant General:	*General*
Major General:	*General*
Lieutenant Colonel:	*Colonel*
Lieutenant Commander:	*Commander*

TO AN OFFICER BELOW THE RANK OF LIEUTENANT COLONEL, COMMANDER OR GROUP CAPTAIN

Formal letter opening: *Dear Sir*
Formal letter closing: *Yours faithfully*
Less formal letter
opening: *Dear Lieutenant Warren*
Less formal letter
closing: *Yours sincerely*

CHAPLAIN IN THE ARMED FORCES

Although a chaplain is given military rank, it is not used verbally or in correspondence.

Envelope:	*Chaplain James Warren*
Letter opening:	*Dear Chaplain Warren*
Formal letter closing:	*Yours faithfully*
Social letter closing:	*Yours sincerely*
Verbal reference, introduction, address and place card:	*Chaplain Warren*

SOCIAL CORRESPONDENCE

Any officer of the rank of Colonel, Captain, Group Captain or above may be addressed in the opening of a social letter simply by rank without a name. For example: Dear Group Captain. Lieutenants, sublieutenants, flying officers and those below them are addressed simply as Mr, Mrs, Miss or Ms.

On social correspondence, the envelope should show an officer's full rank but some ranks may be shortened in the opening to the letter. They are as follows.

SHIPS OF THE ROYAL AUSTRALIAN NAVY

The Captain of a vessel retains his own rank. Letters to him should be addressed
Commander James Warren, RAN
Captain HMAS *Seagull*
C/o GPO
(No further address is necessary, since the Navy Office keeps the postal service informed of the whereabouts of RAN vessels at any given time.)

Business correspondence should be addressed to The Commanding Officer, HMAS *Seagull*, C/o GPO.

RANK

Vice Admiral:	*Admiral*
Rear Admiral:	*Admiral*

OFFICIAL FOREIGN CORRESPONDENCE

In writing official letters to heads of state, heads of government and other officials of a foreign land, it's wise to check the correct forms of address from the relevant embassy in Canberra or visit the web site of the Department of Foreign Affairs, www.dfat.gov.au, for guidance.

Broadly, in the United Kingdom and Commonwealth countries, 'The Right Honourable' or 'The Honourable' (shortened to Hon.) is usually the correct term for members of parliament. In most other countries, particularly those with a President as head of state, the term 'His Excellency' or 'Her Excellency', sometimes shortened to HE, is preferred. Just to complicate matters, this is not always the case, so be wary.

For instance, in Austria, Lebanon, Mauritius and the Seychelles, HE is never used and a letter opens with 'Dear Mr President' (as it does in the United States of America, where 'The Honorable' precedes the President's name on an envelope and letter superscription). In Ireland, while the head of state is referred to as 'Your Excellency', the correct salutation for the head of government is 'Dear Taoiseach' (pronounced Tee Shock).

The opening of a letter addressed to His Excellency The President of Germany should read 'My Dear President'. The head of the German government is titled His Excellency (first name and surname) Federal Chancellor, and he is addressed as 'My Dear Chancellor'.

Although the King of Belgium is addressed as Your Majesty, you simply pen 'Mr Prime Minister', and 'Mr Minister' for members of the Belgian government. In the Republic of Korea, the President is addressed as 'Excellency' without a 'Your'.

A King, a Queen (when she is the monarch, such as the reigning queens of Great Britain, Denmark and the Netherlands), an Emperor or a Sultan is addressed as 'Your Majesty'. The kings of Bhutan, Cambodia, Jordan, Lesotho, Morocco, Nepal, Norway, Spain, Swaziland, Sweden, Thailand and Tonga are all called 'Your Majesty', as are the Emperor of Japan and the sultans of Brunei, Malaysia and Oman. In a departure from the norm, the salutation for the King of Saudi Arabia is simply 'Dear King Fahd'.

An Amir, such as those who rule Bahrain, Kuwait and Qatar, is called 'Your Highness'. The reigning head of a principality, such as Monaco or Liechtenstein, is called 'Your Serene Highness'. The head of state of the Grand Duchy of Luxembourg is called 'Your Royal Highness'. The title of Libya's head of state and of government is Leader of the Revolution and he is addressed as 'Supreme Leader'.

CONTINENTAL EUROPEAN NOBILITY

Although the monarchy has been abolished in European countries other than those mentioned above, the old ways die hard in some countries, including France, Germany and Italy, and among some expatriates from central Europe who still use family titles. These are courtesy titles, not legal ones, and are sometimes used socially or in business as a mark of respect for an ancient blood line. Before writing to such a person, it is wise to ask the relevant embassy or consulate for advice on an acceptable form of address. If necessary, you could use the British form, although it may not be strictly correct.

ASIAN NAMES AND TITLES

In China, Japan, Korea and Vietnam, the surname comes before the given name but do not take anything for granted because, in business, the order is sometimes reversed to conform with western practices. In India, the order of names varies from one region to another. As for titles, they are a great mystery for an outsider, mainly because there are so many of them and they change from one age group to another and from one country to another.

Unless you are confident of the correct form of address, feel free to ask the individual concerned or a native of that country. Invariably, I have found Asians very willing to enlighten, although sometimes they are so polite it's difficult to get straight answers. Persevere. It's worth it.

Chapter Twenty-one

GOODNIGHT SWEETHEART

I t is said that there are only two things in life you can be sure of: death and taxes. Well, you fork out plenty of tax as you go along but one day it's time to pay your ultimate dues. The light goes out and it's all over.

THE WILL

The most thoughtful, courteous and sensible thing any of us can do is leave our affairs in perfect order. Since most of us have no idea when, where or how our demise will take place, a will should be made as soon after the age of consent as we have any possessions of our own. When the will has been made, the original should be kept in a safe place with your solicitor or bank and you should keep a copy somewhere that would be readily accessible after your death.

Legally, you are perfectly entitled to make the will yourself by buying a special kit for the purpose. Or you might prefer to have it drawn up by a specialist in the making of wills; that way there can be little risk of misinterpretation or missing bits. The last thing most of us would wish on those we leave behind is an undignified family wrangle over who is entitled to the seventeenth-century armoire or the Arthur Boyd over the fireplace. When you sign your will, no matter where, how or by whom it is put together, your signature must be witnessed by two people who are not beneficiaries or the spouse of one.

EXECUTORS

In appointing an executor of your estate – that is, a person responsible for carrying out the instructions in your will – you should be aware that this can be an onerous and time-consuming task, therefore it lightens the load if you appoint co-executors. One could be the public trustee, a private trustee company or your solicitor, who will be paid for the function, and the other should be someone close to you, a beneficiary of a sizeable portion of your estate. For obvious reasons, this person is younger than you are, a trustworthy character who will be fair in distributing items and will understand the intention, as well as the letter, of your will. Before you appoint this person, it is customary to ask if he or she is prepared to take on the responsibility.

BENEFICIARIES

Although how and to whom you leave your worldly goods is entirely up to you, your spouse is usually the beneficiary. If you have no spouse but you do have children it is customary to divide your estate evenly between them. If there is no will, the term is that you die 'intestate'. While ultimately the law will see to it that your estate goes to your nearest (whether or not they are dearest), the process can be lengthy, sometimes complicated and possibly expensive. One example: if you have lived in another country, its records may have to be searched to find out whether you had any family there who may be entitled to claim.

Stories of revenge beyond the grave are amusing in the telling but when you are making a will is not the time for settling old scores or being vindictive, for the simple reason that you won't be around to enjoy your own questionable joke, face the consequences or set someone else's mind at rest. It is a coward's way.

PERSONAL PAPERS

Bear in mind that nobody is as familiar with your financial and legal affairs as you are, so make it easy for your family and executors to find the necessary documents. Inside an envelope marked 'To be opened in the event of my death', put details such as the whereabouts of the original will, birth and marriage certificates, bank accounts, tax file number, keys to safe deposit boxes, passport, share certificates and insurance policies. Give contact details of your solicitor, accountant and other key people to be notified. What is to be done with your pets, if you have them? Make all the decisions that would otherwise be left to others, who may not do things the way you want them to be done. If you can afford it, a thoughtful gesture is to allocate a certain amount of money for a reception or wake after the funeral.

FUNERAL ARRANGEMENTS

Make your wishes explicit in every detail. You may choose to pre-pay your funeral so that there can be no misunderstanding about where or how it is to be done and nobody will be out of pocket. You may arrange this with the administrative office of a cemetery or crematorium or through a person who used to be called an undertaker but is now gentrified to funeral director. (Be careful, though, to choose a firm that is not likely to go out of business before you do.) This will mean that there is no confusion over whether and where you are to be buried or cremated, the kind of religious or other ceremony that should take place, and so on. Your loved ones will be spared the responsibility of arranging and funding the funeral at a time when they are distressed, burdened and sometimes in a state of shock.

Another possibility is to do some research into the kinds of goods and services on offer from various funeral directors. Decide on the kind of coffin you want and the general level of expenditure and make sure your next of kin knows of your decisions.

DEATH AT HOME

If death occurs in hospital, formalities are taken care of by the authorities there. If it occurs at home, this is what you do.

- Telephone a doctor immediately. He or she will need to conduct an examination and issue a death certificate.
- Telephone a close, competent family member or friend to be with you for moral support and to help make decisions, including notifying other close family members and friends.
- Look for the envelope marked 'To be opened in the event of my death' and abide by its instructions. If there is no envelope, try to find a copy of the will and contact the person or company holding the original.

NOTICES IN THE NEWSPAPER

Choose a reputable funeral director to make all the necessary arrangements for the funeral, including the death and funeral notices (although only after consulting about the wording with the family). These should be kept simple and without undue sentimentality. Such notices might read:

> STANDAWFISH   Angela Jane, beloved wife of William, mother of Simon and Sophie, grandmother of Gabrielle, Monty and Lulu.

If a private funeral is preferred, just add the words 'Private funeral' to the end of the death notice. In that case and for obvious reasons, no funeral notice is published. However, if you would prefer to have a separate funeral notice, it might read:

STANDAWFISH   Angela Jane, at St Mark's, Swankton, on
Thursday, 7th May at 2.30 p.m. Cremation at Rookwood.

If the funeral details are finalised in time, both notices may be published together, in which case the notice would read:

STANDAWFISH   Angela Jane, beloved wife of William, mother
of Simon and Sophie, grandmother of Gabrielle, Monty and
Lulu. Funeral at St Mark's, Swankton, on Thursday,
7th May at 2.30 p.m. Cremation at Rookwood.

If you wish donations to be made to a nominated charity instead of money being spent on flowers, add words such as 'Donations in lieu of flowers to Australian Cancer Research Foundation' (or other charitable organisation) to the funeral notice. The funeral director should notify the suggested charity, which may make envelopes or forms available at the funeral service to make it easy for mourners on the day to give whatever they choose, in cash or by cheque.

THE CEREMONY

The wishes of the deceased should always be honoured regardless of the beliefs of anyone else. If the death notice specifies 'private funeral' outsiders should not attempt to be included; if feelings are deep enough, they should be expressed in a letter. A divorced spouse of the deceased may attend a public funeral but should not expect to be included with the immediate family. A funeral is not a place for children, although that may depend on age, circumstances and religious belief.

A eulogy may be given by someone – usually a close friend or relation – apart from the presiding minister, although in the Greek

Orthodox Church it is not customary for anybody but the officiating priest to deliver words of praise. In most other religions, there is no limit to the number of people who may get up to speak, although care should be taken that these do not turn into lengthy, self-indulgent monologues prompted more by ego than appropriateness to the occasion. Whether speakers volunteer their services or are asked to participate, it should be done ahead of the day. The final decision rests with the next of kin.

Tributes

The flowers placed on the coffin are from the chief mourners. Flowers sent by other mourners, to the funeral director or to the place where the funeral is to be held, should carry an envelope addressed to the deceased, 'Mrs William Standawfish' or simply 'Angela Standawfish', containing a plain white card with 'In loving memory' and a signature. Every effort should be made to have these words written by the sender, not the florist. Such niceties count for a lot at any time, but they are precious in times of emotional stress. It is the funeral director's role to collect these cards and make sure they are given to the immediate family for acknowledgement later.

Flowers sent to the bereaved at home are addressed to 'The family of Angela Standawfish' and carry a white card that reads 'With deepest sympathy' or 'With love and sympathy'. A handwritten letter of condolence is equally appropriate.

If the deceased has nominated a charity, you can take the initiative by telephoning the nominated charity to say you wish to make a donation on behalf of that person. You will be asked your name and address, the name of the person who died and the name and address of the next of kin. In due course after your donation has been received, the charity will send a card or letter of condolence to the next of kin, advising him or her of your contribution, although the extent of it will probably not be specified.

Or, if you prefer, bring to the funeral an envelope containing a card and your cheque made out to the charity, and hand it to the funeral director. Unless you are an intimate of the family, remember to include your address and make sure your signature is legible.

BURIAL

By law, humans must be buried in land zoned for the purpose – that is, a cemetery, where you buy a grave site. Although it is part of crown land, the plot is yours for the purpose of interment. Depending on the cemetery and the location of the grave site, the cost of a plot is upwards of about $1600 for two people, one on top of the other, not including burial fees.

If you own land measuring more than five hectares – say, a property in the country – you may be given permission to bury a loved one there, but there are strict rules governing such interments and you must apply to your local council for authorisation.

CREMATION

A burial occurs immediately after the funeral service, often with the chief mourners at the graveside, and that's that, but a cremation, which is done without the presence of mourners, means that a decision must be made about what to do with the ashes. The thoughtful person specifies his or her wishes in the will or in a note that accompanies it. These wishes must be honoured to the letter.

If there are no such instructions, the next of kin decides what to do with the ashes. There is no right or wrong thing to do with them – keep them in an urn on the mantel or a box under the bed, if you wish – except that permission is required before the ashes may be scattered in certain places. Some people pay for them to be placed under a rose bush or in a niche in the wall in the gardens of the crematorium with a bronze plaque to mark the place. Others put them in a family mausoleum or on the grave of a close family member. Some scatter them over the sea, in the bush, across a park or in the garden. It was the request of one man who died too young to have his ashes sent off in a rocket with fireworks from Bondi Beach one evening, while his friends toasted his progress to the stars with champagne.

THE WAKE

After the funeral, there is usually a gathering of friends and family at the home of the departed's family or close friends. There's no need to send out invitations as most people expect that there will be some kind of get-together after the service. You don't have to attend the wake, but in that case it's important you see the bereaved family immediately after the service to let them know how special the service was and to express your condolences in person. Close friends and neighbours usually offer to make sandwiches and cakes for the event. This is a time to gather around and fondly remember the life of the departed, if that's appropriate. Make yourself useful by refilling teacups and washing glasses.

OBITUARY

If you were a notable person, you might receive newspaper coverage in the form of an obituary, a potted history of your life, dwelling on your achievements rather than the circumstances of your death, although they may be mentioned briefly. Most reputable Australian newspapers publish obituaries in the editorial pages which, unlike classified advertising space, cannot be bought. The content is decided by the editors. If you feel that the life of someone newly departed merits such attention, the best way to get an obituary into the newspaper is to telephone or email the editor of the obituaries columns with all the details. If your suggestion is accepted, you may be asked to write a piece of a certain length and to provide a photograph.

MEMORIAL SERVICE

High-profile people remain that way in death as in life. As a tribute to them it is customary to hold a public event in the form of a memorial service or requiem mass some weeks after the funeral. An announcement in the newspapers might read as follows:

> A memorial service for Angela Standawfish will be held in
> St Andrew's Cathedral on 28th May, at 11 a.m.

FUNERARY DRESS

Black is not obligatory at funerals or memorial services but sober colours and modest clothing are, out of respect for the occasion, the chief mourners and the dead. It is a courtesy to be seen to be more concerned with decorum than with vanity. Unless it is a state funeral, when men might wear morning dress, the appropriate apparel for a man is a dark suit and a subdued tie. A woman's clothes should be equally unassertive, with little jewellery, and a hat if desired.

THE AFTERMATH

There are no rules of dress or social behaviour any more for women and men who have been widowed. But for those who grieve, there is sometimes an internal time span that should be honoured.

Widows and widowers sometimes don't want to go out, except with loved ones, for several weeks or months after the funeral. Sometimes they do. Either way, they should not be pestered with requests or urged to do what they do not want to do. Bereavement is not a disease but a perfectly normal reaction to loss. Let nature take its course. Let tears be shed in private or among kith and kin. Bereavement has its own pattern and time schedule that must be gone through in order for recovery to be possible.

People in whose company the bereaved feels comfortable, safe and protected are particularly important at this time. Immediate relations and close friends should be sensitive in continuing their support in practical ways, long after the event. For example, a thoughtful person might send a letter of condolence at the time of death but wait for several weeks before sending flowers to the next of kin, timed for when all the other tributes have faded and been thrown away. Family members should ensure that the bereaved has a well-stocked fridge and cupboards, particularly when they are too grief-stricken to shop or cook.

One of the most painful social encounters the widower or children of Angela Standawfish could have is with someone who does not know that she is dead and asks, 'How's Angela?' It is up to others to do what they can to avert situations such as this by discreetly spreading the word, never in a gossipy way, as widely and quickly as possible.

It is extremely inconsiderate and ill-mannered to suggest to the newly bereaved the possibility of amours to come, much less make any attempts at match-making. Similarly, anyone interested in the bereaved in a romantic way should back off and make an approach only if and when things seem to be back to normal.

Expressions of sympathy

While commercial cards with printed messages of condolence are widely used, they are a poor substitute for a handwritten letter, prompted by kindness and concern rather than social obligation. Black-bordered paper is no longer used but the colour should be plain white or something subdued. Although what you say and how you say it are more important than the stationery that carries your missive, use the best quality you can find or afford.

A spontaneous and loving letter need not conform to a pattern but sometimes guidelines are helpful: begin with an expression of sympathy, make a personal observation about the deceased, say some words of comfort and, if you mean it, offer assistance. For instance:

> *Dear Sophie,*
>
> *Although we had all been expecting it for some time, news of your mother's death has come as a great shock to us, so we can imagine how you must feel. Please accept our deepest sympathy. Angela was such a*

> *loving and spirited woman, she will continue to be the inspiration to us*
> *that she has always been. It must comfort you to know how proud she*
> *was of you and how much she appreciated your support, particularly*
> *when she needed you most. If there's anything at all we can do, we'd*
> *regard it as a compliment if you'd just say the word.*
>
> *Sincerely and with love,*
> *Polly and Ali*

It is not correct to refer to the deceased as 'the late' until after the funeral. Similarly, if there is a title to be inherited, such as Baron or Duke, that is not conferred until after the funeral.

Letters of thanks

If you receive lots of letters of sympathy – say, thirty or more, in addition to the cards from flowers at the funeral – it is acceptable to respond with a notice in the newspaper or an engraved or printed card, followed up later by a handwritten acknowledgement. Depending on circumstances, the notice or printed card might read:

> *The family of Angela Standawfish wish to thank everyone who sent*
> *tributes after her death and will reply to each of them personally*
> *when they are able.*

or

> *William Standawfish wishes to thank everyone who sent tributes after the*
> *death of his wife Angela and will reply to them personally when he is able.*

Although there should be no pressure on the bereaved to write individual thank-you letters, you should try to respond personally. It is important to realise that other people are grieving, too, and your response will reassure them that their reaching out to you has been helpful. The effort sometimes has secondary rewards, in keeping alive the presence of the one who is physically no longer there. Doing the right thing also carries a sense of completion in honouring the loved one in a proper way. Like dealing with the clothes and other personal effects of someone you have loved intimately, it is a ritual that, however painful, helps to cleanse and heal.

This is a perfect time for other members of the family, particularly young ones, to be useful in gathering together the writing materials, addressing envelopes, buying stamps, posting the letters and being generally helpful with suggested words, if they are difficult to find. Each missive need not be lengthy. As few words as these will do:

> *Dear Clarissa and Tony,*
>> *Your note is an enormous comfort to the family and me.*
> *Thank you.*
>>>> *William*

or

> *Dear Kirsten,*
>> *I really did appreciate your wonderful letter.*
>>>> *Love, William*

THE LAST RITES

How Australians pay their last respects depends on their individual religious and cultural traditions. These are many and varied, as you can see if you spend time at a vast and long-established cemetery, such as Rookwood Necropolis and in the gardens of Rookwood Crematorium in the western suburbs of Sydney. Although they are not as numerous as members of the Catholic and Protestant faiths, the people of all other denominations are catered for here, each in a special section whose character reflects the people laid to rest there.

THE CHINESE FUNERAL

Before the burial or cremation, the body of the deceased stays at home or at a funeral parlour and the family keeps watch over it for three days and nights. When people come to pay respects, the coffin will be open and they are expected to light joss sticks (incense), view the body and bow to it in recognition of the transitory nature of life. Drinks and food will be provided, including something sweet to help neutralise the bitterness of death.

Often, the most appropriate time to visit is after dusk when your presence might help shorten the long night for the vigilant family. In the old days, the chief mourners wore sackcloth. Nowadays, they wear black or something equally sombre. Visitors to the house and mourners at the funeral should be similarly self-effacing in their dress. Nobody should be seen in cheerful colours, although white is permissible. If flowers are sent to the bereaved or to the deceased, traditionally they should be white, although westernised Chinese now sometimes choose other colours, such as yellow. Money is an acceptable gift as long as it is an uneven amount and comes in a plain white envelope.

At a traditional Chinese funeral there is often an uninhibited display of grief. It is also customary to have an effigy of something dear to the heart of the departed – a car, a mah-jong set, a house – made out of paper. This is set on fire to accompany the departing soul on its journey.

THE GREEK ORTHODOX FUNERAL

The Greeks bury their dead after a service at the church; cremation is not usually practised. The chief mourners wear black and sit in the front pew on the right-hand side of the church. Other mourners, wearing black or something equally subdued, arrive at the church and bless themselves by making a sign of the cross, touching head, chest, right side, then left side, ending on the heart. They sit down before being invited to go to where the coffin is placed. It is usually open. The procedure is to say farewell by bowing and kissing the cross or icon placed on the chest of the deceased.

Funeral services are conducted by priests, bishops or archbishops and one of them, rather than a member or friend of the family, delivers a eulogy. At the end of the service, the chief mourners say their last farewell to the deceased, then move to the left-hand side of the altar. The congregation then files past the family to shake their hands and give condolences. They wait until the casket is taken out and put into the hearse before following it to the cemetery where the priest conducts the final ceremony. Each guest may place a flower on the coffin in the grave.

A wake is always held afterwards and while alcohol, such as brandy, may be served the food is more austere than lavish, with dry biscuits rather than rich cakes.

Seven days later, the priest goes again to the graveside with the family to conduct a service. Every three months for the first year, the deceased will be remembered at a ceremony at the church after a regular service on a Sunday. Mourners light candles and are given altar cakes made of flour, honey and spices. A widow wears black for a period of up to two years after the death of her spouse but the idea of her wearing it forever is now a thing of the past.

THE INDIAN (HINDU) FUNERAL

Wear white, not black, to a Hindu funeral, which is usually a cremation, except for the funerals of children, who are buried when they die. It takes place as soon as possible after death. Flowers are placed at the feet of the body in the coffin, which is open. Mourners are expected to view the body without touching it. Ten or thirty days later, depending on the caste of the deceased, a ceremony is held at the home of the next of kin. Called a *shraddha*, it is intended to free the soul of the departed from earthly constraints. Visitors to the house should arrive with gifts of fruit.

THE ISLAMIC FUNERAL

To a Muslim, life is a journey and death an inevitability that can happen at any time. It doesn't mean the end. It means going back to God to be judged. To complete the life cycle, the last words a Muslim should hear is the *shahada*, a proclamation bearing witness that there is no god except God and that Mohammed is the Messenger of God.

After death, the body must be washed, wrapped in a clean white cloth and buried, not cremated, with a simple prayer, preferably on the same day or as soon as possible. The body when buried must come into contact with earth. Friends and family members attend the burial.

Relatives and friends make themselves useful by doing domestic chores for the bereaved and making supplications for the departed. Mourning should end after three days because Islam emphasises accepting death as intertwined with life, moving on and not dwelling on the past.

The prophet taught that three things can continue to be useful to the person after his or her death: charitable deeds they had done during their lifetime; knowledge they had been taught; and prayers said on their behalf after death by a righteous child. A tribute such as subsidising the digging of a well in an impoverished area, or helping the homeless and needy anywhere in the world, would also benefit the departed.

THE JAPANESE FUNERAL

Many Japanese have more than one faith (see page 23) and many believe that they leave this world as a Buddhist. Of the two sects of Buddhism, *mahayana* (meaning 'great vehicle') is the one practised in Japan. The belief is that for a few days after the body dies, the spirit does not realise it until confronted by an awakening light. If the spirit gravitates to the light, it attains nirvana. If it recoils from the light, it will go on to search for parents who will create a body in which it can be born again. Prayers from monks and mourners are important over weeks and months after the death because they are thought to be beneficial in helping the wandering spirit to undergo an auspicious rebirth.

In Australia, a Japanese funeral service is usually similar in ritual to a Christian one, except that Buddhist monks may preside. Traditionally, after a body has been cremated, the family uses chopsticks to pick the bones from the ashes and pass them to each other. The ashes and bones are put in an urn and kept at the altar in the family home for thirty-five days before being buried in a Buddhist cemetery at a site that is subsequently visited regularly by the family.

Black or dark colours should be worn to the funeral. White or very pale flowers – chrysanthemums are ideal – may be sent to the house of the bereaved or to the funeral. It is not appropriate to send food but it is quite in order to give money, if you wish. It is very important not to use new banknotes as this indicates the death was expected. Put the money in a plain white envelope with your name written in black ink on the front at the bottom, and the amount written on the back of the envelope, take it to the house or the funeral – whichever you are invited to first – and present it with both hands to the family member or friend who is at the reception desk. Any financial offerings are acknowledged forty-nine days after the date of death when the mourners respond with gifts of green tea, symbolising purity, and handkerchiefs, to indicate sorrow.

THE JEWISH FUNERAL

Flowers are not sent but a donation to charity is customary. At the funeral service, conducted by a rabbi and a cantor and held in a synagogue or temple, or in a chapel at the cemetery, men should wear skullcaps (yarmulkes), which are available there. Cremation is practised only in very rare circumstances. Only family and very close friends should be present at the graveside. After prayers, if the chief mourner is a male he puts the first spadeful of earth on to the coffin and each of the other mourners follows suit. Later in the day, a *minyan* is usually held at the home of a close relative. Mourners gather and prayers are said. There is a week of intense mourning after the funeral during which friends and relatives may pay their respects for a short time in the day or early evening.

It is customary to light *yarzheit* (memorial) candles on the anniversary of the death each year and on the Day of Atonement – Yom Kippur.

FROM THE CRADLE TO THE GRAVE

One of the purposes of all tribal rites, from the joy of birth to the sorrow of death, is to bring together people linked by blood or friendship. They are bonded by the experiences and emotions they share and the knowledge that each can bank on the support of the others in bad times as well as good. If the old saying 'charity begins at home' is true, the same may be said of courtesy, the civilised person's means of smoothing the way from the cradle to the grave.

Acknowledgements

Behind the scenes at Penguin Books is an army of people who never get their names on the books they spend their working lives helping to make. They have inspired me to keep writing, tweaked my words when necessary and beavered away to make me do my best and ensure this book is as accurate, stylish and beautiful as possible.

First among them is Julie Gibbs, whose faith kept me going when I thought I'd never make it; she finally gave up setting deadlines and put Kirsten Abbott on the case. As the book's editor, Kirsten guided me expertly and benevolently to make our collusion as pleasurable as it has been productive. The designer, Debra Billson, has such a light touch and an understanding of the importance of legibility. She has made the book friendly and approachable when it might have been a bit forbidding. Tracie Grimwood's whimsical illustrations have just the right contemporary spirit, bringing wit and humanity to the pages. The fact that I look so glamorous on the back flap is entirely due to photographer Earl Carter's mastery of the dual arts of lighting and camera; he has ensured that you wouldn't recognise me if you saw me putting out the rubbish bin or grappling with shopping bags on the bus.

It might seem absurd to be grateful to a bookseller, but if it weren't for the wondrous Amazon.com, I would never have been able to assemble the reference library that now forms an impressive wall behind me as I work. The gems that laid the foundation of my research are works by those great pioneers of etiquette guides, Emily Post, Amy Vanderbilt, Debrett's, Letitia Baldridge and Miss Manners, along with local pundits, such as Robert Hyslop, ISO, for his treasury of forms of address titled *Dear You* and Sir Asher Joel for his *Australian Protocol & Procedures*.

Then there are the people who gave me their time, scholarship, contacts and know-how on the huge range of subjects that had to be covered, including many beyond my personal experience, such as riding a surfboard, dining at the Governor-General's residence, dressing for the mosh pit and being a follower of certain religions. I have learnt so much in tackling these subjects, thanks to the generosity of others. My one regret is the absence of significant coverage of Aboriginal culture. I did quite a bit of research but, since it's difficult to do justice to the diversity of their rituals and customs without making generalisations, I have excluded almost all reference, so as not to offend any particular tribe.

Quite apart from those patient friends and acquaintances who've put up with my banging on about this project for so long, I must acknowledge the many people who have helped me with this book. I don't know how to thank them except by listing them alphabetically here and hoping I haven't forgotten anybody. I asked them all (except for the few I could not reach) how they wished their names to appear and that accounts for the inconsistency in forms of address.

Jodi Adams; Zoghera Allie; Wolfgang Angyal; Chris Ashton; James W Ashton; Ben Aylward; Christine Barro; The Hon Emeritus Professor Peter Baume AO; Nadia Benussi; The Hon Bronwyn Bishop MP; Myram Borders; Bob Brenner; Elizabeth Bryan; Lesley Brydon; Jim Buckell; Paul Budde; Ms Sue Bussell; Maureen Campbell; Mr Santo Cannata; Renzo Colla; Rabbi Allison H Conyer; Margaret Cox; John H Cutler; Giovanna D'Abaco; Joyce DiMascio; Suzanne Du Val; Bob Egerton; Philip Engelberts; Keith Fallick; Andrée Fitzgerald; Pat Forster; Annabelle Furphy; Ms Eleanor Galvin; Ulfa Gamildien; Penny Gerdes; Bruno Giagu; Gerard Gooden; Strath Gordon; Julie Gorrick; Ken Groves; Campbell Hanley; Kathryn Harris; David Harrison; Saskia Havekes; Mr Trevor Kennedy AM; Barbara Higgs; Donald Hollingsworth; Jane Hooper; Dr Thomas Jancik; Yun-Sik Jang; Mr Paul Kelly; Ms Kathy Lane; Neil Lazarow; Ilmar Leetberg; Lindy Leonhardt; The Rev Dr Paul G Logan; Ilaria Logi; Dr Pamela MacDonald; Megan Magarey; Nicole Makin; Caroline McFarlane; Patricia Manolas; Jackie Mawson; Harley Medcalf; Don Michelborough; Harry M Miller; Justin Miller; Nando Mogianesi; Brian Moore; Adrian Newstead; Glen-Marie North; Susanne North; Rachel O'Brien; Françoise Parsons; Frederick Paruta; Greg Paton; Luisa Perugini; Damien Pignolet; Ann Ramsay; Ms Satu Raunola; Janet Reid; Anne Rogan; Janine Rohrlach; Nada Roude; Lisa Sheehan; Ms Alana Sheil; Kenneth W Shields; Leo Simons; Mrs Maree Smith; Joel Solomon; Mr Wayne Spencer; Des Sullivan; Carol Summerhayes; Mrs Janna Tang; Jennifer Tang; Andrew Tatrai; Giri Tenneti; Mrs Mangayi Tenneti; Mr Sundara Tenneti; Dr Paolo Totaro AM; Helen Tribe; John C Vaughan; The Reverend Bruce Walker; Brendan Walsh; Father Hugh Walsh OFM; Norma Watson; Eon Waugh; Georgina Weir; Mark Williams; Ms Norhan Youssef.

INDEX